W9-AKC-620

SWEET DREAMS
AND FLYING MACHINES

The Life and Music of

James Taylor

MARK RIBOWSKY

An A Cappella Book

First edition
Published by Chicago Review Press Incorporated
814 North Franklin Street
Chicago, Illinois 60610
ISBN 978-1-61373-376-9

Library of Congress Cataloging-in-Publication Data

Names: Ribowsky, Mark, author.
Title: Sweet dreams and flying machines : the life and music of James Taylor / Mark Ribowsky.
Description: Chicago, IL : Chicago Review Press, 2016. | Includes index.
Identifiers: LCCN 2015047190| ISBN 9781613733769 (cloth : alk. paper) | ISBN 9781613733776 (pdf) | ISBN 9781613733783 (kindle)
Subjects: LCSH: Taylor, James, 1948– | Composers—United States—Biography. | Singers—United States—Biography.
Classification: LCC ML410.T2 R53 2016 | DDC 782.42164092—dc23 LC record available at http://lccn.loc.gov/2015047190

Interior typesetting: Nord Compo

Printed in the United States of America
5 4 3 2 1

CONTENTS

INTRODUCTION

The Troubadour

Although eight presidents have come and almost gone since he first broke onto the pop cultural scene wearing the lean and hungry look of Cassius, James Taylor still walks the earth with purpose and haunted eyes, not quite as lean or hungry and certainly not as hirsute, but, like Julius Caesar's foil, a man who indeed thinks too much. "Such men are dangerous," said Caesar. At a firm and hardy sixty-seven, Taylor may be still fairly described as dangerous in that sense, though often forgotten is that Marcus Antonius counseled, "Fear him not, Caesar, he's not dangerous. He is a noble Roman, and well given." And *noble* is really the best word for Taylor, a man very well given and very wealthy, who today is in better physical and probably mental condition than during the whirlwind when he influenced music so heavily and magazines and newspapers—there were no tabloid TV shows then—used to print feverish stories about him, his gawky hunkiness, his *liaison amoureuse* with Joni Mitchell, his glittery, bollixed marriage to the sublimely sexy Carly Simon, his endlessly carried-out heroin habit, and sometimes even his music. Taylor would surely have been *People* magazine's Sexiest Man Alive, if they'd committed that crime back then.

However, while these pages reanimate those years in great detail, it is not with the intent to leer at his bedroom and shooting-gallery scenes, of which there are many. Rather, this book was conceived from a broader purview, as a historic journey through a time when the waters of the rock evolution—revolution?—parted for Taylor as a perfect trademark of his times, easing from the frenetic, soul-sapping 1960s into the '70s, when hair-relaxing soft-rock retrenchment grabbed the fast lane in a traffic jam of other evolving idioms such as country rock, redneck rock, seminal punk, lush romantic soul, and socially conscious funk.

The James Taylor in these pages emerges as a rather strange man, one of impeccable, implacable Southern-bred manners, awkward social skills, and, for many years, sexism and outright stupidity. He always existed in a strange warp. He was never the biggest-selling artist in the world, or in America, yet despite other acts selling more units, he was the fulcrum of a movement growing from L.A. that fully converted rock from an impulse behavior to a corporate behemoth. The focus here is how and why Taylor and that decade got there at the same time. Not that Taylor stopped doing important work; rather, by the next decade his work as a mover of earth and sea was done, his legacy set. His skill, timing, and calculation had implanted an identification with burden and relief that played to the masses, its ingredients those of the broad spectrum of American music. Taylor, a child of wealth, cashed in on his grasp of middle-class angst to the extent that few of his contemporaries are now able to rouse inner emotions formed so long ago in their fans quite like he does.

Any time his voice is heard on the radio, on one of those periodic DVDs of concerts in intriguing locales like his own barn, or on one of his perpetual tours, it notifies us that at sixty-seven, Taylor is the nearest thing to rock royalty in America. You damn near feel like curtsying to him. While such an imprimatur is far more easily given to men who boast literal nobility cred—Sir Paul McCartney, for one (though please, let's not talk about Wings)—such is the James Taylor brand that the most preeminent rock royalists themselves bow to him, and Sir Paul can take a bow for unearthing the Taylor brand, even if only for a fleeting moment in time: Taylor's failure as the first non-British act in the souring Apple Records orchard in the late 1960s. Another winning argument is that Taylor's best songs have aged with less rust than anyone else's best songs, not artifacts as much as still-glowing pieces of eight.

Back when, at a pivotal time in history, popular music sought direction following the Beatles-stamped decade of volatile, smoldering convulsions and open rebellion—all the stuff that convinced John Lennon that "the dream is over"—Taylor's voice was calming, a perfect match for the times *he* would stamp, reminding '60s survivors that there was still room for pain and personal baggage, which could all be told in a pretty song. It worked because Taylor's own pain could be felt, in his voice, in his balladry, even in his feel-good deviations. As he puts it, Zen-like, "I think people are isolated because of the nature of human consciousness, and they like it when they feel the connection between themselves and someone else."

Taylor wasn't the only one who tapped into this rich vein—and *rich* was the operative word. As Jules Siegel, one of the idiom's many critics, once wrote, the folk-rock crowd was "an audience suffering from hardening of the bank account." Jackson Browne, Neil Young, Carole King, Randy Newman, Dan Fogelberg, Gordon Lightfoot, Don McLean, Tom Waits, Loudon Wainwright, Leonard Cohen, Taylor's brother Livingston, and even John Denver added different elements to the same rough formula, which would mutate into the soft, faintly folk, faintly rock, fervently emotional genre that rose in time and space with the troubadours. Some of it was good, some of it was . . . well, remember Morris Albert's "Feelings"? If you wanted someone to credit, or blame, it was generally James Taylor.

He is, then, the epochal, essential, and existential troubadour of pop music, whose travails are as much legend as is his music but so removed now from them that it all seems a blur. Even back then, his frightful demons seemed cute and adorable, and because of Taylor, weakness became an allowable, even necessary, trait in a human being. And this, too, is why he can retain so much of his old-time twinkle and, yes, his *honor.* No one ever played victim or provoked curiosity as skillfully as Sweet Baby James, his alter ego. But Taylor can no longer be called a baby, nor does he make garish, catnip headlines as horny James, dating or marrying female singers with neuroses as obvious as his. Not that he will ever shake the residue of his marriage to Simon, a one-act, sweet-and-sour fairy tale with music that foundered under the weight of its overwhelmingly far-fetched expectations.

At one time, well into his thirties and a decade beyond his prime, it might be said that the great love of his life was neither performing nor Carly Simon but rather heroin. It is almost preternatural that Taylor once said, had he not become a performer, he probably would have been a chemist, which he had once intended to be after high school. For years, he *was.* But he now has taken a wife three times and has four children and two grandchildren. He kind of knows what love is supposed to feel like, has no problem calling himself "an addict in recovery" after thirty-plus years, and is sort of content that he stands firmly with his fellow surviving icons like Sir Paul, Jagger, Richards, Dylan, Paul Simon, and Brian Wilson. Though roughly the same age as Elton, Crosby, Stills, Nash, Young, Springsteen, Browne, Stevie Wonder, Bob Seger, Sting, and Bowie, Taylor keeps the busiest schedule, and even more so than U2, the most socially conscious one, which by some definition makes him more endearing. Which is not to be confused with *biggest.* Troubadours don't play football stadiums, he once said, adding that "Bruce Springsteen's a rock star. Elton John is a rock star. I'm a folk musician. Honestly, I think that's true."

At the same time, he has survived the same drugs and psychoses as harder-living rock stars, so that qualifies him, on some level, as a victor. Yet while some, like the preposterously still-alive Richards, the famously dubbed "Walking Death," look it, Taylor, who did at least as much heroin, does not. He is the still-sprightly elder, sometimes in his cobbler's hat looking something like a malnourished Tevya on loan from *Fiddler on the Roof.* Always in good voice, too old and too rich to really bitch about much, he can transport one back to when his songs reached from the darkness. They don't now, but still weave cathartic spells, having gotten us through so much, for so long. Can that be said of anyone else's work?

Taylor's first massive hit, the inextinguishable and undrenchable "Fire and Rain" (1970)—incidentally, a song Taylor himself can't stand to hear when it comes on the radio, as it still does, a lot—came when he was lost in a miasma of heroin and inner pain. Yet its clarity is legendary, not flinching in its checklist of dark-side impulses about suicide, mental illness, failure, weakness, and self-pity, with a plea to Jesus to "help me make a stand." These are themes he had already expressed in songs he wrote as a teenager during and between visits to sanatoriums. As a trust-fund kid looking for a path to sanity, he wrote songs about breakdowns that sometimes held an impishness that could turn a stay in a nuthouse into a Felliniesque fun house. Consider "Knocking 'Round the Zoo," his prequel to "Fire and Rain" from the days of his teenage band the Flying Machine, its imagery streaked with "bars on the windows," "counting up the spoons," and being "hit with a needle" when misbehaving. A *Rolling Stone* review even called it "*kicky.*"

When Taylor had mastered the art of melancholia in 1971, he found himself, almost as a cultural hybrid, in a Peter Max–style psychedelic illustration on the cover of *Time*, under the words "The New Rock: Bittersweet and Low." Taylor's personal trail of family dysfunction stoked an in-vogue notion at the time, that he and his talented and equally troubled siblings, Livingston, Kate, and Alex, had fashioned a Kennedyesque dynasty, updated to the squalid scape of rock and roll. It was almost *cute* that Taylor's whole *family* was fucked up, two of them confined to the same loony bin where he had been! "The family that sticks together, breaks down together," ribbed one rock scribe. In the new culture, American royalty need not hide their secrets the way the Rockefellers and Roosevelts had. But only Taylor prospered. His records were therapy sessions on vinyl and reassurances to baby boomers that this man of wealth and looks and talent was as fucked up as they were.

His way with self-revelation can still escape from his pen and guitar today. Kicky, though with less urgency and barium, it has always been compatible with the pleasant MOR pop that balanced the dark and complex with the simple and warm—often within the same song. But none had greater impact than his rendition of Carole King's "You've Got a Friend" (1971): its melancholia and oppressive fear of loneliness would be suffocating if not for the lilting and lifting nature of his sparkling, tickling acoustic guitar licks. Back then, he *did* look the part: long, lean, shaggy, sallow, hollow-cheeked, and unkempt—in other words, the prototype of the new American macho in the late '60s and early '70s. (Best forgotten is the phase when, to his regret, he tried to make suspenders worn over T-shirts into a "look," or that white-suited Gatsby thing, mercifully soon discarded.) In the early '70s, he even starred in an *Easy Rider*–inspired, independent movie, *Two-Lane Blacktop,* with the intent of being seen as a new James Dean.

For maturing baby boomers who had gone through too much trauma and broken idealism in the '60s, he provided fertile turf for angst-and-a-half masked in easy listening reverie. This is what has gotten him here, now: the fact that, as a host on NPR noted, "Even in the saddest songs, it's always had a kindly nature to it." He was of such loft by the '90s that when Bill Clinton went sailing off Martha's

Vineyard on a presidential summer vacation, he did so on Taylor's boat. And when the Red Sox went to the World Series in 2013, Taylor was invited to sing the national anthem before the second game at Fenway Park, like the old stadium, a beautiful relic born in Boston. It didn't matter that he committed an error; booked to sing both the anthem and "America the Beautiful" that night, he sang the first line of the latter song instead of "Oh, say can you see." But then, that was one classic he *didn't* write.

Rock's old dogs have a real hold on pop culture. If it seems unreal that the bestselling compilation album of all time is the Eagles' *Greatest Hits Volume 1*, moving forty-two million units, it is surreal that Taylor's own original greatest-hits album, released around the same time in 1976, still sells around half a million copies a year. One simply cannot dismiss Taylor's survivability and ability to be intact and hearty after so many years and scars—compared with wobbly legged compatriots such as, say, Gregg Allman, who once sang of surviving by letting one's soul shine through the darkest hours. Taylor agreed. Relief, he seemed to be saying in his songs, was damn sure better than fire and rain. And the happy ending is that he somehow found it with time. Ever the optimistic pessimist (pessimistic optimist?), Taylor proved Allman's point. And seeing him perform so breezily these days, one can almost feel his relief.

Not that all the boomers, coming out of the 1960s but reared in the '50s, bought into the acceptance of overt vulnerability and Taylor's way of moisturizing the hard calluses of rock. Arguably the crankiest critic to ever haunt Taylor, Lester Bangs became renowned for a poison-pen essay titled "James Taylor Marked for Death," mourning the trend Taylor set to "moulder in the Dostoyevskian hovels of dead bardic auteur crap picking nits out of its navel." Kim Fowley, the now departed, magnificently subversive founder of the Runaways, once explained, "What caused glam rock? Simple: James Taylor and saggy tits and granola." The acrid Brit Nik Cohn fires away: "As far as I could tell from Taylor's whiny none-dare-call-it-folk music, JT's only claim to fame was that he was both terminally wealthy and terminally privileged, attributes I hardly connected with true rock 'n' roll. If 'Fire And Rain' was a 'harrowing' piece of music, then I must be deaf, dumb, and blindsided."

British music historian Barney Hoskyns writes that "back in the protopunk wars of the early '70s, we were all supposed to revile James Taylor and his kind. [They] represented the death of everything dionysiac and incendiary in rock [and] all that was smugly narcissistic about singer-songwriting bards of the time. Forget the fact that James may have been a worse junkie than Johnny Thunders: this music was wallpaper balladry for the new consumers of the post-counterculture."

But, dropping the other shoe, he adds, "We all mellow as we ripen and rot . . . and what sounded wimpily self-satisfied in 1975 now soothes and even moves."

David Crosby, a man who should know, says of Taylor, "If he isn't one of the half-dozen best singer-songwriters in the world I'm Napoleon." From the country side, Garth Brooks calls Taylor his favorite artist. References to Taylor proliferate in rock literature—good, bad, in between, and some from outer space. By example, one sure to make Taylor blanch, when Charles Manson's pre–murder spree recordings were released in 1970 as the album *Lie: The Love and Terror Cult*, one reviewer wrote that "Manson shows a vocal resemblance to James Taylor."

From a strictly personal perspective, that of a cynical New York child of the '60s, Taylor's appeal was indeed not readily apparent then. In time, though, his stark, soulful melancholia would touch a collective raw nerve. Guitarist Danny Kortchmar, his childhood accomplice who became the premier studio sideman during Taylor's ascension, says of his old confrere, "Think Kurt Cobain unplugged." On a surface level, indeed, there certainly are parallels between them: both were misfits with looks, haunting voices, and open-wounded vulnerability. Taylor saw much of himself in Cobain, saying after the latter's suicide, "I really dug his music," and recognized the scars left on Cobain by industry "vultures" and the "delusionary system" they both worked within. But, to get real, it's always hard to get down with someone talking about being a victim of totalitarian oppression from the wooded gazebo of a hundred-acre estate in the Berkshires. Cobain, who lived in squalor, spewed cool nihilistic rage, never stooping to ask God to help him. His songs seemed to say, "Fuck it. I am who I am. Leave me alone."

Taylor, by contrast, seemed a little too needy, geared to making young and old women want to give him a big hug. Little wonder that audiences at Taylor concerts were generally weighted two-to-one female. John Rockwell, the erudite *New York Times* music writer during Taylor's rise, touched on his timelessness, calling him "a hipper, younger, folk-rocking update of the great crooners of the between-wars era." Taylor, who seems renewed each time he performs, is still just such a generational bridge, even as he is less hip and not really updating his mien. Rockwell also writes that Taylor's "sly and lonely" and "sexily intimate way" with a tune is "almost always a delight."

But how honest a sensitive man is he, really? The venerable *Village Voice* music critic Robert Christgau ventures that Taylor became "a star because he's an egotist [who] vaunts his sensitivity so expertly." Maybe it was that suspicion that, to these ears, made him just too cloying, his covers of Marvin Gaye and the Drifters dilettantish. More palatable was Jim Croce, once dubbed a "James Taylor . . . with a broader, blue collar appeal"—or, for Lester Bangs, a guy who "looks like Frank Zappa and sings like James Taylor"—who could get down with junkyard dogs. (All things in music being cyclical and regifted, it's tickling to read the critical observation that Taylor's "Gorilla" was "reminiscent of Jim Croce on Seconal and bananas.") In Taylor's favor, though, was that while he exploited the crude avarice of the Southern California music jungle, he rejected its pretensions of pseudohip eminence and entitlement. In a subculture riddled with the cavities of empty souls and ruled by common thieves, he was happy to be the East Coast outsider.

Today, to an older and if not wiser at least less cynical author with less sharp ears perhaps, Taylor's body of work cuts deeper than it did then, to places unknown. While some thoughtful critics called these inward journeys "faux reality" in a post-'60s world of mundane routines, further age would make the discoveries found on those sentimental journeys valuable, a kind of self-therapy. While Croce's "I've Got a Name" and Harry Chapin's "Cat's in the Cradle" are intense homilies that can make one cry, Taylor's tales of woe are simpler. An easier road to introspection, his overarching metaphor is to "brighten your night with my day." If Taylor made sentimentality a viable option—and perhaps, for some, a curative—he has nothing to apologize for. Well,

OK, maybe for breeding the sensitive personae of Alan Alda and Phil Donahue. That's totally unforgivable.

Like Dylan, who paved the way for ethereal, poetic lyrics, Taylor has gone about his work mainly alone, as if unwilling to share his darkest fears with anyone until he himself has honed it into words and music. Of course, one notable exception was "Her Town Too" (1981), his last major chart hit, written with fellow lonesome traveler J. D. Souther, whose Roy Orbison–type plaints about pain that never heals made him a perfect partner for Taylor. Lonely, angular figure that Taylor is, Sting once said, "James always reminded me of Abraham Lincoln because of his height and his lugubriousness." He added that Taylor is "the archetypal southern gentleman and a great storyteller." The octogenarian arranger and pianist Dave Grusin, a later habitué of Taylor sessions, recalls a full room of studio musicians once greeting Taylor with a standing ovation. Grusin, who has worked with, well, *everyone*, made a mock introduction, saying, "This is James Taylor, who should be chosen the next poet laureate of the United States." That would mean he surpassed Dylan and "Rhymin' Simon," in his role as the proverbial poet and a one-man band, to crib from the latter, and kept a step or two ahead of contemporaries like Van Morrison, Cat Stevens, Leonard Cohen, Tim Buckley, Jesse Winchester . . . and on and on.

During this five-year fold of the 1970s, Taylor coated agony in gossamer, poetry, and soft acoustic guitar chords as his metaphors and parables got a tad stretchy, such that he was no more than a gorilla that "dreams about the world outside from behind those bars of steel." Yet his influence was such that John Lennon veered from the nightmare of "Cold Turkey" to the daydream of "Imagine." As the softer side of hard men's tried and tired souls got even softer, formulaic pop thrived. A subculture grew that to many seemed like well-off yuppies perched in open-air cafés sipping chamomile tea or lattes, James Taylor music on the speakers framing melancholy tales of alienation. Carly Simon recorded one of the most overwrought, cynical "soft"-rock songs of all, "That's the Way I've Always Heard It Should Be"—which actually portended the same horror of "drowning in love's debris" that she wanted to avoid, but that was inevitable with a cruelly inattentive Taylor as a husband.

All this decadent wallowing stretches out from the hub of Taylor's polite, profitable wounds of the heart. During his peak of influence, even lower-wattage bulbs like Stephen Bishop, Andrew Gold, or Jonathan Edwards could soft sell Taylor-like pop angst into a good-sized hit. Cynical as he is, Randy Newman once semijoked that he felt out of the soft-rock loop by dint of not having enough inner turmoil for a song. "What am I gonna write about?" he asked. "Sitting at home and reading and playing with the kids?" When Newman composed his 1995 musical *Randy Newman's Faust*, updating the classic Goethe war of wits between God and the Devil, he called on Taylor to not only cowrite and perform three songs with him for the soundtrack but also assume the identity of the Lord, opposite Newman's Mephistopheles—which seemed about right, given Taylor's hard-earned conversion from prickly to prudent. (Faust was played by Don Henley, also perfect casting.)

Of course, some men will never own up to having a feminine side, and if truth be told, Taylor's manipulation of women for most of his life ridicules his own musical images. But give him props: he knew how to come off as needy. When he sighed, "Don't let me be lonely tonight," could any woman have failed to comply? Could any man pretend not to have thought the same thing, way too many times? *That* is why Taylor has survived divas, hip-hoppers, rappers, nasty boys, and twerking girls, even if he had to change his skin a few times, take a tumble down the pop chart, and make the easy listening chart his refuge. And let's give him props for something else: he may have receded, but he never sold out. In an age when rock evergreens sell everything from cars to Corn Flakes, never have we, or will we, hear "Fire and Rain" in a charcoal grill commercial or "Shower the People" in one for Dial soap. For that, we owe him.

Certainly, Taylor has been honored, and well. Somewhere in some basement or attic in his cloistered aerie in the Berkshire Mountains are stored five Grammys, hardware signifying membership in both the Rock and Roll and Songwriters Halls of Fame, the *Billboard*'s Century Award, a Grammy Lifetime Achievement Award, and many similar, lesser honorariums from the industry. To this stash he could add, late in 2015, arguably the most coveted bauble, the Presidential

Medal of Freedom. The *Time* cover is no doubt there, too. He has honorary doctorates from big universities, a Gershwin Award, a Jazz Spirit Award, the Chevalier de l'Ordre des Arts et des Lettres from the Ministry of Culture and Communication of France. A permanent James Taylor exhibit sits in the Chapel Hill Museum in North Carolina, not far from where he spent his youth and not far from the bridge over Morgan Creek that he sang of in "Copperline." Taylor must be a pop culture icon: his cartoon image and his voice graced a memorable 1994 *Simpsons* episode in which he's called in during a disastrous space flight to calm the astronauts' fears by singing "Fire and Rain," stammering to alter the line about "flying machines in pieces on the ground."

These are the spoils of recording sixteen studio albums, ten live and compilation albums, and forty singles, twelve of them Top 40 hits, all told selling around 40 million records and amassing a personal fortune of around $60 million. Seven of these albums went gold, fourteen platinum, one of which—the 1976 *Greatest Hits* set—is today an *eleven-time* platinum seller. Even his two Christmas albums, in 2004 and 2006, went gold and platinum. Bridging eras from vinyl 45s and LPs to eight-track to cassette to MTV-bred video and digital formats, he's released seven video albums. He's performed with the Utah Symphony and the Mormon Tabernacle Choir. He sang "Sweet Baby James" on the final *Tonight Show* of Jay Leno (the first time Leno left). When he was married for a third time, in 2001, the pomp and guest list seemed suited to a state wedding.

Even though his most recent successful Top 100 single was over thirty-three years ago, his singles ever since have found a reliable home high on the adult contemporary charts. And the albums recorded after his fiftieth birthday—*Hourglass* (1997), *October Road* (2002), *Covers* (2008)—carefully intermingled between regular repackaged greatest-hits albums and collaborations with Yo-Yo Ma, Shawn Colvin, and Branford Marsalis, sold surprisingly well. All charted Top 10 (the latter two Top 4), greasing the way for the unlikeliest rise to the top of the charts in 2015, when his long-awaited *Before This World* album became his first *ever* to hit number 1, a forty-five-year waiting period. That recent history netted him three Grammys, one more than he took home in the '70s, though this may have been a factor of his longevity and decades of dues-paying. Similarly, his most recent Grammy, a 2003 duet with Alison Krauss, "How's the World Treating You," which won for Best Country Vocal Collaboration, testifies to the wide range and idiomatic scope of his work.

None of which can remove what is forever quintessential in him: a man painfully shy and a bit awkward and out of place, not quite knowing how to look or what to say—though who, when at ease, can be a scream. Still long and shambling, the now beautifully bald Taylor can safely don designer tuxes for award shows. But, at his core, he is a walking, singing wraith of times past, with no one more freaked by his longevity than Taylor himself. Even now, isolation is his thing. His 1972 epitaphic single "One Man Parade" was followed by his 2007 album *One Man Band.* Weary as he has been at times, he once said, "I thought I'd passed the midpoint of my life when I was 17." And as far back as the early 1970s, he could wistfully sing of events that were "Long Ago and Far Away" and plead to find a place in his head that was "Anywhere Like Heaven." By '77, he could temper the outward optimism of "Secret o' Life"—"Enjoying the passage of time / Any fool can do it, there ain't nothing to it"—with a fatalistic plaint that "Nobody knows how we got to the top of the hill / But since we're on our way down, we might as well enjoy the ride."

By the '80s, having battled through marital strife splayed all over the papers and the near death of his son, he could write optimistic chanteys and write a song and album called *Never Die Young*, which one review said "floated on a sea of yuppie contentment . . . reminding his listeners why they had liked him in the first place." Call it a redefining of purposes, in a new light. As it happened, Jesus *did* look down upon him; it was his year-older brother, Alex, who didn't make it out of the darkness, dying after downing a bottle of vodka in 1993, on James's forty-fifth birthday. Only then was James ready to cop to it, writing a tribute to him, "Enough to Be on Your Way," in which he recognized "this fucked-up family." The father whom he waited decades to find common ground with died a decade later, before that belated bond could happen. In a strong sense, then, staying alive was a mocking triumph, producing more pain, having to live with more loss, and that was something Jesus could not help him out of.

Like everyone else of the old ilk still ambulatory enough to pull in a nice payday for an hour or three of work, he doesn't need the bread, but he surely needs to hear the applause. The journey has been a long and epic one, with a far happier ending than Taylor at times would have believed was possible, with a list of songs one can reference almost too easily. Read on and it will become clear why they have the subconscious hold on us that they do: it's because they came at precisely the right time in history that they needed to.

1

HOW SWEET IT IS

Sunrise, Florida, November 15, 2014

Sunrise, a city sitting on the west end of Broward County that borders the swamps of the Everglades, one of those wistfully named Florida hamlets that draws people of all sorts to its sleepy hollows, gets James Taylor tonight. Which means the newly rooted baby boomers will congregate in the town's glittery corporate jewel, the BB&T Center, for another exercise in uncluttered nostalgia and yuppie contentment, as they did when Elton John christened the place in 2001. On a cool night on what passes for autumn here, under the palm leaves encircling the parking lot of the arena, only half the spaces are filled just minutes before Taylor will take the stage. Though lines wait to get through the doors, the pace is orderly, calm; no one seems in a hurry. Wedged between two midlife-crisis symbols, a BMW and a Porsche, a card table has been set up, and two couples who look to be in their late fifties or early sixties sit around it, lounging, sipping, talking, laughing, the men in pleated slacks and short-sleeve Hawaiian shirts, the women in white jeans and low-cut tops.

"What's going on here?" a stranger joshes them.

"Having a little wine and cheese party," one of the women says.

"Shouldn't you be getting inside? Show time's eight o'clock."

"James will wait for us."

"Why? You guys know him?"

"No, but with James, it's like he knows *us*. You know, we're his audience. He'll wait for us." She has a thought. "You know, I probably never had wine and cheese before I heard James. Something about him, it makes you feel like you want to have wine and cheese."

The party at the table laughs, then goes back to their Whole Foods crackers and breezy conversation.

Inside, the feel is of a larger but still intimate wine and cheese party. The spacious arena seems full, every opulent luxury box lit, but the entire top tier of the hall has a dark curtain all around it, closed off because not enough tickets were bought for up there, sparing embarrassment to Taylor, who can still move tickets but not as many or for as much money as the next two high-level acts who'd come through Sunrise, John Mellencamp and Fleetwood Mac. To his relief, though, tickets were moving quite well for a Taylor show at Madison Square Garden in early December.

In the now teeming lower level, the almost all-white crowd waits, still without impatience; the two couples in the lot will indeed make it in time. At around 8:15, the place is darkened but for an illuminated stool on the stage. With no introduction, a solitary six-foot-four-inch man emerges from the dark, at first to silence, then building applause. He walks to the front of the stage, shakes a few hands, then sits on the stool, guitar in hand. The face is overly familiar, recognizable even from a distance, craggy but soft, the square chin and eagle-like eyes of a Grant Wood portrait. Indeed, *Time* magazine as far back as 2001 noted that Taylor had "a great American face . . . a face out of Steinbeck, long and spare, radiating intelligence and surprising strength for a man known for his soft lyric." Fourteen years on, one could almost call that face Rushmore-like.

But not *old*, really. Eagle eyes don't squint and they don't sink. They peer into other animals' souls. James Taylor is about to do that, once again, just looking at his audience. As he does, the feeling is palpable through the hall: Does this man, who has long been shrouded in self-imposed, semi-isolation from society, ever change? Not only are his songs frozen in time—*Taylor* is.

"He's wearing the same thing he wore on the Troubadour Tour in 2010!" a woman who has known Taylor for years muses, referring to the Taylor "uniform": loose, dusty pants, white and well-worn shirt, linty brown sport jacket, all looking like he'd slept in them.

He is a proud kind of fossil. Even now, he can neither write music nor read it; he only plays and sings it. As he eases into his first song, the now antediluvian "Something in the Way She Moves," it is like almost every other title in his long catalog, reflective of himself. Years after he lost his freak-flag hair and Harry Reems mustache, there is surely something in the way *he* moves through a song. The voice. Good God, the voice. No instrument on earth that has been around as long as his throat has accumulated as little rust or evidence of age. It has the same timbre, the same faintly Irish-folk hue, the same restrained power. This must be a tribute to the most obvious irony of all for Taylor—clean living. Bell-clear and nuanced at every rise and fall, Taylor's tight baritone range is unconfined because of nuances that constantly color different aural-visual images, allowing for a typically eclectic set list on this night, a remarkably deep and broad palette of musical styles, meters, and influences, and of one man's ability to perform them flawlessly.

It will take him three hours to render them all, with an intermission, in the manner of a Bruce Springsteen concert. The set list is a far-reaching buffet that, after "Something," includes "Today Today Today," "Lo and Behold," "Copperline," "Everyday," "Country Road," "Millworker," "Carolina in My Mind," "One More Go Round," "Sweet Baby James," "Shower the People," "Stretch of the Highway," "You and I Again," "Raised Up Family," "Handy Man," "Steamroller," "Only One," "Fire and Rain," "Up on the Roof," "Mexico," and "Your Smiling Face." The encore begins with "How Sweet It Is (To Be Loved by You)," and "You've Got a Friend." And he will seem as fresh and energetic at the end as he was at the start, kept buoyant by the backing unit billed as Taylor's "all-star" band—Andrea Zonn on fiddle; horn men Lou Marini and Walt Fowler; guitarist Mike Landau; bass player Jimmy Johnson; pianist Larry Goldings; percussionist Luis Conte; drummer Steve Gadd, who first teamed with Taylor in '91 on the *New Moon Shine* album; and backup singers Zonn, Kate Markowitz, Arnold McCuller, and David Lasley, the last a Taylor accomplice since the early '70s.

For decades, Taylor was probably the least animated and *happy* act in rock to see live. In 1971, one review of a Taylor performance began: "As opposed to coming on strong in the time honored tradition of super-stars—James Taylor comes on weak! He is the first and the foremost of the low-key rock and roll stars and onstage presents the public image of a vulnerable, ambulated American string-bean with braces." Another scold sniffed about the then new wave of singer-songwriters that "the basic problem with both British and American artists in this genre is an overpowering intensity and a shocking lack of humor."

By that, he really meant James Taylor—who one writer said had "massive egotism and exhibitionistic tendencies"—fought tooth and nail with his natural depressive tendencies, agoraphobia, and insecurity. Not surprisingly, future holy man Cat Stevens's first impression of him was that he was "James Taylor of the disturbing voice and eye." Taylor's justifications for being antisocial often reeked of pomposity. "I enjoy selling my music. I don't enjoy selling myself," he said in 1971. "Photographers and reporters are mostly after me. They want to know what I read and what I'm like and I don't really know myself so how can I tell them? I'd just like to see a lot of this confusing rubbish go away and get back to those old times. If I could go back I would. I'm looking forward to being able to retire from being a public figure and being able to afford to be myself!"

He was all of twenty-three when he said that.

It has taken decades for it to happen, as an elder statesman and national asset, with a Medal of Freedom medallion to show for it. And so here he was, one-nighting in the glades of Southern Florida, exhibiting a shocking sense of humor, telling stories about songs so offhandedly that one could forget that there are maybe two humans in the world who could say something like this, as he does after "Something in the Way She Moves":

"That song means a lot to me. Um, in 1968 I played it for Paul McCartney and George Harrison in a little room in London. They were starting Apple Records. It was my audition and, well, um, you know the rest."

Taylor can also crack on himself. "Don't pay attention to the lyrics," he coos before embarking on "One More Go Round," a song from the 1991 *New Moon Shine* album that he had not sung live before this tour. Funny enough, given its nonsensical rhyming—"Running around the room / In my Fruit o' the Loom / A cup of coffee from King Tut's tomb." He also makes mocking reference to one or another of the most familiar tunes as "old" or "a sixties song" or "a little bullshit thing I did for the *Sweet Baby James* album," bringing lusty laughter from the hoary boomers, not above a little self-effacement themselves.

Some songs will run in stark minimalism, others enlivened by a light show—not one that Pink Floyd would lift an eye at but one that, for a Taylor gig, is dazzling to the eye. And there is the Taylor, well, inscrutability. Telling as he has for four decades the genesis of "Sweet Baby James" and the baby famously named after him by his ill-fated brother Alex ("It's touching . . . if you like kids"), he further muses, "Just goes to show that anyone can have a kid," to nervous titters, the tragic demise of Alex being known to all, except perhaps Kathie Lee Gifford. An alternate line he often uses about Alex Taylor is "You take your eyes off them for a minute and they divide." Maybe only a shrink would understand why lines like *that* seem funny to him.

What one is left with, however, is not his attempts at humor but how he can still keep an arena spellbound with a few notes. During "Fire and Rain" and "You've Got a Friend," when the place becomes a mass, quiet sing-along, sniffles can be heard as old tears begin to run again. But not for long. With Taylor, pop bleeds into blues, and tonight when he reprises his funky blues foray "Steamroller"—written as a send-up of white blues bands in Britain during his sojourn there, and first played live on February 6, 1970, at the Jabberwocky in Syracuse—his long legs unfold and he rises into a happy dance across the stage, making his face a rubbery mask of Louis Armstrong.

"Who is that guy?" says someone in the audience. "I've never seen him like this. It's like . . . he's having *fun.*"

Of course, his signature emotion is and always will be that of loneliness. Of all his peerage, his voice is closest to that of the human heart. A song like "Don't Let Me Be Lonely Tonight," heavily influenced by Roy Orbison and subsequently influencing other great soft-rock pleadings like Bob Seger's "We've Got Tonight," carries an essential truth—that of, as Cheech Marin once said, "the greatest pickup song in the history of the world. If you can't get laid to *that* song . . ."

No one knows this better than Taylor, who can make any song an aphrodisiac and has tried strenuously to *not* make himself into Barry (Very) White. His song catalog is so long, so diverse, that he has always been able to indulge his lesser-known but personally edifying numbers, and when the heat of the crowd cools a bit, crank up a master work. Thus, making them wait for "Fire and Rain" until the eighteenth song, deep into the second act, a wonderful case of not shooting one's wad too soon; in fact, it strategically shifted the show into its home stretch, with four humdingers culminating in "Your Smiling Face" and the rousing encore.

Even here, though, Taylor had a curve ball, the last song of the night being his folksy, searching cover of Francis McPeake's 1957 arrangement of an old Scottish folk tune by nineteenth-century poet Robert Tannahill, "The Wild Mountain Thyme." Its refrains about "the blooming heather" bring to mind a reviewer's take that Crosby, Stills and Nash's "Clear Blue Skies" was "the kind of dippy 'aren't-trees-nice' song that makes James Taylor so annoying." And while it sent many baby boomers out into the night while he was still singing it, such is part of the price of admission to see Taylor, a man who needs you to know he is comforted not by fame but by God's good earth and his place in a great universal *something.*

After the last note is sung and the last chord played in Sunrise, Taylor took bows with his band and backup singers, then engaged in individual and group hugging, then some handshaking with the fans. It took him a good fifteen minutes before he was ready to take his leave. As a parable for his enduring popularity and viability, it worked; the guy who once couldn't run from the stage fast enough is happy to overstay his welcome.

"We love you!" a woman screams from further back, piercing a softening din.

He looks up, trying to locate where it came from. "Love you, too . . ." he is compelled to call out, awkwardly, then seems to wonder if he's given a little too much of his inner self.

". . . I guess," he adds, almost under his breath.

For James Taylor, love is never given or taken easily, or without cause. Jokes he can do. The working of the human heart and the baggage it always seems to leave, that's nothing to trifle with. He probably was writing a song in his head about it as he shook his last hand.

2

"IF YOU'RE TAYLOR AND A MALE . . ."

"Southern gentleman" James Vernon Taylor was not born in the South, nor was his lineage filled with many gentlemen. Indeed, in the matter of the Taylor men, perhaps the most charitable thing that can be said of them was that they knew how to make an almighty dollar, and asses of themselves. Unlike the famous scion who would sing so movingly about spiritual soul searching, the Taylor ancestral males were irreligious or outright atheistic, and frequently in a bunch of trouble. This heritage of rounders and bounders has been traced back, on his mother's side, to seafaring commercial interests along the Angus coast of eighteenth-century Scotland. The late *Billboard* editor Timothy White, whose longtime close relationship with Taylor allowed him access to a sheaf of family research into Taylor's lineage, dutifully shaped an obeisant 2000 authorized biography of Taylor written for a British publisher into a stupefying tale of intrepid seafarers and merchants, their wives only pertinent for the children they delivered. That odyssey labored on for forty-seven pages before Taylor's birth seemingly intruded on the story.

The trail began in the early 1600s with one John Tailyeour, treasurer of the town council in Montrose, and his son, the intrepidly christened Hercules Tailyeour. Their descendants bled through Scotland, raking in money and sailing the wide seas, with perhaps apocryphal tales of being shipwrecked and daringly rescued. The first James Taylor—Hercules's grandson—prospered along with his brother Robert in the mid- and late 1700s, and it was his son, Isaac Taylor, who moved the narrative across the sea, sailing with his brother John to the British colonies in America in 1790 to plant the Taylor flag in the New World. They settled in North Carolina, in the port town of New Bern, just off the snakelike Neuse River inlet—though maybe a more poetic destination might have been Scotland Neck, to the north—anglicized the family name, and planted that flag squarely in the soil of the most peaceful and thriving sector of America's antebellum South, on a cotton plantation. Meaning James Taylor, who no doubt reeled at the thought, would be connected by blood to a common slave owner.

When John Taylor died in 1796, his brother, named the administrator of his estate, seemed to mourn only long enough to fret about John's many creditors. Only days later, Isaac purchased an announcement in the local newspaper that "John Taylor, late of Newbern [*sic*], is dead" and that "all persons having claims against said estate are hereby ordered to bring them forward, as they will not be paid after the time limited by law." As for anyone to whom John had extended credit, "All those who are indebted to the estate are desired to make payment to Isaac Taylor, Admr."

The Taylors of New Bern were proud Southern men who believed they were doing what their good book said, even as they continued importing black men to tend their fields and serve their wishes. But being members in good standing of the American Confederacy was only part of what future Taylors would have cause to wince about from their lineage. Isaac Taylor's lone son, Alexander, was bred to be his scion, full of hope and promise, but he fell into the old Taylor mold and by his twenties was so, well, Taylor-like, that his father cut him out of his will for what he called "excessive" drinking and other depraved behavior. And yet Alexander went on to become a respected doctor and fathered two sons. Tim White saw the Taylor men as something quite different, their bad apples aside. His say-what consecration was a classic of purple prose.

"The annals of the Taylors," White wrote, "are also the story of the ebb and flow in the fortunes of the British Empire, and its collateral impact on the economic, social and cultural destiny of the United States, from its colonial origins and the Civil War, on through the Civil Rights Movement of the mid-20th century and its unsettled aftermath."

In truth, there is no discernible evidence the Taylors of North Carolina ever had much of an impact on the annals or economy of either country—though White specifically omitted the Confederate States of America—and particularly in the arena of the civil rights struggle, beyond helping to make it necessary that there *be* such a movement by owning and keeping men in chains. If anything, the first American-based Taylors were the personification of why five hundred thousand men died in a civil war, during which the only Taylor woman of note, Sarah Ann Cole, Alexander Taylor's wife, was a nurse in a Union prison caring for wounded rebel soldiers and, in White's hyperbolic view, was a Confederate "spy." Actually, all she did was smuggle in letters to the soldiers from their families.

Several Taylor men served under the Stars and Bars, one dying in battle and another fighting at Gettysburg. And if White is to be believed, the Taylors were a different breed of manor-house patricians, taking a cue from Isaac, who "treated his slaves like longtime friends, a rarity in America at that time." But if they boasted that some of their best friends were slaves, and that future generations would include fine, upstanding, and patriotic men—an uncle of James Taylor, Hannis Taylor, was the US minister for Spain in the 1910s—Isaac Taylor's great-grandson Isaac Montrose Taylor II, born in 1921, would have reservations about mythologizing his forbears. Said James Taylor's father, "If you're a Taylor and you're male, then people should stay clear of you because you can erupt at any time like a volcano."

A Taylor woman by marriage had many years hence seen enough of the nature of one Taylor man in particular to confirm that supposition. "It seems that sons cannot help following in their fathers' footsteps," said Carly Simon, "whether they like the path or not."

Directly descended from the "black sheep" of the family, Isaac Montrose Taylor II's birth was cause for the biggest Taylor family tragedy. In 1920, Alexander Taylor II, son of the original Isaac Montrose Taylor—the constant recycling of the family's nomenclature was becoming comically confusing—married a woman who, after becoming pregnant, had serious complications. Dr. Isaac Montrose Taylor was called upon to deliver the baby but could not prevent Theodosia from falling into a coma. Two weeks later, she died, a loss so devastating to Alexander that for years he wallowed in whiskey and depression, leaving his new son essentially an orphan. The abandoned Isaac would be raised by his aunt Sarah and her husband, Dr. James Vernon, within a tight-knit Taylor clan. Alexander died later in the year.

The surviving Taylors moved westward to Morganton, in the lap of Pisgah National Forest, near the majestic peaks of the Appalachians. But the bucolic atmosphere did little to relieve the child whose birth had caused so much pain, and he became wracked by guilt over his birth leading to the death of his parents. He, too, would find a bottle of booze a comforting escape in his life. Yet "Ike" Taylor, as he was called, could not escape the family legacy; it was up to him to become the next in line in the succession of Taylor physicians, and he did so impressively, excelling in studies at a prep school in Asheville, then as a member of both the Phi Beta Kappa and Sigma Ki fraternities at the University of North Carolina (UNC) at Chapel Hill. Graduating at the top of his class in 1942, he would earn his medical degree at Harvard Medical School, where he was president of his class all four years. By twenty-four, he was tall and handsome and had found a wife, Gertrude "Trudy" Woodard, a debutante from Newburyport who called herself a fisherman's daughter, though hers was one of the richest New England commercial fishing and shipbuilding families, tracing itself back to 1600s England. Trudy was studying at a Beacon Hill finishing school when she crossed paths with Isaac at a Harvard frat party in 1944. They were mutually bedazzled: she by his tall, confident swagger, Southern manners, and puckish charm. Trudy was already a polished soprano with aspirations of singing professionally and taking classes at the New England Conservatory of Music, tutored by no less than Metropolitan Opera diva Marie Sundelius.

After Ike graduated from Harvard Medical School and served a brief stint as a postwar lieutenant in the navy, he put off his remaining two-year requirement with a medical school exemption as he worked his internship at Massachusetts General Hospital. He married Trudy in 1946, was named chief resident, and the couple moved to a house in suburban Milton. In February 1947 came their first offspring, a son named—what else?—Alexander. By now the dashing young doctor had been appointed assistant medical adviser at Harvard and a research fellow in biological chemistry. He could afford another move, to a bigger house on Randolph Street in Weston, a country idyll Trudy described as "Cambridge Bauhaus."

It was here that they brought home their next child—James Vernon, born on March 12, 1948, at Mass General under Ike's watchful eye. As a nod to the uncle who had raised Ike when his own father had a meltdown, he named his second son after Dr. James Vernon. With an enviable home and a growing brood, their winters spent in serene, snowy calm and their summers in the elite sands of a Martha's Vineyard beachside bungalow, the Ike Taylors were for all the world the perfect couple with a perfect family, able to imbue their children with culture, wealth, leisure, and endless opportunity. Again wasting no time, a third child, a daughter, Katherine "Kate" Taylor, arrived in 1949, and a third son, Livingston, in 1950, these last two leading Ike to deviate from the anachronistic, dynastic child-naming tradition, at a time when a bustling, culturally changing America was in the midst of updating its own traditions.

Ike had some hard decisions to make. As chief resident at Mass Gen, his swath was so wide that he had been receiving offers from many other states' medical institutions, one from the medical school at the University of North Carolina at Chapel Hill as an assistant professor teaching body metabolism to medical students. This gave him a portal to go home again, his prestige intact, the soil and warmth of the South an added comfort. Trudy favored the move, and the Taylors had Carolina in their minds again. Ike found an eleven-room farmhouse in the woodlands on Old Greensboro Road in Carrboro, appropriate digs for a big doctor and professor with a Harvard pedigree but one that left no greater impression on his second son than to call it years later "the place where I used to crash."

Ike wanted to make the family happy, but he would become only more morose, unable to break free of the guilt he felt about his parents' deaths. Worse, he would grow apart from his own wife and kids. Tim White quoted Livingston Taylor as saying rather archly that his father "was not ever able to overcome that reservoir of sadness, and it continued to drag him down." Nor was he able to keep that mordancy from affecting his children. James Vernon Taylor once ventured that his parents "should have stayed in Boston," and that by not doing so, his father "basically re-engaged his family drama," which was now handed down to his children.

Ike maintained ties with Beacon Hill. Each summer he would take the brood on vacation to Martha's Vineyard, where they could sail their boats and rub elbows with the idle rich. Ike never really could get comfortable in Dixie, his liberal leanings clashing with the heinously conditioned Jim Crow laws and mindset all around Chapel Hill—not that he came into contact with many black people in the Vineyard. Ike had to take progress in small doses; he would come to accept that the South would not mend overnight, or perhaps ever—in 2015, long after his death, three American Muslim students in Chapel Hill, a married couple and her sister, would be gunned down by an avowed Islamophobe in what the mayor called a hate crime. Even so, in the thick of the civil rights movement, things were changing at the school, with a small but positive trickling of black students into its classrooms.

The fifth Taylor child was born in 1952, Hugh Cole. By then, James Taylor was four and already possessed of a melodic voice, a gift from his mother. The Taylor family would sometimes have sing-alongs in their living room. Again probably apocryphally, Ike would later say that when James was two, he could hold a tune. "Right then and there I knew my boy was gifted." The first recording his son made, to be generous, was when he was two and sung "Little Red Wagon Painted Blue" with Ike into a bulky wire recorder, a recording Ike later could have kicked himself for losing. Still, it was almost blasphemous that in the Taylor family a male child would sing for a living. And as he grew, James seemed on track to follow his father into professional success. He seemed like he knew big words, could make conversation about social issues, buried his nose in books. He could alter lyrics of familiar songs, making funny rhymes of them. Progressing through elementary and junior high school, he was a good, attentive student.

But as the second-eldest child gradually became aware of his family history and tendencies, his increasingly fleeting images of his father began to turn him inward, and he grew aware that, as he once said, "there was some shame involved in how my father was reared," meaning the dark saga of Alexander Taylor. Ike, he said, dealt with it by "propel[ling]" himself to success, even if it came at the expense of spending time with his own family. Ike Taylor was a stringent, prickly man, short of temper and toleration for knaves and fools. He was a good father, not overly strict or outwardly cruel, but the moments he had for the children were evaporating. Intense and a chain-smoker, he had brilliant ideas. An early proponent of socialized medicine, he encouraged his wife to speak her piece. And Trudy could act like Carrie Nation, joining civil rights demonstrations in Chapel Hill. She was, as James recalled, "a committed foot soldier. She picketed the local businesses to get them integrated." Needing support, she would sometimes take her young daughter with her into the fray. Ike didn't try to stop any of this; indeed he beamed at such activism—from a distance, recalcitrant to join up in the civil rights movement in any significant way, accepting how things were as the price for not rocking the boat and possibly crimping his career advancement.

Nor did Ike make any apologies about his atheism. While he was baptized, his Catholicism had lapsed, and he did not put his children through rituals of the church he believed were useless. He generally avoided the subject, though he did put up a Christmas tree each December and endorse the Ten Commandments. In matters more personal, he also seemed not to have the ability to say or show that he loved his children, or bespeak a desire to be around them for any great length of time. His children would adopt his ambivalence about religion as they grew older, with a bit of regret. As his son James once remarked, "I consider myself a spiritual person, with a lot of spiritual motivation, but I just missed the boat with religion." This would help explain why he calls many of his songs "this kind of religious music without having any obvious religion in them." That only happened after years of introspection, making the connection between his environment and spiritual truths that did not involve church doctrines. In the interim, though, Ike's atheistic tendencies added to a sense of indifference and confusion about those concepts, and a lack of anchoring beliefs that someone—some*thing*—was watching over them.

Trudy lamented to friends how lonely she felt, also rueful about the loss of cosmopolitan living. She felt, she once said, "as though I was living on the end of the earth." Ike tried to appease her by changing scenery again, moving when James was five to a more modern home in a less rustic setting on Morgan Creek Road in Chapel Hill, just across the wide byway of Fordham Boulevard from the main campus of UNC and the school's football and baseball fields. There, Trudy began to entertain neighborhood kids who mingled with the Taylor kids—but usually not James, who would normally hide in his room. Much of the fabric of the Taylor family was unraveling. Maturing as they were, and aware that something was wrong, something was *missing*, they didn't really know how to be close to each other, psychologically or spiritually.

The second son seemed to be the one most tortured by factors that normally would blow right by young children. It almost seemed a guilty pleasure if he smiled; goofing around, playing ball in the schoolyards and sandlots, walking along the railroad tracks, exploring the woods—these were the sort of diversions alien to him, and it began to concern Trudy that she would hear the same words about him from his teachers: awkward, shy, loner, sad, a little angry. Some in school called him "strange." A kid who couldn't assimilate with others his age. He could call few of his classmates a friend, and he didn't seem as if he wanted or needed to. One time he was said to have dissolved into tears when, giving an oral report in front of his second-grade class, the other kids laughed at his squeaky, adenoidal voice. The one that would make him far more money than even Isaac Montrose Taylor II would ever see.

3

CAROLINA IN MY MIND

James Taylor spent his teenage days mainly by himself, developing a tightly inward personality, his happiest moments spent on that Martha's Vineyard beach where, as he would say, he could "go outside in his bare feet." And if he turned inward for his simple pleasures, that digression only escalated when Ike took his leave, something that became all too common in 1955. The turning point for the worse began when the call came that Ike had to pay the piper for delaying his military obligation; he would need to put in those belated two years. At first he took a short-term assignment at the Bethesda Navy Medical Center in Maryland, which allowed him to take the railroad there, do his service during the week, then return home on weekends. But that lasted only a few months, and the remainder of his hitch would send him a very long way from home.

In fact, it seemed he could go no further than the end of the earth when, in October that year, he applied for and was granted work on a high-level military project in *Antarctica,* on the McMurdo naval base. An adjunct to Admiral Richard Byrd's polar explorations, the work there had grown into a multinational project called Operation Deep Freeze, charged with developing bases and satellite stations. Ike, promoted to lieutenant commander in the US Naval Reserve Medical Corps, was placed in Task Force 43, which performed all manner of medical research.

James Taylor was seven when he waved good-bye as his daddy embarked on this adventure at the bottom of the globe. He would be nine when he saw him again, two years deeper into the malaise that would turn common misery into uncommon music.

The entire Taylor family was ambushed by their patriarch's withdrawal, the damage to be fatal to every member's relationship with him, and to Ike Taylor himself. While serving in the coldest wasteland on the planet, bereft of any contact with the outside world, any culture, any beach or ocean to sail upon, he began a more intimate affair with the bottle to keep warm. All Trudy had of him were his letters and paychecks sent back home. Suddenly living her life as if a single mother, she had to raise four restless children on her own, and grew embittered, which hardly helped the kids' state of mind or their weakening bond to their father. When Ike returned in 1957, it was not to a family overjoyed to have him back; rather, he seemed a daddy they had to make room for and had learned to get along without.

In his midthirties, balding, and rounding, he was not the dashing young doctor now, but he was wealthier than ever and in some circles a celebrity for his work. During his absence, the local paper ran a story about him stitched from his letters to Trudy: DR. TAYLOR RELATES ADVENTURES NEAR SOUTH POLE. He had also received special commendation for helping victims of a deadly plane crash at the base survive. But what the stories didn't say was that he had battled continuous depression while being holed up almost like a prisoner of war in a meat locker—"We're in a lonely place here," he wrote with great understatement in one of his letters—and came home with insomnia, terrible headaches, and slowed reflexes.

During Ike's sabbatical, one of his boy's letters that found its way to the South Pole read, "I wish you were home. It would be so good to have you back." Later, the son would surmise that his father had taken the assignment, even if subconsciously, to run from his family ghosts, echoing Livingston in saying the antarctic adventure was "an escape from the harness of his shamed existence in Carolina." After Ike returned to his family, said James, he "was never the same. He was almost like a stranger for a long time."

An easy, too easy, induction is that, lacking a steady father figure, James Taylor, like all the Taylor children, has gone through life at the mercy of some sort of Oedipus complex, seeking unconscious payback by doing what his father believed was beneath him: rock and roll. Taylor has lent some credence to this theory, saying that he did indeed bond with Trudy in what felt oedipal, that every upward step in music carried "inherent and impending retribution" for Ike. Like his brothers, James would say, "I got very much into my mother." He told *Rolling Stone* in 1974:

> I think the idea of success would be to have her love me instead of my father. That kind of an Oedipal idea, that mind of an Oedipal striving, carries with it the idea if you're successful you'll have your eyes pulled out. It's the kind of thing which you know you can't be successful at. And you know you mustn't be successful at it because you're not a man, you're a child. On the other hand, being successful might have carried with it an inherent anger at my mother or father for their wanting me to perform, their wanting me to do well, and therefore if I'm successful there's an element of having done it for them and not wanting to have done it at all.

Similarly, he had told the same magazine three years earlier: "I used to be really hung up on ambivalence and dichotomies, especially when I was having a lot of trouble with my head about conflicting things . . . about something going into your mind and striking all the resonant frequencies that belong to it, and the fact that one thing from without can strike about a million things at the same time and half of them can be positive and half of them can be negative. I felt as though I was being ripped apart by dichotomies."

These were the kind of proverbs and perorations that helped explain why Taylor so often would find himself alone at the punch bowl, or wondering if it was the heroin talking and not him. What's more, these issues would never be resolved, and probably still aren't. His stained memories of his mother living a marriage in name only didn't help him cut Ike any slack. Trudy, for her part, knew the marriage was not going to work when Ike returned. She would describe the man she now hardly knew as "full of himself," "enormously agitated," and "very frightening." Making matters worse, stories had been getting back to her for years about his womanizing. Exerting her independence, she had also gotten back into music, becoming a member of the arts and concert committee at UNC, helping book performers for shows at Memorial Hall.

Ike, so mindful of the scars left by his father's abandonment, vowed that he would not even think of ending the marriage, not while his offspring were still children. And so he would playact the role of a dad until 1972, when the kids were all adults and he and Trudy mutually—mercifully—agreed to divorce. But did he do them all any favor waiting so long? Considering the widening gulf between him and the family, the sham of living like the Cleavers or the Nelsons left the same scars on James Taylor and his siblings as Alexander Taylor's disappearing act did on Ike, by subjecting everyone to continuous pain.

Taylor's dodgy relationship with his father was an open blister, one that, much like Ike's with regard to Alexander, never would fully heal, causing him the same enormous regret. Unlike Ike, James would have leeway to try to repair the damage, but that came late in the game, probably too late. And Ike, for his part, would not go out of his way with any of his kids to make up for the years he lost raising them. He was there; that was the main thing, as he saw it. But with so much else to do in his life, too often he was there as an effigy, not to any real effect. His wife and kids learned to get along without him when he'd been away. And for all of them, what filled the void was the great lure of baby boomers everywhere within the borders of Nowhereville in the 1950s, when the norms of the so-called greatest generation weren't enough for their children. For James Taylor, such was the timing of his maturation that the confluence of music and his generation's markers and anxieties seemed predestined. When he was seven and Ike had bid adieu for those two years, Trudy had bought her son a cello. It was the kind of safe, traditional, "proper" instrument that parents were amenable to. But that didn't last long as his instrument of choice. Too many other voices beyond Carrboro were calling.

By the time James Taylor heard the voices, a whole new cultural identity had grown up with him. It was called rock and roll, and it didn't exist when he was born. That week in 1948, the showbiz trade paper *Billboard*—"The World's Foremost Amusement Weekly," as it said on page 1—was still running reviews of vaudeville shows, such as one at Chicago's Oriental Theater featuring Yvonne DeCarlo (pre–Lily Munster), "in a Turkish dancing gown," and the Nat King Cole Trio; Jackie Gleason was starring at the Hippodrome in Baltimore. On the "Best-Selling Popular Retail Records" chart, based on sales figures from retail record stores, number 1 was "I'm Looking Over a Four-Leaf

Clover," bandleader Art Mooney and his orchestra's cover of the 1927 pop tune. Next were Peggy Lee's "Mañana," Bing Crosby's "Now Is the Hour," and Vaughn Monroe's "Ballerina." This was the heyday of Tin Pan Alley, when the structure of the recording industry formed a trough that flowed from the powerful labels—MGM, Capitol, Decca, RCA Victor, London, Columbia—to favored radio disk jockeys primed with promotional copies and, shall we say, *inducements* to play and hype the latest release. Among *Billboard*'s other charts, "Most-Played Juke Box Folk Records" was code for country music, the top spot held that week by "I'll Hold You in My Heart" by Eddy Arnold and His Tennessee Plowboys. The only space for records by black artists was "Most-Played Juke Box Race Records," which had two songs by "dirty blues" singer Julia Lee and her group the Boy Friends, "Snatch and Grab It" and "King Size Papa," as well as Louis Jordan's "Barnyard Boogie" and T-Bone Walker's "Call It Stormy Monday but Tuesday Is Just as Bad."

Isaac and Trudy Taylor were music lovers; no surprise given the latter's opera tutelage. They had an extensive record collection, encompassing everything from Mozart to Al Jolson. Like many couples their age, they had a particular preference for show tunes—Trudy had made a splash in a senior high school play with a rousing rendition of "Smilin' Through," the title song of a 1919 Broadway musical, and more quietly sang tunes of that sort as lullabies for her children. Her own favorite song, she once said, was "What's the Use of Wond'rin'?" from *Carousel.* Their children, prompted early on to play and sing, had been tutored to sing folk and show tunes as well as the highly charged protest songs of Woody Guthrie—including the ingenuous children's song "Riding in My Car" and "This Land Is Your Land," with the pungent verses almost always omitted by singers who recorded the tune, but not by the Taylor clan, such as:

In the shadow of a steeple I saw my people,
By the relief office I seen my people;
As they stood there hungry, I stood there asking,
Is this land made for you and me?

But the Taylor siblings enjoyed a versatile musical education by osmosis, and more and more the sounds from the radio coincided with the explosive birth and nascence of rock and roll, a roiling thunder that emanated from the South and found its voice in the big cities in the North. There, from the great black migration foretold by the great Delta blues musicians in the 1920s, having formed a bustling inner-city jazz/blues club scene across the continent, the first chimes of a new, sweatier blues arose. Often acknowledged as the first rock-and-roll song is Ike Turner's rumbling, honking production of "Rocket 88," a song about an Oldsmobile 88, recorded in Sam Phillips's Sun Records studio in Memphis and credited to its writer and lead singer, sax man Jackie Brenston and his Delta Cats, when released by Chess in April 1951. It went to number 1 on the "race" record chart. But, like many "new" sounds, the song had its roots in R & B, done originally in 1947 as "Cadillac Boogie" by Jimmy Liggins and as an instrumental in '49 by Pete Johnson as "Rocket 88 Boogie."

There was a new vernacular, cadged from "race music," taking hold in America, and a new sound to propel it, even if the mainstream was still resistant. In November 1955, *Billboard*'s "Honor Roll of Hits," ranking the top thirty records, was nearly all white artists; only two black acts were deemed "mainstream" enough to make the list: the Platters' "Only You" at number 8 and Chuck Berry's "Maybellene" at 29. (Number 1 was the clean-cut Four Aces' "Love Is a Many Splendored Thing.") However, only three years later, just two months after the "Hot 100" chart debuted in August 1958, the top rank was "It's All in the Game" by Tommy Edwards, a black singer, followed by another, Bobby Day, with "Rockin' Robin," and yet another at number 4, Little Anthony and the Imperials' "Tears on My Pillow." That year, too, the black market as a whole was given a nod, with an R & B chart.

No longer fighting the funk, the mainstream now looked and sounded very different; even back in '55, *Billboard* ran a brief story that foretold much—"1955: The Year R.&B. Took Over Pop Field," pointing to Atlantic Records' thriving roster of black acts led by Ray Charles and the rise of Chuck Berry and Fats Domino. By the time James Taylor was in his midteens, Elvis Presley had united pop, country, and race idioms, and initiated a new style of crooning and preening. Writers, some old pros, some barely out of high school, were composing not simple movie themes and big-band covers but operettas of teenage heartbreak and even death ("Teen Angel," "Moody River"), sung by innocent-looking, fresh-faced white and, increasingly, black pop singers, brilliant ones like the gospel-bred James Brown and Sam Cooke and the thunderously gifted Jackie Wilson. Sometimes it seemed that, little by little, the placid Eisenhower years were going to break apart at the seams.

Like other kids seeking a new sound and a new path different from the one their parents had traversed, Taylor could take conscious and subconscious cues from the rapid and radical change of popular musical tastes. By the time he was twelve, in 1960, his head rang with music, as did his brothers' and sister's. Trudy, who was never fully resigned to nipping her own budding career to play wife and mother, had become something of a stage mother, paying for lessons for nearly all of them: Livingston and Kate on piano, Alex on violin. With James on his cello, they'd do pubescent jam sessions in the living room, playing folk songs; she'd coach them on how to sing. If Ike was around, he usually blew past them on his way out the door. While he diligently learned how to play it, and did so in his school bands, James hated the intricate lessons and having to lug the thing on his back. He had sprung up by now to nearly six feet tall, his frame skeletal, fleshed with around eighty pounds, and by the time he unpacked his cello, he'd be exhausted. This provided a convenient excuse for him to switch gears, at a time when all that rock and roll was swarming between his ears. As far as he could tell, not one song he heard on the radio had a cello part. Besides, who ever sang while playing the cello?

The guitar, on the other hand . . .

This long-necked, six-string (sometimes twelve) slice of wooden, heavenly manna, which may look to some like a shrunken cello, was arguably the single most trenchant symbol of a metamorphic America in the '50s. Its name derived from the Latin *cithara*, the guitar had been around since the ninth century in a multitude of shapes, sizes, contours, and names. Baroque guitars were the core of classical Renaissance music, and their derivative acoustic guitars were part of the big jazz bands, small combos, and symphonic orchestras through the first half of the twentieth century, in tandem with the quiet brushstrokes of drumsticks and the steady thump of its musical cousin, the stand-up bass guitar. The folk crowd often adopted it as often the only instrument necessary to meld with carefully articulated lyrics.

Once all the rules of music began to be rethought in the new shakeout of rock and roll, the guitar was metaphoric, especially in 1940 when Les Paul, née Lester William Polsfuss, a Wisconsin-born jazz musician of Prussian descent, invented an amplified guitar with much greater wattage than the plug-in guitars by Rickenbacker and Fender—not to mention T-Bone Walker, Johnny Shines, Howlin' Wolf, Muddy Waters, and the dozens of other great electric blues pioneers. Nearly electrocuting himself in the process of his work, Paul began to play hopped-up chords, reflecting the "hot" freestyle jazz style of his idol and mentor, the great French guitar master Django Reinhardt. And he would shake up the industry once the Gibson Les Paul model hit the market in 1952, to become the bestselling guitar in history.

Sending electric current through guitars liberated ungodly screeching, whining sounds that were expertly mellowed by Chuck Berry, whose fictional alter ego played guitar "just like ringing a bell," and Bo Diddley, who fashioned his own box guitar and chugging "hambone" skew on the African Pattin' Juba, or hand-jive, beat. As much as the folk purists hated the amping, musicians everywhere were juicing their guitars. Jazz bands were going electric, the four-string electric bass guitar, capable of more color and texture, replacing those big Buick-sized stand-up basses. Blues offshoots like bluegrass and hillbilly jug bands were suddenly *rock and roll.* Those six-string monsters—"axes," in the musician's vernacular—were fast becoming the means of propulsion for the new strain of mainstream R & B–cum–rock. And James Taylor, struggling to keep his cello on his back, wanted to catch the new wave, wanted to be Johnny B. Goode.

As his twelfth birthday neared, coincidentally in the same year that would turn the page to a new decade sure to bring social and cultural upheaval, "Stringbean," "Jamie," or "JT," as people had taken to calling him, began to bug his mother about springing for a guitar as a Christmas present. Always willing to oblige her children's fancies, she agreed, on condition that he not abandon the cello. He promised he would not, and meant it. And so she purchased a guitar from the mail-order Schirmer company catalog, and he rarely let it out of his sight—though one time when he did, his puckish brother Alex spray-painted the thing blue, even the strings. But that only made it seem cooler and more unique, and he quickly taught himself to play by listening to Trudy's albums and hanging out at music stores where he could pick up pointers from the real players. The songs he first learned were those in the songbooks of the largely Southern tradition of folksingers at one with the soil under their feet and dreams of pie in the sky: Woody Guthrie, Hank Williams, Pete Seeger and the Weavers, and the later breed of Ivy League–flavored folk groups like the Kingston Trio and the Limeliters, who were all the rage in the intellectual corridor of Cambridge, as were even folk parodists like Tom Lehrer, Allan Sherman, and the Smothers Brothers.

Although Taylor might not have known, this music had its roots in English and Scottish ballads from his ancestors' times, which came over on the boats with people just like them. Indeed, early American folk music was concentrated in the very Appalachians where he grew up. British folklorist Cecil Sharp mined them on folk expeditions through the mountains of the mid-South in the 1910s; his discoveries led to a folk revival in his native country and prefaced similar expeditions by left-wing folk revivalists Charles Seeger and Lawrence Gellert and folk preservationists John and his son Alan Lomax in the 1930s and '40s, the latter recording thousands of hours of latter-day folk songs based in grassroots cultural traditions that found a home in the Library of Congress. Their recordings of a primordial Woody Guthrie, Muddy Waters, Blind Willie Johnson, Bessie Jones, and dozens more virtually exhumed a lost South of broken dreams and common love of soil and skies, and their discovery of Huddie Ledbetter (a.k.a. Lead Belly) in a Louisiana prison unleashed the brilliant, pockmarked career of the self-styled "king of the twelve-string," whose songs were like chapters in a grand novel: "Cotton Fields," "Midnight Special," "Gallows Pole," "In the Pines."

These were the traditions that gave life to the twangy, homey country folk of both Hank Williams and the Weavers in the late 1940s. Yet there was often a price to pay for idealism. Guthrie, like Williams, would die disillusioned and alone, consumed by illness and depression; he had been—like the Weavers—branded and blacklisted during the Red scare witch hunts. Similarly, Alan Lomax was hounded by the FBI as a "Communist agitator." And even as Lead Belly was being heralded, a typical headline ran in *Life* that read, LEAD BELLY—BAD NIGGER MAKES GOOD MINSTREL. Such martyrdom only made the music more salient. For Taylor, the long tradition of simple narrative verses, oral storytelling, and the minimalist chords and dry, nasal intonations of Guthrie, were his biggest influences, as they were for Bob Dylan, who followed Guthrie and the Weavers' folk trail to Greenwich Village in the late '50s. It was only in the '60s that Pete Seeger, who had been so ostracized for writing now standard protest folk anthems like "Where Have All the Flowers Gone" and "If I Had a Hammer"—songs that James Taylor had learned to play on the guitar during Seeger's forced exile—could come out of the shadows for a renaissance.

Also, the Taylor children were in the advantageous position of hearing folk meld with blues, even in upscale Chapel Hill. In what seemed like frozen time, there were still African Americans tilling in them old cotton fields back home. Liberal as Trudy was, she befriended a black sharecropper's family and paid the wife a hearty salary to be the Taylors' housekeeper. Not reticent to play with the housekeeper's children, though this was still not commonly done by white kids in the South, James also observed the Sunday morning rituals of the black church her family attended, perhaps on some level seeking some informal salvation from a God not overly welcome in the Taylor home but more so to groove to the choir singing spirituals.

He would, years later, reflect to Tim White, more at length than about most subjects, that human beings' emotional response to music was not learned but imbued. "I think that one of the main motivations for writing music is to get out, to get off, and ultimately to get relief from separation. That's why music has lived forever in church in the South, and elsewhere, and it probably comes from that religious setting, from that need for connection. I have that need, and that's why a lot of songs that I write can turn out to be this kind of religious music without having any obvious religion in them." The need for such a ligature, he said, "suggests an underlying or overlying reality and a huge emotional content for us, regardless of what the lyric is. . . . I believe, most of all, that just by being music, it's religious." As a metaphor, religion of course would be a useful tool in his music, conveniently showing him the light any number of ways. As he said in 1973:

> It's religious sometimes when you take acid and lose your ego and dissolve completely. I think what people are trying to get away from in their religious experiences is the isolation of the conscious mind. . . . Being a conscious being

> means that you divorce yourself from certain aspects of life that are worthwhile. . . . The unknown represents death to men, represents that which he does not control and which eventually kills him; and what you're left with is a very lonely and isolated place.

Another time, he would admit that whenever he would bring Jesus into his longings to help him survive and see the light, it was "really as a way of expressing desperation" but also calling out the true believers who used the same such pleas to the heavens as a crutch or magical potion. On "Country Road," he explained, when he sang about good boys and girls sailing home to Jesus, it "doesn't suggest that I want people to do that. I'm mocking people who do it." Asked if he actually ever did look to Jesus, he said, "Only under the most desperate of circumstances. I think Jesus is interesting as a phenomenon that permeates this culture." One might almost believe that, for James Taylor, religion mattered only when it most felt like a good line, or a good drug.

The elixir of the blues flowed freely in the Taylor home, coexisting with white gospel music. And inevitably these elements found their way into Southern music of all stripes, giving an earnest, down-home folk context to the Southern id, a recognition that the South of legend was now just a state of mind, buried in a morass of undeveloped backwoods, mountain roads, and barren fields, the old pristine topography slowly being covered by miles and miles of superhighways and strip malls. Perhaps if *that* South had come to the Piedmont hills, James Taylor would have had more to write about his surroundings being spoiled, been more of a country crooner like Woody or Hank, or a protest singer like Pete and the Weavers. Instead, this land was not his land, as he saw it.

"Chapel Hill, the Piedmont, the outlying hills, were tranquil, rural, beautiful, but *quiet*," he once said. "Thinking of the red soil, the seasons, the way things smelled down there, I feel as though my experience of coming of age there was more a matter of landscape and climate than people. 'Cause there was nobody around! . . . Carolina in the early '50s was a culture shock for somebody used to Boston, so [Trudy] focused on us kids."

But what would *they* focus on? By default, and just as she did, on music. All across the South, elements of gospel merged with blues and folk, and rock prospered from the basin of the old Delta cats; and in New Orleans through the piano-based boogie-woogie of Fats Domino, Huey "Piano" Smith, and Ernie K-Doe; while up in Norfolk, Gary "U.S." Bonds recorded the R & B/rock "party" song "Quarter to Three," which went to Number 1 on the Hot 100 in '61. The young Taylor couldn't help but feed his musical appetite across the radio dial, most of which was white country stations on which he heard, he once said, "Hank Williams, white gospel, *The Grand Ole Opry*, and jingles for Valleydale Smoked Ham, Penrose Pickled Pork Sausage [and] Toddy Time Jerusalem Artichokes." Nashville was close enough for him to hear the nation's biggest country station, WSM, but the treat was that at night the fifty-thousand-watt WLAC would beam in R & B and doo-wop, Chuck Berry, Little Richard, Frankie Lymon, Howlin' Wolf, and the early R & B records from Sam Phillips's Sun Records studio in Memphis.

As far as Ike Taylor would be able to recall, when James first fooled around on the guitar, his playing was "awful." But he soon could reasonably play bluegrass boogie, a style executed with the thumb and next two fingers of his right hand—taught to him, he later said for a time, by an unnamed blind black man who used to play for change on the street. He worked on mastering the style of the bluegrass finger pickers—not using a full hand and a pick, but the fingers of his right hand delineating in varying ways the left and right hands of a pianist, usually with the thumbnail and forefinger acting as the "left hand" plucking melody, the other fingers the "right hand" rhythm. He would later speak of the method as "Travis picking," and said, "I suppose Elizabeth Cotten is probably more to be credited"—a shout-out to the tragically overlooked black folk/blues guitarist who lived ninety-four robust years as a legend of finger pickin'—playing guitars upside down because she was left-handed, with a style some call "Cotten picking."

Cotten was a Chapel Hill native, though Taylor never met her and only saw her play when she had moved north and played the Boston/Cambridge folk circuit, including the Newport Folk Festival. James's playing wasn't polished, but he could make slick chords ring without a pick, a style also perfected, among millions of other kids his age learning the cosmic properties of the guitar, by one out in Palo Alto, California,

Lindsey Buckingham, who fashioned a guitar-pickin' style based on the banjo licks of John Stewart of the Kingston Trio. Such incubation of future talent would soon seem to reach critical mass all at once, armed with a guitar and a philosophy of musicianship Buckingham defined this way: "I've always believed that you play to highlight the song, not to highlight the player. The song is all that matters." Taylor would say amen to that.

Sucking up the new vibe of popular music, Taylor as a fifteen-year-old was nonetheless tempered by his shyness and isolation. As fate had it, though, on the family's summer jaunt to Martha's Vineyard in 1963, the gawky teen with enormous, if untapped, talent happened to run into a kid close to his age who had gotten close to mastering the guitar. This was Daniel Kortchmar, at seventeen two years his senior and quite nearly everything the introspective Taylor was not. Already bearing the nickname of "Kootch," he was a fixture in the coffeehouses and beach bars around the Vineyard, a brash, forward, big-talking guy with an Elvis sneer, black clothing, and a spit curl. His home was the Westchester County, New York, suburb of Larchmont, the area that seemed so perfect for the windy, pretentiously liberal upscale Maude character played by Beatrice Arthur in the '70s sitcom. Like Taylor, Kortchmar was the second son of a wealthy man, this one's fortune made in manufacturing screws and washers, and an artistically inclined mother, Lucy Cores, the daughter of violin player Michael Cores and known in literary circles for her romance and mystery novels of the late 1940s and 1950s. A short story Lucy wrote for the *Saturday Evening Post* was adapted into a TV show starring Loretta Young.

The Kortchmars, again like the Taylors, were addicted to the sand and society spoils of Martha's Vineyard, summering there each year; a later Cores novel would be set in the Vineyard. They were also politically liberal, outspokenly at yacht parties but in quieter ways in their lives. Cores's boldest stroke was a truly horrifying parable in a sci-fi anthology in which Richard Nixon remained president until 1994. Their son also had an open tap of family money, and it must have amused less well-off teenagers in the Vineyard that the guitar-playing pair had become so tight and spoke wistfully of performing together as a duo—what would they call themselves, so the thought went, the

Trust-Fund Two? Also amusing was how polar opposite they were: one tall, spindly, and disassociated, stunted in the social graces, woefully unsophisticated; the other short, wiry, gregarious, and suave in a swarthy, pushy way—a Steinbeckian Lenny and George. One difference was that Danny's family members, their wealth notwithstanding, were expressive, friendly people of Eastern European sensibilities with whom James would enjoy spending time at backyard barbecues and such more than he did with his own. Kortchmar could see why when he would meet the Taylor clan. He recalls the children as distant from Ike and Trudy, eager to fulfill whatever time they thought they had to punch in with their parents before going off on their own. When they were together, such as on Ike's boats, they had strange, almost ritualistic patterns, communicating not verbally but in something like sign language, with little facial tics, nods, and hand gestures. It was, for all purposes, the law of least involvement. Not surprisingly, few who knew Taylor can recall him saying much of anything about his brood. One to whom he did uses "*Looney Tunes*" to describe what he heard.

Ike, who hoped he could counterbalance his neglect for his children by opening the money spigot for them, had established trust funds for each, not a cent of it to buy anything but more anxiety and fretting from his second son about why he *didn't feel* more contented, nor any closer to Ike. Nor did it help any that, when the Taylors summered that year, Ike and Trudy (but mainly Ike), with no input from their son, had already decided that James would be coming back to Carolina with them after Labor Day, only long enough to pack up his things and head right back for the Bay State, having been enrolled at a pricy boy's prep school. The exclusive Milton Academy boarding school, located in the city of Milton (where Ike and Trudy lived when James was born) and founded in 1798, has in recent times been tarred by scandal but its history is inviolate, its graduates a who's who from Robert and Teddy Kennedy to Buckminster Fuller to recent Massachusetts governor Deval Patrick and sundry Pulitzer Prize and Medal of Honor winners, ambassadors, politicians, filmmakers, and industry captains.

Ike Taylor could not have earmarked a more stately or portentous incubator of success for his son, room and board and tuition there setting Ike back only a reasonable, for him, $2,700 a year. But for

James, it was all a lot of self-important hooey that felt like one more expectation of walking in step with the Taylor heritage. He dreaded the passage of each day as the summer dwindled and Milton beckoned. Those three months were a real tease. Hanging out almost exclusively with Kortchmar on the beach, the hours were fused by instructions from the older kid on the guitar, who tutored him on how to play twelve-bar blues figures that Taylor never could have taught himself. He gladly allowed himself to be dragged to clubs where Kortchmar, a real go-getter, had a schedule of gigs lined up playing for the tourists, sometimes backing up other bands. Not surprisingly, the fringe benefits were also enticing, with the sudden presence around him of the very personification of what Steely Dan would one day identify as "sweet things from Boston, so young and willing." Lesson learned. As Taylor would posit, "I realized right away that girls are attracted to musicians," even weird ones. Kortchmar, who had his pick of girls as well, can easily recall with admiration his new buddy playing off several sweet things at a time, seeing him with a different teen girl each time he saw him.

To Taylor, whose virginity was swept out to sea that summer, Lord knows with whom, it was easy enough to call this sudden burst of attention and affection "innocent adolescent fun," making no exception when he hopped into the sack with women, not *girls.* As Kortchmar recalled in wonder, "At fifteen, he was dating twenty-year-old chicks!" It was more than just recreational sex—it was an addiction, seemingly harmless enough, as was another rite of maturing in the crucible of music, money, and leisure: smoking his first joints, usually passed to him by Danny or other hip teens in clubs or beach hangouts. He quickly and easily fell into a lifestyle of drugs and easy sex, able to consume mass quantities of both, to everyone's surprise given his awkward, bookish appearance—which not incidentally seemed to morph into actual *coolness* with each hit of weed; his walk would become slower, manlier, his voice lower, his remarks hitting the right literary and musical references. He could play guitar and sing with more confidence and improvisation, and could let loose his tightly wound inner spring into free-flowing vocalization, and later on, more cohesive writing.

He could be tall without being gawky, and from what the girls told each other, under the influence he was a hell of a lay. Even his natural way of keeping a distance from people seemed to work for him—to Tim White, it came off as "a kindly indifference." Taylor even then knew the score, *why* he was a different person under these conditions. It was because he didn't have to conform. Losing himself in the music scene, he has said, was "a feeling of being wanted," this feeling not being possible under the usual conditions of his life. Another time he said his insecurity was suffocating and thus, "I didn't feel like facing the world every day." Music, sex, pot, it all "gave me the escape I needed." If only that feeling of ascent didn't rub off when he came down from the bud and became the nerdy, goofy James again. He felt most repressed when he would come home to the family's cottage or spend time with Ike sailing, his function most often to be getting his father enough packs of cigarettes to last through the trip. The solution, of course, seemed simple enough: what if he never *had* to come down? It was something he seriously pondered in the years to come.

As it was, even at fifteen these rituals of youth mixed with posing as a music savant were a kind of deliverance, a gradual one to be sure, since the highs were so irritatingly short. Still, it was clear that he had a special instrument in his voice. When James would do a turn on "Michael Row the Boat Ashore" or an old blues riff like John Lee Hooker's "Crawling King Snake," Kortchmar immediately knew this was his friend's main strength, if he could learn to master singing in front of a crowd without his voice cracking in cold fear. The problem was that, just as he had dreaded, when the summer ended, so did the reveries. Kootch went back to Larchmont for his next year of high school. And James Taylor swallowed hard and packed with all the anticipatory élan of a man on his way to prison.

4

THE NEED FOR CONNECTION

James Taylor was uprooted for his own good, as he was told—a measure of how Ike demanded that all his children be privately schooled, as he had been, as all good Taylor men had been through the ages. Livingston received his marching orders to the Westover School in Pennsylvania, and Kate to several summer boarding schools in New England. Alex was left free to continue at Chapel Hill schools, spared the dreaded train or plane ride out of town on grounds that he was neither smart nor well behaved enough for a place like Milton. The irony was that James, as gentle and intellectually gifted as he was, was even less suited to it, something Ike might have realized had he admitted to himself that he really didn't know his own son very well and listened to him when he pleaded not to go to Milton.

If he had, it would have occurred to Ike that his son was a nonconformist, a trait sure to be trouble at the vaunted prep school, and his unresolved anxieties and alienation would hardly be assuaged far from home, alone among preppies hard driven to follow the lead of all those famous graduates, to places like Harvard, Yale, and MIT. But none of James's arguments, and none of the clues all around him pointing against sending him away, did a bit of good. And so off he went, with a kind of self-fulfilling prophesy of detesting the Milton Academy and doing as little as he could to fit in there. The first time Ike and Trudy drove up to visit him at the school, one of his teachers confided that their son was having a disconcertingly hard time and had already said he wanted to drop out. Ike, of course, wouldn't have taken such a notion seriously; his son had all the privileges he needed, and he'd surely become more inured to the place, given time. James wasn't about to repeat what he told the teacher; then, and even years later, he would pass off his unease in school as "typical adolescent crap," but it was obvious to Trudy he felt alone, friendless, and homesick.

If there was a good side to wearing a jacket with the Milton crest, it was being able to impress the girls he could entice back to the cottage that his parents now kept year-round in Chilmark, by the ocean. Sometimes he'd ride his bike from the cottage to the coast and take the boat out on warm days—at fifteen a sailor in the tradition of all those Taylor men—or else simply bicycle along isolated roads, not coming home until late at night. "When you were alone, you were really alone," said Kortchmar, who was normally the only one Taylor allowed into his life, and was with him on many a summertime hitchhike excursion to nowhere. "When it was dark, it was absolutely black, and when it was quiet, there wasn't a sound. I think it was a profound experience for James and me, too—a romantic trip. I think that's where his song 'Country Road' came from." Of the summers, Kortchmar said, "You did all your living in two months. You'd expect incredible, romantic things, to happen. Sometimes they did, sometimes they didn't. You'd go there to really be alive and then go back to school, back to sleep."

During the winter, with little else to do, he had waded deeply into music. Keeping his promise to Trudy, he had taken his cello to Milton along with his guitar, and it might have seemed like extortion to her that when she and Ike arrived there, the son had but one request: he wanted to sell the cello and buy a newer guitar. Trudy, who made these kinds of decisions, relented. He *had* kept the promise for several years, and it was clear his musical tastes were more plebeian than she hoped. She gave her assent, with one caveat—that the guitar he would buy had better be a "good one." During a visit back home, he bought a Gibson, a J-50 acoustic, on a side trip to Durham, and it would be the only one he would play until 1973. Back in his room at Milton, he could be heard strumming it at all hours. As he would surmise years later, had it taken "any kind of discipline, any effort or will or strength of character for me to develop a musical style, it never would have happened. . . . It was lucky for me—it actually saved my life."

In the autumn of 1963, when the entire nation was paralyzed for months following the dark day of November 22 when the young president and signet of generational change was murdered in a motorcade in Dallas, the music industry in particular seemed frozen in place. Record sales lagged, appearances by top stars were canceled, and a shroud-like pall descended over the Christmas season. The gloom was broken in February when four British mop-tops in tight suits and boots came to America to perform a new-sounding rock and roll on *Ed Sullivan.* That, as with most everyone else his age, was an epiphany for Taylor as he hunkered down in the snow of Milton, further crystallizing his objectives. But Taylor was reluctant to perform alone and wouldn't have even known how to pitch himself for club owners, what to play, or how to do it without being guided by Kortchmar's swagger and bold guitar licks. Worse, he would have another trying year at Milton to slog through, every day in misery.

By then he had already composed a song, titled "Roll River Roll," which existed only as a historical footnote, as he would never record it, finally singing it onstage in 1995 for a National Geographic TV show about rafting the Colorado River. While the lyrics were ingenuous, they were cultivated for a fifteen-year-old with no formal music training. Created as he strummed his new guitar, it referenced his long hours staring at Morgan Creek as a youth: "When I was a little boy I played along her side / Built myself a raft of reeds and on her I would ride." Stuck in Milton, the river represented to him a metaphor for rolling "past fields and towns" toward a brighter destination—"And the ocean is the biggest thing I will ever be." (In 2007, British troubadour Richard Hawley would write and record a similar kind of song with the same title.) It would also, as an element of nature, be one crucial part of the equation of many songs, a building block that could make a lyric metaphoric of numerous things.

"I started being a songwriter pretending I could do it," Taylor would say, "and it turned out I could."

Taylor had the sort of nasal, high-pitched voice that country singers usually featured, but sang with only a faint distillation of Southern twang and the crisp diction of Beacon Street, both bluegrass and blue blood at once. The only time anyone would hear him talk *Suth-uhn* was years later when he mimicked a drawl telling the cowboy lullaby genesis of "Sweet Baby James." There was also that curious, clipped Irish-folk element no one could figure out. All this would help delineate him from country singers south of the Mason-Dixon Line as something different—a quality that *Rolling Stone* would aver later "suggested Dylan as a North Carolina country gentleman." Dylan, indeed, was the standard template for pubescent folk rockers. The constructions and vernacular of his songs followed no industry rules, and while his machine-gun blasts of syllables always seemed to require great analysis to figure out, he almost singly killed off the days of "I need you / I miss you / I love you" fluff, at least if it wasn't done in some cynical fashion. Now "vandals" and "handles" made for a good rock rhyme. A metaphor like "Maggie's Farm" could be applied to any job or any regime under which one could sit simmering, between cultural pincers, and think:

Well, I try my best to be just like I am
But everybody wants you to be just like them
They say sing while you slave, and I just get bored

During these formative years for the young understudy from Carolina who was assimilating various music idioms, his main thrust was clean, straightforward pop with a touch of poetic piping and a talent for storytelling, but never with the snide tone of a personal cudgel. There was one thing missing from Dylan's poetry: an expression of his own humanity and life; they weren't about him. Whereas the future Taylor could have written a line like "And you want somebody you don't have to speak to / Won't you come see me Queen Jane?" (from "Queen Jane Approximately"), his would have gone "And you want somebody you *can* speak to." Even if he was as insular as Dylan, Taylor didn't stew in discontent. He didn't do mean; he wanted everyone to like him too much for that—maybe he really wanted to be pitied.

Taylor made it through another year, barely making passing grades, the reward for which was another summer go-around in the coffee and beach bars with Danny Kortchmar, who was certainly moving far more surely and steadily up the ladder. The Vineyard circuit was good to him, earning him invitations to play guitar on recording sessions in England upon his graduation from high school, meaning he'd once again leave the beach after the summer of '64, when the two had resumed their act, Taylor playing rhythm guitar or harmonica, another self-taught instrument. Danny never conned himself into believing he could sing, so he kept vocalizing to an occasional harmony part.

"From the first time we sàng together on old blues stuff," Kortchmar recalls, "and I heard his natural sense of phrasing, every syllable beautifully in time, I knew James had that *thing*." He calls it "a gift" and says that "he was smart enough to know *what* to sing and when."

Even then, that could be just about anything, and the inclination was to play folk as the twosome followed the noble path traveled by Joan Baez, the swarthy, half-Mexican daughter of a Methodist-converted Quaker minister and physicist who taught at MIT. She played the same coffee bars and summer beach hangouts in the late '50s, her remarkable high-trilled tremolo helping rewrite a new folk idiom, and she recorded her first album in the basement of a friend's home. Baez was just one of many folkies who performed regularly at Club 47 in Cambridge, the place to be for rebellious young folk and R & B devotees. By the early '60s, she had gone to California and was being called the "Earth Mother" of the folk revival, performing with Bob Dylan and recording widely selling albums for Vanguard Records, an important folk and blues label. Her folk ballads and updating of old Negro spirituals and labor-movement laments like "Joe Hill" began moving ever more to protest—first as a leading edge in the civil rights cause, then as a unified voice against the mounting toll of the Vietnam War.

It was only natural for Jamie and Kootch to plumb those records for musical guidance, and Danny remembers playing Baez's albums, marveling how she took Dylan, Woody Guthrie, and even some hoary folk standards to higher ground in ways that could bring even a hard heart to tears. On her 1965 *Farewell, Angelina* album was a song that caught Taylor's fancy, derived as it was from the Scottish highlands of his ancestors—Francis McPeake's "The Wild Mountain Thyme," reserving a place in his mind for its sweet lullaby melody and scenic lyrical clarity:

I will build my love a bower by yon clear and crystal
And all around the bower I'll pile flowers from the mountain

That kind of poetry was more to James's sensibilities, while Danny's was more Ray Charles and Lightnin' Hopkins. When they'd play a set at a club, folk would alternate with R & B, a rather unique repertoire that they hoped could bridge any gap between the two idioms. Sometimes it did; other times the audience would sit on their hands and wallets when the plate was passed around, the only means of compensation the unknown acts had at the open-mike nights. One source charts a typical set—four songs before clearing out for the next act—as Hopkins's "Custard Pie" and "Rocky Mountain Blues," Charles's "Hallelujah I Love Her So," and the Hoagy Carmichael "Circle 'Round the Sun," which indicates that while Taylor would write mainly in the folk poet vein, they were circumspect in their use of folk, sensing that the greener fields of pop music lay in the roots of rock and roll and mainstream pop.

Another source recalls that they even won a hootenanny contest in a beach bar, proving they could get people's feet moving and hands clapping, earning fifty bucks and an appearance at the Unicorn on the Vineyard, with a promise from the owner of that Unicorn and the bigger one in Boston. They shared the stage for that gig with the great blind blues/gospel guitarist Reverend Gary Davis, who had cut his teeth in North Carolina, his thumb-pickin' guitar style one of Taylor's early influences. Davis was almost seventy at the time, yet when the owner refused to pay up, he displayed a most unpastoral side, pulling a gun on the man. Still, these steps, small and halting as they were, convinced the younger men, especially when they got stoned, that they would one day make everyone forget about Simon and Garfunkel.

The two dreamers indeed seemed to be following in the path established by the equally odd couple from Queens, New York, a small, cocky guy paired with a bigger, more reticent guy who was a better singer. Simon and Garfunkel's 1964 debut studio album *Wednesday Morning, 3 A.M.*, on Columbia Records—Bob Dylan's home label—and produced by Tom Wilson, who had produced Dylan's work, was a rock landmark, though in real time it was buried in the landslide of the Beatles and the British invasion, a bitter taste shared by a good many American acts. Simon's "The Sound of Silence" and their cover of Dylan's "The Times They Are A-Changin'" were markers of the itchy marriage of rock and folk, and Dylan was said to resent the duo for stealing his thunder. But that didn't happen right away. A disillusioned Simon went to live in England before "Silence" was remixed by Wilson, without his permission, in the clanging guitar style of the Byrds' cover of "Mr. Tambourine Man" and released. The track immediately struck a nerve of cool alienation, which made it the ideal theme of Mike Nichols's brilliant movie milestone *The Graduate* in 1967, solidifying Simon and Garfunkel as the singing bards of rock.

Still, Taylor could not be pigeonholed into any category. Unlike the Yankee folksingers, he had been imbued with the gospel of country; of Elvis, Carl Perkins, Buddy Holly, the Everly Brothers; and of the *new* country rooted in the '50s by Sonny James, Marty Robbins, and Merle Haggard, and continued by Willie Nelson, Johnny Cash, and Waylon Jennings, who strayed from the classic Nashville/Grand Ole Opry comfort zone. Country music, with its lineage of hard but fancifully good-hearted men who happened to drink and cheat on their suffering women by rote, pulled at the emotions harder and more sincerely than anything in the white pop market, evoking a near-crippling loneliness and isolation, themes that Lennon and McCartney would expand for the mainstream market when they turned from formulaic pop to almost monkish introspection and melancholia with "Nowhere Man," "In My Life," and "Norwegian Wood," a trinity on *Rubber Soul.*

The songs in Taylor's head as a midteen strove for introspection, much like "Roll River Roll," reflective not of Southern man machismo but a Southern boy's sentimentality for the land and sea. The words he wrote would be about pubescent yearning. However, he was looking not for a party or a double shot of his baby's love but rather for acceptance and love he didn't really know how to give but needed to take. Such emotional undertow was no affectation, though sometimes Taylor seemed to like wallowing and playing the victim. He was ever the lost soul, not easily figured out and prickly as all get-out to be with. The teachers at Milton had branded Taylor as a different sort of rebel, one who could cause damage only to himself. As one teacher would recall, unaware of the irony, "James was more sensitive and less goal oriented than most students of his day."

By the first days of spring 1964, Ike and Trudy allowed him the extraordinary concession of temporarily leaving the prestigious school before he could flunk out, or worse. His parents agreed to ease his burden and let him come home to finish his junior year at Chapel Hill

High, provided he would ultimately graduate from Milton, as planned. Ike, who in 1964 had become dean of the UNC School of Medicine, a position he would hold until 1971, was to become even less a hands-on father. James's path was then far more influenced by his ambitious older brother, who had also been bitten by the music bug. Alex had even put together a band, the Fabulous Corsairs, pilfering the name from the North Carolina singing group the Corsairs, whose superb and then daring post-doo-wop tale of an adulterous affair, "Smoky Places," was a big pop hit in 1962. Alex was pleased to take his younger brother into the band, provided that he accepted who was boss. James had no problem with it, playing rhythm guitar to Alex's lead on his Fender and singing backup to Alex's lead vocal. Neither did Alex ask for any input about his band's format, which contained not a drop of coffeehouse folk but rather all rock-ribbed R & B, commanding the group perform songs like "The Midnight Hour," "Searching," and "Stormy Monday" at sock hops, dorms, and other small-time gigs around Chapel Hill.

There was an underlying competitive reflex that also led Livingston to claim his turf. When Livingston was learning the guitar, he recalled of James, "He'd show me things . . . no, as a matter of fact, he wouldn't show me anything. He was a real bastard about it. What I'd do is watch him play something and I'd go up to him and play it wrong and it would make him so furious that he'd grab the guitar and show me how to play it right." Of course, James might have kept a distance musically from his siblings as they grew so that they *could* find their own identity and style, which is exactly what happened. Moreover, with the Fabulous Corsairs, James willingly receded to his more aggressive brother, ceding most of what he had learned up on the beaches of the Vineyard to revert to gospel-pocked, foot-stomping Southern soul, which he would later recall as "party time, Shag music."

Both Alex and Livingston Taylor seemed to be poised and primed for success as a singer far more than their reserved brother. Livingston could be as quiescent as James—who defined him as "observant and fairly quiet" and said that he "always held his cards close"—but more calculating, at least at this point. Alex, on the other hand, was never loath to speaking his mind, usually to the slow-burning discontent of Ike Taylor, by whom Alex, probably to his delight, was consigned the label of "rebel." Burly and barrel-chested like Livingston, and as blond and pug-nosed as James was dark and sharp featured, he most resembled his now balding father, and it was almost as a protector that his siblings wanted him around. Alex nobly took on that role. About the brother who was having such a rough go of it, Alex once said that by playing music with him in a band, "I tried to make sure James kept out of trouble. . . . I had to keep a close eye on him."

Indeed, when Kate would make the short trip up to DC to march in antiwar protests or participated in student demonstrations at UNC, Alex came along to see that she'd have a human shield. But the notion that Alex, the bad boy, would be anyone's moral sentry seems ludicrous, as he himself was neck-deep in drugs and running with the wrong crowd—which, to be sure, was normally anyone and everyone Ike saw hanging around the music scene. In reality, the Taylor brood were *all* rebels, out of step with the Carolina worldview. As is often the case with towns dominated by a college environment, it was assumed by those outside the town to be a hotbed of liberal rabble, by dint of so many in the population holding jobs on campus. The execrable Dixiecrat Jesse Helms regularly called the town "Communist Hill." Racists like Helms were feeling the heat. Central North Carolina in the '50s bucked the Jim Crow intransigence all around the South; nearby Greensboro had been the first Southern city to comply with the Supreme Court's 1954 *Brown v. Board of Education* ruling and was the site of what is sometimes mistakenly regarded as the first lunch counter sit-in, at the Woolworth's in 1960.

While James took a pass on marching and protesting—a characteristic of his that would not change, similar to Bob Dylan's cherry-picking of "safe" causes—he would by osmosis have a political component to his worldview, such as it was in '65, even if any leftward statements would not go beyond Woody Guthrie–style allegorical plaints about the preservation of the soil and sea. If he ever was as outraged as, say, Barry McGuire about the Vietnam War and the nuclear menace, and would lend his name to concerts to rescue the imperiled environment, he seemed content not being a firebrand. Some naturally believed he was a classic cop-out. Even Ike, despite his own reluctance to mix it up politically at the risk of his prestige, was disappointed that James, the "quiet" one—alternately, the "smart" one—begged off an activist approach. This of course was hypocrisy, but Ike apparently believed that transference of his sharp political edges to his children, once they renounced a career in the professional upper class, would assuage his own cop-outs and minimalism. He openly told his son to "take a stand," a phrase the son would remember well, and deliver in a punchline fashion. Still, for now, he was not ready to stand on his own two feet.

The Fabulous Corsairs gig was a kick. The band dressed in turtleneck sweaters and tweed sport coats, looking "pretty collegiate," the rock-and-roll look then, James recalled, and it was with them that he gained his first entrée into a studio. That happened when they pooled their resources and rented time in a studio in Raleigh, where they recorded a song Alex had written called "You're Gonna Have to Change Your Ways," with James coming up with a similarly innocuous song for the flip side, "Cha Cha Blues." Looking to get a nibble, Alex sent the few copies he had of the disk to local record labels, in vain, and the band was soon history. For James it was a couple months of head-clearing respite before going back to Milton in the autumn of '65 for his senior year. Having given Carolina a last shake, he felt he *needed* the separation that he had once felt was destructive. Those few weeks of living with Ike were hellish, mainly for how he had taken to treating Alex, who was now his whipping boy and becoming more of a delinquent by the day, as if by cause and effect.

What's more, Ike would be snide about James's own motives for finishing school; even years later, he couldn't help putting down the fact that his boy wasn't going to follow in his steps as a professional man. "If he dropped out of school," Ike said, "he knew he'd have to go get a job. If he got a job he wouldn't be able to play guitar. . . . So he decided to go back to Milton." True enough, his influences now were those in the folk-rock venues around Boston and the Vineyard. That was his *real* education, his classrooms the smoke-filled rooms of bars and coffeehouses. That was the case with many kids his age, one of whom was another child of wealth, Bonnie Raitt. A year younger than him, the pert redheaded daughter of the Broadway actor John Raitt, she, like Taylor, attended elite prep schools and would enroll at Radcliffe in Cambridge two years later, but her classroom was Club 47, the Cambridge beehive of folk and blues. "The first person I saw there was [blues guitarist] Spider John Koerner, who I fell in love with [and who would record her 1971 debut album in his studio]. . . . I saw Canned Heat. I saw Joni Mitchell, wearing that little, red satin, pleated mini-skirt with her hair rolled up." Soon she hooked up with Dick Waterman, a much older, well-connected promoter, and was running with Buddy Guy, Junior Wells, and Lightnin' Hopkins, "hangin' out with seventy-five-year-old blues guys who drank at ten in the morning. I was serving them drinks." Why? "I wanted to be the female Muddy [Waters]."

This scene, she said, "was one of the navels of the cultural period, and a lot of influence came out of it. It put a lot of intelligence into the guitar movement. . . . Between Elvis Presley and the folksingers, the guitar movement believed in youth and the correctness of their own thinking." For Taylor, the closest thing to a mentor was Tom Rush, whom he saw perform at the Unicorn, the big folk hangout in Boston. Rush, then in his midtwenties and only a few years out of Harvard, was working toward defining a new wave, the folk-rock troubadour era, performing acoustic folk songs from the Alan Lomax archives of ballads derived from the Scottish lowlands and Appalachians. When Taylor heard Rush, he recalled, he "instantly became a big fan. I copied and learned a lot of his arrangements, so I guess it's fair to say that Tom was not only one of my early heroes, but also one of my main influences." Rush would get his big break in 1963, signing a deal with Paul Rothchild of Prestige Records. He made two albums there. Then when Rothchild went to Elektra Records, an L.A. label branching into rock, Rush cut four milestone albums, including the classic *Take a Little Walk with Me,* and found himself godhead of the primordial folk-rock scene.

Rush indeed seemed something like an oracle for the young Taylor. Folk rock had pretty much lost its way ever since it fell under the spell of the electric guitar, something that got Bob Dylan booed off the stage at the hoary Newport Jazz Festival in 1965, when "Like a Rolling Stone," fitted in a clear rock style, went to Number 2 on the Hot 100. By year's end the L.A. country-rock band the Byrds had taken their electrified cover of Dylan's "Mr. Tambourine Man" with Roger McGuinn's piercing twelve-string Rickenbacker guitar line to the top of the chart. Another soft-rock L.A. outfit, the Turtles, had covered Dylan's "It Ain't Me Babe" and made Number 8. Folk was still accounted for but was fused into pop (e.g., the Limeliters' Glenn Yarbrough's theme song for the movie *Baby the Rain Must Fall,* a Number 2 pop hit). Yet Rush seemed resistant to trends; he could still transfer to poetry and song the aching of a human heart, perhaps best expressed in the song that became a much-covered elegy, 1968's "No Regrets," in lines like

The hours that were yours echo like empty rooms
Thoughts we used to share I now keep alone

Taylor would appropriate Rush's "you were gone" phrasing in the song "Fire and Rain," and getting into the mindset of writing songs was an undercurrent of his life—that is, when he wasn't so depressed he started to alarm people. Most days he seemed lost, and Ike and Trudy didn't know, but may have suspected, that drugs had played a major part in his slide. His marijuana consumption had become a daily habit—no doubt another reason he preferred not to stick around at home—and at Milton he became quite expert at dodging detection and expulsion. Only by getting high could he play his guitar, the feeling he got during those interludes "my medicine," he would say, a delusional crutch that would plague him for years to come. And when he came down, he was at risk, any kind of withdrawal leading to deepening depression. He began telling people he was having thoughts of killing himself. Whether or not he really meant it—according to psychiatrists, those who openly threaten suicide are normally less apt to go through with it than those who harbor it silently—he figured he had to address his disoriented mind. Accordingly, he never got through that senior year at Milton, suffering what is usually described as a "breakdown." In the Taylor family's circles, there was a long precedent for dealing with fear and self-loathing: booking residence in a "designer" institution where being an inmate had cachet and even conveyed *status.* The twist was that apparently it wasn't Ike or Trudy who took the initiative to do this—it was their son who did that, on his own. Given the name of a psychiatrist in Cambridge, he went there and, he would recall, broke down in the office. "Listen," the shrink told him, "I'm going to put you under observation for a while."

For cases like Taylor, the place chosen was the McLean Hospital, a chichi sanatorium where no less than Sylvia Plath, Anne Sexton, Zelda Fitzgerald, and Ray Charles had taken their neuroses and drug habits—and of more recent vintage, Steven Tyler and Rick "Super Freak" James. It was a place Ike Taylor indeed knew well, the hospital long affiliated with Mass Gen and the site of important neuroscience and brain tissue research. How he got there is a little hazy. At separate times

Taylor has contradicted himself, saying that "people around me put me in a mental hospital for a spell," other times that he indeed booked himself in, a very adult thing to do. But whatever the circumstances, it was something his mother and father were quick to sign off on and had no problem letting it be known. Whether their son was ill in the head or had a case of, in contemporary parlance, "affluenza," he was welcome within its four brick and ivy walls.

Taylor's own explanation, in hindsight, for why he was there: "I was shy. I went to a boarding school that was all male, and I think that was an absurd thing. . . . I had a rigorously academic direction that ratified me not even in the slightest. I didn't think I could break out of it. That was mainly why I went to McLean, because I saw no way out of it." In fact, the idea seemed so righteous to Ike and Trudy that they would eventually contribute two other of their unhappy children to McLean as well. With the Taylor family, some scripts just seemed to write themselves.

5

A VICTIM OF HIPPIEPHRENIA

McLean Hospital in Belmont, Massachusetts, fifteen minutes west of Boston, is on a lovely piece of splendidly manicured acreage, looking more like a rolling golf course lined with fruit trees than a mental institution. Its storied history is something akin to the Grand Hotel of infirmaries. Ray Charles, when he entered to kick a never-ending heroin habit in the '50s, famously remarked, "Brother, for $50 a day I could be staying at the Plaza, and I'm staying here!" Thousands of well-heeled patients had come through its doors since it was built in 1811 and moved to the Belmont grounds in 1895, with more than a few occupants quite in need of help—for one, Sylvia Plath, whose stay there in the 1950s led her to meet the poet Robert Lowell but did not head off her sticking her head in an oven and committing suicide a decade later—and more than a few others simply there because someone thought it was a good idea.

Like James Taylor, quite a few younger patients had no clinically definable mental disorders, and thus were generally lumped under meaningless catch-all pseudodiagnosis "adolescent turmoil." The term was applied to author Susanna Kaysen when after a suicide attempt at age eighteen she too confined herself at McLean in 1967, a two-year stay that provided the material for her bestselling 1993 roman à clef and later movie, *Girl, Interrupted.* Kaysen's characters, based on fellow patients—an array of sociopaths, manic-depressives, obsessive-compulsives, schizophrenics, and drug addicts (none based on James

Taylor, whose time there preceded hers)—tread a netherworld in which, like Ken Kesey's famous "cuckoo's nest," insanity isn't an affliction but an alternate world. In the end, being "cured" is nothing more than being able to act out what society deems as "sane" behavior.

Getting to that point meant waiting out "treatment" approved according to a diagnosis, and the level of payment made for entry to McLean, which for Ike and Trudy was $36,000, prepaid, for one year. But the diagnosis and course of treatment for James Taylor was not cut and dried, it being unclear just why he believed he was so maladjusted. While he spoke of suicide, he hardly seemed as sincere about it as was Plath, who wrote of the "owl's talons clenching my heart" before she took her life. Taylor had a similarly poetic description for himself—"It felt like someone had cast my hand in concrete." In 2000, Dr. Alan Stone, professor of law and psychology at Harvard, coined a retro pseudodiagnosis for such malcontented '60s refugees. As he wrote in the *Boston Review,* for he and his colleagues back then, "It was by no means easy for us to decide when someone had crossed the border from hippie to hippiephrenia," a sort of mockery to deride what seemed like self-absorbed teenagers. Even so, for the price of the treatment, there would be deep discussions with staff psychologists, and for many of the patients, this was exactly the kind of concern and attention they had never experienced at home.

McLean was considered a modern facility, eschewing Stone Age means like Scotch douches—the colloquialism for painful, needlelike or ice-cold showers—electroshock treatment, and icepick lobotomies. Yet the windows were blocked off with bars—actually, two-thousand-pound "security screens"—and patients were permitted to eat in the cafeteria only with plastic utensils, as metal utensils could be used as weapons, or a means of suicide. McLean also still routinely dispensed antipsychotic drugs that were popular in the 1950s, like Thorazine, to calm hyperactive teenagers, causing them to aimlessly wander about zombielike—the "Thorazine Shuffle," it was called. Taylor, who hardly seemed in need of calming, least of all with a strong narcotic, spoke of being injected with the drug nonetheless. "It's really a heavy and stultifying tranquilizer," he said, "a blunt instrument, and a very heavy-handed way of dealing with mental health problems." Little wonder that he would give as a short answer to what it was like at McLean, "They lock you up in a chemical jail."

Apparently that wasn't the worst of it. For some reason, the doctors found it necessary to apply a "modern" form of electroshock therapy called electroconvulsive therapy (ECT), which he would speak of only in broad metaphor in song. However, that had less effect on him than classes he attended accredited under the name of the Arlington School, whose military-like regulations forced him to concentrate on his books. "We didn't have that jive nothingness that pushes most kids through high school," he would tell *Time* magazine years later, when he had little compunction in revealing details that would counter his leisure-class background. "You can't tell a whole bunch of potential suicides that they have to have a high school diploma. . . . The day was planned for me there, and I began to have a sense of time and structure, like canals and railroad tracks." One book he read cover to cover was *Oedipus the King*, the patricide and incest undercurrents of the Sophocles epic tragedy perhaps giving him a fatalistic context to his life—to be reinforced when the FM radio stations played Jim Morrison wailing about these very themes in the Doors' 1967 song "The End."

The scenarios that swam endlessly in the roiling sea inside his head gave vitality and purpose to his writing. He had come a good way in the art of composing, and it seems beneficial in retrospect that his own inward path landed him on the lonely highway of rock in the mid-'60s, when pop lyrics had become very needy and self-centered. Who could have ever foreseen a few years before that Frank Sinatra could have crooned a song about needing to die knowing he did it "my way"? Or another that yearned to find a one-night stand with a "stranger in the night," a song Sinatra confessed he regarded as "a piece of shit" and "the worst fucking song that I have ever heard," yet his blunt vocal and its swirling strings gave him a rock-era number one hit, one that would be covered even by *Connie Francis.*

The tenor of the times was alienation and separation—even among the live-wire songs from Motown, Levi Stubbs urged the world to "ask the lonely how vainly a heart can yearn, for losing a love that will never return." Riding on this river of tears, Taylor's musical mien flowed from the core of his own soul, but a rudderless core. In ways similar to Roy Orbison, his material was his own life. And, mostly, that was something he saw as a sad story but one he needed to tell, hopefully without self-pity. It was as if he heard, years before the fact, the slowly intoned vow by Van Morrison to find a way to purge his own barriers in the latter's 1972 song "Listen to the Lion":

I . . . shall . . . search . . . my . . . soul.

That he did, owing his time at McLean a lot for compositions that arose from cold industrial gray corridors decorated with vomit and echoing with primal screams in the night. These would arise from inside his head soon enough, in haunting verbal images of sights and sounds that were all too true, yet also convenient. In truth, at his age and with his hormones, none of it, not Thorazine-filled needles or low-voltage electroshock, seemed to freak him out as much as the horror of not having any girls around, creating an intimate eight-month relationship with his hand. And Taylor himself admitted that he owed McLean big time, as boys his age were being shipped off to Vietnam and many dying there. As the story goes, on the day of his draft board hearing, two white-coated McLean attendants accompanied him, and as one source puts it, he was "uncommunicative" as officers interviewed him. He got a deferment as a mental case, laughing all the way back with the attendants.

Ike and Trudy assumed their boy was being well taken care of, and within a year of James's release they would bundle off Livingston and Kate, who also seemed troubled enough for a stay at McLean. One chronicle of Taylor history has it that "the McLean experience would soon become [for the Taylors] what Harvard is for the Saltonstalls—something of a family tradition." Indeed, the chief psychiatrist at McLean for twelve years, Dr. Shervert Frazier, has said that the families of kids like the Taylors were clueless about why their children were really there. The kids, he said, "were addicted and their behavior while under the influence was erratic. They were not themselves, and at times they were dangerous to themselves and to others. Their friends didn't recognize them and vice versa. Many of them had disowned their families. Nobody in the old-line families had ever seen anything like it—all they ever did was drink martinis."

Neither did the Taylors come out of McLean anything close to being "cured" of whatever ills they may have had, to say the least, given that they were hardly done with drugs, not by a long shot. And James left feeling contemptuous of the "elitist, rich white kids" whom others might have assumed he had a lot in common with but didn't, and shrinks whom he believed had less attachment to reality than the patients had. "Once," he remembered, "when I was feeling outasight, I went in for a weekly consultation with two psychiatric residents. And they questioned me, they said, 'Why are you feeling so good?' as if this were an abnormal situation. That was really strange—to have to remedy that." Perhaps how he really felt about McLean can be deduced from the fact that in Tim White's authorized biography, Taylor's stay there was given two pages, half a hundred or so fewer than those Scottish seafaring ancestors. If McLean meant anything to him, it may have been as a different kind of relief—as he said, "My exit from the family agenda, as I perceived it."

Having gotten what he needed out of McLean—a diploma, a draft deferment, and nine months of exile from the outside world and his own family—James would be generous about his diversion, calling McLean "a lifesaver," "a pardon," "a reprieve," "a sort of medical stamp of approval," his main worry being that "they wouldn't let me stay." And why not? For the musically gifted, McLean was something of a launching pad. The place even had a music therapy department, and in 1967 it would hire a young rock musician, Paul Roberts, to conduct classes, which included guitar instruction. Besides the Taylor siblings, flutist John Payne would jump from McLean into a music career, playing on Van Morrison's acoustic album *Astral Weeks*. A doctor at the hospital once said, popping his buttons, "Music therapy at McLean was the path to greatness."

James, Livingston, and Kate would be far more prepared to sing and record professionally when they came out than when they went in. And for years afterward, when introducing "Knocking 'Round the Zoo," James would jauntily tell audiences, "Here's a tune I wrote at McLean to make a million bucks." Livingston and Kate would record similar songs about their McLean stays. Indeed, McLean was fertile ground for scary-enough truths to baste with hyperbole and convenient fiction and cook up into commercially rewarding songs and tales. Much would be made by journalists in future years of James's "escape" in the spring of 1966. Why this would have been necessary is unclear, though, since the doors were unlocked and unguarded. With its minimal security, McLean has been called "a country club, with barred windows" and a "rock and roll high school." Then, too, if Taylor had admitted himself voluntarily, he couldn't be kept against his will. By then, as he later told *Rolling Stone*,

> I really wanted to leave and they were going to discharge me and let me out but they don't let go very easily. And I was self-committed, so I could have signed a yellow sheet, they call it, and gotten out a.m.a. [against medical advice] that way. But that involved spending three days locked in the ward and usually by that time you change your mind. I had a friend with a Dodge truck. He came by and I told the nurse on the hall—I used to be in love with her, and it's very frustrating to be in love with a nurse when you haven't had any ass for eight months and you've been cooped up in that joint. At any rate, I told her that I had gotten my discharge and that I was going to get out in two days but that I was going to carry some of my heavier stuff out to my friend's truck just to move it into Boston. She said OK, so my friend and I picked up all of my stuff in one trip and carried it past the aide who had the keys and put it in the truck and tore off down the hill.

After nine months knocking 'round the zoo, seriously backed up and straining to write music somewhere other than looking out a window with "security screens," he kept right on driving, as it turned out, all the way to where the lights and drugs are never shut off and people never sleep, and usually get themselves into trouble. With a capital T.

Once again, James Taylor's path on the day he got out of McLean was determined not by an Oracle of Delphi but by the Kootch of Larchmont. That spring of 1966, Kortchmar had settled in Greenwich Village among the post-Dylan folk-rock crowd. He was married and had held a day job in the mailroom of a small ad agency uptown before quitting and living the rock-and-roll dream again, starting up a rock band called the King Bees, who played summertime gigs at a hotel in the Borscht Belt. They then scored a big break, winning an audition to be the house band at Arthur, the hip discotheque on East Fifty-Fourth Street where celebrities like Sinatra went to be seen and do drunken facsimiles of the twist and the jerk on the dance floor. A young rock and roller could go far in a joint like this—the front man of the last band there, the Wild Ones, married the owner, Sybil Burton, who'd been thrown over by Richard Burton when Liz Taylor threw over Eddie Fisher for *him*.

Such was the vibe of the mid-'60s in New York, all hot lights, miniskirts, go-go boots, and self-conscious, ring-a-ding-ding cool—one of the less admirable effects of the Beatles as they reshaped culture in the mold of Fleet Street's puffy-shirted, high-collared dilettantes. The King Bees, whose lead singer was John McDuffy, later a member of the Blues Project, filled the need for infectious grooves to get people dancing. But as important to Danny was that the scene there was a nest of rockers also looking to be seen, the tables and VIP rooms commonly occupied by sundry Stones, Rascals, Hermits, and top-shelf producers and record executives. Just such a visit by the British invasion duo Peter and Gordon, of "A World Without Love" and "Lady Godiva" fame, led to an invite for the King Bees to back them up on what would be some of the pair's final tours.

But Kootch could only take the nightly grind for so long, quitting the Bees and going to the Vineyard to play less-stressful clubs before returning to the Village in the early summer of '66. He got the drummer of the now sundered King Bees, Joel "Bishop" O'Brien, to play in a new band, with a bass player named Jerry Burnham. As fate would have it this was precisely when his old Vineyard confrere made his drive down from McLean. More than anything, the band would need a singer, and when James, after asking around where Kortchmar was living, showed up at his door in a walk-up apartment on East Sixty-Fifth Street, Danny must have felt it was divine intervention.

Taylor believed in something like that, as well. A few years later he would call Kortchmar "the central figure in my karass," appropriating the word from a Kurt Vonnegut novel, which Taylor explained meant "teams that do God's will without ever discovering what they are doing." He arrived in Greenwich Village sort of bright-eyed and painfully naive, but his offhanded stories of nuthouse "bondage" would surely make for some damn cool songs for the sophisticated neurotics who frequented the Village clubs. As 1966 was nearing its end, folk, jazz, and blues clubs clustered around Washington and Tompkins Square Parks, while the West Village, Chelsea, and Lower Broadway were going rock. Jimi

Hendrix had arrived, performing blues songs as Jimmy James and the Blue Flames at Cafe Wha? and the Cheetah Club, where Rolling Stones manager Andrew Loog Oldham saw him and took him to London. The drag queens of the Andy Warhol crowd had also latched onto rock, hanging out at Max's Kansas City, the dive bar/music club on Lower Park Avenue. Warhol's house band at his Factory home/club, Lou Reed's Velvet Underground, that year recorded *The Velvet Underground and Nico.* Backed with electric violas and "ostrich"-tuned guitars, the then little-known work is recognized now as what *Rolling Stone* calls "the most prophetic rock album ever made," with Reed's haunting, hunted poem-songs—influenced by William Burroughs and Allen Ginsberg—about heroin, sadomasochistic sex, and inspired deviancy.

Kortchmar was enmeshed in the scene, sold on the idea of making rock with an edge and with a perfect front man. When James showed up, Kootch wanted to call his new band the James Taylor Group, in the same manner as the Brit blues band the Spencer Davis Group, a heady honor that James winced at, being a nobody. Instead, cadging from the recent British comedy flick *Those Magnificent Men in Their Flying Machines,* they settled on the Flying Machine as a simple yet inexplicably cool name. James completed the band by bringing in a former chum at the Vineyard, another bass player, Zach Wiesner, and set out to write original songs for them to play. Although he could have afforded a room at any posh hotel in town, he was now running with the Bohemians, getting off on the starving artist motif that fed his writing, and so he crashed wherever someone let him sleep, sometimes at Danny's, sometimes with Zach in the Village at the Albert Hotel, which had been nearly destroyed by a fire but continued renting rooms for almost nothing. There were no lights in the halls, no plumbing, and room service meant cockroaches and mice looking for crumbs. Taylor would recall it not with disgust but as molto cool for a young man who had known only luxury, smilingly saying it was "a charred experience."

The band rehearsed in similar squalor, in what Kortchmar remembers as the "rat-infested, shit-box basement" of the Albert, and damn if all that dirt and sewage didn't create some cohesion and purpose. They held off taking gigs until James had finished enough songs to carve an identity for them. And as he made some progress, it was clear that the Flying Machine was going to be a hybrid creature; the material would be in the Velvet Underground mien of "wild side" reality, but Taylor could only bathe it in the varnish of folk and R & B, not the frenetic, barely listenable din of the rock and roll being played at clubs like Max's Kansas City, nor the inoffensive hauteur rock uptown. Taylor could only write of things he had lived, and the Village added a few more. From nearly the first day he arrived, his pot smoking—one of the things McLean was supposed to take care of—was abetted with harder stuff he had no hesitation in trying. The Village was a virtual supermarket of drugs, reefer being a given, spiked with God knows what; but not many lingered with it, dropping acid, mushrooms, and ludes on the way to the assumed nirvana of cocaine and heroin.

Veterans of the scene were invariably hooked on something hard. Danny Kortchmar was one of the very few who managed to stop before it would become a monkey, but his bandmates had no such self-control, especially the one they called Bishop. Joel O'Brien, born in Great Neck out on Long Island, was the fortunate son of a big DJ at WMCA, one of the most listened-to AM Top 40 stations in the country. He had gotten into heroin while hanging out in the Village in the mid-'60s, contracting a case of hepatitis that almost killed him and left him blind in one eye. He never kicked the stuff and was by now absolutely buried in white powder. And for the new guy, it was the most natural thing in the world to share in Bishop's stash. It was so easy to do that Taylor would, even after getting clean many years later, theorize that he was "probably genetically predisposed to substance abuse, so I didn't stand a chance. It just felt like an amazing release. It felt like it solved all kinds of problems for me." It also sharpened or dulled his senses in ways that could add the final touch on a song that bared his soul, and conceal from him that he himself was a lost soul. What's more, the band seemed to get better during rehearsals when the snow was heaviest.

"It was a very good group, I'll tell ya," Taylor recalled. "And we really flashed on ourselves." Kortchmar was amazed at that. "We were fairly conscientious," he says, "considering how fucked up we were."

Sometimes it seemed that down in the Village all you needed to do was reach your hand out, and someone would put a plasticine envelope in it with white powder; it was that easy. But for Taylor, addiction meant obsession; he not only had to have it, he had to have the best shit going up his nose or, more to his liking, through his veins. He had to feel the burn of a needle—ironic indeed, given how those needles at McLean had made him wince—and the wave of soothing warmth spreading through his whole body until he could feel even his toes getting comfortably numb. When in this condition, he could breathe, think, write music. Everything in the world was in a good place. The right place.

Considering his troubled mind and weakness for getting stoned, it wouldn't have taken much to get him started on it, and for that, the blame would fall to Bishop. Said Kortchmar, "Joel O'Brien was doing heroin, and then one day I realized James was, too." While this seems somewhat implausible, since by Kortchmar's description they all were "messed up" and living in such close quarters, Taylor and O'Brien gradually broke off into a subbranch during nonperforming hours. As Mark "Moogy" Klingman, another Great Neck teenager prowling around the Village scene, soon to be Todd Rundgren's keyboardist, once recalled:

> I remember having to walk through various dingy basement rooms and hallways complete with puddles of water on the floor when I got to a room where those guys had a set-up with a small drum set and small amps. It was just the Flying Machine and me. My mind was definitely blown that day. Joel, laying it down on the skins and Danny Kootch playing and singing like the monster I always knew he was. And that skinny string bean kid, James Taylor, boy, could he sing. And with his long hair, he looked a bit like Jesus, I thought maybe this was the second coming. After that day, I spent as much time as I could hanging out and listening to the Flying Machine. I'd go listen to them play til midnight at the Nite Owl [*sic*] and then walk with Joel and James back to Joel's sixth-floor walk-up on Charles Street. Joel had an endless supply of records new and old, and would play them for James and me until dawn. He'd explain each part and how the musicians decided to play what they played. Joel was an expert on all styles of music. Jazz to bluegrass to blues to rock and R & B. Joel knew and could play it all.

He did not add that O'Brien had an endless supply of heroin, which probably made listening to all those records an out-of-body experience. After Taylor had gotten himself in too deep, Danny felt he'd failed his old buddy. "I think if I had been a better friend," he said, "I'd have found a way to intervene [but] we got into a schedule where I didn't see James each night until it was time to play—because of the dope. Both he and Joel hid it from me. James was ashamed for me to know." And so as guilty as Danny felt, rather than pity Taylor, he pulled back, hurting him. "He shut me out, never let me see him doing it, and it put a veil between us that remained for years."

It was classic Taylor, however, that getting it easily wasn't good enough. There had to be better shit out there than the Bishop's. Soon he had fallen in with street lice, guys who most people, even the musicians with the worst habits, would keep a distance from. Guys with long rap sheets, with the bulge of guns under their coats. Kortchmar describes them as "shady characters." Taylor once told Tim White: "I had fallen in with some people who could have done me some harm if I'd stuck with them. There were warrants out for these two guys staying at my place. I knew them by no other names than Smack and Bobby, and they were robbing people for a living. I was addicted. I was beginning to get desperate." It's not known what happened to Mr. Smack and Mr. Bobby, but for Taylor the dividing line between sanity and insanity, good and evil, was obliterated. He had crossed over with an astonishing ease and sense of normalcy. Sometimes he'd be found, God knows where, passed out on a dirty, needle-strewn floor, and people would merely step over him. It was just that James guy, they'd say, knowing he'd soon snap out of it and be on his way. Indeed, when he'd get to the Night Owl, he'd look none the worse for it. The eyes might be bloodshot and his speech slurred, but when he sang, the voice was clear and commanded the room. That was his gift, or his con.

His looks and body language were those of a reticent rebel. No one scored women more easily. Sex was his other great rush. Young, very young, girls and older women would wait for him at the bar, and he would leave with two, maybe three at a time. Was there a stranger bird than the interloper from Carolina? While he lived the Bohemian life, he was the most sartorially splendid one in Bohemia; while the others in the band had long shags and mustaches and wore jeans and leather—Bishop a Victorian ruffled jacket and bowler derby—Taylor was clean-shaven and donned striped, starched Arrow shirts and preppy slacks, his hair now neat and short. In a publicity photo taken in '66, he looks, well, *rich*, standing tall and stiff to the side of his mates, who lounge easily on a pushcart. Few besides Danny and Zach knew that his father was sending him money, some of which came from a recent inheritance. Taylor never really had to fend for himself, and he wasn't about to send the cash back. "They were interested in me doing something that pleased me," he reasoned a few years later, "and they never implied that I was doing the wrong thing, not even once." Nor did it pose a conundrum about how he was spending it. "I had some expensive habits at that time that took up most of the money," he put it, belying the killer irony that, unwittingly, Ike and Trudy were financing his new and dangerous addiction, an irony he justified as only a junkie could: that it kept him from descending even lower. "I had it pretty easy, I had enough money to support my habit. I never had to knock over a grocery store or anything."

The Flying Machine was ready to go live in the fall of '66. The band's first paid gig, if passing the hat qualified as such, was at Cafe Bizarre, an early folk club that opened in 1957 on the ground floor of a dingy three-story brownstone a block south of Washington Square Park. It was the same bandstand where Ken Kesey used to read poetry and the Velvet Underground did whatever it was they did. There, the Flying Machine was good enough to get a better gig at the Night Owl on West Third Street just off McDougal Street. The house band a few years before was the Lovin' Spoonful, whose members all lived in one room at the Alfred (thus the line in the Mamas and the Papas' autobiographical song "Creeque Alley": "Zal, Denny, and Sebastian sat at the Night Owl"). This may have been Taylor's biggest challenge as a singer, given the narrow dimensions and weird acoustics of the room. The stage was situated lengthwise, facing a wall and forcing Taylor to sing to the sides of the room, around a church pew called "the crotch watchers' bench" in front. The speakers were aimed at the walls, which absorbed most of the music and left vocals naked, unmasked. The rule was that you had better sing on key or not sing at all. The owner's son, Joe Marra, would turn the stage lights on and off in a low-rent strobe light effect.

Here, where a Night Owl Burger was a buck, an espresso seventy-five cents, and the hardest drink was a cold cider, the Flying Machine earned their dinner, and not much more. With the band contracted to play three or four sets a night, before, after, and between sets by other acts that included the Turtles and the Ragamuffins, Taylor virtually learned to sing, really *sing*, battling the acoustics by training his voice to loudly accentuate syllables, then peel back to almost a whisper. The Machine didn't exactly rock out—one patron of the place says he expected a "straight-up garage" band but got "wimpiness not far removed from Taylor's later work"—yet there was something about the skinny guy with a sometimes off-key but strong voice who never said a word to the audience. At the beginning, they were still doing mainly bar-band-type covers of British blues songs, their sound as dark as possible and not a bit like the refined folk rock laid down by the Village acts that had gone Hollywood, like the proverbial McGuinn and McGuire. About the only folk left for the erstwhile Jamie and Kootch was the Hoagy Carmichael tune they'd played all over the Vineyard. They also did some shtick, doing versions of commercial jingles for Coca-Cola, Falstaff Beer, and Tube Rose Snuff, a change-of-pace riff that Taylor would continue when he went solo.

It was Zach Wiesner who convinced Taylor he needed to write original material in the manner of those brooding, depressing blues songs that seemed so righteous to Taylor when he was blitzed. Wiesner may have been the smartest person his own age who Taylor ever met, the son of Jerome Wiesner, a remarkable man who in addition to becoming dean and then provost of MIT's School of Science (he would be named its president in 1971) was also a leading folk music authority who had toured the South with Alan Lomax. He would, as well, make Richard Nixon's infamous "enemies list" a couple of years later with twenty other top academics. Zach, whose wisdom seemed endless, had the band model its sound on the Rolling Stones' "Paint It Black," which as it happened included the very images burned into James's brain from his stay at McLean, with its screened windows no different from the darkened curtain of the song that blotted out the sun from the sky. As Wiesner explained it, anyone who lived in the web of darkness could not and should not be cheered up; before that could happen, he would say, "you need to go down, all the way to the bottom."

After getting the hang of fronting a band, James turned to writing, a thousand shards of ideas in his brain. Making few friends and less dependent on Danny now, he wrote alone in order to wind himself as tightly as he could and have the intensity roll out of his pen. At times the radio in his room would be on too, or a scratchy forty-five would be spinning on a turntable to provide some clues about where music was and where it was going, his windows indeed blackened. These might include pop tunes, Otis Redding or Motown soul records, Tom Rush, whatever. This was also during the rollout of songs by singing/songwriting women inspired by Joan Baez, such as Buffy Sainte-Marie. Taylor, with so much still unresolved angst, could not help but listen hard to a line in her "Cod'ine" that went:

And my belly is craving, I got a shaking in my head
I feel like I'm dyin' and I wish I was dead
If I live till tomorrow that'll be a long time

He had begun piecing together songs based on what had formed word pictures in his mind, following the guideline that anything, even the inhumane, could thematically fly if it was massaged and even tickled by a good melody and simple structure (i.e., to take a sad song and make it better). Strumming his guitar, he made the words and melodies mesh darkly. And the first to be completed, "Rainy Day Man," showed that no matter how dark he could get, there was no way he could sneer like Mick Jagger. Taylor could only write in the winsome folk meter of Simon and Garfunkel, looking toward "another fall" when "your friends they don't seem to help at all," pledging that "when you're feeling kind of cold and small just look up your rainy day man." While he wrote it as an appeal to a girl, metaphors such as making a hole much too big to mend and store-bought treasures not being good enough were all about him. He meant it as stripped-down folk, a languid ballad of slow death. In many ways, though, this was the James Taylor the world would get, and even a phrase like "cold and small" would be recycled into a far bigger song that detonated his reign as a major star, so major that he would believe he had to deny the seemingly obvious—that "Rainy Day Man" was about heroin—while conceding it was "a reasonable interpretation."

In truth, he was on much more solid, poetic ground with "Something's Wrong," enumerating the hardest moment of a relationship, when it had to end:

Something's wrong, that restless feeling's been preying on your mind.
Road maps in a well-cracked ceiling, the signs aren't hard to find.

There were moods of empathy, anger, dismissal. He wrote of a lover who had become "wind-blown leaves," a "third or fourth hand," who would "wrap your hands around that small change and tiptoe barefoot out the door"—only he was referring not to a lover but to *himself.* All he really needed was an acoustic guitar, a sad bass, and brushes quietly tickling a snare. Indeed, most of the songs of this period were written as folk blues, Lead Belly–style, and he would sing some of them in clubs on a stool with his acoustic guitar, sometimes while the others took five. This would cause some quiet speculation that he was looking beyond them, using the band as a platform to pimp himself to record-label honchos who might be in the audience. And, truth be told, he was.

The song intended to get the most attention was "Knocking 'Round the Zoo" (its original title), with those knife-carved lyrics inspired by McLean about "the chick who's paid to be my slave" who will "hit me with a needle if she thinks I'm trying to misbehave." This sort of realism—though he would never convert his own needle experiences into anything but oblique references in a song—had never been heard in mainstream pop, and it too portended Taylor's later work. He would get funky with it onstage, make the grimmer references a subject of derision, even laughter. It was a hell of a concept in the super-serious, self-important culture of rock, wherein few were able to laugh at themselves, or laugh much at all. Not that Taylor was *happy.* Far from it.

6

SOMETHING'S WRONG

Armed with a quiver of original songs to blend with the blues busters and shtick, the Flying Machine had found a niche and became the featured attraction at the Night Owl for seven months, though they never were bumped up from the standard pay of seventy-two dollars per band per night, or roughly three hundred a week, which when split among them left peanuts to live on. Of course, James wouldn't have needed the scratch if he didn't squander everything Ike sent him on smack—but the fact that he actually *was* a starving artist didn't exactly hurt, this being the image he wanted to purvey. Indeed, in later years he would enjoy relating a story to *Rolling Stone* that went like this: "Once James showed up at his manager's office on speed and an empty stomach to ask for some bread. 'Here, have a sandwich,' the manager said, pulling a corned beef on white out of his desk drawer. James cried."

The story sounded more baloney than corned beef, and the *Rolling Stone* writer was moved to note, "It seems strange that James often found himself down and out in New York. The Taylors have a great deal of money." Taylor did concede that "there was some scuffling going on, but I wasn't completely poor, I was just mostly spending the money on the wrong things." But his Zelig-like adaptation to his environment seemed authentic—his draft board could have confirmed what a good actor he was—and that poor-man's pose may have even given his music a sharper bite. An oft-heard remark by club patrons of the era would be, "I'm no big James Taylor fan, but I'm impressed that he paid his dues as part of the Albert/Night Owl scene." Taylor, in turn, did what John Sebastian had when he wrote a Spoonful instrumental called "Night Owl Blues"; as a solo act Sebastian would write another, "Night Owl Cafe." Taylor's paean was "Night Owl," though it made no reference to the bar itself, which a year later would convert to a head shop and then be occupied for three decades by the wondrous, and quite overpriced, record store Bleecker Bob's.

Even so, it had a dark undertone, reflecting Taylor's daily routine of hibernating all day in a heroin stupor—actually, *he* was the night owl, saying:

Turn off that bright light, baby
You're just about to drive me blind
Draw them curtains for me, mama
You watch and you'll see how my love light shines

Taylor used it as a rare upbeat tune, hoping for something like "Sunshine Superman," though without the psychedelic element. Another, "Brighten Your Night with My Day," was the first hint that Taylor's antidote to despondency was dependency—that is, the codependency of love: "Girl, you can count on me / Watch those shadows fade away and brighten your night with my day." In hindsight, this may have been a tortured metaphor about heroin, all his days looking like night now. The line "It's no good concealing a feeling it hurts you to hide" was pure Taylor angst, again trying to convince *himself* to cleanse his soul. But he wasn't ready for that.

Taylor and Kootch hoped the right industry bird dog would see them play and offer a big record contract. Danny also tried calling in chits. And whether James really wanted to be discovered as a standalone act, it was again Kortchmar's groundwork that made something happen. One of the many industry bumblebees he had crossed paths with was John Wesley Voight, known professionally as Chip Taylor, who at the time was more successful than his older brother Jonathan Vincent "Jon" Voight, whose acting had taken him only as far as TV dramas and off-Broadway shows. Taylor was a mover in the music game, having written "Wild Thing"—which the British garage band the Troggs had taken to number 1 earlier that year—and "Angel of the Morning."

Indeed, Chip Taylor recalls that when Danny introduced James to him, and Chip played the latter song as performed by Evie Sands, "he went mad over it, especially the line 'just touch my cheek before you leave me, baby.' That was right in his ballpark. He loved that kind of stuff." Chip Taylor was also impressed by James Taylor, and in the music business, that meant something. The former's fingerprints were all over the rock map. He had recorded as Wes Voight and in the early '60s was a staff writer at April-Blackwood, the tentacle-like music publishing house that is part of the CBS empire, and still had ties to it. In fact, when Kortchmar, who'd met Chip during the King Bees run, kept pimping the Flying Machine and particularly James to him, Chip fell in love with the oddly fetching nasal voice and some of the lyrics he'd written. But before doing anything with it or the group, the first paper he stuck under their noses had no music on it but rather terms for future publishing rights: half the writing royalties of any songs James Taylor wrote that would be recorded—in *perpetuity*, whether a day from then, a year, or *ever*. It was outrageous, a fast shuffle, but the men of the Machine were in no position to quibble. As James Taylor spoke of it later, it was "a simple mistake. . . . I had no idea what I was signing"—one of the most often heard refrains in entertainment.

As it happened, Chip Taylor was starting up a record label and had gotten financial backing from Jubilee Records, an independent label that had some big doo-wop hits in the '50s but now was floundering—it would go under in 1970. Whatever he had made he sunk into Rainy Day Records, named for "Rainy Day Man," signaling that the label was to be built around the Flying Machine, who he rushed into Jubilee's Select Sound Studio at 1790 Broadway in early '67. As he heard James's voice, Chip believed it was suited to the emerging album-oriented corner of rock. It was, he recalled, "not what you would call a good voice for the radio"—only proving that even brilliant record men can be titanically wrong. Rather than looking for a quick single that might fly, an album would be the priority, hopefully breaking the band—but mainly its singer—as a vanguard of the new rock. Taylor and his production partner, Al Gorgoni, also a top studio guitarist, brought in Trade Martin, a hip writer and arranger, to do charts of the songs and then turned the microphones on. Even though James came in with a fever of 102, it didn't dampen his enthusiasm.

"Hi Mom. Hi Dad. This is our first record," he chirped into his microphone before the first song.

It was so rush-rush an affair that Gorgoni announced from the booth, "Okay, this is 'Brighten My Night with Your Day.'"

"Brighten *Your* Night with *My* Day," corrected James with a nervous chuckle.

The songs on these tapes were just this side of dreadful, promising pieces of work drowned by hackish production. Chip Taylor wanted it to sound soulful and young, like the Rascals, but despite some self-conscious embellishments—such as speeding up and adding a funky Joel O'Brien drumbeat and walking bass line to "Zoo," on which they did a take with Danny hoarsely singing lead, and James Brown–like grunts of "*uugghh*" here and there—it never congealed as anything discernible. Trying everything, Gorgoni came out on the floor and played harpsichord, piano, organ, synthesizer, and keyboards. The producers bathed each song in ridiculously thick echoes, sacrificing all intimacy. With only two rudimentary recording tracks, vocals leaked into microphones meant for instruments, making for an early sort of garage-band rock, especially with the impromptu shouted backing vocals, yelps, claps, and whistles. Two acoustic guitar tracks were used, stripped of vocals, "Kootch's Song" and "Something's Wrong"—the latter depriving Taylor of some of his best, most heartfelt lyrics.

Indeed, on the whole, the tapes in no way showcased Taylor's voice. All it did was give Chip Taylor something to bring to Jubilee, and perhaps not surprisingly, the honchos there were cool to it. Not that there wasn't some buried treasure in these songs. On "Rainy Day Man," Taylor's acoustic chords rang clearly enough to have the mournful but springy air of syncopation, adding an optimistic nuance. Later, he would redo and extensively rearrange the song in the more refined '70s mold of sweeter and dreamier folk rock—keeping pace with Tom Rush, who released a song in 1970 with the same title but a different theme, coated by romantic strings. "Night Owl," uneven as it was, had a definable folk-blues quality, such that it would be covered by Alex Taylor and Carly Simon—and recorded by James Taylor several times. And "Zoo" was instantly infectious, its bouncy melody more so when it too was sped up on tape, though it made Taylor's vocal almost unrecognizable, more like one of the Chipmunks.

Perhaps with some decent distribution, an album could have made a ripple—had there *been* an album. Instead, Jubilee passed, leaving Chip Taylor and the Flying Machine pissed. As a sop, Jubilee waived through a two-sided single, "Brighten"/"Night Owl." Even Chip Taylor, it seemed, wasn't sold on his big discovery. The disk, with the catalog number 45-8001, is an artifact—the one and only product ever released by the soon defunct Rainy Day Records, one that was heard maybe a couple times on some FM stations around the Northeast but sold probably less than a hundred copies, any of which would be a collector's item today. As Chip Taylor surmises, it wasn't production flaws that kept Taylor from earlier fame; it was that the world wasn't ready for that kind of voice or the conjunction of sweet and sour. But how could it have been, if judged by these songs—with the one about needles and spoons done so hurriedly, and merrily, that it was all but impossible to even know what was being sung about? His take is that "everyone knew James's songs were great. As a songwriter he just made me feel like two feet tall by comparison," but being rejected was more the result of realities in the industry. "Look, James was in trouble, you knew he might not be around to see the next sunrise. They were wrong, very wrong, but in their defense, it's hard to bank on a guy like that, who was new and not a star. We all loved James but he was a risk, mainly to himself."

Chip Taylor, his work done, saw no reason to stick around before turning to other things. The Flying Machine continued playing the Night Owl and other haunts, until James began missing shows and could not be found anywhere. Yet he was so comforted by junk that he didn't think anything was wrong. A few years later, he recapitulated his addled outlook this way: "There was a junkie-sized hole in my soul at one point [but] I really dug it, and I stayed with it as long as I really dug it." Such delusions, he would admit, were in truth "a waste of time; I feel as though I did deadhead miles." All those miles happened before he turned twenty.

Even putting aside the damage done by Taylor's addiction, Kortchmar could read the tea leaves and conclude that James wasn't built for singing in a band, especially in an era when amplification and isolation were rudimentary. "I think we were doomed from the beginning partly because this was before stage monitors and James had to sing way louder than he should have had to," he says. "James's voice is a delicate instrument; if he's yelling and straining, you get none of what James Taylor is about, and that's what happened. On that album, with him trying to sound rock and roll, I honestly didn't recognize the voice I was hearing as his. I think that's when James started realizing that he was gonna be better off as a singer/songwriter as opposed to member of a rock band."

Taylor was not too strung out to lose sight of his ambition. Still intent on pimping his work, it was not as a singer but as a songwriter that he came uptown one day that autumn, ambling into the offices of Elektra Records looking to sell some songs to Paul Rothchild. Timing. No matter what other attributes Taylor had, he seemed always favored by good timing, because while Rothchild said he was too busy, it so happened that Tom Rush himself was in that day and was walking by Rothchild's office just as Taylor came in. Rothchild introduced them, and the great folk icon agreed to hear what the kid had. The irony was that Rush had indeed heard of Taylor—while in Cambridge, Rush's roommate happened to be Zach Wiesner, who after coming to New York would occasionally tell his old roomie on the phone about this Taylor guy with the incredible voice. Now that guy was right here in front of Rush, droopy shoulders, old guitar, and all.

As Rush recalled: "We sat down on the floor of a vacant office and he played me some songs," including "Something in the Way She Moves" and "Sunshine, Sunshine." Rush was impressed enough to put those two on his impending, third Elektra album, 1968's *The Circle Game*, a brilliant concept work tracing a relationship from beginning to end, along with songs by two other rising folk-rock singer-songwriters, the title track and "Tin Angel" by Joni Mitchell (before she recorded it herself for her second album) and "Shadow Dream Song" by Jackson Browne. As such, this album can now be regarded as a rock-and-roll oracle. Taylor would learn of this coup while in England, and those songs would become the first by James Taylor the public at large would get to hear.

Taylor's voice had already begun to give out from the nightly grind onstage. The album sessions blew it out further, inflaming his throat and vocal cords. He hung in, but Danny could sense the feeling was gone and the end near. The Night Owl run ended and gigs were scarce, no doubt due to James's reputation as a screwup and junkie. The last one came in the winter when the band was invited to play an engagement at a disco in Freeport in the Bahamas called "Joker's

Wild," appropriately since the gig was a disaster. Audiences had no interest in them, and after a couple of nights, sunbaked, drunk, and stoned, they were sent home, never seeing what they were supposed to be paid.

When they returned they sat idle for the long months of those horribly cold, depressing New York winters Paul Simon wrote of "bleeding" him. No Flying Machine business was conducted. They merely spent whatever cash they had getting stoned. In the spring, rather than feeling renewed, by mutual agreement all of the members agreed to go their separate ways. In Kortchmar's words, "We busted up 'cause we were all fucked up, man." Especially Taylor. Says Kortchmar, "James couldn't stand scuffling and being fucked over, hungry and miserable, and he had to escape," meaning to somewhere other than his own world. Escape he did. For that, he turned to a man who had become a distant memory to him: Dr. Isaac Montrose Taylor II.

Figuring he had no other way out, James did what he had done only sparingly since McLean. Not even having a record out had prompted him to call his father. Now, awakening on the floor late one night, he picked up the phone and somehow managed to dial Chapel Hill. According to Ike's later recollection, he could barely understand what his son was saying, so slurred and incoherent were his words, but it was obvious it was a call for help. So estranged had they been that Ike had no address for him in New York. Demanding to know his location, he barked through the phone, "Stay put! I'll be right there!"

Ike never moved faster than he did that night. He caught a red-eye flight, rented a station wagon at LaGuardia Airport, and found his way to the burned-out pig pen of an apartment where his son had stayed put. Getting there, he reeled at the dreadful conditions, the smell, and most of all the shocking sight of his son. James had lost probably 40 pounds, down to around 120, all skin and bones. He had calluses, zits, dirt all over him, and Ike could see track marks on his forearm. It was all Ike could to keep from vomiting as he went all around the place, stuffing his son's clothing into a suitcase he found in a closet. Grabbing James's guitar in one hand and the ragamuffin James in the other, he led him down the creaky stairs to the car, got him in, and headed out of town through the Holland Tunnel and down the New Jersey Turnpike, not stopping until ten hours later when they were back in Chapel Hill, all without making a word of conversation.

James, who drifted back into never-never land, slept the entire way, mumbling something here and there, and seeing him this way must have produced a myriad of emotions in the strict, proper father whose son had made such a mess of his life. There were moments of anger, of betrayal, but also of guilt that he must have done something horribly wrong as a father to have repelled his son like this. He could only hope that out of this abyss might come a rapprochement, that James might get out of his system the stimuli of this dance with death. To James, who slept for days in his old bedroom while Ike and Trudy hovered over him, it indeed meant something that his father had made such a rescue mission and not sent a plane ticket, which he would have no doubt sold to buy more drugs. When he had dried out—apparently able to weather whatever withdrawal aches and pains he had without medical assistance—and gained back his weight, he did enjoy some downtime with both his parents, with Hugh, and with Alex, who had entered the University of North Carolina at Wilmington.

He had a belated appreciation for his father, perhaps for the first time actually feeling the bonds of kinship with him. However, there was no real rapprochement. Ike was still distant and rarely at home, and soon would separate from Trudy and end the sham of that marriage. And things began to go bad with James when Ike began to hound him about going to college. The walls started to feel like they were closing in on James. Again, he would need to flee Carolina. Danny Kortchmar was relieved to hear James tell the story of his escape from New York. Though he would harbor a varying degree of resentment against him as both moved on to other things, they spoke regularly on the phone, and once again it was Kootch who would set the stage for Taylor. This time, it came when James told him what he really wanted to do was go to England and see what was cooking over there.

To be sure, Jimi Hendrix had made the right move doing so. And Danny, who truly worried that Taylor would kill himself if he returned to New York, *wanted* him to go as far away as he could. He told James to ring up Peter Asher, for whom the King Bees had opened on that final Peter and Gordon tour, once there. Maybe Asher could do something for him. Taylor believed, with remarkable naïveté, that England was different from New York; that drugs were less prominent, less *necessary.* Only he knows if he seriously believed that. But he knew he wanted to give it a go in another port of rock and roll, where someone would be ready to buy what he was selling—himself.

7

APPLE SCRUFF

When Taylor traced the time line of his rise in *Rolling Stone* in February 1971, he made the transition from New York to London out to be seamless. "I didn't enjoy living in New York City and I didn't very much enjoy living with myself, either, at the time," he said. "I decided I'd fuck that, I'll travel around some and see if I can get into something interesting." In reality, there was a six-month interim in which he rested his weary bones but had a serious setback after he went with the family again to the Vineyard, hung with some old peeps smoking pot, and further irritated his throat. When he returned to Chapel Hill, it hurt so much he was unable to speak above a whisper, much less sing. Ike stuck a tongue depressor in his mouth, took a look, and told him he needed to have tests done at an ear, nose, and throat ward; when he did they found polyps on his ravaged vocal cords and scheduled him for surgery at the university hospital late in the summer.

Fortunately, there was no lingering damage. He gradually began singing, and by Thanksgiving of 1967 he was delighted that his voice seemed stronger, able to hold a note longer, and not tire so easily. If for that reason alone, coming back to Carolina had been well worth it. He once again began to have visions of going to England. He had dried out sufficiently in Carolina, done some more songwriting, and convinced himself that he was sane, healthy enough to want to pick up the pieces of his career. Alex agreed that he should, that he had to grab for that dream or he'd never forgive himself if his career fizzled. Ike and Trudy, of course, tried every way they could to talk him out of it, to get him to go to college and grow up. It had been just a few months since he went through hell; hadn't he learned from that?

Yet he was so disoriented and so intent on going that Ike and Trudy, who always bent over backward for him, sprung for his ticket and were there at the Raleigh airport to wave him good-bye when he flew to New York for the connecting flight to London just before the turn of the new year. There, in the land of his ancestors, walking where past Taylor men had made their fortunes—and practiced their madness—he set out to reach several goals, which as he defined them, were to "emote and really get as much attention and gratification as I could. I wanted to perform, I wanted to write songs, and I wanted to get a lot of chicks."

The latter objective would play out as he hoped, even if he had to slink behind the back of his new girlfriend, Margaret Corey, who had come to England with him. Five years older than he, the daughter of the wacky comic "Professor" Irwin Corey (a.k.a. "the World's Foremost Authority"), she and her brother, Richard, had met Taylor in the Village, both becoming part of his tight circle. No common groupie, she was petite, pretty, and intellectual, a fervent advocate of liberal causes. She had seen the effects of right-wing paranoia in the '50s when her father—who turned 101 years old in 2015—was blacklisted for openly supporting the American Communist Party. She was also an aspiring actress, taking classes in the Village, and as brash as Taylor was introverted, prone to saunter through the Village in micro-miniskirts and see-through blouses. Through her father, she had been friends with Lenny Bruce, and developed her own ribald sense of humor and dirty-mouth jargon. In other words, she was just the sort of hip, committed woman who could indulge Taylor's long hours of soul baring. He soon took to introducing her as his girlfriend to more important people, such as photographer Richard Avedon. She, in turn, sank her teeth into him like a bear trap and patiently waited for him to recover at home.

In London, where "Maggie," as everyone knew her, would continue acting classes, they moved into an old, weathered Victorian house in Notting Hill, a now affluent, then run-down district in the Royal Borough of Kensington and Chelsea in central London where a large hippie population had settled, then in Pont Street Mews in the Belgravia section. Not long after, Richard came over as well, along with Joel

"Bishop" O'Brien, and this coterie made the scene all around Soho. Taylor played Bohemian as a street performer singing and strumming for spare change. Urged to record something he could use to pitch himself to the English record people, he soon paid eight quid to rent a cramped studio in Soho and recorded forty-five minutes worth of new demos, including a redo of "Knocking 'Round the Zoo," "Something in the Way She Moves," and "Something's Wrong." It was just him and his guitar, making the sound bigger by double-tracking with an engineer, laying identical tracks one on top of the other. He called around to producers and label executives, who knew nothing of him and politely begged off listening to the tapes. That's when he pulled out the number Danny had given him, and made the call to Peter Asher.

Talk about *timing*. Without knowing much about the wee half of Peter and Gordon, Taylor entered Asher's life just when it had taken a major turn. With the Peter and Gordon thing no longer viable financially, Asher and Gordon Waller had recently ended the act. Asher, a much-admired man in the industry, was soon after given a new job by Paul McCartney, who until 1966 was the boyfriend of Asher's younger sister Jane and had written "World Without Love" for Peter and Gordon. He remained close with McCartney, and the job he got was no less than head of A & R at Apple Records, the center of all operations and aspirations for the Beatles. Asher remembers the first time he heard the voice that would make his second career far more enriching than the one he'd just given up as a rock star.

"It was quite late on a rainy winter evening in early 1968," he says. "I was at home in my flat and I got a phone call out of the blue from a rather nervous-seeming American with a very pleasant speaking voice. I didn't know him, but he told me his name was James Taylor. James explained that he was in London in search of some kind of musical success. He had made a demo the day before and wondered whether I would like to hear it. I listen to everything. I told him that I would love to and we made a plan for him to come over the following day."

Taylor could hardly believe it. He grabbed up his tapes and guitar and the next day met the ruddy-faced little man with giant glasses—reputedly Mike Myers's model for the absurdly flouncing but historically accurate Austin Powers character (Myers's costar Elizabeth Hurley believes it was British DJ Simon Dee), down to the snaggleteeth and Cockney accent. He was just one of a slew of musicians who streamed through the Apple offices every day, many of them Americans, whom the Brits had a hard time making sense of to begin with. Taylor was a particularly strange Yank. Tony Bramwell, who headed Apple Films before becoming CEO of Apple Records, remembers laying eyes on Taylor:

> Paul and John had announced in New York that Apple was signing up new acts and producing records for their own label. They repeated this mantra on their return to London—and even took out ludicrous advertisements that showed lads with huge cars and saying something like: "If you want to be rich, Apple is looking for your talent." Not surprisingly, the offices became like a glorified international rock and roll social club, with people constantly dropping by. . . . Bob Dylan and Janis Joplin came in and almost diffidently said that they would love to be on this fresh and original label, but I especially remember the day when James Taylor happened to show up. I believe "happened" is the right word. He was one of those funny little people who arrived at just the right moment.

As Bramwell says of the audition, Taylor "just sat down cross-legged on the floor and sang a lovely song. [Sings] 'The way she moves . . . forever . . . ' [from 'Something in the Way She Moves']. It was so good that I sat up very straight, stopped working and listened hard." Taylor, he says, was a sight, dressed in "Levi's, a black shirt and Greek car-tire-sole versions of the usual Jesus boots. But he had a beautiful guitar, a Martin or a Gibson, which he could most definitely play, and which showed he was serious."

"He's a bit good, isn't he?" Bramwell said coyly. Asher certainly agreed. Looking back, Asher says, "I was totally knocked out, because here was someone who looked like he was just going to be an ordinary strumming folkie [but] he played the guitar with the skill of a classical guitarist. He had been listening to Segovia and Julian Bream as well as pop music. Even though he had an almost folkie-ish flavor to his voice, his phrasing owed more to Sam Cooke and Ray Charles. He played classical guitar, but with sort of jazz voicing as well as all the folkie [suspended] chords and stuff." When Taylor was done, Asher rose from his desk and climbed to the top of the staircase leading up to the offices where the Beatles irregularly hung out.

"Is there a Beatle in the house?" he called out.

Again—*timing.* On this day, one was. Paul was asked by Asher to come down and listen to the American from off the streets. Taylor's smoothly romantic but edgy voice was right up McCartney's alley, making the approval unanimous. Taylor would embellish the fairy tale at times during concerts to include George as being there as well; but though he wasn't, "Something in the Way She Moves" would become a common thread between them soon enough. Asher's take on Taylor's material was that

> these were not traditional rock and roll songs. They had elements of folk to them but with an R&B groove. The guitar parts had the elegance of classical Spanish guitar playing but used occasional jazz chords. The vocals were intense and soulful but introspective and thoughtful at the same time. The songs were brilliant blends of poetic eloquence, humor, precision. I was overwhelmed. I asked him to play a couple more songs live and he did so. I told him how very good I thought his music was and I would like to sign him. I also discovered that he had nowhere to stay and invited him to move into our guest room where he ended up staying for several months.

Of course, he *did* have a place, in Notting Hill, Belgravia. But when opportunity knocked as loud as this, Taylor was apt to tell anybody anything if it could nudge him a little further along. He'd done that in New York and would do the same now, with far higher stakes. He and Margaret moved in, and up, with Asher and his wife, Betsy, a former Rolling Stones publicist, in their splendid house on High Street in the ritzy Marylebone section. And, to think, only weeks before, he was lying incoherent and rotting, in a pool of his own urine in a burned-out slum. But the Ashers weren't particularly eager to provide him with free aid and comfort. Betsy Asher soon began leaving hints for him. When he'd come down for breakfast, on the table would be a newspaper open to the classified section, specifically "Flats to Let."

Taylor shot straight with Asher about his heroin hell in New York, and Asher did the same in telling McCartney. "Peter explained to me that [Taylor] had just got clean off drugs and was in a slightly difficult time in his life," McCartney looked back. "But he was playing great, and he had enough songs for an album. Peter said, 'I think it'd be good to sign him.' So I said to the guys [the Beatles], 'We should sign him.'" Whether they had qualms about it, they had more pressing matters to think about. The nature of rock was changing, in no small way because of how the Beatles had made deep and probing introspection a rock stanchion. In the early months of 1968, they were readying themselves for the follow-up to the profound, avant-garde albums that had left rock breathless, *Sgt. Pepper's Lonely Hearts Club Band* and *Magical Mystery Tour*, seeking more personal revelations. The result would be *The Beatles* double album, its symbolically simple, white-bathed jacket embossed with the title and serial numbers (which would reach to around five million), prompting fans to call it *The White Album*. They had come back from their ballyhooed retreat with the Maharishi in India disillusioned, with the horny holy man trying to hit on their women, and still devastated by the sudden, sleeping-pill-overdose death the year before of their dominating manager Brian Epstein at thirty-two.

Their path uncertain, with Lennon and McCartney having grown apart and tension all around, they had founded Apple Corps to be the corporate umbrella of the Beatles' tangled business ventures. Its objective, as Lennon adumbrated, was "to see if we can get artistic freedom within a business structure and sell without charging three times our cost." It was all very noble but it went south fast—witness the lamentable *Magical Mystery Tour* movie. As far as music was concerned, Beatles products would be released on Apple Records, with EMI and Capitol distributing the label. The rise of intraband feuding led to frightful studio scenes and the discordant vibe of John bringing Yoko Ono to sit beside him, with each of the two chief Beatles despising each other's songs—Lennon calling "Ob-La-Di, Ob-La-Da" "granny music shit." How such immortal pieces as "While My Guitar Gently Weeps," "Blackbird," and "Revolution" (1 and 9) ever got recorded is a magical mystery indeed.

Taylor dropped into the Apple orchard just as all this was happening, judged by the band as a good fit for what they wanted Apple product to be. *Pretty* was a must, to be sure. At the time creamy instrumentals like Paul Mauriat's "Love Is Blue" and Mason Williams's "Classical Gas" sold in the millions, as did vocal flan like "The Girl from Ipanema" and "Guantanamera." As well, 1968 seemed to be the year when the first stirrings of a new singer-songwriter era were being felt. Jackson Browne, a baby-faced California analog of Taylor, who also had migrated to the Village, would be signed by Elektra Records, landing him on *The Circle Game.* And Van Morrison, a laconic Irishman, had his first solo hit in '67, "Brown Eyed Girl," coming out of, as he sang, "transistor radios" like a gusher of folk, pop, and rock.

Asher was willing to go out on a limb that the reflective singer-songwriter scene was money. Before even signing Taylor to an Apple contract, he had big plans for the young man. Asher was so taken that he wrote an internal memo to the president of Apple Records' American division, Ron Kass, who had been brought in to oversee the entire label. The memo read: "1st June 1968. Re: James Taylor. He is an American songwriter and singer who is very good. We intend to start recording about the 20th of June, by which time he will have enough songs rehearsed and arranged with me. He is ready to discuss contracts as soon as you are." When the contract was drawn up, Apple had to iron out a sticky situation about the publishing. Because April-Blackwood owned half the rights to any old and new Taylor-written songs, Apple claimed any new songs recorded for a non-American label. The percentage of publishing royalties for Apple Music Publishing Company on these records wouldn't give Taylor half—it gave him zero, the same as his advance.

Thus did James Taylor become the first non-Brit act signed by Apple, joining an elite club that over the next two years would include Mary Hopkin, Billy Preston, the Modern Jazz Quartet, the Iveys (soon to be Badfinger), Jackie Lomax, Ronnie Spector, Hot Chocolate, and Ravi Shankar. The announcement of the original signings was made by McCartney at an elaborate press conference in which he said the label would be in the hands of record artists, not corporate hacks, with control over their work. It was all very heavy, and heady, and Taylor may have thought he was caught in a whirlwind. As Asher notes: "Thousands of American musicians and fans were no doubt setting off for London around this time with vague hopes of getting into Apple somehow or even of actually meeting The Beatles. Only in retrospect can I imagine how extraordinary and scary it must have been for a sensitive, nervous artist with a history of psychiatric issues and drug use to come to London and do so within just a week or so of his arrival. And his life was only going to get more complicated from now on." Asher needed more songs from Taylor, and so Taylor, needing to clear his head and veins, sailed off alone on a charter boat ride to the south of Spain to the island of Formentera, a favored hangout of wealthy European hippies. Waiting there were warm ocean breezes, isolated bicycle trails, another willing woman, and the birth of a song:

> I spent two nights on the island, drinking Romilar [a cough syrup] and riding a bicycle, just chanting. It was a hypnotic, anti-psychedelic experience. I met a girl there named Karen, and she and I took a boat to the next island, Ibiza. . . . We were just walking around there and missed the last boat back and didn't have any money for a room and we stayed in the street that night and waited for the next morning when the boat would run again. . . . She was asleep and I was up and I was thinking about my home in North Carolina and what it meant and stuff and it just sort of came down out of the air.

The song, which he would finish in Marylebone, was of course the bittersweet "Carolina in My Mind," ostensibly a hosanna to his home state in the manner of Hoagy Carmichael's 1930 chestnut "Georgia on My Mind," immortalized by Ray Charles in 1960. The song, however, seemed to rub off John Lennon's vita "Norwegian Wood," interspersing native pride about the sunshine, moonshine, and "geese in flight and dogs that bite" with now classic oblique lines—"Karen she's a silver sun"—and "a holy host of others standing 'round me," famously meaning the Beatles. And there was the always effective color word—"fire": "Whisper something warm and kind / And hey babe the sky's on fire, I'm dyin'." For Taylor, certain words or phrases like these would resurface, as a sort of code. Words like *fire* and *warm* and any variation of death, the dark, the moon, or both (e.g., "dark side of the moon" in this same song), broken glass—or even the restorative/destructive powers of women—may also have described the effects of and sure consequence of heroin in his veins. Only he knew when this was so. And the softer and more intimate he could make these words sound with shimmering, gently weepy guitar chords, the more personal the song became. The "Karen" reference expressed wistful sadness; when he returned to England, he became haunted by her without really knowing why. Four decades later, says someone who knows him, he actually tried to locate her, without success, and even had a sketch artist do an illustration of what she might look like, joking that because of the sketch, he would now see her as a criminal instead of a wraith.

Of "Carolina" he would say many years later: "When I wrote it, I knew I had something. It was very early on and it did a job on me. It did some work for me. Internal work for me. Well, there's no better feeling when one comes through and it falls into place like that. And somehow solves a puzzle for you. In a way that comes from inside of you but it's outside."

He also wrote "Sunshine, Sunshine," yet one more example of the Taylor code, or in his parlance, the puzzle, its swirl of beautiful poetry linking rain with something ominous, sunshine with salvation:

Things ain't what they used to be, I say pain and rain
And misery, illness in the family
And sunshine means a lot to me, I say sunshine

Its last line was repeated: "Sunshine means quite a lot to me / I say sunshine, whoa sunshine."

Asher, wanting to ride into new territory on Taylor's bony back, worked closely with him. Needing musicians to aid him, the adjutant of the Beatles almost quaintly put an ad in the British music paper *Melody Maker*, from which came bassist Louis Cennamo and keyboardist Don Schinn. Taylor, who would have loved to have Kortchmar, was pleased that he at least had Bishop O'Brien to play drums (back home, O'Brien was in a new band of his own, the psychedelic jazz-soul group Glitterhouse). And after James saw veteran jazz piano player Freddie Redd, who was living in England (and was still touring in 2013, at age eighty-five), in a club, Redd agreed to play the session as well. There would also be the selective participation of two other sidemen of note, blokes named McCartney and Harrison. Asher, who would be producing an important work for the first time, hired guitarist Mick Wayne and a harpist named Skaila Kanga, and relied heavily on Richard Hewson, a producer whom McCartney had hired as arranger of Mary Hopkin's "Those Were the Days," the old Russian folk tune Paul produced that went to the top of the charts.

The sessions began in early May at Trident Studios in St. Anne's Court in Soho. Asher sat behind the glass with Hewson and engineer Barry Sheffield, who owned the studio with his brother Norman. The sessions were running concurrently with those by the Beatles, who were recording *The White Album* there—Taylor got to hear early versions of "Hey Jude" and one day wandered into their usual studio on Abbey Road and heard the mixes of "Revolution." As for his sessions, he recalled, "We just got all the basic tracks down as good as we could. Then Peter would take the basic track to Richard Hewson" for further work, then send it back to Asher, a process that Taylor thought was "pretty confining." Since Asher was a novice at production, Hewson's ideas carried much weight, and coming on the heels of "Those Were the Days"—which was overstuffed with noisy layers of exotic instruments and choirs—he couldn't leave the hushed, intricate simplicity of Taylor's songs as is, adorning tracks with similarly unrock appurtenances such as his own violin and bassoon parts.

The song Asher and Taylor thought had the most hit potential was "Carolina in My Mind," which would be track 1, side 1. As Taylor remembered, "McCartney used to come up every once in a while and see what we were doing. I think he took an interest in me. I'd say the only song that Paul really had any influence over was 'Carolina in My Mind.' He liked it a lot. That was the only one he played [bass] on and George Harrison sung harmony on that one, too." Thankfully, a track backed by the thirty-piece London Philharmonic Orchestra was discarded, and Taylor's voice rang splendidly clear, driving every track, even when Asher had him sing some songs faster than he had written them. Asher's design was, as one music writer would call it, "a sort-of concept album" with two distinct sides: the first the newer songs fused in a "unified multi-song suite incorporating several distinctly Baroque-flavored links connecting the larger compositions," the second the older ones in "a more traditional collection of individual tunes." In the main, it was charming, clever, cohesive, and full of character, as uniquely calming a record as there was at the close of the riotous '60s.

Not that Taylor was completely sold. Few tracks were as unadorned as he would have liked. Some he couldn't have asked for more—for instance, "Sunshine, Sunshine," recorded as a tidy violin/harp concerto, with his voice violin-like. But "Something in the Way She Moves" left him a bit cold, another time when he sang too hurriedly for the sentimentality of acknowledging the power of a woman's love to make him "feel fine anytime she's around." However, as was common in his words, innocent-sounding plaints about feeling fine or feeling not so fine may have been an allusion to heroin; another example being from "Don't Talk Now"—"I know she can't hurt me less by talking more / She can't make good what was bad before."

These were songs of quiet power, indeed. The opening stanza in particular—"There's something in the way she moves or looks my way or calls my name / That seems to leave this troubled world behind"—stayed with George Harrison for months, until he would find the phrase "something in the way she moves" a perfect opening line to the song he called "Something," an emotive, slide-guitar-driven valentine to his wife, Pattie Boyd, that would appear on *Abbey Road* and be the only Harrison-written song ever released as the A-side of a single—not that this distinction mattered, as the B-side was Lennon's "Come Together"—"Something" going to number 3. If Taylor thought this was dirty pool—Harrison gave him no writing credit—he kept mum, later explaining that "all music is borrowed from other music. I've stolen things much more blatantly," and pointed out that his song's last words were "I feel fine." Taylor would redo the song years later by *adding* strings and a choir, but with more subtlety than had Asher the first time around, minus the harpsichord transitioning from the bouncy "Taking It In" that bled into the opening of "Something in the Way She Moves." (A similar Asher affectation was layering Taylor's lovely acoustic rendition of the old English folk romanesca "Greensleeves" between "Don't Talk Now" and "Something's Wrong.")

Asher and Hewson had crafted quite a masterful work, with artful, if often pretentious, flourishes that tried hard to isolate the beating heart of rock and roll to the point where it could be *felt*. Mixing the tracks with great care and dubbing whatever new stir-in they believed would help, they did what Chip Taylor could not: make "Knocking 'Round the Zoo," "Rainy Day Man," "Night Owl," "Brighten Your Night with My Day," and "Something's Wrong" compelling pop songs. A quiet chorale sang behind him in a nicely nuanced "Rainy Day Man"; Motown/Stax-style horns played on "Night Owl"; nimble acoustic guitar runs are heard on "Brighten Your Night"; and a stirring horn flourish appears between the last two tracks. Still, Asher will admit that the album was "overproduced."

> I was so anxious to make everyone pay attention to these remarkable songs and the genius of James's musicianship that I suggested a lot of overdubs. I had only produced a couple of records before, but I had a real sense that this was the important one—and I was quite certain that James was an extremely important artist. Despite all of this we made a record of which I am certainly still very proud—and began a professional relationship which was to last for almost 30 years and an invaluable friendship which continues to this day.

It was hard for Brits like Asher and Hewson to really "get" Taylor or that what he was going for was a sign of cultural clash, not between old and new but between British and American. Although the Brits would eventually grasp the new intensely personal folk-rock idiom—*after* it had been produced properly, in time, by a wiser Asher—a grittier strain of blues, metal, and glam rock was starting to percolate in England. It would boom in the early '70s cheek by jowl with soft rock, with bands like Led Zeppelin, Deep Purple, and T-Rex already paying dues in clubs or artists like Eric Clapton in established rock bands. David Bowie was in a band then called, of all things, the King Bees. All Asher could do was guess what soft rock could be, and he did so commendably, as Taylor knew, but just not optimally. As they had worked on his album over the summer and into the fall, however, factors that had to do with his nationality or the propensities of British music were already complicating things. Most important, there was the brewing storm over Apple as Lennon and McCartney jockeyed for control. But, more immediate, there was the fact that James Taylor was right back where he had been: in New York, in smack hell.

8

"IT'S LIKE BEING DEAD"

This turn was probably inevitable, given Taylor's seemingly fatal inability to exercise some willpower. Again, having Bishop O'Brien around didn't help. "Oh, Jesus," O'Brien once recalled, "it was a laugh a minute." Or, as the mod crowd would have said, a gas. Taylor would confess, "I was addicted all the time I was recording the album on Apple. I was stoned for most of the sessions." And: "I'd shoot speedballs of smack and meth, all pure stuff over there. But pure stuff is just pure poison. Peter didn't know I was on junk. I guess he just thought I was really sleepy or something." The contrast between all that sensitive singing and writing simply didn't add up; how could such pretty music come out of a person with such a large, ugly hole in his soul? The latter was a fissure Taylor would need decades of introspection and professional help to close. Until then, it was as if he *needed* to creep up on death, to see how close he could get; to sleep with as many women as he could, giving and taking phony vows of love, to temporarily fill that cavity; to move from place to place like a gypsy moth.

"I used to get crazy on this drug," he once said, relating episodes when he was flirting with acid, "jumping great gaps between the roofs and swinging on fire escapes." One time, he unwittingly left a plate of matches burning in the flat where he was staying, then went out and "walked along a ledge, stories and stories up, and jumped into a tree in a park along Baker Street," then jumped in a car and "blasted around the West End doing about 80—just screaming." When he got back, the plate had exploded and sent pieces flying, leaving a hole in the ceiling. "I later thought of that as being pretty irresponsible," he recalled, though for him irresponsibility was not reason enough to *take* responsibility. And he was damn lucky too. Striking a guy in the street with his car sent Taylor "into some heavy freaker right there." But the bobbies busted the *victim*, whom they had been chasing for three blocks.

Taylor indeed faced little legal consequence. The drug scene in England was far less given to psychodrama and hysteria than in the United States. While pot was illegal—McCartney could vouch for *that*—the harder stuff was not technically illegal at the time; rather, cocaine, morphine, and heroin addicts were registered by the government and made eligible for methadone treatment, which could be just as addicting and destructive. Taylor felt much less pressure using smack. But he was pushing his luck. Asher, who preferred to see things from the sunny side of the street, came to see that Taylor "was still dealing with some personal and addiction issues during the making of the record." Still, Asher, pleading ignorance, not avoidance, adds, "I was far too naive to recognize the symptoms for what they were," and Taylor happily took advantage of his credulous nature. And so things moved ahead, slowly but surely, and in the end it was nothing if not mesmerizing, all the evidence needed to justify his line in "Rainy Day Man" that "You can't hide the truth with a happy song."

The album was completed in October. The cover featured a photo taken by Richard Imrie of Taylor reclining in front of a rock wall in a London park, his bony frame clad in a baggy gray suit Taylor bought from a London secondhand store for the shoot, suspenders, and a psychedelic tie, a dying amber leaf stuffed into his lapel, and a dead brown leaf on his thigh. His eyes are cold, glaring under a mop of unruly hair. The back cover had the lower half of his frame, down to his scruffy brown boots. What Asher wanted it to say was unclear—it seemed to be that the era of flower children and psychedelic optimism was as ill-fitting to the new era as the suit and as moribund as those leaves—but it suited his exigency to present Taylor as dark and a little disturbed underneath his engaging, but dark-hearted, folk-rock brand—the Apple scruff, as it were.

Taylor was breathing rarefied air indeed, sharing studio space with the Beatles, boating around Gibraltar, getting high as a kite in swinging London town. To be young and a favored Yank in England, he understated, was an "exciting time. . . . The whole thing was like a swirl. I stayed at a lot of different places, I lived with a number of different women, writing a lot of songs . . . and forming and breaking off and exchanging volatile romantic attachments." And: "It was like a door had opened up, and I'd been given the key." In fact, the *least* exciting thing about London for Taylor was the Beatles, who struck him out of the studio as rather pedestrian. "The Beatles were a phenomenon," he would say, "but they were also ordinary blokes like anyone else. I was lucky enough to see that side." The contrast with his scabrous experiences in New York was vivid. As it happened, Taylor's "exciting" time in London coincided with what seemed like a clusterfuck back home. That spring, Martin Luther King and Bobby Kennedy were murdered, and when the smoke and confusion cleared, Richard Nixon, the lowest sort of political animal Taylor could conceive of, would have the key to the Oval Office. There was no end in sight to that wretched war in the jungles. Bouts of homesickness aside, he began to wonder if he should stay permanently in England, where he was finding satisfaction. At one point he slagged the country he had left, saying, "I learned a lot about America there. I learned America has no culture, except that which exists in terms of there being no culture. The philosophy of no philosophy, y'know?" He went on:

> That's the difference between the United States and England. Age. Tradition. People in England aren't uptight about long hair because there's still the pub, tea time and the Queen. There are those constants. They're not afraid. They don't feel threatened. But in the United States everything is changing. There aren't the constants. People are afraid. . . . There's no responsibility with power in [the United States.] Because power is money and money is available to everyone—even to those who are not responsible, or worse, totally irresponsible.

Of course, this was a prime cut of Taylor hypocrisy. But being a burgeoning rock star meant never having to explain personal inconsistencies, only strike a good pose and a good message. The album seemed to prove it. But, again, he would be the only thing that could have thrown his train off the rails. Taylor's heroin habit was fast growing out of control, threatening himself and all that dolce vita, not to mention the album Apple was banking so much on. Even in the studio now, a place held sacred by rockers as a no-go zone for their drug habits, he needed to shoot up. The credulous Asher recalls him "disappearing into the bathroom for long periods" during the Apple sessions—not that he demanded to know if he was shooting up in there.

It had become too much for Taylor as well. Friends again became scarce, now avoiding him. Margaret, humiliated by Taylor's constant trolling for other women, had gone back to America. Again he wasted down to a scrawny skeleton, always feeling sick, passing out for long periods of time, the "excitement" now nothing but counting the minutes till the next time he could pump a needle in his arm. He entered a treatment program and was prescribed visepdone, a form of methadone, the synthetic opiate that mimics the effects of—and is as addictive as—heroin, but for a longer period of time, thus decreasing the urge and frequency of use, and in theory, lessening dependency. It was a good theory, but it failed him. He would say a few years later:

> What the junkie is looking for when he picks up his syringe or goes out to cop is something that will be the same every time and completely supersede all other goings-on. And smack does that. It's the circumstances around it that kill you. Heroin maintenance has worked well in England. But, it's like being dead. It knocks out your sensitivities at the same time that it gets rid of the suppressed emotion that you can't stand anymore. I was incapable of writing on heroin. I imagine even methadone does that to me, to an extent, except that after a while the presence of methadone disappears. You can't feel it.

These would continue to be his conundrums—needing heroin to create but unable to write until he was clear-headed—for some time to come. Soon after, with Taylor still in dreadful shape and his yearlong visitor's visa due to expire, he and Asher caught a flight to America. James had told his mother he felt sick and needed rest in a controlled setting. Ike, who didn't know how close he was to having to rescue his son again, made arrangements for him to check into a hospital in New York. After they landed, Asher dropped him off there in a cab. James told his parents nothing about heroin, and they didn't ask. It was his intention to go cold turkey and fight his way through withdrawal while doing what always could relieve—or sometimes stoke—pain: writing songs. Being laid up in a hospital bed, however, was a debilitating drag, with bad food and nowhere to wander about. Soon he was on the move again, to another of those rich-folks manor-house-style infirmaries on rolling acres with leafy woods.

With places like this, only the name and location seem to change. Now it was the Austen Riggs Center, deep in the recesses of the Berkshire Mountains. It was named for its founder, a doctor influenced by an alternative branch of psychiatry known as the "mental hygiene movement," a belief that disordered humans had to be kept under constant surveillance and control, mainly with occupational therapy like weaving, carpentry, painting, games, and so on. Opened in 1919, it earned a reputation as what a medical journal called "a fully integrated conceptual system of ego psychology" that eschewed lobotomies and electroshock methods for round-the-clock therapy sessions. Drugs *were* administered—it was called "medication dispensing"—to "lessen distress, improve the patient's behavior and increase his accessibility to psychotherapy." Almost as if in a rest home, patients paid a fortune to spend months or years sorting out their lives, free to come and go at will.

Though Riggs was only tangentially a drug rehab hospital, drug abuse was a behavior that fit into the mental disorders that needed to be reprogrammed. It sounded good to Taylor, and Trudy came up and drove him there herself. When word got back to England, no one seemed surprised Taylor had wound up where he was. Hewson many years later said he had found Taylor "an easygoing guy, but he was really out of it at the time. Quite weird, actually. He went to a mental hospital shortly after that." For a time it occurred to Apple that leaking his drug problem to the press might be a PR tool, heightening the dark side of Taylor's pretty folk rock. But it was ultimately decided this would not be the best image for Apple or the Beatles, considering all the tiptoeing and labored denials they had to make about, for example, "Lucy in the Sky with Diamonds" not actually being about LSD. After all that, the first act they signed was . . . a *junkie*? What if he turned up dead in that bathroom, needle in his arm, the way Lenny Bruce had been found?

Asher was highly offended by the notion of exploiting Taylor's woes. But Apple had a most unusual situation on its hands: it had an album it highly valued but by a troubled artist nowhere near England or near ready to go on tour promoting his work. And, already, there was some regret that they had erred in their fascination with him.

As Taylor languished in the Berkshires, his days filled out with meetings, basket weaving, and methadone dispensing, Apple released *James Taylor* in December 1968, with "Carolina in My Mind" as a single and "Taking It In" on the flip. When Taylor was told the song would be a single, he asked Asher if he could redo it, but it was too late in the game. Two years later he would say, "I still don't like that version of it. I do it now and I think I do it a lot better." He was right about that; the marching beat tempering the yearning, the record barely tickled the chart, making it for one week as number 118 in the United States, and not at all in England. The album, by contrast, seemed positioned well and won critical praise in one significant notice by Jon Landau, who, nearly a decade before he moved up as Bruce Springsteen's manager/producer, was a freelance music critic. Assigned by *Rolling Stone* to review the album, his notice sat beside reviews of Joan Baez's *Any Day Now*, Miles Davis's *Les Filles de Kilimanjaro,* Johnny Winter's *The Progressive Blues Experiment*, the Beach Boys' *20/20*, and the *Elvis TV Special.* It began: "James Taylor is the kind of person I always thought the word folksinger referred to. He writes and sings songs that are reflections of his own life, and performs them in his own style. All of his performances are marked by an eloquent simplicity. Mr. Taylor is not kicking out any jams. He seems to be more interested in soothing his troubled mind. In the process he will doubtless soothe a good many heads besides his own."

Within a mix of "country, blues and some antique folk style," Landau noted Taylor's understated reserve as a "sign of his maturity. . . . He refuses to let himself get lost in anything that obscures his identity as an artist," each song "reflect[ing] a different shade." And while "on first hearing the album may sound a bit repetitious," Taylor "is capable of making unusual chord changes while never jolting the ear, all such changes . . . absorbed by Taylor's coherent and naturalistic lyrics." Pegging the two most "deeply affecting" cuts, "Carolina on My

Mind"—the title by which it was originally released—and "Rainy Day Man," Landau raved the former as "a beautiful song . . . an absolutely perfect arrangement" and the latter for the "perfection with which the simple but important transitions are made."

That he found "Knocking 'Round the Zoo" to be an example of Taylor's "subdued sense of humor" proved that Taylor was no ordinary songwriter—though this was hardly unanimous. Jules Siegel, a self-admitted egomaniac who wrote frequently for *Rolling Stone*, and seemingly made every effort *not* to understand what Taylor sang, blew it off as "a sadomasochistic fantasy," and jabbed that "even in the mental hospital, James Taylor is still the aristocrat. . . . The female attendant is paid to be his slave. And she'll hit him with a needle. I wonder what Bob Dylan would have thought of all this? And Joplin. And John Lennon. And RFK."

If he was asking that, why not just go all the way and ask what *Jesus* would have thought of Taylor?

Rock journalism was that deformed, that self-absorbed, its practitioners more stoned-out crazy than any rocker. And actually, the answer to that lazy question might have surprised Siegel. Lennon had already given Apple money to Taylor, and every performer who heard him seemed to groove on his music. And the Kennedys? All that needed to be said were two words: Martha's Vineyard. Landau's verdict was the template; the takeout line being that "this album is the coolest breath of fresh air I've inhaled in a long time." It has weathered time well, too. Deep into the age of the Internet, the AllMusic retro-review of the album called it "a multidimensional layer of surreal and otherwise ethereal instrumentation," and says that the McLean references "actually do a disservice to the absolutely breathtaking beauty inherent in every composition. . . . [With] equal measures of wit, candor, and sophistication, James Taylor created a minor masterpiece that is sadly eclipsed by his later more popular works."

Danny Kortchmar, when he heard the album, had a different reaction. It was, he said, "terrible, too much production going on, too much gimmicky bullshit."

Without the buzz of an in-the-flesh Taylor to promote the album, his debut work would sell poorly. Although apple-polishers at Apple Corps would parrot that Taylor's failure to promote was the problem, the truth was that Apple had mismanaged itself into an abyss. All that palaver about "artistic freedom within a business structure" was just so much shepherd's pie; in truth, there had been so little money available for anything other than Beatles business that no promotion had even been planned for the Taylor album. The arrogance was implicit: anything it put out, according to the executives, would automatically sell because of the Apple éclat. It would be as simple as that, never mind that Taylor would see almost no money in royalties from the album until years later when his success prompted sales of previous work.

His future at Apple looked grimmer as the Beatles lurched toward their bitter end and the ugly power struggle between Lennon and McCartney shifted into high gear over who should manage the sagging fortunes of the badly bungled Apple. Lennon's candidate was Allen Klein, the tough-talking, cigar-chomping former manager of Sam Cooke who had moved his way up to managing the Rolling Stones. McCartney's choice was Lee Eastman, the powerful lawyer-father of his girlfriend Linda Eastman. The battle was won by Lennon, but it was Pyrrhic. Klein would negotiate a huge extension deal with Capitol/EMI as the Beatles' incipient solo careers began but be ousted in '77, with a $4.2 million buyout, before going to jail for tax evasion, having defrauded the Concert for Bangladesh.

As of mid-1969, Apple was a clunking, looming disaster. Peter Asher, feeling the heat for the Taylor album not having done better, asked himself, *Why do I need this shit?* and devised a plan whereby he and Taylor would leave Apple, with him as Taylor's manager. Both men had a meeting with McCartney and asked to be let out; as McCartney recalled it, "Peter said, '. . . We don't like this Klein guy and we don't like what's going to happen.'" Klein adamantly refused, but Paul overruled him, saying, "Look, man, we're artists here. . . . He's given us a great album, he's made money for us, why do we need to keep him in a slave thing?" Asher then moved to New York, where he became A & R director of MGM Records, still Taylor's de facto manager, for a very simple reason, according to Asher: "I didn't really know anybody else that would particularly want to do it, and I had some ideas of what to do, if only based on mistakes that had been made in our career."

But Taylor wasn't let out of Apple that easily. Klein, not buckling to the Beatle who was his enemy, threatened to sue Taylor for $5 million for breach of contract, and the wrangling over the "weird" American went on for months. Klein also couldn't believe that Asher had not taken *all* the publishing rights on Taylor's songs, leaving the Chip Taylor–produced songs in the grip of April-Blackwood. Asher, Klein told *Rolling Stone*, was a "wonderful kid, but he never even signed James Taylor to Apple Publishing"—never mind that CBS, Blackwood's parent company, was threatening to sue Apple for taking *any* cut from *any* Taylor song, a mess that would crawl through the courts for years.

As Taylor's biggest—maybe only—booster, it was Asher's assumption that the skinny American with the golden throat and self-destructive impulses would soon follow him and that he'd make a deal for him. In the meantime, he and Taylor had an odd agreement, with Asher working as his manager even though Taylor was still contractually obligated to Apple. And Taylor, terrified that Klein might shut off the spigot to any money he had coming, or even derrick his career out of spite, wanted to remain on the label. But Klein did nothing to keep him occupied; thus there was never any reason for him to go to London. Stuck in limbo in the Berkshires, Taylor was a mess. So much so that Margaret Corey, his beleaguered girlfriend in between his diddling with other girlfriends-for-a-day, referred to him as "my boyfriend who's in the looney bin."

Again bored out of his mind in a sterile environment, he was not at all interested in joining the games of sedate badminton and volleyball on the impeccably manicured lawn. Rather, he considered his stay done, four months shorter than the McLean sojourn had been, and no more cured now than he was then. Packing his guitar and belongings, as well as a supply of and prescriptions for methadone, he went to where life always felt right, the Vineyard, living at his family beach house. The album had been out for around a month, going nowhere fast, and so he also now began to tentatively perform at small clubs, a long way down from the tour Apple had wanted to string together. Asher meanwhile was becoming itchy to do something more for himself than be an A & R guy. He wanted to produce and make managing his prime function. To do that, he had to join the buffalo run heading west, to the land of the angels and more than a few devils. And his move would bring another fateful turn in James Taylor's life. He, too, by necessity rather than choice, needed to graze in the land of milk and honey, with a side of hedonism and a chaser of derangement.

9

CALIFORNIA SCHEMING

Los Angeles, as one might assume, developed within the rock universe in an orbit completely different from any other. With an ocean on one side, barren mountains and a desert on the other, and an untold crop of fruits and nuts in between, the onetime pueblo of Mexican colonial days may have been the movie capital but was maligned by music students as an arthritic, smog-filled wasteland with no discernible music heritage of its own. But, as the ultimate American magnet, the sun and celluloid Oz of Hollywood and Vine had drawn so many millions of migrants from across the country that the town-turned-metropolis became a player during rock's 1950s nascence, mainly in the area of dreamy rhythm and blues like that of the Platters, and then restless, scabrous rock—Eddie Cochran—and ethnic rock—Ritchie Valens.

All these ingredients, good and bad, gave the town a loose, eclectic, anything-goes feel by the time the big studios—with Capitol Records getting the lion's share of talent, having been founded there in 1942—began to recognize the synergy and wide-open, dreamy, smoggy traits of the town were transmuted in the airy recording studios with their fat echoes. The leeway felt by singers, musicians, and producers translated into distinctly freestyle, sometimes over-the-top recordings and a "Southern California sound." Characteristic of the airy sound were large background chorales and high, lushly echoed harmonies perfected by the Beach Boys, the first great American band of the '60s and, appropriately, natives of L.A. When folk became alloyed with rock, the Byrds took those high, ethereal harmony background vocals as counterpoint to Roger McGuinn's pungent, clanging chords on a twelve-string electric Rickenbacker. Voilà—a new idiom had sprung up.

As of the mid-'60s, the race was on, with musicians far and wide packing up vans and jalopies and heading for L.A., the rush immortalized by songs like "California Dreamin'" and "Creeque Alley." L.A. was the place where, according to the latter, "[Roger] McGuinn and [Barry] McGuire couldn't get no higher." The folk old guard was right about one thing: folk *had* sold out its political base to live in the sun and wallow in cheap drugs and sex on Sunset Boulevard, even if, as McGuire warned, the world—and by that perhaps he meant L.A.—was on "the eve of destruction." Still, folk ran ever more deeply into rock—one watermark being when the pop-tart Monkees in a moment of genius covered John Stewart's banjo-driven "Daydream Believer," taking it to number 1.

By 1968, scores of nascent bands had formed. Buffalo Springfield had even made Sunset Strip an unlikely site of protest when an anti-curfew protest on the street outside the Pandora's Box nightclub, at which Peter Fonda and Jack Nicholson were present, prompted Stephen Stills to write the band's lone hit, "For What It's Worth," telling of "A thousand people in the street / Singin' songs and a-carryin' signs / Mostly say hooray for our side." The song furnished the perfect folk-rock flavor, with a thump-beat and echoed high-range guitar chiming by Neil Young, fronted by Stills's gentle warning to the new generation that if you step out of line, "the man will come and take you away." Under the surface was an escalating darkness of mood and far more blatant drug use than anyone had seen. One of San Francisco's rising bands, the Grateful Dead, proudly wore the label applied to them as a "drug band." Another, the Jefferson Airplane, had a huge hit based on Lewis Carroll's acid trips, with Grace Slick cawing, "Feed your head, feed your head." L.A.'s attitude about drugs may have been summed up unwittingly by Paul Simon, who when the grass supply at a hotel ran out, groused, "I don't mind that there aren't any girls. I can always jerk off. But I can't think up a joint."

Cocaine, heroin, acid, weed, and all manner of needles and pills blanketed the Sunset Strip, almost guaranteeing that James Taylor would partake freely. He eased right into the scene, one that Jim Morrison, after his March 1969 arrest in Miami for exposing himself in concert (a bogus charge the city finally owned up to in 2010, posthumously pardoning him), would upbraid for being *too* sick. "The initial flash is over—the thing they call rock, what used to be called rock n' roll, has gotten decadent," he said. Actually Morrison would help romanticize it in "L.A. Woman," objectifying the "city of night" town as an irresistible *mala femmina*. With rock acts staking their ground now for the shakeout of the next decade, L.A. was the epicenter of it all, seeing and breeding a soft brand of rock mixed with the blues that had fueled so much of earlier rock. The Byrds got out in front, but not to be overlooked is Bob Lind's 1966 "Elusive Butterfly," a soothing tonic asking to be understood for irrationally chasing after love—"Don't be concerned, it will not harm you / It's only me pursuing something I'm not sure of." Then came New York–born, St. Louis–raised John Hartford, who augured the tone and texture of the new folk rock with the Grammy-winning "Gentle on My Mind," the lyrics of which seem positively Taylor-like:

. . . I'm not shackled by forgotten words and bonds
And the ink stains that have dried upon some line
That keeps you in the back roads by the rivers of my memory

Most of the music crowd lived not in the ritzy corners of the city, not out on the beaches of Santa Monica, Pacific Palisades, or (God knows) the millionaires' playpen of Malibu, but in small, ramshackle cottages dotted along the prosaic boulevards of Laurel Canyon and swallowed up into the Hollywood Hills. Most everyone in the music kibbutz had lint in their pockets, and there'd be a carousel of people sleeping on someone else's couch in shacks with no air-conditioning or heat; but as John Phillips had written while California dreaming, there were no brown leaves or gray skies. Joni Mitchell, after coming out from New York, loved "the ruralness of it, with trees in the yard and ducks floating around on my neighbors' pond. And the friendliness of it: no one locked their doors."

Sadly, not locking the door would prove fatal in August 1969 for the seven people murdered by the foam-mouthed gang sent to the Hollywood Hills by a failed rock singer named Manson, an event that cast a neurotic pall forever on the city. As Jules Siegel summed up L.A. in '71, "In Los Angeles, they commit suicide during the long rains when they cannot get out to the beach, or the golf course, or the ball park. Television is not the universal antidote for the poisons of loneliness.

And loneliness is the great disease of Los Angeles." To Siegel, it was a modern Babylon, not a particularly novel metaphor—Kenneth Anger had long before written his deliciously salacious book about the movie colony, *Hollywood Babylon*—but it fit. A little too well even for Taylor's amoral tastes.

From his perspective, Taylor may have left Carolina but not the Vineyard. Asher confirms that James "always hated L.A." But while he was there, he would leave his stamp in the sunbaked turf. He entered this reservoir of gently bubbling, cutthroat competition as a novelty. The Beatles connection, though a failure, sparked scuttlebutt around him that he had to be a rock savant, a poseur, or a drug-addicted screwup; as always with him, contradictions abounded. He was a rich kid with a history of living through hell for undetermined reasons. Many who heard of him hadn't heard him sing, only through word of mouth, and some were obliged to ask: "What the hell does *he* have to bitch about?" Yet his James Dean–like angst played well, his reputation as a problem child preceded him. Those who were able to penetrate his hard shell were less wary of him; his messed-up tendencies were too scary to be fake, his talent too deep to come out of anything but a damaged soul.

Keeping a distance from the other hustlers, he slept on a couch in Peter and Betsy Asher's Canyon home. It was an elegant colonial on South Longwood Avenue in the Wilshire district, a few miles south of the two main music cantinas: the Troubadour and the Whisky a Go Go—convenient that Taylor needed to make only a short trip if he was to be somebody. Once again playing Bohemian, it was no different from the Village or London. Many women fell for him. But now he didn't need to settle for chaff. He had made an immediate impact on the girl everyone in the community lusted after. And it was more than remarkable that Joni Mitchell fell into his lap so quickly.

As gifted as she was and as picky as she had the right to be, the fey, doe-eyed Mitchell simply could not resist James Taylor and his roguish charm, fully formed at age twenty. As together and driven as Mitchell was, she had a cavity in her soul. A breakable woman, her songs were as personally confessional as were Taylor's and had similar psychological baggage about abandonment and self-doubt. An art school dropout who had overcome childhood polio in Alberta, Canada, she fell for a man in 1964 who, she later said, in language much like her morose lyrics, "left me three months pregnant in an attic room with no money and winter coming on and only a fireplace for heat. The spindles of the banister were gap-toothed fuel for last winter's occupants." She had a daughter but gave her up for adoption, something else she would sing sadly about. She married American folksinger Chuck Mitchell, moved to Michigan, migrated to Greenwich Village, met Tom Rush, and, like James Taylor, gained first attention when Rush sang her song "The Circle Game" and titled his album after it.

Although the object of flirtation by tons of men, her assets obvious, her hard-set but aching vulnerability seemingly etched by her soft blonde hair and big, sad eyes, she had little inclination to become involved with anyone but the artistic young singers who could help her move her career along. Divorced and living in the Canyon in 1968, it wasn't as if she was selling herself to the most influential bidder, but she surely had something the biggest and brightest rockers could not resist. The one who came in handiest was David Crosby, even as he himself was begging for work. Having seen Mitchell at a club in Florida, he then made the Village folk scene with her in New York and, when they got to L.A., he produced demo tapes that won her a contract with Reprise Records, with songs that included "Michael from Mountains," "Both Sides Now," and "Chelsea Morning." These were revelations; as Mitchell would recall, "My songs began to be, like, playlets or soliloquies. My voice even changed—I no longer was imitative of the folk style, really. I was just a girl with a guitar that made it look that way."

As L.A. became an incestuous music commune, with male singers shacking up with female singers, then discarding them when something better came along, Mitchell gained ascent by doing the reverse, going from Crosby to Graham Nash, who also was absolutely smitten with the sad-faced, sensual young woman from Canada. Crosby, who was already looking elsewhere for his stepping stones, had no objection; well known were the volatile screaming matches between these two highly sensitive and temperamental artists, and Crosby, who insisted the relationship was platonic, in effect, passed her to Nash, the mild-mannered, and married, Brit. In no time Mitchell would be his "Yoko," leading him to quit his band, leave his wife, and traverse half the globe to take up with her in L.A. Nash of course found a real pot of gold as a result with his new supergroup bonding him to Stills and Crosby, but the romance was typically doomed after two years, even if it spawned one of the great vinyl valentines, enshrining the very, very, very fine house on Lookout Mountain where the couple lived. The reason for the split was the spindly, Buddha-like expatriate from North Carolina by way of the Village, England, and at least two stays in the loony bin.

Mitchell first laid eyes on James Taylor not in L.A. but in Boston early in 1969 when he opened a show for Mitchell and Graham Nash at the Unicorn. He was flattered by her attention—it always fed his ego how easily women were attracted to his flame—and eager to couple with a woman whom he actually admired as an artist. And it was a moment when ambition met opportunity. Taylor may have been a totem pole for the "sensitive man," but in the areas of sex and the heart, he was not overly interested in sincerity or monogamy, though when he made a play to get her to leave Nash he could pretend as well as the next cad that he loved her, without even having to say so. There were enough women up and down Sunset Boulevard who could have, and did, warn Mitchell that Taylor would use her as he had them. In the matter of women, says Danny Kortchmar, who first saw this in 1963, "James always has had the same profound effect on people, especially girls. They always say he's the most honest, sensitive guy they've ever met. They make out he's some kind of messiah with special wisdom."

As Taylor surely had noticed, McLean had paid certain fringe benefits. Says Kortchmar, "James's mental hospital trips only add to his *mystique.*" Indeed, Taylor could have personified the Jackson Browne–Glenn Frey refrain in "Take It Easy" about "four that want to own me, two that want to stone me, one says she's a friend of mine." He still had Margaret Corey back east, and one of the world's hottest singers on his excursions west, with a lot of others as backup. To be sure, few men could be as convincing a rogue as Taylor, with his hair down to here and plenty of money, when he cast his dewy blue eyes into a woman's helpless eyes and played that "smoky" voice like a Stradivarius. Once Taylor began to sit down and sing for her and then exchange song ideas, Joni was smitten, as hard and hopelessly as Nash had been with her. For his part, the deal clincher was her, well, bed skills. Taylor made a valiant effort at saying this in euphemisms: that she was "a love goddess," "so sensual and free with her body," and "a real artist who likes to search down deep," who was "not afraid to experiment," the kicker being that "we share a lot of common ground. We're very compatible."

The upshot was that in this new maw of demented culture, Nash never held a grudge against Taylor; rather, he accepted the strange new guy on the periphery of the scene as a real mover who had gone after a woman he wanted. While Nash moved to other pastures, Mitchell, who was so busy playing the same game that she could go from one rocker to another without blinking, seemed to think the tall, gaunt newcomer was different; he was one conquest not based on what he could do for her but the other way around. She probably figured he was too insecure to play her. Taylor indeed entered eagerly into the relationship, allowing him to leave Asher's couch to sleep in Mitchell's big, frilly pillowed bed in her airy house on Lookout Mountain overlooking the whole San Fernando Valley. Here, they were "compatible" for days on end, getting off and getting stoned, out of reach from the world. And when they weren't doing that, they were arguing about something or other, then making up and starting the cycle all over again, a mode of behavior that could be expected from two such train wrecks.

Yet as good as he was at playing these games of feigned love and collecting chits, the whole L.A. states of mind and being disgusted Taylor. He absolutely detested the city, many of its music crop, and the acts of smiling in people's faces while wanting to take their places. To Taylor, there was no soul in L.A. beyond the kind that was unearthed on records by men like Stills, Crosby, and Nash. Even the vernacular of L.A. was the stuff of parody:

"Hey man, wanna hear something weird man?"

"Yeah man."

"Yeah man, like my old lady went out for cigarettes man and I don't know where she went, and I need cigarettes man."

"Bummer man."

A good song idea would elicit an obligatory *"Far out, man."* Musicians would congregate at the clubs, mostly the Troubadour, communicating in the tribal lingo. Even so, Taylor came off as something intrinsic to the culture—witness his quick entry into Joni Mitchell's arc. His *image*, as conceived by Asher, was distant and troubled, a melodic James Dean dragging on a cigarette, looking only at the ground or into a distant horizon—but also at times cuddly, naive, needy. In this construction, Taylor was *begging* for love—for a night, for a year, whatever. It didn't even matter, he would soon sing, whether he was done right or done wrong.

The problem for Asher was that Taylor still could not extricate himself from Apple. It was now six months since *James Taylor* was released, and Taylor had still heard nothing about a follow-up album; about *anything* from Allen Klein or whoever might have been running Apple on any given day. Taylor kept himself busy playing whatever small appearances Asher could book for him. What may have been his first was on May 3, 1969, when he opened for Ten Years After at Atwood Hall at Clark University in Worcester, Massachusetts. The summer of '69, however, loomed as a pivotal time for rock-and-rock social climbers like James Taylor, and though he was admittedly on the lower end of the food chain, Asher could pitch him as the next big thing about to burst. And the most critical gig he would ever play came when Asher got him booked for a six-night engagement July 7–13 at the Mecca of L.A. rock and self-absorption: the Troubadour.

Nothing, not even a place at Woodstock (had its promoters even heard of James Taylor), could have served Taylor's interests better than the "Troub," as it was called in the shorthand of the L.A. rock colony. Opened in 1957 on La Cienega Boulevard before moving to West Hollywood in '61, it was owned by a ubiquitous figure, Doug Weston, a six-foot-six lamppost with long hair before it became fashionable. Weston literally made his name synonymous with the place, spelling out "Doug Weston's Troubadour" in big letters on the long black marquee along the storefront, a landmark that still stands unchanged, and reveled in being called "the godfather" first of the Southern California folk movement then its regional singer-songwriter movement. Weston, says J. D. Souther, was "totally self-absorbed" and considered himself "the epicenter of music," and indeed careers were made by a good buzz at the Troub. The roster of bands, singers, and comics who had earned regular gigs includes Lenny Bruce, the Byrds, Buffalo Springfield, the Doors, Judy Collins, Bill Cosby, Arlo Guthrie, Richie Havens, Joni Mitchell, Laura Nyro, Mort Sahl, Nina Simone, and . . . *everybody.* Robert Hilburn, the sage *L.A. Times* music writer, was a regular at the Troubadour and today likens the place and the crowd it gathered to a "spaceship that landed on earth" carrying an entirely new species, one that by the late '60s was almost officially branded as the singer-songwriter tribe. Of those formative days, he says, "It was a new discovery as exciting as rock and roll was when it began."

The Eagles—or, as they kept trying to tell people, vainly, just *Eagles*—had met each other at the Troub bar, and would later coin another metaphor for the place—it was, they sang, "The Sad Cafe." Taylor probably thought so, too. He never would really bond with the crowd of musicians and hustlers at the bar—all of whom had to pay the cover charge to get in, famous or not, per Weston's anti-"aristocracy" decree. As Carole King recalled of Taylor, "He wasn't outgoing then, he was very, very shy, and he lived more internally than he does now." To Danny Kortchmar, he hadn't changed a bit since the Village. "As the expression goes, he's an interesting bunch of guys. He can be the complete opposite today of what he was yesterday. He is very shy but he also can be very outgoing. He's an outstanding performer even though he doesn't try too hard to be one." People didn't really know what he was, but they would know he was *there*, assimilating, using that affected Southern gentleman accent he could turn on and off and suddenly become a Southern California folk rocker. It all made for intrigue, though at this stage with limited buzz, thanks to Asher. But the best Asher could do by way of pimping the Troub gig was the least the media gave him. The only advance word came in a blurb the day of the concert in the *Los Angeles Times* on page C12, which if one blinked, would miss it:

> James Taylor Opens
> Singer James Taylor, who records for the Beatles record company, the Apple label, opens a week's stay at the Troubadour tonight, his first Los Angeles appearance. Sharing the bill is the Sunshine Company, a folk-rock group making its fourth appearance at the club.

It's a matter of conjecture in fact how much of the audience for the run came to see Taylor or the Sunshine Company, whom Hilburn recalled as "a pleasant but unstirring group." For both acts, as with everyone else, the gig meant they had to take almost no pay—a hard bargain Weston could drive, further requiring all acts to play the intimate, five-hundred-seat club on the same terms, a headlock some would later pay to get out of. Weston himself was almost always drunk and stoned, but he had an ear for talent up until his death in 1999. "The people who play our club are sensitive artists who have something to say about our times. They are modern-day troubadours," Weston once said, the term given new life by the club's imprimatur. Taylor's path there had surely been greased by a recent gig by Neil Young, which convinced Weston "there was an avenue that other people would identify with. . . . When Peter brought me James, I could hear him moving in that direction. People were sick of music that looked outwards all the time. They wanted to hear what was on the inside too."

Taylor rose to the occasion. In that intimate room you could tell who had real talent, or so Weston believed. You would know who was a big fucking deal. And this was one of those times. Harvey Kubernik, then a rock scribe, later a producer in L.A., recalls Taylor, accompanied only by a drummer and a bass, was "very cool, very nervous. He came out, sat on a stool, and played acoustic guitar. He was doing 'Fire and Rain' before it was recorded and it was hypnotic. You knew he had that *thing.* It's like porn; you can't define it but you know what it is." Robert Hilburn knew. Recalling that he had been cool to Taylor's Apple album, on which his voice was "a cross between Dylan and Jose Feliciano," Hilburn revised his opinion. Tracing Taylor to the "country-folk-blues tradition," he wrote in his review that he "showed enough promise Tuesday to warrant close attention," though only on his own songs, the "borrowed" numbers like "A Little Help from My Friends" and "Hallelujah, I Love Her So," he said, "not overly impressive." Of the Taylor compositions—the others including "Carolina in My Mind," "Knocking 'Round the Zoo," "Steamroller," "Sunny Skies," "Country Road"—they "capture the warmth and memories of familiar places" and were "noteworthy."

Even a somewhat restrained rave like this was of inestimable value to a young Turk like Taylor, and helped fill the room the rest of the week. David Crosby, despite his own far more ascended standing at the time, says that when he saw Taylor play during the gig, "the first thing I thought was, 'Gee, I wish I could do that.' When people like that show up and hit the stream, they'd make an eddy, that's for damn sure." Taylor, who earned his praise, couldn't seem to avoid being in the right place at the right time. He was up in the big league now, he had Joni Mitchell, and men were about to walk on the moon. The wonder of being twenty-one, diffident, calculating, and James Taylor seemed infinite.

Things were getting hot between him and Mitchell. They were being seen everywhere, arm in arm, snuggling like teenagers. When she was signed to perform at the Newport Folk Festival, which came up a week after Taylor's Troubadour run, he arrived with her, though he had not been assured of a place in the four-day affair—which would be the last edition of the hoary concert series for twenty years, victim of the dominance of rock and roll presaged by Dylan going electric in '65. Folk purists had booed but couldn't hold back the tide. Thanks to Joni's henpecking, the Newport promoter George Wein allowed her obscure boyfriend a slot, not in the evening prime-time shows when crowds of fifty thousand jammed in but at an afternoon "workshop" on the next-to-last day, Saturday, July 19, hours before Mitchell's evening set (which was recorded for a live album).

There, with Joni giving a symposium of folk, he sat with several young musicians sitting in folding chairs behind her, his guitar in his lap, wearing a purple shirt and safari hat. The next day, he was given a meatier spot, though again not under the lights but during the daytime Young Performers concerts. He took the shot and ran with it, again blessed by timing. The festival that year seemed almost tepid to critics. With no Dylan, no Joan Baez, and no Janis Joplin, who had blown people away at the event the previous year, the biggest names on the marquee were Mitchell, Arlo Guthrie, Buffy Sainte-Marie, Ramblin' Jack Elliott, and of all people, Johnny Cash with June Carter, though the most noise had come on the second night when Muddy Waters made a surprise entrance and Big Mama Thornton sung the blues into the night. And so, even as the rain started to fall, Taylor had a chance to win notice for something other than being Joni Mitchell's par amour.

Taylor mounted the stage, in a red long-sleeve shirt and loose blue pants, possibly with thoughts that, two days before, Van Morrison had played and, as it was reported, the bored crowd had "fidgeted" through his set. In fact, Morrison, like all who played Newport, was prohibited from playing any rock and roll—there being a ban of it at the event, passed by the Newport City Council, one very good reason why attendance fell from a high of 71,000 the year before to 51,000 this year. Taj Mahal, scheduled as the festival's closing act, never even showed up, leaving the closer to be a tribute to Lead Belly. Little wonder the festival could not sustain itself any longer. Taylor, no rocker, dusted off his folk chops, and as the rain fell harder, a few thousand fans who lingered for curiosity's sake stood in rain slickers and hats as he braced his guitar and began playing his fetching, chiming chords, before intoning, a bit nervously, "I'd like to continue with a song that I wrote myself not too long ago. It's called 'I've Seen Fire and I've Seen Rain.' It goes something like this. . . ."

If it's possible to grab an audience with just a few acoustic guitar notes, he did, suddenly singing with confidence and intensity, stopping people in their tracks on their way out. He would also do a couple of other songs, and when he finished "Carolina in My Mind," he seemed to be prepared for more. However, when it came to timing, this day sold him short. Four days before, Apollo 11 had shot into space headed for the moon. Just as Taylor had begun singing, 280,000 miles away it landed in a cloud of moon dust. And George Wein, thinking it unseemly that a concert should go on as this was happening, came onto the stage, grabbed a microphone, and announced, "The concert is over," leaving Taylor sitting on his chair, not really knowing what to do. After a few more minutes, the crowd was congregating around transistor radios listening to the news, waiting for Neil Armstrong to step from the capsule and descend down a ladder to take "one small step for [a] man, one giant leap for mankind." Those steps down that ladder had brought America to a standstill, millions holding their breath as they watched on TV. But Taylor had little interest in it, too pissed off to care. Walking offstage, he looked even more chafed.

"I waited all weekend for this," he told someone, "and they only let me play 15 minutes."

Unimpressed as he was by these vital stepping stones—in Tim White's authorized biography, there is, astonishingly, no mention of Newport or, more astonishingly, the Troubadour gig, the latter of which he would much later in life resurrect as a profitable means of nostalgia—Taylor did leave a mark; as Jan Hodenfield wrote in *Rolling Stone*, "Those 15 minutes set a standard for clarity, wit and magnetism that was never equaled during the four days of the Festival. . . . If 1965 was Dylan's year at Newport and 1967 Arlo's, then 1969 should have been

James Taylor's." Yet it *was* his, even if just as a taste. And neither the moon nor the tides could seem to alter James Taylor's locus.

Following Newport, Taylor and Mitchell hung around New York, during which time she would write "Woodstock" while watching news reports of the staggering event on Yasgur's farm in their hotel room a day before she appeared on the *Dick Cavett Show.* The song, its delicate images of song, celebration, and bomber jet planes turning into butterflies, was soon to be perfectly elucidated by Crosby, Stills and Nash—albeit with a rock feel, not the slow, hushed wail she intended. It was the anthem not only of an event but also of the new rock-and-roll order. And, at the time, it was a tremendous asset to Mitchell. Indeed, when she and Taylor took off for England, where he had a gig at London's Queen's College, as if fusing into her aura, he performed a ten-song set, only four being his and the rest hers: "The Gallery," "The Priest," "Carey," "California," "For Free," and "The Circle Game."

During this interim, many Americans got their first impression of Taylor in a late-August *Rolling Stone* article that stemmed from an interview with the then two-year-old, thirty-five-cent rock rag during his Troubadour gig. In the interview he had calmly sipped on Beaujolais and chain-smoked cigarettes he rolled from Lloyd's Old Holborn rolling tobacco he had brought back from England—what Mick Jagger meant by a real man smoking "the same cigarettes as me." He was not shy and retiring, that's for sure. Nagged by the Apple snafu, he told of going back to London in recent weeks. "I wanted to record. We were ready to record. They knew I was coming to record. But we couldn't get moving. So I did two television shows, a radio show, two guest appearances and came home again." Of Allen Klein, he said, too green to be cautious, "That man worries me. We all know what his reputation is, right? . . . I can't understand why the boys ever signed with him." *Now* he realized caution was wise. "I shouldn't really knock the man. I don't know him that well, really. I've just met him a couple of times—yet I feel that is enough." Described by writer Jerry Hopkins in the piece as "gentle and articulate," Taylor went on, anguish in his words:

> I don't know what's going on over there. I know what it was like a year and four months or five months ago, when I signed. But it's different now. That old craperoo, the bullshit music biz thing, is creeping in. I think the Beatles have discovered the business trip isn't fun. You can't goof off. I get the feeling Apple is like a rich toy. I'm bitter, I guess. I feel they've let me down. . . . It's a mess over there. Everybody's been fired or quit. There's just [PR man] Derek Taylor left now. Even some of the Beatles are getting confused. John's gone away for two weeks, just to get away from it all. . . . In a way [my future is] all up to Allen Klein. He's got my record contract and now he's after my writing. I know he is. He's also responsible for my career. And it terrifies me.

It was quite the rant for a guy who copped a pose of frigid existentialism, never mind the oddness of a trust-fund kid calling out someone *else* for his rich toys. But the Apple shuffle had left him bitter indeed. For twenty-one, he seemed world-weary already and had no compunction identifying the disposable chick he was with, named "Maggie"—it was unclear whether this was Margaret Corey—as his "girlfriend," perhaps for Joni Mitchell's attention. Grooving on being interviewed by *anyone*, much less *Rolling Stone*—which ran the interview in August with a half-page black-and-white photo taken of him by San Francisco photographer Baron Wolman at Newport, mustached and long-haired, intense eyes staring hard—he discoursed on many things, including drugs, saying people who got stoned "for a mystical or religious experience are full of shit, man. It gets you high. That's its only redeeming feature." At least it was for *him*. Taylor was so chafed that when he spoke of McLean and his "girlfriend" began gesticulating in spastic fashion, mocking "half the people in his graduating class," he didn't blanch or rebuke. He merely took another sip of Beaujolais.

10

ACTS OF GOD

Shortly after the summer, Allen Klein finally gave in to the other Beatles besides John and took James Taylor's key back, allowing him to break his Apple contract. Taylor was hopeful it would mean he could finally record again for somebody new. Then, while back in the Vineyard in September, he had either borrowed or pilfered, depending on who tells the story, a stolen motorcycle that the sheriff was holding until the owner could be found. What Taylor didn't know was that the bike was damaged, its brakes not working, and when he hit fifty miles an hour it went out of control, hit a tree, and threw him off. He rolled head over heels down a dirt road, fracturing both hands and both feet. That was actually the second time in recent months he had fallen off a cycle, and while luckier than Duane Allman was in 1971 when he was killed in a motorcycle accident, Taylor would be out of commission for months, bringing to mind Bob Dylan's own 1966 motorcycle crash and exile.

Roaming restlessly around the Vineyard, his hands and feet in plaster casts, Joni Mitchell busy in L.A. and never particularly eager to fly across the country, he dropped mescaline, a new dalliance, as he read *The Teachings of Don Juan*. He picked up a new hip phrase, something said by the maybe-real, maybe-not Yaqui Indian and spiritual guide Don Juan Matus made famous in thirteen of Carlos Castaneda's jive-talkin' philosophical books—"Mescalito has opened my eyes." Taylor would repeat it like a mantra at times, intending it to use in a song somewhere down the line when it fit his mood. He also wrote two complete songs about acid and another about peyote, neither of which he would ever resurrect after he suddenly resolved to give up the mescaline, when he determined, "Acid wears me down"—as opposed to smack, which never made him want to leap from rooftop to rooftop. He wouldn't be ready to bag that high for another decade.

He had already written the song that fairly defined his journey through the landscape of life, "Country Road," the song Kortchmar says Taylor began years before in his periods of isolation on the Vineyard. But the lyrics seemed to be especially pungent now, the road being one that set him free from his family—"Momma don't understand it, she wants to know where I've been"—on a path where he could hear "a heavenly band full of angels, and they're coming to set me free," which conceivably might have meant dying young. Clearly, he was still sinking. He had served notice within the industry but seemed stuck on the bottom rung; it was cool that the Everly Brothers that year covered "Carolina in My Mind," but it didn't make the chart. Asher had to keep insisting to record people that Taylor was whole enough to actually sing and record. And that he *could* was amazing, given that, post-Riggs, he was using methadone so compulsively that he would run out and the scrambling would begin to find him some of the stuff before he imploded. Asher, who would accompany him on periodic gigs at whatever clubs would book him, recalled, "There were bizarre moments, like scouring Chicago with some doctor friend to find methadone so James could finish his last show, with the attitude, Let's just get him through these shows and *then* figure out what the hell to do." That, however, was easier said. Stories of this sort of behavior by Taylor were becoming common, trailing him wherever he went. As if he needed that sort of attention, *Rolling Stone* got wind of the chopper spill and reported in November: James Taylor Crash: Breaks Both Hands.

And so, before Taylor might do more damage to himself, Asher threw himself into his new work. Having quit MGM, he created his own production company, Marylebone Productions, named after the section of London from where he hailed, and a publishing company for those non-Apple royalties Taylor shared with April-Blackwood, Country Road Music. He and Taylor co-owned each of these entities, fifty-fifty. For Taylor's legal representation, Asher retained a high-powered attorney named Nat Weiss, a big, windy, shade-wearing former divorce lawyer who had handled the Beatles' legal interests in America. Asher and Weiss became comanagers of Cat Stevens and began producing records for Tony Joe White and John Stewart, though in short order everyone else pretty much fell away save for Taylor and, soon, Linda Ronstadt. Concentrating on Taylor, Asher put Shelly Schultz on what would become a thirty-five-year retainer. Schultz, an old-time Tin Pan Alley agent, was the booking producer on Johnny Carson's *Tonight* show, and he would carry Taylor and Ronstadt as clients on his tenures at MCA, William Morris, and the Trident talent agencies.

Looking to score a contract for Taylor, Asher pitched him first to his bosses at MGM, who didn't bite. Then Asher signed him to a five-year agreement with Warner Brothers Music, which was already a conglomerate but would become much more so. Already its sublabel, Reprise Records—created in 1960 by Frank Sinatra—had Joni Mitchell, Neil Young, the Kinks, and Jimi Hendrix. And the famous Warner Brothers corporate imprint had been purchased by the enormous parking-garage operator Kinney National Corporation, which in 1970 would acquire Atlantic Records, then a year later Elektra Records, elevating the head of Reprise, the leprechaun-like Mo Ostin, to the presidency of Warner Brother/Reprise Records.

It was a dizzying spiral, and Taylor became a small cog in it when Warner Records' vice president, Joe Smith, a onetime DJ in Boston (and future successor to Ostin), offered Asher a five-year deal for Taylor, with a $20,000 production advance, another $20,000 upon completion of each album. But it was a whole lot more complicated than that. Once the lawyers and accountants had sifted through all the little details, Warner wasn't buying only Taylor; they were actually buying Marylebone Productions, through the sale of the Asher/Taylor company's stock at forty-four dollars a share. That stock would now be *Warner* stock, held in escrow for future disbursement of royalties—when Taylor would, in effect, be earning Warner stock. For every forty-four dollars he reached in royalties, he and Asher would each be given a share. As Taylor recalled, "The way [Peter] had structured things, I wouldn't be getting any more if I had been in a straight royalty situation so I agreed to it; I took his advice on it."

It was unorthodox, to say the least, and risky, entirely at the caprices of the stock market. But everything about the Warner name—and stock—had a rich and powerful scent, and Asher leaped to sign James Taylor, and himself, into that elite fold. For Taylor, it meant something else: that he, too, would be coming westward, as Smith required that his acts record in L.A. For Taylor, that was the downside. But it would all be upside for the community, and an integral step in the booming fortunes of soft rock.

A compulsive bloke, Peter Asher was nonetheless quite the small fry in the broadening clambake of L.A., the home of people who prided themselves on their sharp eyes and ears for talent—and fondness for making money, lots of money. Arguably the most ambitious of them was David Geffen, a squirt from New York who seemed to have a classic Napoleonic complex, his bravado and arrogance in inverse ratio to his scrawny anatomy. Almost as ambitious was his right-hand man, another windy homunculus, Elliot Roberts. The two of them had worked together at the William Morris Agency in New York before Geffen made his move in 1967 when he convinced New York folksinger-songwriter Laura Nyro that he should manage her, spinning her head so much with his jive that Nyro, whom he saw as the next big thing in social-consciousness folk, sued her old management firm to be let out of her contract.

Reluctant and shrouded, the incredibly talented Nyro indeed seemed the next thing, writing winsome, quirky pop-folk songs like "And When I Die" and "Save the Country" covered by numerous acts, which earned her a cult following and a major deal with Clive Davis at Columbia Records. Moving westward to mine more gold, Geffen and Roberts gambled, and won big, with Buffalo Springfield and the nascent Crosby, Stills and Nash. In 1972 when her contract would be up at Reprise, Joni Mitchell also came aboard, bringing her plaints of longing and disaffection to their new custom label, Asylum Records. A year later, so would Linda Ronstadt when she bolted Capitol, coming under Asher's wing when she called him in to save her debut Asylum album *Don't Cry Now* after producer John Boylan had walked off the project.

In retrospect, Mitchell and Taylor were in a race to see who would get farthest, neither having broken out big yet. Joni seemed to be ahead. In July 1968, Robert Shelton had focused on her in a prescient *New York Times* article about the changing dynamics of rock, the L.A. corner of which was setting out to prove that "the high-frequency rock'n'roar may have reached its zenith." By mid-'69, Happy Traum, the editor of the prime folk music magazine *Sing Out!* wrote in a *Rolling Stone* article called "The Swan Song of Folk Music" that the new singer-songwriters—led by the "swans," Joni Mitchell and Judy Collins—were an "an aural backlash to psychedelic acid rock and to the all-hell-has-broken-loose styles of Aretha Franklin and Janis Joplin." Their acoustic message, he said, "is gentle, sensitive, and graceful. Nowadays it's the personal and the poetic, rather than a message, that dominates." Taylor was too new to be included in Traum's tract, but he would soon be the black swan. Indeed, if not for Taylor's emergence, the soft-rock movement may well have been one made for women only, or mostly.

Mitchell's infatuation for Taylor was gushingly romantic, but perhaps there was more to it; by being seen as the more powerful of the two, was she making a statement about who had a hand in the forming music and social culture? To be sure, she tried to push his career along. But she had no intention of ever being in anyone's shadow. For all their mutual shyness, neither was prepared to accept that condition. David Crosby, in fact, who had brought her to prominence, now had no reluctance saying that "Joni Mitchell is about as modest as Mussolini," which was said to infuriate her. Perhaps qualifiers about Mitchell heard around L.A. like that only gave added weight to Taylor's refusal to move in full time with her and be thought of as her houseboy. He didn't need head games, and besides, he despised L.A. so much that he convinced himself he simply could not write there. He needed the intellectual and natural air of blessed isolation in the Vineyard, where he could find new ways to write of himself and his personal demons.

By the middle of '69, he'd finished the most personal and complex of them all, "Fire and Rain," which he had unveiled at Newport as "I've Seen Fire and I've Seen Rain," the verses of which he had gradually filled in, first in England, then at Austen Riggs. When he first had played it for Asher, the manager was floored. Not knowing when Taylor would be up to recording again, he didn't want to wait to produce it, if not with Taylor then someone else. After arriving in L.A., Asher had once again run into Danny Kortchmar, who had also relocated there, as well. He had married and for a time in New York been the third member, with Carole King and her husband Charley Larkey, in a band called the City. Danny then started up another band, Jo Mama, resurrecting at least some of the Flying Machine by reconnecting with Bishop O'Brien, who himself had left a good thing at Apple, having parlayed his work on Taylor's album into session work for Paul McCartney and George

Harrison. Jo Mama secured work playing on some Carole King demo sessions in L.A., then landed a contract with Atlantic Records. Asher agreed to produce their eponymous debut album. He asked Taylor if he'd allow them to record "Fire and Rain." He readily agreed.

"This is sort of a secret," Kortchmar says, "but Peter will tell you if you ask him nicely that he produced a version of 'Fire and Rain' with Jo Mama, with me on lead vocal. Very ordinary pop with big drums and guitar, making it impossible to make sense out of those incredible lyrics, which needed a lot of subtlety." A laugh. "Well, we were learning. Everybody was. To his credit Peter tossed it and saved it for when he could do it right, with the only person who could sing it right." Another laugh. "And we took the pledge not to ever mention what we did."

That was a break, for sure, since Taylor would now be the one who could break the song. And, fortunately, by the time his first Warner's session came around in early December, Taylor's methadone addiction seemed at least manageable and his injuries had sufficiently healed, though he was on pain-killing medication, another addictive thing he had an excuse to abuse. Tuning up for the session, he performed at the venerable Bottom Line nightclub in Greenwich Village. Tony Bramwell, who was in New York at the time, recalls that night. Taylor, he says, was "out of this world. It was just him and an acoustic guitar, but what made his performance particularly poignant was this was the first time he had played [since the motorbike accident]. He was just great. I sat there and listened, thinking back to how different things had been when he first walked into Apple. We had been excited, fresh and looking to the future. Now all we were doing was scattering."

Returning to L.A. just around the time of the Altamont disaster that would be captured for the world in the ensuing *Gimme Shelter* documentary, Taylor played Asher demos and the redheaded bantam sat himself down behind the glass at Sunset Sound Studio. Brimming with ideas about swathing some very grim lyrics in careful nuanced and shaded melody, he would solder all of Taylor's innate influences into a brand-new fountainhead folk: personal, intimate, melancholy, even painful, yet irresistibly *listenable.* This time, Kortchmar would be on the session. Both men realized that, as cooled as their personal friendship had become after the Flying Machine breakup, they shared the same frequency, how to intuitively and seamlessly contour Taylor's words to his music and the music to an emotional context. And yet again, it was a Kootch connection that abetted him even more, forming another fateful bond. That bond was with Carole King.

This queen of '60s pop was stumbling at the time. Only a few years back, the Brooklyn-born Carol Joan Klein had been half of the most successful Brill Building songwriting team of the pre-Beatles era, writing with her husband, Gerry Goffin, lovely, at times caustic tunes about the battlefield of teenage love, such as "Take Good Care of My Baby" and "Will You Love Me Tomorrow." Somehow, the Goffin-King "Chains" made it onto the radio, with as daring a title as could be for a black girl group, the Cookies, to sing. King-Goffin had a profusion of megahits and two of the best songs of 1967—the Monkees' "Pleasant Valley Sunday" and Aretha Franklin's "(You Make Me Feel Like) A Natural Woman." By '68, however, they were divorced and King was living with Charles Larkey, who had come out of the Village trough, playing bass for the Fugs, the part-satirical, part-Beat, part-hippie folk-protest band, with whom Danny Kortchmar also played for a time. When King packed up with her two daughters for L.A., forming the City with Kortchmar, her legendary stage fright kept her from promoting it and soon they disbanded. King was then rescued by Lou Adler, one of the industry's majordomos, a man Kortchmar calls "the coolest guy I ever met," who had ushered the Mamas and the Papas and Johnny Rivers to fame in the mid-'60s as a prototypical superstar producer. When Adler opened his own label, Ode, in '68, he signed King as a solo act, with cause.

King had a built-in audience of mainly females who had aged into their thirties with her. Petite, her kinky, stringy blonde hair and makeup-less face striking in a nontraditionally pretty way, she had an unorthodox sexual allure, that of a "hippie chick" with a New York accent and attitude. Her voice was nasal and direct, folky but louder and jazzier than other female acts, and she could write a line every bit as vulnerable as Mitchell could. But she still needed to contour her introspection to the new pop-rock market, something she and Adler would need to work out. And so it was supremely good timing—for both—when she and James Taylor came into each other's orbits. She had seen Taylor sing back in New York, when she and her short-lived band the Myddle Class came into the Night Owl—a moment that had been a highlight for James and Danny. It seemed provident that Danny and King had bisected, leading inevitably to King and Taylor doing so, which happened when she, Larkey, and Kortchmar attended one of his shows at the Troubadour, after which she had Danny ask Peter Asher to introduce her to Taylor. Thrilled to no end by that request, Asher told Danny to bring her to his home, where Taylor was rehearsing in a makeshift living room studio, seemingly oblivious to the world.

"James, you remember Carole," Danny said coyly, referring to the Night Owl days.

"Sure!" said Taylor, breaking as if from a catatonic trance.

King wrote in her memoirs: "Soon James and I were playing and singing songs we both knew—some by him, some by me, and some by other artists. Magical . . . ? Transformative . . . ? Timeless . . . ? Adjectives fall short. It was as if I were playing with an extension of myself. Every time I thought of a chord or note that I wanted James to play or sing at the moment, he was already there. Our musical vocabulary was the same, and we found we had an impeccable vocal blend."

Though she was as powerless as any other woman to resist Taylor's *kavorka*—as Kortchmar puts it, "James had a powerful *allure*"—and marriage vows in the showbiz universe meant about as much as drug laws, it was a nonsexual magnetism between them that created what Charles Larkey called "a mutual admiration society," though he easily could have substituted *remuneration.* As excited as Taylor was to have King play on his sessions, she was intrigued by adding a sensitive layer of plaintive, acoustic sensibility to her generally upbeat songs. It would be a relationship with incredible returns for both, and for King a lifeline when things looked bleak.

But the first to profit from the union was Taylor, whose debut album came around before hers. Strapped by Warner and limited to $20,000 for production—tipping money for the Beatles and other big bands—Asher was blessed to have King on keyboards playing her proven pop-style riffs. He then turned to Chris Darrow, who after the Linda Ronstadt gig had become a member of the L.A. bluegrass-folk outfit the Nitty Gritty Dirt Band. Darrow would play fiddle on the date and suggested future Eagle Randy Meisner, the bassist formerly of Poco and then Rick Nelson's Stone Canyon Band, and Russ Kunkel, who was married to Cass Elliott's younger sister and whose only experience was in a nascent metal band, Things to Come, that once opened for Cream. Though Kunkel had not yet played a session, Asher went with him. During the sessions other sidemen would stream through, including veteran steel guitarist Red Rhodes, bass players Bobby West and John London, and horn man John Bielan. The Sunset Sound engineer Bill Lazerus worked with Asher on the board.

The title-track-to-be, the first to be cut, as James Taylor would tell audiences ad infinitum, had been written during the time he was at Riggs, after his brother Alex had become a father. Alex's wife, Brent, delivered a son who Alex named James after his brother, in keeping with Taylor christening traditions—over objections from Brent, who wanted to call him Richmond, where he was born (Richmond became his middle name). The event stunned James Vernon Taylor, who even decades later was telling the same gentle put-down lines about Alex and fatherhood (another example: "That's the trouble with some people; they divide"), weirdly, carrying it on even after Alex's death, and he drove down to Richmond in the middle of the winter to see the child. The trek itself became part of the song, in lines now famous about "the turnpike from Stockbridge to Boston," through the frosted Berkshires, ten miles behind him and ten thousand more to go. Within the intricate phrasing of the "cowboy lullaby," as he liked to call it, the boy took on the guise of a cowpoke thinking about women and beer sitting by a fire on a moonlit night, singing himself to sleep. The chorus flourished into one of rock's most memorable hooks, that whimsical conjunction of "moonlight ladies" and "deep greens and blues" prefacing the wish to let him "go down in my dreams, and rockabye sweet baby James."

When it was recorded, his acoustic guitar backed only by Red Rhodes on pedal steel guitar and Kunkel's metronomic brush sticks, it was mesmerizing, certainly tugging at the old heartstrings, and Warner immediately earmarked "Sweet Baby James" as the breakout single he needed. But lurking right behind it was "Fire and Rain."

As Asher had known, this was no ordinary song, in neither its thematic content nor how it had evolved, and he was raring to produce it the way it could only be, with all the currents of mourning, self-pity, and optimism conveyed by the sparsest arrangement he could give it. The song was similar to, but much more refined and thought out than, "Knocking 'Round the Zoo." It abridged into three verses the last year of his life, like acts in a play, metaphorizing the pain and misery of artistic failure and personal weakness—but also the reminder that he had seen sunny days that seemed unending. Of course, of all the affecting and mysterious lyrics, the most enigmatic was "Suzanne, the plans they made put an end to you," raising all sorts of conjecture about who this was and what happened to her—a not unhelpful bit of scuttlebutt and residual speculation to potential buyers.

The identity of the character, Bishop O'Brien revealed in 1971, was one Susan Oona Schnerr, whom he said "was this friend of my brother's—we both really liked her and she had killed herself six months before. No one had told James—they were afraid I guess. One night late we got drunk and I told him, 'cause I'd wanted to. In a week and a half, he had that song written." Actually, there was a bit more to it; Taylor had met Schnerr while both were institutionalized at McLean, and when they were both out of the place they had a brief sexual liaison in the Village but parted ways before James left for England. He knew nothing of her death when, on one of those group benders in London with the Coreys and O'Brien, he was told the tragic news. That led to the unforgettable opening line "Just yesterday morning they let me know you were gone."

The song lay incomplete for another several months after, the second and third verses knitted into it after the Austen Riggs stay. The resulting song was frightening in many ways, inviting all sorts of imaginary sad scenarios—one of many being that fire and rain knocked the "flying machine" out of the air and into "pieces on the ground," killing poor Suzanne. Of course, anyone who had followed his career, and admittedly there weren't many, would have known the name of his first band, but many had no clue that the verses were about suicide—Schnerr, a drug addict like him, had been, Taylor would say, "put into an isolation cell and she couldn't take it and committed suicide"—kicking junk, and electroshock treatment, though the last occurred at McLean, raising the possibility that, in this instance, it meant the fire of burning heroin in his veins, the cooling rain of Methadone. Whatever the exact derivations, Taylor composed the song by fitting these enigmatic lines with some of the saddest yet prettiest acoustic guitar chords ever heard, which were echoed by Kortchmar on a second acoustic guitar.

Asher, with a lot on the line for *him*, to his credit resisted any temptation to overdo his role. As he recalls, he kept from falling into the almost universally adopted method of recording by the late '60s, in which technically perfect instrumental tracks were labored over for hours, even days, before the vocal tracks were done and slapped onto the master tape. This piecemeal technique was high craft but problematic in retaining the essential qualities, emotions, variations—the *feel*—of a live performance, the kind that made Taylor shine. "Most of the vocals are live," Asher said, referring to the body of his work; though he would make use of heavy overdubbing to fill out a sonic field, and there would be a good deal of disagreement about how to shade a song, he would always cut vocals live. That pleased Taylor. However, in regard to "Fire and Rain," he would be surprised himself that it became a minefield of emotions, which was not his intent.

"It wasn't any kind of premeditated attempt at knocking down an audience," Taylor said to *Rolling Stone* in 1979. "It's just a hard-time song, a blues without having the blues form." Rather than streaming fully formed from his head, he admitted, "I stole the chord sequence from something my brother Alexander wrote." At another time, he added: "When you write a song, it may come from a personal space, but it very seldom represents you. It comes out of a sort of mood of melancholy, somehow. It's almost theatrical."

Still, by opening the door and his mind to the philosophical minefield of suicide, he had to reconfront his own unresolved miasma about suicide, and neither did it help that he might have used a human being's death as a commercial prop. He told *Rolling Stone* eight years before, in 1971:

> I don't think there is such a thing as suicide, or if there is . . . there's no other kind of death, except for accidental death and "acts of God" as they say. I think circumstances always kill, that's what killed her. I often wonder if her parents know that the first verse is about her and about me. Sometimes I feel kind of mercenary—I talked to Joan [Mitchell] about this too and she sometimes feels guilty about using people for songs. But that's what writers do.

He also embellished to Tim White, "I always felt rather bad about the line, 'The plans they made put an end to you,' because 'they' only meant 'ye gods,' or basically 'the Fates.'" The Fates had made his song necessary, and for him, it carried unexpected cathartic qualities. "It was a great relief," he went on in *Rolling Stone*:

> That song relieved a lot of sort of tension. There was things that I needed to get rid of or at least get out of me or get in front of me or at least have some other relationship than feeling them internally, either by telling somebody else or by just putting them out in a form in front of me so that I could say, "There they are," you know, externalizing it somehow. And that part was hard, having the feelings that needed to be expressed in that way. But it was actually a relief, like a laugh or a sigh.

Not that his conscience didn't bug him enough to stop him from altering the line to "the plans *we* made put an end to you" long into the future.

As with all the songs on the album, Asher had learned not to drown them in bathos, nor excess; they would sob, not bellow, though every once in a while on "Fire and Rain" there'd be a primal scream in the form of a building tempo and a peal of roiling drumbeats (played only with brushes by Russ Kunkel). Taylor's haunting and haunted voice grew stately as he went along, a feel boosted by a gently rumbling cello played by Chris Darrow and King's bluesy melodic piano runs. In the time frame in which it was recorded, with the idealism of the '60s dying, it was cool to maturing baby boomers that a guy their age was singing about having seen "fire and rain." For those who'd fought in war or marched in peace rallies, it was a mental image of artillery fire, acid rain, napalm. For those who'd manned the civil rights front, it could have been the gunfire that killed Martin Luther King and the heavy rain that gushed out of Bull Connor's fire hoses. Dylan, too, had written of rain—as in nuclear rain—in his 1963 song "A Hard Rain's a-Gonna Fall" as the world stood on the brink of annihilation during the Cuban missile crisis. (Dylan, for the record, denies this was what he meant.) Dylan wrote his song not knowing if the world would survive; Taylor, for far more personal reasons—more contemporary reasons in 1970, which had to do with *self*-preservation.

All these conditions, combined with staggeringly original and compelling songs—the best one having summoned up his father's wish that he make a stand, with the help of a Jesus he had never bothered with before—Asher's deceptively minimalist arrangements, and the way Taylor's voice, given just the right amount of echo, cooed about simple pleasures and hinted at terrible tragedy, turned *Sweet Baby James* into a killer, a tour de force. That is, if Warner Brothers had known what it had. The rest of the tracks similarly boasted Taylor's range and affinity for all idioms. The weakest were the ones like "Lo and Behold" that sounded like only slight variations of "Fire and Rain." But beauty met darkness even in cuts like "Sunny Skies" and "Blossom," quietly upbeat tunes that had a sing-along *Sesame Street* feel yet were more melancholy than they sounded, with Taylor's earth/wind/fire allusions never far off—on "Blossom": "There's a song inside me, take these chains away / Now send the sunshine down my way whenever you call my name." There was a nod to his country-folk roots, "Anywhere Like Heaven," again flavored by Rhodes's pedal steel, walking his mind back from the bitter reality that as life passed meaninglessly, nowhere on earth is there anything like a heaven, nothing like "a pasture in the countryside I used to call my own" where he could take refuge:

I think of that place from time to time when I want to be alone
It's been a long way from anywhere like heaven to your town, this town

There was even room for an elaborate joke, "Steamroller," a blues riff he had been performing in concert, spinning caricatured pseudosexual metaphors, joining "I'm a—" with everything from "cement mixer" to "churning urn of burning funk" to "demolition derby" to "hefty hunk, steaming junk." The climax came in a vow to "inject your soul" with rock and roll and "shoot you full of rhythm and blues," which with its full-blown brass section was itself authentic blues even as Taylor, a critic would note, "effectively mocks the straining pomposity of then current white bluesmen." A shorter blues riff, "Oh Baby, Don't You Loose Your Lip on Me," was just as convincing, Taylor cawing, "Poor old loving man JT, (Pick it, James!) / I don't know nothin' but the blues," and adding some squealing whoops. "Country Road" was given an upbeat tone by Asher and even a potentially corny turn like "Oh, Susanna" was reworked into chiming guitar folk pop, Taylor comfy enough to sing of "my girl Susanne." The closer, "Suite for 20 G," an allusion to the advance tab for the album—which Asher made quite good use of, bringing the album in for $7,600—rollicked on for nearly five minutes of fill time, Taylor stitching together fragments of songs into a blues with more bellowing horns and Kortchmar vamping funky electric guitar boogying.

One thing was sure: no one would be able to call this album derivative, not even of folk. Instrumentation was so spare on all the tracks except the blues songs that they made "Eleanor Rigby" seem overblown. But how would it play? How would *Taylor* play? How could songs that were suitable for bowling alley lounges possibly fill up arenas? Taylor was a real gamble. He was not well known nor overly liked, even in the Canyon commune he was now fleeing after his session work was done, proud of being the classic loner, and outsider, no matter where he was. In fact, no one ever seemed to know where to find him. When *Rolling Stone* wanted to get some pictures of him just before the album would come out, they put photographer Norman Seeff on his scent. Given an address, Seeff found it on a large, barren plot of land in the Vineyard, Taylor working on the wooden skeleton of the house he was building for himself.

Seeff recalled:

> I remember carrying my equipment into all this construction, and there was no one there at all except James, who was single-handedly building this house. He's a very quiet, reserved person—no pretense, no performance. We didn't have a lot of conversation, because he wanted to keep building. The fact that I was there was fine with him, but he was having his day alone, building his house. . . . It was kind of magical, just a one-on-one with someone who was the furthest away that you can imagine from being a star. He folded me into his day. At the end, I packed up my equipment, said thank you and left, with him still working away.

Seeff's shot of an unsmiling, staring, long and lean Taylor in an undershirt and jeans with an oversized belt buckle, arms on his hips, standing in front of a wall with saws and other tools hanging on it, was just one of a host of similarly hunky, iconic poses from those days—a dewy-eyed Jesus, or a guy from a Marlboro ad, an attitude of the reluctant rock star. And there wasn't a thing he could do about it.

In the run-up to the album's release, Warner Brothers sent promotional materials to newspapers and magazines about Taylor, and they were not at all reticent to play up his history as something less than a Boy Scout, wanting to help create some buzz about the genesis of his songs. One part of the release, with Taylor relating his past, read: "In the fall 1965 I entered a state of what must have been intense adolescence . . . and spent nine months of voluntary commitment at McLean Psychiatric Hospital in Massachusetts." However, thinking better of it, Warner deleted that sentence from the materials—of course, too late for it not to get around, or for Taylor himself to have related the same details in brutal detail, a practice he would only continue. And when they agreed on a title for the work, rather than the obvious grabber of *Fire and Rain*, it was the much more winsome *Sweet Baby James*, the title track of which would be preferable to the third-rail images of "Fire and Rain."

Issued just after the New Year, a month ahead of the planned album release, "Sweet Baby James," as beautiful a song as has ever been recorded, died in a sea of apathy. The album then hit the market, a Henry Diltz photo of a clean-shaven, almost preppy-looking Taylor in his usual pissed-off pose on the cover. The first reviews hit in early spring, with *Rolling Stone*'s Gary Von Tersch hearing the influences of the Band, the Byrds, "country Dylan, and folksified Dion" yet avowing that Taylor "pulls through it all with a very listenable record that is all his own" with arrangements "gentle" and "intelligent"—even if Von Tersch misheard one of the indelible lyrics as "sweet dreams and *fire* machines." He averred: "Taylor's persistent lonely prairie/lovely Heaven visions work their way up to the intensity of a haiku or the complexity of a parable. . . . Taylor seems to have found the ideal musical vehicle to say what he has to say."

Ben Edmonds, in *Fusion* magazine, confessed:

> I must admit that [the album] took me nearly by surprise. Taylor's work has a marvelous capacity for growth, a time-release quality, so much so that upon the arrival of this

> album I was still very much captivated by the Apple disc. If he had never produced another thing, I am of the opinion that his first release would go on sustaining itself (and me) forever. But the new album is here and it serves to reinforce the picture of Taylor we got from his initial effort. His songs present a vivid portrait of the man. Indeed, no division between the two can be made. . . . James Taylor is a permanent resident in my home. Yours too, I hope.

Sales moved slowly but were enough for Warner to cut bait on "Sweet Baby James" and rush out "Fire and Rain," backed with "Anywhere Like Heaven." The first time Taylor played "Fire and Rain" and "Sweet Baby James" together in concert was on February 6, 1970, at the Jabberwocky Cafe at Syracuse University, setting in motion Asher's plan for building up a college market for Taylor. There, alone on a stool, he played a twenty-eight-song marathon that also included some of the Apple stuff, covers of the Beatles ("Yesterday," "If I Needed Someone"), Woody Guthrie ("Pretty Boy Floyd"), Wilmer Watts ("Duncan and Brady"), the Impressions ("People Get Ready"), the Carter Family ("Diamond in the Rough"), Ray Charles ("Hallelujah I Love Her So"), and goofs like the "Things Go Better with Coke" jingle, a smug reference to cocaine. Next up would be Worcester State College, Sanders Theater in Cambridge, and Berkeley University Community Theater. And each show would gain him more of a foothold.

At the time, and now all but forgotten, another Taylor-style folk prodigy, who had also come of age in the coffeehouses of Boston, Norman Greenbaum, late of Dr. West's Medicine Show and Junk Band, was on the same upward path with his "gospel-rock" send-up of religious hucksters, "Spirit in the Sky," which would sell two million copies and also go to number 3, in April. Going step for step with Creedence's "Green River," the Guess Who's "American Woman," Crosby, Stills and Nash's "Woodstock," and the execrable bubblegum studio concoction "Sugar Sugar" as the freshest flavor of the day, Greenbaum seemed poised for a breakout as a troubadour, and would release a number of fine folk-soft-rock songs such as "Canned Ham" and "Dairy Queen"—the last in particular sounding indistinguishable from Taylor. But then, out of nowhere, "Fire and Rain" finally caught hold. Taylor, touring tirelessly—heroin helped—got more buzz over the summer when he played the Mariposa Folk Festival in Ontario, Canada, a slice of the market pie Asher did not overlook—though when he bluffed the promoters by saying he wanted *$20,000* for Taylor, he wound up settling for seventy-eight bucks.

By late September, with airplay getting heavy for "Fire and Rain," a cover of the tune with banjos and brass was issued by Johnny Rivers (who replaced "Suzanne" with "girl"), quite a coup in itself for Taylor, and it too was on the charts, though it would be left in the dust at number 94 once the original took off, not stopping to gain until, with *Sweet Baby James* in its thirty-first week on the list and still at number 5, the record hit number 3 on October 31, behind the Jackson 5's "I'll Be There" and the Carpenters' *really* soft rock sedative "We've Only Just Begun," and just ahead of Neil Diamond's "Cracklin' Rosie" and Sugarloaf's "Green-Eyed Lady." It was apt that "Fire and Rain," harrowing in content as it was, reached its apogee on Halloween. By then the song had risen as well to number 7 on the easy listening (later adult contemporary) list. It did even better in Canada, where it went to number 2, and also charted in England and the Netherlands. *Sweet Baby James*, meanwhile, peaked at the same number 3 on the album chart in the United States and Canada, number 6 in England.

Robert Hilburn attaches all sorts of profound significance to the burgeoning sales of the record. "The rock and roll generation was almost exhausted from the '60s and wanted to calm down. And 'Fire and Rain' was a perfect song for that. Enough of the drugs, enough of the war, they just wanted to regroup. The '60s had lost steam, rock and roll needed to take a breath. And that's when the singer/songwriter movement was at its most powerful." No small wonder that the dulcet refrains of *Sweet Baby James* were heard so much, particularly through the nooks and crannies of the place where it was made, where the forces had pointed it to be made. Like no other before it, said Barney Hoskyns, "*Sweet Baby James* became the sound of the Canyon."

Not really able to figure out why himself, James Taylor suddenly found himself in demand all over the rock topography; concert invitations poured in from at home and abroad, especially England, where Allen Klein rereleased "Carolina in My Mind," which had a second-chance run up the chart, to number 67 in the United States. However, for Taylor and Asher, it was hard to take a victory lap. They suspected some funny business was going on that undercut the singles that spun off the work. The first, the title track, did nothing, not smelling the chart. Yet "Fire and Rain," which carried the album, was heard *everywhere*, getting loads of airplay on both Top 40 and the album-oriented FM stations. In December, it was licensed by producers for the soundtrack of the NBC television show *Bracken's World*. Maybe it was because those who bought the record played it *so* much—"Endlessly," says Danny Kortchmar, "wherever I'd go someone had that damn song on a turntable"—in group situations, and especially in college dorms, as long as *someone* owned it, others didn't need to.

But stopping short of number 1 seemed baffling, even for the inexact science of record charting, which is based on any number of arcane criteria. What's more, the official status of "Fire and Rain" is *still* in doubt. It would be ingrained in the loam of music forever—for what it's worth, number 227 on *Rolling Stone*'s 2011 list of the five hundred greatest songs of all time—and sell one and a half million copies in 1970 (over three million to date—reflecting the new paradigm, in 2013 it was decided that one hundred audio streams on the Internet equaled one unit sold). *Sweet Baby James* would stay on the chart for two years and be certified gold in October 1970 (the Recording Industry Association of America would revise downward the gold-level standard in 1981 to 500,000), yet for reasons unexplained, the RIAA has not to this day given "Fire and Rain" gold record certification, surely a glitch in the system.

Or is it? As Liz Kennedy, communications director of the RIAA, explains, "The RIAA itself does not track music sales by artist, title, or genre, but we can offer certifications when the label or artist has requested certification after certain U.S. sales thresholds have been met. Since RIAA awards are only certified upon request, it's not up to us!" If the explanation is that simple, it means that—amazingly, and for whatever reason—neither Taylor nor Asher nor anyone at Warner Brothers has ever requested gold status for "Fire and Rain." As Kennedy laughs, it's about time someone got on the phone and made that call. Still, Taylor did earn a Grammy nomination for Best Album—losing to Simon and Garfunkel's *Bridge over Troubled Water*—and four others, for Contemporary Male Vocalist, Contemporary Song, Record of the Year, and Song of the Year, and only Ray Stevens and Miles Davis had that many nominations.

However, he did not win any. Sitting in the audience in his rented tux at the drafty Hollywood Palladium with Joni Mitchell, glowering all the while, his contempt for the tawdry self-congratulatory rituals of awards like these was set into cement; even decades later, as the winner of a brace of Grammys, he would say, "I have a love-hate relationship with the Grammys because I don't see the music world as a competitive sport." It was a relationship he would need to get *very* accustomed to. Yet the shutout of *Sweet Baby James* did not sit well. If there was any comfort, it was that the album had put him in the fast lane, in a new stratum, one that would leave James Taylor in a position that he could not have imagined a year ago. Along with Joni Mitchell and Crosby, Stills and Nash, he was a team leader as L.A. soft rock charged hard into the 1970s.

11

"WHERE'S JONI?"

The turn of a new decade came with the usual sense of incipient change. When the clock struck midnight 1970, everywhere one looked there was a clearing out of and moving on from old business. Like the boots made for walkin', the psychedelic groove had nowhere left to go but out of the picture. *Laugh-In* was no longer a must-watch, and the spy craze and the Smothers Brothers' TV gig were over. Vince Lombardi was gone from Green Bay and the NFL merged with the AFL in another typical corporate monster. A country shell-shocked by disorder and medieval violence, political and spiritual leaders gunned down like rabid dogs by bottom feeders, and secret peace plans that led only to more war, looked warily to the future for some sort of reformation. As did rock, as the idealism of Monterey and Woodstock seemed erased by the ugly, symbolically violent end of the decade at the Altamont Speedway. The fatalistic ending of *Easy Rider* allegorically warned pilgrims of a new order, in the innards of America, in which a certain kind of freedom was not an option. Still, to those in the rock-and-roll colony, L.A. seemed to be an oasis, or at least a smokescreen, shielding them from all that cold, ill wind.

Their solipsistic view that the music world would revolve around them was an early warning shot that the '70s would in time be called the "Me Decade" of sex, drugs, and rock and roll. All the "me's" in L.A. were ready to conquer, even if they would need to find a way to do it all by themselves. Indeed, the big New York record houses had been slow to take a chance on the emerging L.A. acts—Joni Mitchell, James Taylor, and Crosby, Stills and Nash. The latter had been signed by Atlantic only because it had Stephen Stills under contract, Buffalo

Springfield having disbanded before their deal did. That started a big ball rolling for David Geffen, who had Stills and David Crosby in his management purview. Finding few takers for them, Geffen got an extension of Stills's contract, with Crosby thrown in, a relief for Geffen since Crosby's angelic high-pitched voice was betrayed by a man so completely self-destructive he'd gotten himself kicked out of the Byrds.

Ahmet Ertegun, the wiliest and one of the most charming men in show business, whose appreciation for the art of the deal was almost as deep as his appreciation for the R & B music he had brought to the public for over three decades before expanding into rock, had *all* the leverage. He got Nash out of his still extant Hollies contract with Epic, working out a deal with Clive Davis, who had moved to Epic in what would be a continual hopscotch by the man through the meridians of the record business, to essentially "trade" another lingering Springfield member, Richie Furay, to Epic once Davis agreed to stoke Furay's next project, the L.A. soft-rock band Poco. By the time Woodstock rolled around in August 1969, Crosby, Stills and Nash (bolstered that day and periodically in the future by Neil Young in an informal Crosby, Stills, Nash and Young) were ready to perform in front of—as they sang in Joni Mitchell's song that celebrated it—half a million strong pilgrims of the new cultural "nation." A year later, they too were Grammy nominated, for *Deja Vu*.

Geffen by now was doing more than all right. In 1969, as well, he and Laura Nyro sold their music company, Tuna Fish Music, to CBS for $4.5 million, making them both millionaires. Geffen and Roberts's label was an allegorical "asylum" on their own turf, though Taylor certainly had a different shading for that word. Geffen had amassed enough pull in the business to inveigle Ertegun to sign an agreement to use Atlantic Records' considerable distribution network. The first act Geffen signed to Asylum was a Taylor analog who'd had almost as long a trip to L.A., or rather, *back* to L.A. An army brat born in Heidelberg, Germany, also in 1948, Clyde Jackson Browne spent his teen years in the Valley and fell into the '50s folk movement. After a spell in L.A. with the nascent Nitty Gritty Dirt Band, he spent time in Greenwich Village and signed on as staff writer at Elektra Records, leading to his being yoked with Taylor and Mitchell on Tom Rush's *Circle Game.* He then returned to L.A., moving into a dilapidated apartment building in the Canyon a floor below an itinerant singer–guitar player from Detroit,

Glenn Frey. Browne, another dark, brooding, skinny folk rocker with Moe Howard bangs, his voice a melodic, pop-friendly Bob Dylan echo, had a cleaner-cut image than Taylor, and was no less able to use his charm and looks to gain ascent through successful women—while in the Village, he had a torrid fling with Nico, playing on her *Chelsea Girl* album. Browne was also a far more successful songwriter than Taylor, his work also recorded by Joan Baez, Linda Ronstadt, and the Byrds, but he was in Taylor's shadow as a performer until Geffen began to guide him—and until Taylor had broken out the troubadour genre just as the new decade arrived. Now folk, country, or soft rock—the cognomen depended on who was talking about the new music—was becoming big business, and the earth would soon move before it.

In July 1970, Warner Brothers acquired Elektra for $10 million, cornering the market on the genre and its biggest names—Taylor; Joni Mitchell; CSN; Neil Young; the Grateful Dead; Van Morrison (whose landmark *Moondance* was released in January 1970); Jethro Tull; Peter, Paul and Mary; Seals and Crofts (not to mention, on the other end of the spectrum, a new British heavy-metal entry, Black Sabbath). As one of the rare acts they missed, Chicago (Columbia got them), sang that year, it was only the beginning. The new decade would indeed begin explosively for the L.A. folk-rock niche. This was the year not only when Taylor broke big but also when Joni Mitchell broke out, making them suddenly a "power couple." Mitchell's 1969 album, *Clouds*, backed only by Stephen Stills, only made it to number 31 on the chart but won her the Best Folk Performance Grammy. The March 1970 follow-up, *Ladies of the Canyon*, a more sophisticated, cohesive work that included "Woodstock" and "Big Yellow Taxi" (as well as "Willy," her paean to Graham Nash), rose to number 27. But the man who had replaced Graham Nash in her life—at least when he was in L.A., and not in the company of dozens of other "Maggies"—kept pace, and then some. And Warner, stoked in no small part by the return on *Sweet Baby James*, wanted more just like it.

No one had to tell Taylor he could not rest on the success of one album, even if it scared him a bit. Though it was what he had been working so hard for, and having a megahit was "gratifying," he would look back in *Rolling Stone* in 1979:

> I think there were some things about it that I really wasn't ready for—perhaps there are some aspects of being a star that I'm not very strong in. Some people can really handle an awful lot of it. And other people just continue to do their work and continue to do it well and have a good attitude toward what they're doing and know how to enjoy themselves and disregard things that are gonna mess with their heads.

But Taylor's own head could handle only so much. Beginning a trend, he refused to be rushed into a studio before he was ready. His writing was good, but not fast. He once said, "I don't read music. I don't write it. So I wander around on the guitar until something starts to present itself. . . . It is a process of discovery. It's being quiet enough and undisturbed enough for a period of time so that the songs can begin to sort of peek out, and you begin to have emotional experiences in a musical way." He'd store up bits and pieces in his mind, file them away to be taken off the shelf when he'd have an associative thought or riff that fit something. He'd rework a song, then rework it some more. While people like Lennon and McCartney would sometimes write an earth-shaking song in ten minutes, he wondered if it would ever be easy for him. Neither did he take easily to the rituals of talking about himself, though when he did he held little back. But that would only happen if he didn't think an interviewer was a prick; if he did, he would get up and walk away. No one ever got him right, anyway, he swore. It apparently had nothing to do with bad reviews; that was something he not could control.

While he built his song inventory, he inveigled himself into the good graces of more helpful people, none more important than Carole King. Returning her favor, when she went into Crystal Sound Studios to cut her debut solo album, *Writer*, in the early spring of 1970, he was there with his guitar, a sideman along with Danny Kortchmar, Charlie Larkey, Bishop O'Brien, and organist Ralph Schuckett. Lou Adler had taken a pass on producing the album, handing it off to John Fischbach, who walked the line between breaking out a new King and venerating the old one; thus, the tracks would do both, with new soft-rock titles like "Raspberry Jam" and "Eventually" and redos of Brill-era ditties "Up on the Roof," "Goin' Back," and "I Can't Hear You No More." Gerry Goffin, who had also moved to L.A., would mix the album, which was released in May to a very indifferent market, going only as high on the chart as number 84, its singles all failures. Again, King did not help matters by shying away from concert appearances promoting it, but the critical response was, as Jon Landau ventured in *Rolling Stone*, that it was a "very worthwhile album" but "the production was poor." Adler agreed. Next time around, he would be calling the shots in the control booth.

Peter Asher had broached King about touring with Taylor, and perhaps only this prospect could have convinced her to do it despite her stage fright and reluctance to leave Larkey and her two daughters for an extended time. But it did permit her to get on a stage and not need to be the one the audience focused on, which wouldn't have been difficult since she was practically hidden behind her piano. Of course, Taylor wasn't exactly Liberace on a stage, either. Even when he wasn't bored, he was never completely comfortable having to be a storyteller and a troubadour. If not for his incredible voice and songs, he would have put people to sleep. The good thing was that the new breed of rockers from L.A. was invariably wooden in performance: Crosby, Stills and Nash, for instance, simply stood erect, playing and singing.

The days of the sharp Beatle suits and clean-shaven faces were over; the "uniform" of the '70s was a plaid lumberjack shirt over a T-shirt, jeans, scuffed boots or sneakers—thus Barney Hoskyns's definition of the era's "laid-back, patched-denim sound." Mustaches and scraggly beards were all but mandatory. Nobody needed to strut around like Mick Jagger; if Taylor would have tried that, someone would have called the medics and reported that he was having a seizure. Having King to lean on was just as reassuring for him. It would be rough for King for a while. Taylor, for all his soft gentility, was establishing a rabid fan base growing out of those college crowds. He graciously ceded some of his stage time to allow King to cultivate the same market in advance of her debut album, but when she would sing one of her oldies, boos would fill the hall—the same sort of sexist treatment Joni Mitchell had to endure when she opened for Crosby, Stills and Nash. But it helped toughen both women, for whom Taylor was an addicting presence, a security blanket, and for Mitchell the beau ideal of the man she wanted to grow old with.

The problem was, Taylor couldn't abide L.A. for long. He would periodically go back to Massachusetts to keep a safe distance from the reptilian insincerity all around him, neither inviting nor expecting Joni to go back there with him to his newly erected, still-unfinished home in the Vineyard. "It's only occasionally I go across country for any length of time," he told a British rock paper. "If I worked really steady say like Ike and Tina Turner or someone like that—well I'd just get so blown out and bored with myself it would be terrible. My throat goes to hell and I start to drink." To some in L.A., that made him an interloper, but he constantly looked forward to being a loner again, to walk those paths he had with Danny Kortchmar, lose himself in the dark and be surrounded by woods.

However, he was not going to get away with not touring to support an album, heroin blues or not. All during 1970, Taylor had to get out on the road, drumming up interest for his follow-up album, hopscotching the country and bouncing to England and back on tours of small clubs with rented musicians. When the venue was large and important, such as a gig at Carnegie Hall in September, he paid the freight for King, Kortchmar, Schuckett, Russ Kunkel, and Bishop O'Brien, who would double on keyboards. To his amazement, audiences knew his songs, *all* of them, even the ones from the little-noticed Apple album. And even though "Sweet Baby James" had done nothing when it was released as a single, when he broke into it, people would sing the lyrics while swaying back and forth. "Fire and Rain," saved for the encore, would elicit not only a sing-along but also tears from the women. He could hardly believe his songs were having this kind of effect, connecting his emotions to theirs.

Because of this, his repertoire long into the future would not be overly dependent on hit singles; he would be able to sing whatever song he wanted, because it was his voice that people came to hear. And when this became a common dynamic, Taylor snapped out of his touring doldrums, becoming more relaxed onstage. Jacoba Atlas noted in *Circus* that "nothing on [his] album prepares you for James Taylor in person. There is a whole different quality, a stage presence that lets you know a seasoned professional is taking over. James is shy, bright, funny, relaxed and entertaining. He is entertaining in the way we have almost forgotten entertainers could be. . . . He has an amazing effect on women, which you wouldn't really think he would.

But there's something there and it attracts like fire." He *was* a more confident guy; when some drunken punk leaped onto the stage one night on a show and confronted him with "You think you're some kind of Eric Clapton?" Taylor never moved a muscle. With a bemused look he watched the punk collared by security and dragged off, then deadpanned a delayed "No."

But the fuss being made over him in America was too much for him. Whether he was naive believing that being the swain of Joni Mitchell wouldn't become a sideshow—or whether he was pretending to be naive about it—gawking became part of the act. Often, audiences would break out of their rapt attention on the music and shouts of "Where's Joni?" would erupt, upon which he would bring her out, to bedlam. Once, on her birthday, she came out and sat in a rocking chair as he sang "Happy Birthday" to her, to a collective chorus of "*Aaaaaaw.*" He had written a song for her, "You Can Close Your Eyes," which would go on his next album. A common moment would be like the one during a concert in Ohio when a teenage girl shouted, "Oh God, I just love you two together. You're beautiful," to which the common reaction by Taylor would be to look uncomfortable. Had it come to *this*, living in a romance novel? At each stop, there would be letters from similar young women or even fourteen-year-old girls for whom he seemed the only one capable of dispensing wisdom, some begging him to call them, some with deeply personal poems they wanted him to make into songs. It distressed him that they put so much faith in him.

"What can I do?" he once said to the *New York Times* of this philosophical dilemma. "Do I have responsibility for people who listen to my tunes? They claim they understand me. How can they? I don't understand myself." He'd even call sometimes, fearing that if he didn't, one of those little girls might harm themselves. He could barely live with his own neuroses. Now he had to be worried about others who saw in him so much, which made him only more neurotic. Even his own mother called him one day to say that she heard the lyrics of "Anywhere Like Heaven," the part about pastures in the countryside, as being about his childhood.

"Mother," he told her, "it means whatever it means to you."

What his songs meant to *him* was more on his mind as the grind and demand necessitated by *Sweet Baby James* intensified. Feeling too close a tie between art and business, he felt that it might sap him of energy and inspiration to follow up with another well-received album. Says Kortchmar, at only twenty-two, "James was constantly saying he had more and more responsibility. No wonder he wanted to hide out sometimes." Still building his Vineyard home, he retreated between gigs to a four-room cottage on the island, his only possessions stacks of *Reader's Digest* and three guitars, self-doubt creeping in, as well as some ambivalence about the spoilage of commercialization. One night, Alex, his wife, and Sweet Baby James came by the cottage. During the visit, "Fire and Rain" inevitably came on the radio.

"That's you!" the little guy exclaimed to the man for whom the moniker was an alter ego.

Not amused, James immediately got up and left the room, as if offended that the outside world *he* had created was intruding on the uncorrupted world of a child.

Worried if he himself could go on, Taylor said in 1971: "Sometimes I wonder if I'll be able to write songs now that things are going better. Because I think a lot of art comes from a painful place. I think fear, or pain or some kind of discomfort is the motivation for almost all endeavor." He could dig that; what he couldn't was being, as he said, "a hypothetical entrepreneur," part of a chain link with "a record company, agent, manager, whatever." Perhaps this explains, if one takes it to a subterranean level of consciousness, his heroin recidivism. In any event, longing again for the lowered pulse rate of London—where Apple, looking to cash in on the surge of *Sweet Baby James*, issued a single of the original "Carolina in My Mind" and "Something's Wrong"—he had Asher book him on a three-month tour over there. Asher kept him flitting from small club to slightly smaller clubs to the Palladium on a bill with the oddity of the British country-folk-rock band Matthews' Southern Comfort, fronted by Iain Matthews, the ex–Fairport Convention leader and perhaps the earliest Brit adherent of the West Coast sound. The concert, recorded for a show on the BBC, drew a common sort of review for Taylor by Jerry Gilbert in *Sounds*:

> The clumsy, gangling, instantly lovable James Taylor conquered the London Palladium and made his eventual

> return to England a triumphant one on Sunday. Taylor groped his way on stage like a blind man, and there was an embarrassing silence as he manoeuvred his colossal frame into the chair provided. He opened with a nervy version of "Carolina On My Mind" [*sic*] but then settled down to warm the audience with a strange almost self-denying humour. After "Carolina" he announced "Er, well to jump right on with the show here . . ." and the audience erupted. He followed with a new song "Riding on the Railroad," then "Steamroller Blues" ("It never ceases to amaze me how people can get off on that kind of garbage").

Asher would accompany Taylor and Mitchell, put them up in a Knightsbridge flat, and Taylor on several BBC music shows, which as intimate as they were still made him get the vapors—"All these cameras floating around are making me nervous," he lamented on *The Old Grey Whistle Test* program. But the geekiness, which had a charm in itself, melted whenever he began to sing and play. Today, the only way to catch the ambiance of an early Taylor live performance is by reliving old but well-preserved tapes of those BBC shows, his presence not yet requested by American TV. (For years, his October 1970 performance with Joni Mitchell on a BBC radio show was bootlegged under the titles "In Perfect Harmony" or "You Can Close Your Eyes.") His first full-fledged American tour would not happen until February 1971, when his third album was scheduled for release. He could hardly wait, saying, "It'll be all friends. It'll be insane!" And of the next album, "It's all just the same old James Taylor stuff except that I'm writing most of it on the grand old folk instrument—the piano, and I guess it sounds a bit different."

James and Joni took London, generating a flood of newspaper stories in the leering British press, who had a hard time picking which one to treat as the bigger name—most going with Joni, who the previous summer played the Isle of Wight festival at Afton Down before sixty thousand people, in a lineup that included Jimi Hendrix; the Doors; Joan Baez; the Who; Emerson, Lake and Palmer; the Moody Blues; Jethro Tull; and Miles Davis—the sheer magnitude of which would have swallowed up Taylor. Typical was the story in the music rag *Sounds* that began: "Joni Mitchell flew into London last Sunday—with James Taylor, the man with whom she is being romantically linked," and went on:

> Joni was here on an "official holiday" and successfully managed to stay fairly well hidden for the two weeks of James' visit. She stayed an enigma hovering in the background like a willow-o-the-wisp—not turning up to her expected guest-spot on James' Palladium show on Sunday and only being seen officially with him when he cut a spot for John Peel's Sunday show at the BBC on Thursday night. James calls Joni "the little lady" when referring to her in veiled terms, and on Sunday dedicated a song—"For Free"—to her announcing that it was for "a very, very close friend of mine who wrote it."

During an interview after Taylor's Palladium show, Mitchell, according to a report, "talked quietly to him and knitted as Taylor disinterestedly answered questions [while sitting] in his bare feet and worn denims. . . . He is a polite young man, but he radiates little warmth as a person. His conversation reflects no depth of emotion, though he has a certain wry offhand humour." As Rodney Dangerfield would have said, tough crowd. Still, Taylor's ennui was palpable, since he was in fact burnt on these tours, which weren't making him much in the pocket. The gigs with Carole King, he inferred, were close to a waste of time. They were, he said, "gonna do some whistle-stops" but added, "I don't think we'll make much money, but that doesn't matter. I think at present I'm boring myself, and probably audiences, too. . . . I believe that if I'm interested, I give a better show, and with a bunch of musicians it's a better show." If that would be the case, he acknowledged, "I can make a lot of noise in the States now."

Perhaps taking a cue from CSN's winning dare with "Ohio"—Neil Young's searing postmortem of the May 1970 Kent State massacre by "tin soldiers and Nixon coming," a song that took as much courage by Ahmet Ertegun to release and radio stations to play as it did for the band to record it—that autumn he had followed the L.A. crowd into chic activism, with the usual Taylor caution. He made no overt political statement in song; rather, he performed in Vancouver with Joni Mitchell, Phil Ochs, and Chilliwack at the aboriginal Greenpeace benefit concert protesting America's underground nuclear weapon testing on the Aleutian island of Amchitka. Taylor sang seven of his songs—"Fire and Rain" would never have a more appropriate context—and sang a duet with Mitchell on "Tambourine Man." (Recordings of the concert were found decades later and released in 2009 on the CD *Amchitka, The 1970 Concert That Launched Greenpeace.*) By participating in such affairs—which helped curtail the testing—he found his middle ground, his voice of protest in song, not screeds. He put it this way:

> I don't think music needs to be so obvious and loud that it shatters and batters the ear drum. . . . The only really good loud group I've heard was The Who—I did a concert with them in the States. I just believe that what I do is best taken in and consumed by the brain at an easy pace. I don't get into heavy political numbers because I don't find them lyrical. I'd like to write for all those commie-fascists but I can't reach them my way. I can't get around to saying "Mr. Nixon will you please go to hell!" I think he's there anyway!

To be sure, Taylor had a visceral loathing for Nixon, whom he believed was the essence of everything wrong with America; by contrast, two years hence, George McGovern was his exemplar of what could have made government right. Of a moment during the '72 campaign, he said:

> We were in a room with him, and we didn't get no wooden smile. . . . He just seemed to be a human being to us. He was and is an honest man, and it broke my heart to see him bust his ass against American political machinery. . . . [But] people aren't going to let George McGovern start to change things until they really *have* to change them . . . most people want the comfort of what America was at the end of the Second World War. They want it to be what their parents have told them it is. They just like to believe that those things are true. Like believing in the Father, the Son, and the Holy Ghost and God is in his heaven, and everything is right with the world. It's a nice lie. But in this case it's keeping us from taking action which needs to be taken.

There was a world of irony in these sentiments—after all, it was those very people, those who sought comfort, who were his base of income. And perhaps, if even subconsciously, that reality overrode all his frustration and held him back from using his music as a political cudgel. Indeed, Taylor adopted an odd construct: that shrill issue rock was *economically* self-defeating. "I couldn't urge anybody to think a certain way politically without feeling uneasy. It's like false advertising. Just because I sing a tune people enjoy doesn't mean anybody should follow my political ideas. . . . If I would sing to people about ending the war in Vietnam—and then pay 60 percent of the money I make to the Government which spends the tax money to kill Vietnamese people, man, that's a dichotomy. If my tunes got any message, I guess it's personal—look deeply into your own self for answers."

He hoped this stance would not be taken as a cop-out, and it wasn't. Taylor, who would do several concerts for McGovern with the usual suspects in the Canyon during the 1972 presidential campaign, was about as socially active as anyone in his stratum was supposed to be, without coming off as a nudge. When Neil Young continued to churn out songs of social outrage, calling out Southern men conditioned to accept the blight of racism that had turned their beloved land into a battlefield once again and failing to "do what your good book says," the reserved Carolinian heir of slave owners took the musical fifth. He remained neutral in this fight, neither agreeing with Young nor feeling the need to rebut the charge and defend the honor of his heritage—that would have to wait a few years before Lynyrd Skynyrd from the backwoods of Florida imposed redneck law, declaring that real Southern men didn't need "Mr. Young" around anyhow.

Young, guitar in his hands and harmonica attached in front of his mouth, Dylan-style, was making some remarkable introspective folk rock during this gestational period for the idiom, for example, "Old Man," a moving parable of fleeting youth, never to find what was never sought:

Love lost, such a cost
Give me things that don't get lost
Like a coin that won't get tossed

Yet his work fell in the cult/album-oriented FM rather than romantic/depressed troubadourial category, his only appreciable hit the brooding "Heart of Gold" in 1972, certain lines of which, such as "I've been in my mind, it's such a fine line," were reminiscent of Taylor's "walking my mind to an easy time" from "Fire and Rain." Such were the shared creative menu and sensibilities of the new rock and roll. Even the semiotics were becoming alike, and in many ways derivative of Taylor's clearing the emotional underbrush. Yet Taylor for his part was now all too amenable to getting away from the music grind for a while and making his bones glowering on the silver screen.

That happened when, late in 1969, Monte Hellman, a protégé of low-budget horror filmmaker extraordinaire Roger Corman, was casting an existential road movie he'd been hired to direct, *Two-Lane Blacktop.* Hellman was of the vérité realism school of cinema, in which personal foibles and failure almost always mucked up idealistic goals. He had made two "acid cowboy" B-films in the '60s starring Jack Nicholson, Old West parables reflecting modern alienation, helping to carve Nicholson's emerging persona, and was looking for actors in that mold—the most important of which turned out to be a nonactor, at least in the celluloid sense. Having seen Taylor's glaring face on a billboard ad for *Sweet Baby James* high above Sunset every day while driving to work, he became convinced that was the face of the '70s. He called Peter Asher, who believed such a turn would be a good way to turn up the Taylor fire even more, and within days Taylor was doing an audition for a role that would require little more than shambling around, sitting behind the wheel of a souped-up Chevrolet 150 drag car, and mumbling a few nasal sentences while looking übercool. (Example: "The thing is, I'm just not in the habit of seeing a Chevy work against a two-bit piece of junk," one of the few lines not littered with scatology, all created by screenwriter Rudy Wurlitzer after he sat in his room for a week reading *Car and Driver* magazines.)

Taylor figured he could do all that, for sure—after all, stick a guitar in that equation and that was about what his life was, anyway. Another inspired casting choice brought one more musical antihero into the movie: Dennis Wilson, the Beach Boys' drummer, the rake-hell Wilson brother, the one who had befriended Charles Manson and paid for his recording sessions, and who was as adept at wrecking cars as Taylor was motorcycles. This made for either the best or worst leading men to ever be cast in a movie—Hellman balanced them with the third lead, veteran actor Warren Oates as another driver, and Harry Dean Stanton as a homosexual hitchhiker—but the malnourished movie, its budget only $850,000, was in step with the cultural rune of Dennis Hopper's 1969 *Easy Rider*, cadging the buddy and road elements by putting two semicrazed, stoned-out misanthropes steering into the bowels of American malefaction, here on a course from Needles, California—subtlety was not Hellman's bag—to Washington, DC. Stealing some more, from Sergio Leone, Hellman's characters had no names; Taylor was "the Driver"; Wilson, "the Mechanic"; Oates, "GTO"; Laurie Bird, "the Girl." Just as Peter Fonda and Hopper suffer a violent end, Taylor and Wilson go down in flames, though their end is unseen, prefiguring Thelma and Louise: as the Driver floors it, the sound cuts out, then the frames of the film slow . . . and stop in freeze-frame, a projection bulb burning it through the celluloid. Upon first look—something few moviegoers thought necessary—the film was grainy and incoherent. And, somehow, Hellman forgot what might have been a natural sales tool—unlike *Easy Rider*, there was no real rock-and-roll soundtrack, just a muted score written by Mick Jagger and Keith Richards, who took no credit for it (an omission rectified three decades later when Plain Records put out a tribute album to the film called *You Can Never Go Fast Enough*, with tracks by the likes of Wilco, Sonic Youth, Cat Power, Calexico, and Roscoe Holcomb).

In the long lens of time, however, its starkness and nonpandering nature has lent it a strange attraction, owing not to Taylor's "acting" but his dark, inexplicable magnetism, just what a counterculture film should have purveyed; it would be cited as the inspiration for the epochal race-car genre. When it was released in July 1971 by Universal Studios, critical reaction was plenty good, if not particularly for Taylor; neither he nor Wilson were even mentioned in Roger Ebert's *Chicago Sun-Times* review and were only in the penultimate paragraph of Vincent Canby's in the *New York Times,* each of whom he wrote had "the proper cool for contemporary mythic characters, and they look so much alike that I can't believe it's an accident. They are the two faces of the same man" yet overall merely the "instrument of a metaphor." J. Hoberman in the *Village Voice* capsulized it as "achingly eloquent landscapes and absurdly inert characters," though Jay Cocks in *Time* raved that it was "immaculately crafted, funny and quite beautiful, resonant with a lingering mood of loss and loneliness." *Esquire*, which printed the entire script in its April 1971 issue, called it the picture of the year. Everyone else . . . didn't.

However, by the flick's release, with audiences staying away in droves, Taylor would be saying almost nothing about it, fortunately having returned full throttle to his day job, with another *big* album out and the subject of an absolute avalanche of media attention. His career as an actor was over, the reward for it dubious at best, though for some, meriting distinction for his one-off role in what would become a cult film that made millions in home release (and designated by the National Film Registry and the Library of Congress for being "culturally, historically, or aesthetically significant"). Not in Taylor's perspective. Having believed Hellman—a control freak whom he called "the most incommunicative cat I've ever met in my life"—had purposely ignored any real contact with him and had given him no room to breathe, much less *act*, he said two years later the whole thing had been "excruciating" and that he had been misled.

"That's what I was furious about," he seethed. "I wasn't let in on what was going on. That's what pissed me off and that's why I've never gone to see it." Thus did his acting join his recording as work Taylor never had any use for once it was done. On the other hand, he did get to make out on film with costar Laurie Bird (another lost soul, who while living with Art Garfunkel committed suicide in 1979, taking an overdose of Valium). But now, with bigger stakes at hand, Taylor's ability to equal or top himself and keep from drowning in the excess of being the most heralded singer in pop music would be seriously tested.

12

GRANFALLOON

James Taylor was annexing more of the rock turf, the *big* rock turf, with each step he took. In late January 1971, he took his acoustic guitar to the stage of Bill Graham's Fillmore East auditorium in the East Village, a place that had seemed a long way off indeed when he couldn't get beyond the seedy walls of the Night Owl and the psychedelic rockers rocked the Second Avenue Theater. But he was a different cat now. Bootleg tapes of the early- and late-evening sets he played at the Fillmore East gig reveal a supremely confident, perfectly relaxed troubadour freely bantering with the cool audience in an affected drawl. Cheered when he took the stage, he protested, "I haven't said anything yet!" Beckoning them to sing a background to his vocal on "Country Road," he joshed the full house, "C'mon, there must be at least 60 people in here." During the long intro to "Knocking 'Round the Zoo," he teased, "I don't know when it's gonna begin," to laughter. Neither his voice nor his guitar were amplified as he worked through fifteen songs, at one point taking a request for Merle Haggard's "Okie from Muskogee." Not thrown off stride a bit, he launched right into it, his nuanced phrasing and mellow voice lending proper irony to the anthem of Southern good old boy hypocrisy. The audience never shifted restlessly and lustily cheered him.

Just weeks later, he finally began to cut the follow-up to *Sweet Baby James.* Peter Asher booked time at Crystal Sound Studios, the intimate acoustics of which he liked during King's *Writer* sessions. This came at the same time that she was recording her next album with Lou Adler at the A&M studio on LaBrea. Two musicians worked both albums—Danny Kortchmar and Russ Kunkel—with Lee Sklar on bass at the Taylor dates, the last a real find. Sklar was, and is, a long, angular man with a bushy beard whose unorthodox five-string bass could shade tones with even more nuance, something critical to Taylor, who believed the bass is "the most important musical instrument on any track that I know of." Sklar, said Taylor, "plays bass like Caruso sings." Yet at times it seemed like one combined album was being made.

Taylor would be at A&M for King; she at Crystal for him; each to provide harmony vocals with Joni Mitchell. Taylor would play acoustic guitar on "So Far Away," "Home Again," "Way over Yonder," "Will You Love Me Tomorrow," and another song King had written, the song he would years later call "maybe the best pop tune ever written" and one that "I never knew I'd be singing every day of my life." King recorded that song, "You've Got a Friend," first, with Taylor playing the tightly melodic acoustic guitar part and singing harmony. King had written the vow for eternal friendship in the plaintive but uplifting style she fell in love with when she heard him at the Troubadour, and which was a direct influence on another song on her album, "So Far Away":

> I had Charlie in mind personally and James in mind musically. James's songs can be deceptive in their apparent simplicity. They're actually quite complex and not always predictable. James creates subtle distinctions that make every verse and chorus not quite like any other, yet each new section feels completely familiar and natural. I was so impressed with James's writing style that I began to incorporate it into my own songs . . . Though I wasn't writing *for* James, it was his voice I heard in my head when I wrote [the song].

Still, she would deny that "Friend," soon to be the most successful song of the folk/soft-rock era, revolved around *him*, telling Lou Adler in 1972 that she "didn't write it with James or anybody really specifically in mind." Another time, she finessed her response by saying Taylor had "triggered" the song in her mind. Whatever the case, it almost eerily channeled his favorite color phrasing—"brighten up even your darkest night." And she was flattered by his request to be allowed to record it first and whether she expected the song to explode, she acceded to it. King was well aware that, but for Taylor, she might not have a successful second career at all. And the synergy between them was now tuned to the same intuitive, subconscious wavelength. He had not shared this telemetry with Joni Mitchell, and it probably mattered that there was no sexual-bred tension or one-upmanship to get in the way of the delicate mechanics of their craft. Whenever yentas would ask through the years whether they ever slept together, her answer was a loud *no*, as if offended by the thought she would have strayed on Larkey with Taylor.

Kortchmar laughs at the thought that Taylor could have been *that* big a cad, being shacked up himself with Mitchell, but also because Taylor and King were so unlike, she the "Earth, Jewish mother," he the "ascetic Protestant vicar." However, in the studio there *was* a sort of romantic chemistry, the romance of creativity. Kortchmar, who played congas on King's version of "You've Got a Friend" and the immortal acoustic chords on Taylor's, says, "It may not have been sexual but there was electricity between them." As incredible as it seems, King's massive insecurity made her look to the younger, much greener balladeer as a mentor. At Taylor's session, Joni Mitchell sang a perfect harmony part on "Friend," striking the mood of underlying sadness in his pledge that "You just call out my name and you know wherever I am, I'll come running," hinting that the vow just might be, well, too late. While King's version shimmered with elegant Tin Pan Alley perfection, piano swelling in volume and violins entering, his minimalist take shivered in foreboding and dread; whenever they would do a duet of it, the difference was plain.

Taylor played on much of her album. She listed him in the credits for acoustic guitar, backing vocals, and, with some very sly humor, "granfalloon"—another of his arcane Kurt Vonnegut terms, this one defined as "a proud and meaningless association of human beings"—never explaining why that applied here. But King was not needed on his cover of "Friend," which Asher says was kept rigorously minimalist, with "two acoustics"—Kortchmar, as in "Fire and Rain," doubled Taylor on a second acoustic guitar—and "a very simple drum part," and very few overdubs after the track was done. But Taylor wanted to broaden the simple arrangements so as not to invite staleness, and he had brought in four sidemen of immense distinction—trumpeter Wayne Jackson and saxophonist Andrew Love, the legendary Stax/Volt

"Memphis Horns"; John Hartford, who provided banjo; and Richard Greene, who'd played fiddle in Bill Monroe's Bluegrass Boys. Asher's job was to add intricate touches without losing the intimacy and tempered emotion that "Friend" evoked with just acoustic guitars and a brush-stick beat backing his vocal.

"Long Ago," which had a similar groove to "Friend"—he called it a "secular hymn"—added quiet percussion to what was essentially a splendid Taylor–Joni Mitchell duet, ruing busted expectations—"What might have been and what has come to pass / A misbegotten guess alas and bits of broken glass"—and the cynical observation that "love is just a word I've heard when things are being said." As Taylor explained the song, it was "a simple song about how things don't turn out the way you planned." And if Mitchell was getting the idea that this truism applied to their relationship, "You Can Close Your Eyes," the lullaby love letter he wrote for her and had been singing in concert, and on which she also sang the harmony part, now sounded less precious and more ominous (e.g., "I don't know no love songs and I can't sing the blues anymore / But I can sing this song, and you can sing this song when I'm gone").

Most of the album was of lesser grade but nonetheless fetching mainstream pop. Again, there was not a clinker in the bunch, not even at its most obviously self-pitying, such as his nod to the easy beat of country blues and Merle Haggard, "Hey Mister, That's Me up on the Jukebox." That was another rueful turn that he wrote right there in the studio, taking an uncomfortable bow as "the one singing the sad songs" on the box, even if no one in the bar knew who he was as he sat drowning his sorrows—a common occurrence for him. He wearily sang, "I done been this lonesome picker a little too long," a similar sentiment to that of the sarcastically titled "Love Has Brought Me Around," which hinted that he was tired of singing those fulsome torch songs, and having to commiserate with other lost souls who took him as an expert in lonely days and lonely nights—"Don't come to me with your sorrows anymore," he hissed, "I don't need to know how bad you're feeling today."

The title track, "Mud Slide Slim and the Blue Horizon"—the name an inside joke, his private moniker for he and the band during moments when he wanted to lighten the mood in the studio—was at five minutes his longest track yet, a shout-out to "sweet soul music" that could "change a lady's mind" and a plan to "build a cabin back in the woods" where "I'm gonna stay until there comes a day when this old world starts to changing for the good," set to a jazzy, honky-tonk piano riff and a closing yelp of "Kootcheroo," some sort of shout-out to Kortchmar. Another, "Love Has Brought Me Around," was an up-tempo pop turn with some mild country tones, gospel-style background choruses, and nifty piano runs. "Places in My Past" channeled John Lennon's "My Life," a sentimental journey—first lines: "There are ladies in my life, lovely ladies in these lazy days / And though I never took a wife, may I say that I have loved me one or two." A buried gem was the one-minute-long "Soldiers," a rare Taylor topical song born of the continued headlines of horror and death in Vietnam, where Nixon's "secret peace plan" was only a plan for more barbarism and death. "Just nine out of twenty was headed for home," he sang, "with eleven sad stories to tell."

Taylor allowed Kortchmar to earn some royalties by putting a song he already had recorded with Jo Mama, "Machine Gun Kelly," plying on the popular fad at the time for gangster movies and inane songs like "Bonnie and Clyde." But the curveball was the song stamped by the Memphis brass, "Let Me Ride," a church-pulpit vibe that leaps into electric boogie blues. It and "Highway Song" were relaxed bluesy road songs, the former with some well-placed banjo pickin' and fiddlin', the latter repeating the refrain "You can miss me when I'm gone," reflecting the dark metaphor of the highway. *Rolling Stone* critic Ben Gerson would point out that it "has an irresistible, sinister allure," and that the inclusion of an old favorite metaphor of Taylor's seemed like "a Biblical introduction, as if Noah were preparing for the Deluge: Father let us build a boat and sail away / There's nothing for you here / And brother let us throw our lot on the sea." The closing track was "Isn't It Nice to Be Home Again," a fifty-five-second chaser about being "so all alone" and thinking, "Isn't it nice to be home again?" If it wasn't a buffet of hit material, the clever chord and mood changes were a sign that Taylor was not a static, boxed-in artist, and that he was capable of great growth. Although the acoustic notes and languid rhythm of "Fire and Rain" would be almost a template, there would not be another "Fire and Rain," by design; he wanted to express broader themes than the harrowing but, as he made it, adolescent crap that he believed had added nothing to his life, though in many ways what he had in mind was even darker. When he sang in "Mud Slide Slim" that "I'm letting the time go by," it was wishful thinking. He couldn't do that without confronting more pain than even he believed was inside him.

Amazingly, by today's record timetables, with sometimes a year of lag time from studio to store, both albums would be out in a matter of weeks. (More amazingly, Asher brought the album in again under $10,000, one more reason why Warner was so eager for Taylor product now.) Working just a bit faster, Lou Adler beat Asher to the market, getting *Tapestry* out in mid-November, an interregnum that broke King out as a major solo act. All over America, millions of mainly young women—the same target audience as for Taylor—sat transfixed, King's imperfect but touching voice sending postadolescent females especially into a trance, playing the record over and over in college dorms, mawkishly applying their own loneliness, yearning, and separation anxieties to "It's Too Late," "I Feel the Earth Move"—the singles released first, as A and B sides. As with Taylor's albums, some prime songs on the album were not issued as singles—"You've Got a Friend," for instance, the field for which she had ceded to Taylor, was called her "most perfect new song" by Jon Landau in *Rolling Stone.* The immediate chord the album struck mandated that she tour on her own. The year before, when she had done her first Troubadour gig, she said she only took it because Taylor had pushed her to. But she captured the in-crowd on that night with her own shy charm. When Doug Weston announced midway through her first show that a bomb threat had been called in, she deftly said, "I hope it's not me," putting everyone at ease.

Both *Tapestry* and *Mud Slide Slim* would own the late spring and early summer, selling on vinyl and cassette tape like nobody's business. But for Taylor the excitement had been undercut in February when, like a ghost from his past, the demo tapes rejected by Apple, which Jubilee Records had sold to Euphoria Records (*not* the underground dance label of today), was released with seven tracks as *James Taylor and the Original Flying Machine*, the qualifier necessary because of the British pop group the Flying Machine, whose late 1969 song "Smile a Little Smile for Me" sold a million copies. Euphoria apparently intended a kind of outtake/anomaly curio of a major act, but unedited session byplay between producer and musicians only added to the unfinished nature of it. And even with both versions of "Knocking 'Round the Zoo," with James and Danny on lead, it sounded just like what they were—demos. (The 1996 CD reissue of the album on Gadfly Records—for which Chip Taylor did some remixing—really *was* a curiosity, with *four* versions of "Zoo," two of "Brighten Your Night with My Day," two of "Night Owl.") Euphoria also released a single of "Brighten Your Night with My Day"/"Night Owl," but it tanked.

That the LP actually charted—*way* down the list at number 67—brought little euphoria to Taylor and Kortchmar, who had not thought to buy the original tapes in order to bury them. (A similar situation would arise with Apple when Allen Klein would refuse to sell or even lease to Taylor the master tapes of "Something in the Way She Moves" and "Carolina in My Mind," forcing him to rerecord the two songs for the 1976 *Greatest Hits* album.) Even with "Kootch's Song," Danny would look back at the album only in anger. "The people involved wouldn't spring for the money for a whole album of James' songs [in 1967]," he said. "So it seemed terrible years later when the same people put out the Flying Machine album of those few sessions."

It *was* helpful in one respect. As the *Stone* review noted, "If you have ever wondered what 'sweet dreams and flying machines in pieces on the ground' was all about, this is it. [But] as an album of music the record falls flat on its face," and needed to be heard "with pity and understanding that this was done four years ago by some very scared people." The intent of "Zoo," it was now clear, was not to commercialize personal travail but to make it into a foot-stomping rag as a way of Kesey-like satire, to wit: "Now my friends all came to see me they point at me and stare / Said he's just like the rest of us so what's he doing in there." But those plaints about not being able to find a friend had been superseded by having a lot of friends count on him being there.

The embarrassment of the bootleg album aside, the impending release of *Mud Slide Slim* precipitated a geyser of press attention three months before it would be released. Within a four-month fold, he would be everywhere one looked in the media, a concentrated inundation few artists beside the Beatles had ever seen, with the spillover of attention benefiting the nascent careers of Livingston and Kate Taylor, as well.

They too had vaulted out of McLean, and not back home but into the Martha's Vineyard community, which might have been why Ike and Trudy had not seen fit to send Alex to McLean, too; they may have believed he was too resistant to structure and that they needed to keep an eye on *him*.

Besides, Hugh needed an older brother around as he grew up in a suddenly empty house, and Alex had laid roots on his home turf with his band. Livingston and Kate rode on the McLean music train, each encouraged and tutored by Paul Roberts as musical therapist. For Kate, who had been a singing waitress at the Galley, a burger shack in a village near the Vineyard, Roberts organized a band, Sister Kate's Soul Stew Kitchen. After she checked out of McLean, she signed a deal with Cotillion Records, an Atlantic sublabel for Southern blues and soul, and in early '71 Peter Asher agreed to produce her first album, *Sister Kate*, with songs contributed by James, Livingston, Carole King, and Elton John. Livingston, when *he* graduated McLean, enrolled at the Berklee College of Music in Boston. He, too, could thank Roberts, who told his old college roommate—Jon Landau—about him. Livingston got his deal—as had his brother Alex—with Phil Walden's "hot" Southern rock label, Capricorn, which boasted the Allman Brothers Band, and Landau soon was trying his hand at producing, his first project, Livingston Taylor's eponymous album of soothing folk-rock ballads, which included one track that referenced McLean, "Doctor Man," and another, "Carolina Day," that cited his therapist, Dr. Harvey Shein.

Landau a few years later would pronounce that he had seen the future of rock and roll, and "its name is Bruce Springsteen." But in '71, that future seemed wallpapered with Taylors. Alex, whose son of course had been the inspiration for "Sweet Baby James," moved to the Vineyard shortly after and in '71 played along with James at a benefit for the Island Children's School; his debut album, *With Friends and Neighbors*, recorded in Macon, Georgia, included James's "Night Owl" and "Highway Song," beating James, who would put the latter song on his next album. They seemed to be a dynasty. Kate and Alex won reviews in *Rolling Stone*, though *Sister Kate* was slagged as was she, even as she was lauded for "a mature, ballsy voice," as a product of nepotism—the "sister of the fellow who became the Next Big Thing," and sounding what "a whole bunch of people [sound] like in 1971." Alex was scolded for purveying "old funk . . . [like] a Swedish lumberjack singing old R&B in a bar," though his "Night Owl" cover was "more *plausible*" than his brother's original. The album had Alex "off to a good start," the main difference between the brothers being that "Alex has James' psychoses knocked off the edges, and there ain't nothin' wrong with that."

Of course, James was really the one everyone in the mainstream media wanted to interview. The first to give him star treatment was Gerald Rothberg's *Circus* magazine, which ran a May 1970 piece titled JAMES TAYLOR: THE SAGA OF SWEET BABY JAMES, with Jacoba Atlas writing that Taylor "is a gentle troubadour who will, within the next few years, emerge as one of the major talents in America"—but it took five months more for the Taylor blitz to kick into high gear. Notably, the *Saturday Review,* the hoary, soon-to-cease magazine, had the first mainstream Taylor blurb, in its September 12, 1970, issue. In it Burt Korall opined that the culture was hungry for "artists who personify themselves." Rebellion was a powerful motivating force for teens, but as middle-class youths moved toward adulthood, the "prosaic details" of their lives took precedence.

Taylor's themes of "lost love" and a "cry for strength," thought Korall, provided "subtle substance for the mind and insinuating provocation for the more basic senses. . . . The only constant [is] the ache that informs both of their light and darker aspects. It would seem life has been a trial for Taylor. . . . One senses he is endeavoring to solve his own problems and, in the process, to help lift the weight of ours."

A national audience would see Taylor perform for the first time when he appeared on the late-night *Dick Cavett Show* on March 9, 1970, sharing the bill with flinty actor Jimmy Stewart and Professor Irwin Corey, who may have believed at the time, like his daughter Margaret, that Taylor would soon be his son-in-law, even if James and Joni gossip was widespread. His first prime-time shot came on the February 17, 1971, *Johnny Cash Show*, the black-garbed country outlaw one of his great heroes. This was a major coup for Peter Asher, as he was able to book another client, Linda Ronstadt, whom he had recently signed to manage. David Geffen also profited when Neil Young was booked, too. (He was at the time cutting his *Harvest* album in Nashville, where the show was taped, and fortuitously it allowed him to conscript Taylor and Ronstadt to sing backup harmonies and Taylor to do some banjo picking on "Heart of Gold" and "Old Man," a little-known fact.) But the centerpiece was Taylor. Ronstadt and Young got to sing a couple songs apiece; Taylor, introduced by Cash as "a rock-and-roll poet," was allowed three, "Sweet Baby James," "Fire and Rain," and "Country Road," alone with his guitar.

But the print media blitz had now escalated into near hysteria, with Taylor *everywhere* that month. He even was the subject of a page-one story in *Billboard* that month, titled "Taylor-Made Disks, Songs Grab Action," with Taylor becoming a cottage industry and April-Blackwood swamped by requests by other artists to license Taylor's songs. There had also been a deal made to issue a folio of sheet music for piano and guitar for twenty-three songs along with photos and article reprints. *Newsweek* had hit the stands weeks before on the eighth, thinking nothing of contrasting its cover story—"Welfare: There Must Be a Better Way"—with a sugary portrait of the son of white wealth. Titled "That Lonely Feeling," its author, S. K. Oberbeck, wrote that Taylor was leading "a new breed of nostalgic, brook-clear lyric that tugs at the heart like a trout leaping in moonlight" and was "one of the purest performers of the new softer, lieder-like sound in rock. . . . His songs, now bouncy, now aching, now richly solemn, always radiate clear-eyed candor and a sympathetic understanding that spans any generation gaps. He sings . . . like a young man back from some painful but revealing ordeal, chastened, but still searching"—quite a stroking for a guy with one chart hit and two albums.

In all these genuflections it was mandatory to cast the singing Taylor siblings as Kennedyesque, a theme of *Rolling Stone*'s February 18 cover story by Timothy Crouse, "The First Family of the New Rock." It began with James saying, "It is very strange making a living out of being yourself"—the perfect meaningless existential creed. Noting that Taylor's songs had elements of "John Lennon's barings of the soul" and "Neil Young's stylized laments," Crouse was ready to crown him, inasmuch as Taylor "stands at the head of this class right now [of] the personal, confessional school of songwriting which promises to supplant much of the hard rock of the Sixties." Crouse also sought out the still-dashing patriarch—"Tall and prematurely bald, Dr. [Ike] Taylor . . . at 49 looks like a handsome, rugged version of [former Secretary of State] Dean Rusk." Ike and Trudy now lived separately, he in a small ranch home in Chapel Hill, and he was said to be "wrapped up in his children's careers," a fable at best, even if he did admit in retrospect, "Aggressive fathers sometimes feel guilty because they have to spend so much time away from their family."

A year before Ike and Trudy would finally divorce, they posed for a picture with James, Trudy thin as a wafer with a close-cropped hairdo, each parent looking beyond each other, all three unable to muster more than a thin smile. As James would point out, "My father was such an academician and none of his children—not *one* of us—went to college." (Actually, Alex racked up a few credits at the University of North Carolina before leaving.) Ike could joke that he would tell friends he *didn't* want James to become a doctor at all but "to get back to his guitar and practice because that's where his future would lie." Then the other shoe dropped. "But that's not true, really. I didn't do that," he said.

Crouse said that interviewing James Taylor "recalled Dylan's exercises in evasion. He throws up smokescreens of trivial details but never makes a cleancut generalization. What statements he makes he whittles down with contradictions until they are almost meaningless. 'No, that's not true,' he says at the end of one story, or 'No, that's all bullshit.' . . . He vacillates between surliness and self-depreciation"—but then a week later, Taylor "seemed a different person. Open, hospitable, and anxious to clarify his points." Crouse didn't speculate why this was; but all such differences could have boiled down to one factor: whether he was comfortably numb.

The February 21 Sunday *New York Times* magazine's puff piece "James Taylor, a New Troubadour," was composed as writer Susan Braudy caught up with him at a Columbus, Ohio, gig, seeing enough to pronounce this "handsome cowboy-Jesus" as the "first superstar of the seventies." In this take, Taylor "sounds like a kid sitting by himself on his bed singing his lonely interior monologues." She also said that Monte Hellman was "talking about starring James as Pat Garrett, the sheriff who shot Billy the Kid," a possibility that existed only until the skimpy box-office figures came in for *Blacktop*. Each of these portraits vied for money quotes from him. Here they were.

Regarding McLean:

> I've never been able to put my finger on any explanation of what was or is the matter with me. It's as innate or incurable as having a size 10-D shoe. I don't know what I would do if I didn't have music to totally engross me. I need it desperately.

On the fact that a Harvard sociology professor was using Taylor's songs in his syllabus, having students analyze the lyrics:

> I don't know. You see, I just write the songs. I don't have to analyze them. I think of myself as being a romantic pretty much. Whatever that means. . . . I don't like to talk about my songs. It's self-defeating, it is the antithesis of what a songwriter wants to do. He writes a song so he doesn't have to talk about it.

On rock's corporatization:

> If it wasn't for the big-business hype behind me, and electronic media, I'd just be some guy singing his tunes. But now, what am I? I sure ain't no troubadour. Ever hear of a troubadour making over a half-million bucks a year?

Drugs, as always, were freely alluded to. "Heroin," he said, "it deadens your senses. You don't think. You take all your problems and trade them in for one problem, a whole physical and mental process of deterioration. . . . You're as low as you can fall in this country as a junkie. I remember once crawling around a strange bathroom floor looking for a stash. You find yourself indulging in an almost romantic self-destructiveness—until you realize you'll destroy yourself unless you get out. I'm out." That was his story, and he was sticking to it, a story that came, Braudy noted, as he was "drinking gin and tonics," a clue that sobriety wasn't in his agenda. Not that any of this mattered to his fans. Outside the arena in Columbus, a fourteen-year-old girl not old enough to be allowed backstage waited for him in the parking lot, sobbing about what a "real person" Taylor was "behind those beautiful sad words." When he got to his hotel room, there were dozens of letters and poems delivered to hotel staff by just such young girls, one of whom left her number and begged him to call. Choosing one, he picked up the phone and dialed, and when a machine answered he drawled, "Amy, this is James Taylor. I sure wanta thank you for your poems. They were very nice." He went on for a good five minutes, giving advice about school and asking about the books she'd read—"You know *Cat's Cradle* by Kurt Vonnegut—that's my book." He even said, "If you're ever in the neighborhood, drop in and see me on Martha's Vineyard Island."

"Anyway, Amy," he ended, "if I don't see you, have a good life."

Completing the blitz, on March 1 *Time* hit the stands with a cover illustration of his face surrounded by outdated Peter Max psychedelic colors and the line "The New Rock: Bittersweet and Low." Beaten to Taylor by the other magazines, its unbylined story, "James Taylor: One Man's Family of Rock," meant to broaden the "family" aspect to the idiom of soft rock itself, the lead reading: "The 1960s reverberated to rock. The walloping folk rock of Bob Dylan sang a striking counterpoint to the sweet-sour, sometimes thunderous eloquence of the Beatles at their best. . . . And now, suddenly, the '70s have brought a startling change. Over the last year a far gentler variety of rock sound has begun to soothe the land. Why? Theories abound, few of them satisfactory," before laying out around half a dozen of them, and quoting Danny Kortchmar—"After you set your guitar on fire, what do you have left? Set fire to yourself? It had to go the other way." The earmark of the sound was "an intimate mixture of lyricism and personal expression—the often exquisitely melodic reflections of a private 'I.'"

Of the new sound's leader, *Time* said, "What [Taylor] has endured and sings about, with much restraint and dignity, are mainly 'head' problems, those pains that a lavish quota of middle-class advantages . . . do not seem to prevent, and may in fact exacerbate. Drugs, underachievement, the failure of will, alienation, the doorway to suicide, the struggle back to life—James Taylor has been there himself." He was, the most widely read news magazine in the world swore, a man who "projects a Heathcliffian inner fire with a melancholy sorrows-of-young-Werther look that can strike to the female heart—at any age."

Everyone was trying hard to come up with the definitive nature of Taylor's art, and of Taylor himself. *Rolling Stone* thought it was "the confessional boldness of his dark folk narratives—inky, anguish-racked songs that would have made for unnerving listening had they not been structured around the bright resonances of his nasal North Carolina twang and the clipped, suspended chordings of his ringing acoustic guitar. He crooned about confinement in a mental institution, about nervous breakdowns and dungeon-deep depressions, and somehow he left such disquieting realities a little gentler on our minds." A shorter version was *Time*'s more cynical spin of a culture in decline. Taylor's rise, it ventured, represented "the tragic slide from activist rage into a mood of enlightened apathy."

13

"THAT'S MY HUSBAND"

The solid month of unabashed exposure—which, in retrospect, makes Bruce Springsteen's cover stories in *Time* and *Newsweek* four years hence seem quaint—caused James Taylor's head to spin in wonderment and dread, but it was worth more in publicity value than Warner Brothers could ever have managed. While Carole King's groundbreaking *Tapestry* went to number 1 and stayed there for fifteen weeks, the longest run at the top by a female artist until Whitney Houston in 1993, *Mud Slide* gave it a good run. It was released the week of March 16, its cover a photo of Taylor not playing hunk but hick, smirking while his hands gripped each side of a pair of suspenders over a wrinkled blue shirt and gabardine pants (though the back cover was a fresco of old-world family, country, and earth). The May 8 *Billboard* carried a full-page color ad for the album, a pricey buy for Warner, which paid off when on the "review" page *Slim* was the first in line, Taylor touted as "one of the premiere artists and songwriters of today, whose talents are appreciated in underground and pop areas"; there was even a huzzah for "Danny Kirtchmar's [*sic*] 'Machine Gun Kelly.'"

That week, its first in circulation, the album broke in at number 22 on the "Top LPs" chart—one slot ahead of *Sweet Baby James*, now in its sixty-first week on the list and still nearly top 20 ("Country Road" only now was released, with a full-page *Billboard* ad, though it only would chart at number 80; and Tom Rush had released a cover of "Sweet Baby James"), and eight slots behind *Tapestry* in its fifth week. The big reviews were coming in, one on a full page in *Rolling Stone* beside another of those antihero Taylor poses, in a tank top. Ben Gerson prefaced the review noting that "this is the season of demolition of James Taylor," provoked by "the sheer vastness of his success, which condemns him. . . . By comparison, his less-talented fellow chart-busters like Led Zeppelin, Grand Funk—in fact, almost anyone—get off easily. [For many he's] the 'cooling of America's' mascot. He represents no political challenge or challenge to a life style [yet] I wonder if people would quite accept his songs on sunshine, blue skies, etc., if it were not for the psychological gloom from which these images spring." Taylor, he wrote, "is one of that rare species which perfectly synthesizes the white and black strains of American music. His singing has the high, lonesome quality of Appalachian music . . . a flat, undemonstrative style which nevertheless bespeaks great emotion." Gerson said the first few times through the record—on which he noted only three cuts had Kortchmar's electric guitar—"is dull listening" but that "once the melodies begin to sink in, and the LP's *raison d'etre* is discovered, [its] subtle tensions begin to appear . . . there is a terrible weariness to it which is part of its artistic statement." However, Gerson had a critique for "You've Got a Friend"—"not enough difference of interpretation from Carole's own to justify its inclusion"—and seemed to think Taylor faced a fundamental "structural" problem, that the reclusive intimacy of his music was lost in concert, where this "becomes hideously manifest." Neither of those two judgments would win Gerson any prize for prescience.

Jon Landau, on the other hand, had no cavils. *Mud Slide Slim*, he would write with a few years' distance, "formed a unity in much the same way that Van Morrison's *Astral Weeks* and Joni Mitchell's *Blue* do. It was his most distant and least accessible work because so much of it dealt with being distant and seeking distance. But it is in that longing for some new psychic and physical space to grow in that James Taylor, American philosopher, starts to emerge full bloom," adding:

> The album ends with Taylor's best work about the search, "The Highway Song." Again [like the album in general] it too could have been better performed, but its opening verse is among my favorite lyrics in all of rock. Bob Dylan may have announced the apocalypse in bolder terms, more suited to an innocent era, in "The Times They Are A-Changin'." But James Taylor conjures up an infinitely sadder, more realistic picture of the future, played off

> against a subtler, more original melody, when he sings of his own and everyone's family, and says, "Father, let us build a boat and sail away." . . . He is singing about the ultimate source of American claustrophobia, the closing of the physical frontier, and with it, the spiritual frontiers that were at once the source of the country's greatness and are now the reason for its decline.

The album received mainly high marks—*Sounds*, sometimes with faint praise ("a nice relaxed album which you don't have to concentrate too hard upon [but] undoubtedly his best yet")—but it was not unanimous; to *Melody Maker* it was "tedious." Curmudgeonly Robert Christgau was merciless: "Having squandered most of the songs on his big success, he's concentrating on the intricate music—the lyrics are more onanistic than ever, escapist as a matter of conscious thematic decision. From what? you well may wonder. From success, poor fella. . . . Taylor is an addict, pure and simple. A born-rich nouveau star who veers between a 'homestead on the farm' (what does he raise there, hopes?) and the Holiday Inn his mean old existential dilemma compels him to call home deserves the conniving, self-pitying voice that is his curse. . . . Interesting, intricate, unlistenable."

No matter. When the LP hit number 5, the May 22 *Billboard* carried word that "James Taylor has been awarded a gold record for 'Mudslide [*sic*] Slim and the Blues [*sic*] Horizon,'" the same week that the Rolling Stones had earned one for *Sticky Fingers* and Aretha Franklin for *Bridge Over Troubled Water*. Still ahead of it was *Tapestry*, already having gone gold, but the paper reported that in a key market—Boston, Taylor's "home" market—a survey of three hundred thousand college students had *Slim* only behind the Stones, with *Tapestry* eighth. Another item quoted Lucky Carle of the Southern Peer music publishing company saying there was a huge spike in middle of the road and country music; specifically citing Taylor and Elton John, he said, "These people have tunes with varying degrees of softness involved and no one can deny the trend." On May 29, the day Taylor's "You've Got a Friend" was released—as well as another cover of the song, by Roberta Flack and Donny Hathaway—*Tapestry* was number 4, *Slim* number 5.

On June 19, *Tapestry* slid into the top slot, as did "It's Too Late"/"I Feel the Earth Move" on the Hot 100, while *Slim* dropped to 6. That week, his "You've Got a Friend" climbed to number 24 in its third week out. On July 24, *Slim* moved up to number 2—"Friend" to number 3—but could not dislodge *Tapestry*, which sat there fifteen weeks and would become the year's second-bestselling album behind only the soundtrack of *Jesus Christ Superstar. Mud Slide* would lose steam and come in twenty-seventh, just behind the *Love Story* soundtrack—a victim as well of the staying power of *Sweet Baby James*, which in its second year was the seventh-bestselling album. "It's Too Late" and "I Feel the Earth Move" were the third-bestselling singles of the year. "I've Got a Friend" hit the top on July 31, displacing the Raiders' "Indian Reservation" (the Flack-Hathaway version peaked at 29), the only time Taylor would breathe that rarefied air, and would come in as the year's sixteenth top seller.

Taylor would also win his first Grammy, Best Pop Male Vocalist for "You've Got a Friend," beating the likes of Neil Diamond, Gordon Lightfoot, and Perry Como. But clearly it was King's year. She would win for Record of the Year ("It's Too Late"), Best Pop Female Vocal Performance, and Song of the Year (as writer of "You've Got a Friend"). Not incidentally, Quincy Jones won Best Pop Instrumental for his cover of "Smackwater Jack." King, petrified of giving an acceptance speech, stayed at home, passing up the ceremonies in the spring of '72. For Taylor, sitting in the audience with Joni Mitchell, the most memorable moment may have been when Best New Artist was announced and the winner sauntered to the stage in a slinky dress to accept it.

Indeed, he had already seen the future when he had been similarly bedazzled by her when she performed at the Troubadour in April 1971 and he just couldn't take his eyes off her. What's more, Carly Simon, knowing he would be there—Russ Kunkel, who was on drums that night, had come into her dressing room saying, "Dig this! James Taylor is coming to see the show!" sending her into flutters—left a welcome card on his and Mitchell's table, signed, "With Love, Carly." After her well-received set, Joni went downstairs to catch Cat Stevens performing in a separate room, and Taylor went backstage to exchange a few words with Simon, whom he had met briefly back in the Vineyard when she and Livingston Taylor once planned to collaborate on a record. It seemed uneventful—to all but Carly. She spoke later of having "this strange, prescient, almost eerie feeling that we were going to be together. . . . I'd think: *That's my husband.* I'd see a picture of him with another woman, and I'd get upset. I've never had that with anybody else. It wasn't good or bad, but somehow, I saw it coming." Later, she amended the story to say that when she saw that bizarre *Time* cover of him, she told her sister, "I'm gonna marry that man!" Her latest incantation, in her 2015 autobiography, was that "the only answer I can come up with" for having such a premonition was that "James was perfect for me in every way. If you believe in predestination or clairvoyance, that would be a terrific example of why you're right to." Whatever it was, either cosmic or common, it was a freight train that couldn't be stopped.

Just as the winds of success were furiously swirling around Taylor, there came a most contrary voice of dissent. Only twenty-three at the time, Lester Bangs, a man with the best name ever owned by a music writer, could sound in print or person like a crotchety old man sending back soup in a deli, but his bilious reviews lit up the pages of papers like *Rolling Stone* and *Creem*—he became editor of the latter in 1971. Bangs regarded Taylor on the same rough level as Eichmann, stamping him "Marked for Death" in the metaphoric title of his famous *Who Put the Bomp?* magazine article that year. Actually, Taylor was only mentioned in a few bloodless sentences; most of it was a cluttered testament to the immortality of the by then dated Troggs, of "Wild Thing" fame ("rock 'n' roll at its most majestic," he wrote).

The piece—written by a "speed-fueled" Bangs, according to his biographer Jim DeRogatis—can be found in the 1988 anthology of Bangs's work, *Psychotic Reactions and Carburetor Dung: The Work of a Legendary Critic*, edited by the incomparable Greil Marcus. (The original was on intentionally cheap mimeograph paper with Bangs's scribbly illustrations.) In this acid-trip meandering through all the stops signs of literary law, Taylor was held responsible for "the emergent Burbank Adult-Rock cartel . . . [of] snotnose minstrels" like Arlo Guthrie. Wrote Bangs:

> I'm just an old fart now—cranking out complaints about the New Generation regular as TB spittle . . . [but] THE LESSON OF "WILD THING" WAS LOST ON ALL YOU FUCKERS . . . and rock 'n' roll may turn into a chamber art yet or at the very least a system of Environments. . . .

> My spleen is reserved for Elton John, James Taylor, all the glory boys of I-Rock. I call it I-Rock . . . because most of it is so relentlessly, involutedly egocentric that you finally actually stop hating the punk and just want to take the poor bastard out and get him a drink, and then kick his ass. . . . Matter of fact, if I ever get down to Carolina, I'm gonna try to figure out a way to off James Taylor. Hate to come on like a Nazi, but if I hear one more Jesus-walking-the-boy-and-girls-down-a-Carolina-path-while-the-dilemma-of-existence-crashes-like-a-slab-of-hod-on-J.T.'s-shoulders song, I will drop everything . . . and hop the first Greyhound to Carolina for the signal satisfaction of breaking off a bottle of Ripple . . . and twisting it into James Taylor's guts until he expires in a spasm of adenoidal poesy.

Bangs, whose cartoon of the "murder" was graphic enough to have turned on Charles Manson, giddily envisioned the mock headline in *Rolling Stone*: "EXTRA! TRAGEDY STRIKES ROCK! SUPERSTAR GORED BY DERANGED ROCK CRITIC!! 'We made it,' gasped Lester Bangs as he was led by the police from the bloody scene. 'We won.'" Whatever fueled Bangs, his dyspepsia upped the PH levels of rock writers considerably, and Bangs alas seemed to go too far in that regard—in 1973 Jann Wenner banned him from the more genteel *Rolling Stone* for "disrespecting musicians" after another mugging, of the boogie-rock band Canned Heat. Indeed, he wondered if his own ego, the self-consciousness in *his* writing, had made his work sound like "James Taylor with a typewriter, which means a suicide."

Dan Kortchmar says of the psychotic nature of the critical backlash that, with Bangs, spread ink-blot-like to other mainly eastern elite critics, "It amused me, because James Taylor, who was supposed to be this wimp, would have made mincemeat out of Lester Bangs in about three seconds. The people decide who's successful, not Lester Bangs or any other critic. At that time, critics had a lot more clout than they do now. And nobody remembers Lester Bangs, but everybody knows James Taylor. The music always wins." And:

> That whole premise was wrong, to begin with. It wasn't about who was tough, who could eat broken glass, destroy

> how many hotel rooms. It was about music coming from the heart, the soul. Do you realize how difficult that is, how much you need to put into it, dredge up things you don't want to, but that's when rock grew up. At the start we were called things like the "mellow Mafia." What do you mean mellow Mafia? Fuck you. I'll kick your ass in five seconds. The fact that we weren't playing loud doesn't mean that we were mellow.

Taylor, a lover not a fighter, didn't feel the need to defend himself. Indeed, one of his most serviceable quotes went like this: "If you think my music is sentimental and self-absorbed, I agree with you." Which is why a bigger gripe for Taylor about the rock press had to do with what he believed—with a gob of hypocrisy—was its prying nature. With a straight face, considering the stream of gossip he himself had fed to the ink-stained set, he complained, "They pick up on the mental hospital, family stuff, try to invent some category of rock that I belong to, or perhaps they pick up on my drug problem." What he neglected to say was that his own songs required that no one "pick up" on any of that. It was all there, in his own words, and a rather big part of the twisted ethos of the new rock and roll. Another of those Taylor bromides was that he didn't need to talk about his life; it was all there in the songs.

Even so, he could be ruthless about enforcing his system of rewards and debits based on his standard of who was a prick. He had gone from amused to annoyed by media dispatches that made him the source of juicy gossip or target of simpleton questions. "Photographers and reporters are mostly after me," he said. "They want to know what I read and what I'm like and I don't really know myself, so how can I tell them?" As too cute by half as this was, considering the Warner publicity department reminding reporters of his troubled past, and as open as he was to discuss it, he was dismayed when local papers would pimp his appearances but add darkly that in the past, shows had been canceled for "unknown" reasons. Rumors always swirled. In 1971, Taylor complained to the *New York Times*, "In one day, my brother Alex got 10 calls consoling him about my suicide, my re-institutionalization, and my split with Joni Mitchell."

Taylor told of a simple rule—if he saw his name in the paper, any paper, he would stop reading. Reviewers didn't really bother him, but rock-sniffing culture writers seemed to push the wrong buttons. For example, there was Jules Siegel, who was not in Bangs's Taylor-hating club but was rather agnostic about him, writing that Taylor's music was "extremely pretty, but thin" and, "It did not seem to me that James Taylor had seen fire and rain. He might someday, and when he did, he had the technical equipment, training and talent to do something really remarkable."

But Siegel, as with everyone else, really pushed it with Taylor. A rambling piece by him had run in the same *Rolling Stone* issue as the cover story about the Taylor family dynasty. It was chock with backstage vignettes before another Taylor show at the Troubadour, including that of a love-struck Joni Mitchell strumming Taylor's guitar. Calling Mitchell "James Taylor's current old lady," Siegel then reported Taylor asking, "Joni, did you re-tune my guitar?" When she "blushed [and] put her hand to her mouth," Taylor, a "sour, hostile, closed kid . . . sulked and pouted." Mitchell then "stretched out her foot to touch his. He smiled reluctantly." There was also the part about joints sitting in aluminum foil on a table being passed around and Taylor saying "People are always giving me dope"—though Siegel did report that Taylor didn't take a hit. And, he wrote, his old friend Peter Asher's face "cleared up nicely" and Betsy Asher, whom Siegel said he once had a crush on, was "a bit chubbier than I remembered her."

Insulting Mitchell and Asher was no way to get on Taylor's good side. Before the piece ran, Taylor had agreed to allow Siegel to come to Martha's Vineyard for an extensive interview, which would have made the writer take a plane and traipse through the snow to get to his home. Lucky for Siegel, he decided at the last minute not to go. And when he called Alex Taylor to tell James, Alex said, "Oh, James split." Realizing how he was going to be punked, Siegel moaned in print: "I wondered if James Taylor had thought about how I might have felt, arriving in Martha's Vineyard and finding him gone." The answer was that he probably would have had a good laugh.

While Taylor sounded sweet and "feminized" to some, he was no model of incipient changes in gender stereotypes. He was not just a product of the '50s but rock itself as a great counterculture vehicle, which for all its flower power had done nothing to counter inbred sexist roles. Some felt a tad guilty about it—when John Lennon sang "Imagine" in concert, he made sure to follow the line "a brotherhood of man" with a shouted "And woman!" But rock, as Bad Company confirmed, was still a fantasy for young men threatened by abstract feminism and solidified by "foxy ladies" who dug "cock rockers," in the term used by pop culture writer Judy Kutulas, epitomized of course by the Rolling Stones but also by Taylor's obsessive sexual conquests. His songs were nothing like the offstage image he was projecting, and maybe only he rather than a Jesus rocker or a member of the Doodletown Pipers could have made the mainstream amenable to feminine-side male folk rock. By contrast, consider Stephen Stills, for whom, as Kutulas wrote, quoting a friend of Stills, "male privilege was so engrained . . . that he had trouble seeing beyond his tortured adolescent soul . . . [to] anyone else's point of view."

Taylor, the accused enemy of rock's authenticity, was actually far more a *rebel* to traditional notions of the male id, in voice and image, and in his songs that begged for love even if it was a metaphor for drugs and an end to loneliness. As well, the refugees of '60s culture were primally wary of unfamiliar, lone wolf sages, even those on their side of the political fence. As Jon Landau wrote in *Rolling Stone* in 1973, Taylor "has been the object of some of the nastiest ideological criticism yet offered in the name of rock. Some of it has been a parody of old-fashioned leftist 'cult of the individual' political criticism. More often it takes the form of genre criticism not just against Taylor but against all the more idiosyncratic individualists who have emerged during the past three years." And:

> Underlying the more generalized attacks is a feeling that because these artists sacrifice the basic *macho* stance of the rock & roll band for a more emotionally complex—adult—attitude towards life, they exist in opposition to rock rather than as a new, evolutionary development of it. The assumption that all rock & roll ought to be boogie-nihilistic-emotionally uninhibited music obscures from view the deeper emotional and thematic content of some of the artists being attacked.

Another eminent East Coast rock scribe of the era, Al Aronowitz of the then cerebral *New York Post*, also would not dismiss Taylor. The bearded Allen Ginsberg lookalike—a man who prompted Bob Dylan, when asked if there was anyone who could save the world, to reply, "Alfred G. Aronowitz"—had partnered up in a label with Carole King and Gerry Goffin for the Myddle Class and was clearly hip to the folk-rock genre, writing that Taylor's songs were "born out of the torture that twice sent him into mental institutions" and that he "speaks for his generation with the kind of cool authority that seems destined to elect him one of the spokesmen of his time." Aronowitz playfully suggested that, given Taylor's "young, thin giant" visage, "he walks through the crowds that come to adore him with a half-smile on his lips and distant visions in his eyes like Jesus in an era when we already have too many, and at the same time one too few. . . . Is James Taylor going to be the next public phenomenon? It's a little early in the cycle for such an event, but that's the league James has applied for. May the Lord have mercy on him."

In fact, if rock had to have this sort of visionary, why not relish one who carved with some intelligence into the uncertainties of the soul, rather than the brain-optional "soft rock" fodder of Barry Manilow, Bread, Starbuck, Hamilton, Joe Frank and Reynolds, Air Supply, Gilbert O'Sullivan, Looking Glass, Michael Murphey, Henry Gross, and so on—and one less mawkish than Dan Fogelberg and less pretentious than, say, Terry Jacks, whose excruciating, treacly interpretation of Jacques Brel and Rod McKuen's "Seasons in the Sun" could almost make one's head explode through the ears. Was *any* song ever more deadly wimpy than "Our House"? Yet many battle-scarred '60s counterculture veterans held it against Taylor more than anyone that his self-examinations *did* require some real thought but accused no one of any depredation.

Even so, rather than turn against Taylor and the new narcotized rock, most aging baby boomers, so tired were they of ramming their heads against the figurative brick wall and suddenly confronted with bills to pay and kids to raise, could put that kind of music on while driving the kids to school and piano class and feel comforted about their own anxieties while hearing out another man's neuroses. If they were clued in, if they read *Rolling Stone*, they could be content that the guy singing those nice songs was as messed up as anyone in rock and roll, or as *them*. This guy was as freaked up on smack as Keith Richards or Eric Clapton! Props for that! Neither did it hurt him that, where in the past society shunned its neurotics, now everyone was *expected* to be neurotic, even psycho (nor that Taylor happened to bear a physical resemblance to Anthony Perkins). Not by accident was the PBS vérité documentary series *An American Family*—killing any remaining pretense about '50s "Father Knows Best"/Beaver/Ozzie and Harriet allegories of infallible kinship—must-see TV in 1973. (Not that Taylor sang overtly of sex, but it also helps define the rapid devolution of taboos that the same year a porn film, *The Devil in Miss Jones*, was among the top ten earning movies of the year—the same Canyon landscape having become the new hub of that stiffening industry as well.)

Reflecting these new realities in song, Taylor was so perfectly timed that he was *subversive* to the aging rock-and-roll guardians. That's what worried Christgau about Taylor: "The reason us rock and rollers are so mad at him is simply that the retreat [from the '60s culture model] has been so successful. We assume that there is something anarchic in all of us, something dangerous and wonderful that demands response, not retreat. In some semiconscious ways Taylor must understand this."

If he did, Taylor would not have considered it a retreat but a necessary evolutionary step, fulfilling something that had been missing from the family of rock, for no reason other than tectonic conceit. Still, he kept his perspective intact: he was not a sociological scold but a simple folksinger, evolved from Dylan but keeping a safe distance from the hot-button issues like Vietnam or racism. Not doing so would surely be bad for business now that he had conscripted into the great American mainstream—another reason for the older critics to hate on him. Taylor also must have understood how dangerous he was as a pinup boy with all the right rock looks and trimmings, the anger, the libido, the Hamlet-like self-pity, but no interest in rock as nihilism. The *New York Times* remarked that "James is gentle. He's not five frenzied speedfreaks blowing your eardrums with amplifiers because they can't blow your mind with a strong emotional message."

The irony: Taylor was a nonfrenzied heroin freak, which was freaky. That he was owned by heroin didn't often seep through his smug front of sobriety. He rose on the heels of the Morrison-Hendrix-Joplin death troika, when people in his position were supposed to be learning from their missteps. Yet his continued usage was not an object of scorn à la

Keith Richards, but of pity. When he sang of love as salvation, there'd be that wave of female voices collectively going "*awwwww*," not something ever heard for Keith Richards.

Accordingly, *he* was finding comfort in performing before audiences small and large. When not with the King troupe and out on the road with pickup bands, he was all over the map. During one spring jaunt in New York City in the winter of '71, he had played a sellout show Saturday night at Philharmonic Hall—on the same Great Performer series as Andre Watts, Beverly Sills, Daniel Barenboim, Jacqueline Du Pre, and Birgit Nilsson—and Monday night at the Fillmore East. In March, he played his first Madison Square Garden appearance, followed a day later by a gig at the Gaslight down in the Village, a basement coffeehouse with a capacity of eight hundred, necessitating that the club turn away two thousand people on a freezing night. Indeed, Terry Knight, Grand Funk Railroad's producer, said that year that the standard gauge for evaluating rock-and-roll acts was no longer who could fill a stadium, citing Lenny Kaye's opinion that one could "count on the fingers of one hand" those who could. In the new math of touring, "three Madison Square Garden concerts equal one Shea Stadium show anytime. Maybe a double bill of Black Sabbath/James Taylor."

And so the deluge continued, with singer-songwriters now rising almost in unison, constantly cooling the temperature of rock. Kent Lavoie, known as Lobo, a music nomad from the South, placed two vinyl sedatives, "Me and You and a Dog Named Boo" and "I'd Love You to Want Me," into million-selling territory; the L.A. duo Brewer and Shipley placed just one with the sly paean to pot "One Toke over the Line," which so confused the American right wing that the insentient Lawrence Welk had a spiritual group sing it on his geriatric program and soon-to-be-indicted vice president Spiro Agnew denounced it as subversive to American youth. In an allegory of the times, British songwriter Albert Hammond had a Top 5 hit that derided L.A., "It Never Rains in Southern California"—only becoming successful after moving to L.A.—a bite-the-feeding-hand approach that would also work to max effect for the Eagles. As Lou Adler recalled, "There'd been a transition from cool to mellow, with James Taylor as the leader of them all." In the newest of the L.A. rock Rat Packs, "Everyone was playing on everyone else's records: Carole on James', James on Carole's, Joni on James', James on Joni's."

Once, bands tried to out-rock each other; now, everywhere one looked there were some soft-rock singers or bands trying to out-bland each other, few able to hone the raw edge of a Taylor or King record. Peter Asher's house was often the cynosure of the scene. Musicians famous and not somehow wound up there. With happy symmetry, John Stewart, who had been so influential in the development of folk rock, had been signed by Asher, and thus was brought into the Taylor-King arc. When Taylor played the Troubadour again, Stewart sent a wreath for luck. One would never know who would flit in and out of this circle.

One unlikely entrant was Billy Mumy, the freckled-faced kid actor known best for a *Twilight Zone* episode, who was sixteen in 1970 and playing in a teen rock band called Redwood. Stewart, whose *Willard* album Peter was producing and on which Taylor played acoustic guitar, Carole King keyboards, and Danny Kortchmar electric guitar, brought Mumy to Asher's house. As Mumy beams, "I'm the first thing you hear on that album, playing cowbell, sitting next to James Taylor, playing his acoustic Gibson. So John was staying at Peter's house. It was a great hang, for me to be sixteen, seventeen years old, smoking a joint with James Taylor, practicing a set with John, and James would be going over tunes with Peter." For him, for *anyone*, he says, "Those were memorable times."

Taylor indeed had been anointed as the leader of this stoned-out, junior league Rat Pack. Chris Darrow has the chart-topper of all explanations for it. While there were many hands in this creature, he says, "J.T. was the penis for the whole thing and made it happen." And the rock and mainstream press seemed fascinated that a penis in 1971 didn't have to roar to command. That was the green light for many, none more so than John Denver, who had turned away from the Greenwich Village folk scene to write and sing about lazy country roads, Rocky Mountain highs, and sunshine on his shoulders—and even more unlikely, carrying the most weight as an activist for humanitarian and environmental causes. Kenny Loggins's smash hit "Danny's Song" was a subtle-as-a-brick-in-the-face derivative of Taylor (written for Loggins's brother upon the birth of his son, imagine that). Arguably the biggest beneficiary of the new equation was Elton John, whose breakout hit, "Your Song," cowritten with lyricist Bernie Taupin, was a huge hit on both sides of the pond late in 1970, its somber hues, simple structure, and piano intro almost a note for note cop of "Fire and Rain."

This caused Lester Bangs to write in *Creem* that he was "drowning in the kitschvatz"—Yiddish for excessively garish or sentimental—of Elton John and James Taylor, though there could not have been more polar opposites on the earth. Yet one wonders why more of the backlash wasn't trained on Steven Demetre Georgiou—Cat Stevens—an absolutely engrossing troubadour with an unlimited supply of anguish about worldly betrayals and soul stealing. Unlike Taylor, this unhappy Greek Cypriot descendent, who'd been a teen-pop idol in England, was so self-absorbed that the sorrowful masses would turn their lonely eyes to him—to wit, his caviling about, well, everything in "Wild World," his finger-waving admonition to then girlfriend actress Patti D'Arbanville.

Taylor, who for all his canny PR sense was intensely private, could never have pontificated like that about the cruel world, nor played for self-pity nearly to the point of open sobbing by injecting his sex partners into his songs and other people's business, as a forum for personal growth or vengeance. Of course, this was a habit his future wife picked up in her songwriting when she had a fling with Stevens, who while she awaited his arrival one night wrote her first hit song, "Anticipation." Taylor may have seen fire and rain and pleaded for redemption, but he never begged for it; and he had his limits on confession. This may be why Stevens could not stand him, which cost Taylor not a minute's sleep. The truth was, Taylor was both up front and safely distant from his personal anguish, which ensured he would endure time better. The same tack was taken by Elton John, who basically reached his peak in self-revelatory music with "Someone Saved My Life Tonight," before moving ahead on less confessional turf, as would Taylor, into pop and soul.

Taylor was a tunesmith, a performer, not a preacher man. Stevens, meanwhile, would become consumed in preacher pity, though not enough to give vacuous Brit techno-pop a go before chucking it all in 1977 to live in ascetic exile studying the Muslim faith—Taylor might have wanted to wave a finger at *him,* such blind faith being what Ike Taylor saw as a false prophecy. Not that Taylor was not still trying to find himself, or on some level trying to kill himself with blind recklessness, but he seemed to be able to see the world clearly, for what it was and what it wasn't. And lately, what it was carried rewards.

The top songs of 1970 had been Simon and Garfunkel's epic "Bridge over Troubled Water" and the Carpenters' "(They Long to Be) Close to You"—with "Fire and Rain," which had in many respects begun the trend, being passed on the highway and coming in at 67; in 1971 the top sellers were Three Dog Night's "Joy to the World," with King's two-sided "It's Too Late"/"I Feel the Earth Move" in third, and Taylor's "You've Got a Friend" in sixteenth; in 1972, the first four were Roberta Flack's "The First Time Ever I Saw Your Face," Gilbert O'Sullivan's "Alone Again (Naturally)," Don McLean's "American Pie," and Nilsson's "Without You." One signpost of the sea change was that John Fogerty was now writing songs that James Taylor could have, one example his 1970 pleading for redemption "Long as I Can See the Light." A lot of songs now sounded suspiciously Taylor-like. And it would only seem more so, for a while longer.

Taylor was keeping a backbreaking, peripatetic schedule. To his delight, Carole King again came out on the road, and this time both musicians were on an equal plane, turning a tour into a two-for-one extravaganza for soft-rock fans. To be sure, there had to be a protocol set that would balance their shows so as not to make it seem as if one was playing second fiddle to the other. Indeed, on some of the billings, both Taylor and King were guest artists for Jo Mama. The protocol, set by Taylor and Asher, was Taylor performing alone, then King and the backup musicians joined him. Despite the egalitarian intent, it never seemed that King was quite on the same plane, nor did she attempt to be. Like many performers, she was intimidated by Taylor, who for all his aw-shucks public stances masked a steely, jaw-clenching insistence on being in control. This, and not seeming to care if an audience warmed up to him, was part of his alienated, who-gives-a-shit pose that served his misanthropic side well. As King admits, "With James, I felt like a 'cat,'" meaning a studio adjutant, "a side man. We all were." The other cats—Kortchmar, Kunkel, Sklar, and Craig Doerge—so benefited as spokes on the Taylor wheel that they were given a serviceable identity similar to Phil Spector's "Wrecking Crew"—"The Section," a name they would make several albums under. To King, as to them, "We were there to serve the song and the performance, not ourselves." King was always given ample time for her hits, but it could almost seem as if even her own songs weren't *all* hers when he was beside her strumming or singing with her.

Because King only committed to a limited number of appearances—demanding to come home each weekend—Taylor would extend the tours for his own benefit. It would only get crazier, the demand to see and hear him live a measure of how needy rock had become. What's more, one never knew when Taylor or one of his cohort would be playing their last gig. Take David Crosby, for example. After his girlfriend was killed in an auto accident in 1969, the already screwed-up Crosby jacked up *his* heroin addiction, one that had repercussions that Taylor, charmed as he was, would never experience, like a stay behind bars a decade later. Even back then, he had that air of inscrutability that could be mistaken for sensibility, a prophylaxis against stupidity. If he was James Dean reincarnate, he'd be luckier than the original. He would only die on an isolated blacktop on a movie screen.

Taylor had returned the favor of Joni Mitchell's backup vocal on "You've Got a Friend" by playing on three songs for her next album, recorded at A&M Studios early in '71: "California," "All I Want," and "A Case of You," his "twitchy" guitar lines singled out by Tim Crouse in his *Rolling Stone* review. He also sang a duet with her on "Carey/Mr. Tambourine Man." However, by the time it came out, in June, it wasn't his work on those songs that aroused attention to the album. It would be on songs she added as the result of Taylor ending things between them. Whatever else Mitchell's motivations for becoming involved with Taylor, when they played house, she would feel positively domesticated, even knitting shirts for Taylor to wear, which he would dutifully don and tuck into his jeans over a big metal belt buckle inscribed "Sweet Baby James." If she hoped he would move toward the ideal of marriage, she was disappointed that he never showed the slightest inclination to do that. Neither did he have any great moral conundrum spending time with other women—he had already been cheating on her with Carole King's long-legged writing partner, Toni Stern, a now longtime consort. And, in mid '71, he had become dazzled, if still from afar, by someone new, Carly Simon, she of the lanky but ample frame and large, enticing mouth and lips.

For Joni, who was no naïf and had never conned herself into believing he was faithful to her, being treated as she had treated Graham Nash opened a wound that would never quite heal. The first sign of that was when she pulled back the album to add the three songs she cranked out after the breakup, including the title track "Blue." Many wondered if he was what lines in the song like this meant: "You can make it thru these waves / Acid, booze, and ass / Needles, guns, and grass / Lots of laughs." There was also "All I Want," which she had been writing when the end came, when the vibes had already turned sour and she felt the walls closing in: "I want to knit you a sweater / Want to write you a love letter / I want to make you feel better / I want to make you feel free." Indeed, the album itself grew out of her tortured confessions about the romance, meaning that Taylor played on a work meant to shame him, or beg him to stay. All Mitchell would ever say about the album, which went to number 15 on the *Billboard* chart, was essentially what she told Cameron Crowe in 1979: "At that period of my life, I had no personal defenses. I felt like a cellophane wrapper on a pack of cigarettes. I felt like I had absolutely no secrets from the world and I couldn't pretend in my life to be strong. Or to be happy. But the advantage of it in the music was that there were no defenses there either."

She didn't stay alone for long, taking up soon after with Jackson Browne. She told people she was over Taylor and that the bust-up was inevitable, since she had no desire to play house with him back east and watch him labor endlessly on his perpetually unfinished house, where he and his brothers would sit on the roof smoking dope all day. She said she wanted to "pass on that," and that now, she was "ready to let him go." Maybe not. She still obsessed over him, her songs pining away for him to bring sunshine "to my apple trees" in "See You Sometime" and wondering if a certain suspenders-wearing man was "holding some honey who came on to you," assuring him, "I'm not after a piece of your fortune and your fame 'cause I tasted mine / I'd just like to see you sometime." Realizing that wasn't going to happen, all she could sing was "It hurts."

By the '80s, there had come at least a professional thawing out between them, at least enough to be able to talk, at the behest of Peter Asher, who had become her manager. In her 2014 book, *Joni Mitchell in Her Own Words*, his name came up exactly once, when asked by the coauthor, Malka Marom, if her connection to Taylor and CSNY had helped her career. Her answer: "At the time that James and I were spending time together, he was a total unknown. Maybe I helped his career." As Marom noted in the text, Mitchell had a good laugh when she said that.

When bony, gawky, postmodern hunk James Taylor broke onto the national scene in 1970, at twenty-three he had already survived family issues, mental illness, heroin addiction, a failed band called the Flying Machine, and being the first American signed by the Beatles' Apple record label. His travails would continue, but now too would come astounding success in a whole new genre.
Photofest

Flanking Taylor in this early photo, Danny Kortchmar (right) and Peter Asher were pivotal to his success. Kortchmar, who himself became a top studio guitarist, befriended Taylor as a teenager and played in the Flying Machine, then on his '70s studio sessions and tours. Asher, who quit Apple Records to manage Taylor, signed him to Warner Brothers and produced all of his epic songs.
Getty Images

Although Taylor detested the plastic, narcissistic Southern California scene, assimilating into it was a must, and romancing Joni Mitchell—here performing with L.A. rock cohort Neil Young in the 1978 documentary concert movie *The Last Waltz*—became his ticket to ride. Mitchell opened doors for him but when he was a star he would dump her for another female singer of distinction.
Photofest

The song on Taylor's debut American album *Sweet Baby James* that turned him into an "overnight" superstar and launched the soft, soothing but trenchant personal sound of rock following the shattered idealism and political defeat of the '60s. Though "Fire and Rain" only made it to number 3, it has been played endlessly for over four decades, like him never seeming to get old.

Taylor's good looks and existential pose of bored alienation won him a costarring role with Beach Boy bad boy Dennis Wilson in the 1971 road movie *Two Lane Blacktop*, saying few words in what is now considered a cult classic of early '70s angst and amorality—though it was a detour that Taylor preferred to forget.
Photofest

The symbiosis between Taylor and Carole King, seen here at Madison Square Garden during their lucrative fortieth year reunion tour in 2010, made history in the '70s. Taylor, whose weepy version of King's "You've Got a Friend" went to number one in 1971 and became his best-selling song, also played and sang on her enormous breakthrough album *Tapestry* that same year.
Alamy

Once, it seemed all the Taylor siblings, gathered here at a rare group performance at New York's Sout Street Seaport in the '80s, were a dynasty, with Kate and Livingston Taylor (second left) even havin gone to the same mental hospital as James. However, only James endured as a major act, while Ale (right) tragically died in 1993 and Hugh (left) avoided the music business.
Corbis

More than any Grammy, Taylor coveted th delectable Carly Simon, marrying her in 1972 t keep her from Mick Jagger's clutches. The mos gossiped about rock couple ever, they had tw children, sang on each others' hits, and seeme to live a fable—but in reality, tortured each othe with jealousy and head games, which, combine with Taylor's endless heroin addiction and adul tery, led to their 1985 crackup.
Photofest

Taylor's country-boy image on the cover of his fourth LP, 1972's *One Man Dog*, belied its experimental alloying of song fragments mating soft rock with blues, and was the first album recorded in true quadrophonic sound. But its failure steered him back to the melodic, brutally introspective songs that set rock's course in the '70s—and had made him the favorite whipping boy for hard-boiled rock critics.
Photofest

Vhile most of Taylor's most cher-shed songs grew from the pain ınd sorrows of his life, addiction, ınd marriage, it took a special ılchemy in the studio to tap into ıudiences' emotions. For that ıe relied on and toured into the 2000s with a tight coterie of musi-ians including Danny Kortchmar, lrummer Russ Kunkel, and, here, ɔearded bassist Lee Sklar, whose ıuanced notes sounded like a ;rieving heart.
'hotofest

After divorcing Carly Simon, Taylor courted Kathryn Walker, who ran with the in-crowd of Martha's Vineyard swells including John Belushi. Walker, who played Belushi's wife in the dud movie *Neighbors* (on Dan Aykroyd's right in this scene), helped Taylor avoid Belushi's drug fate by nursing him through heroin withdrawal, but their subsequent marriage lasted only five years.
Photofest

The late '80s version of James Taylor had him clean and sober, mature, his hairline receding, smiling confidently as he he faced having to fit into a rapidly changing rock landscape that had left many of his '70s contemporaries for dead. Yet his music enjoyed new generational acceptance, with a place found for his sensitive, melodic brand of personal folk rock and clever oldies covers, and a place for his albums on the charts.
Photofest

James Vernon Taylor in 2002, the year his last great album, *October Road*, came out and went platinum. His hair was gone and his forehead lined but the eyes were still intense, mirroring the rivers of ideas in his head to write about. His voice seemed not to have aged a day. At fifty-four, he was the apotheosis of "adult contemporary," the chart he had come to dominate as he once did the Hot 100.
Photofest

Taylor finally found his soul mate in beautiful Boston Philharmonic executive Carolyn "Kim" Smedvig, whom he married in 2001 and began squiring to public events. Becoming a dad again when she gave birth to twin sons, the brood moved to a castle-like home in the leafy Berkshire Mountains, with Taylor serious about family life in marked contrast to his neglect the first time around.
Photofest

Enjoying his cachet as a rock and roll elder, Taylor no longer hid from the public nor spouted contempt for the industry that has made him fabulously wealthy. Apt to be seen just about anywhere there is a red carpet or a red camera light, he teamed up for a duet with fellow warhorse Randy Newman during the 2007 Academy Awards show, looking amazingly fit and sounding amazingly clear-throated.
Photofest

Trying to make up for lost time, Taylor belatedly spent time with his older son by Carly Simon, Ben Taylor, who followed tradition by starting a singing career of his own, as did his sister, Sarah Taylor. Sometimes performing with the hunky son who resembles him, this 2011 appearance at the Adler Theater in Davenport, Iowa, sold out the house, something he still does regularly.
Alamy

Son of rigorously liberal parents, and a fixture at rock protest concerts such as No Nukes and the Rainforest, Taylor campaigned for Barack Obama and sang at the latter's second inauguration in January 2013. In this freeze-frame, he glad-hands the president after he took the oath of office and beams at Vice President Joe Biden, who seem as star-struck with him as he is with them—just one measure of his enduring popularity and noble legacy.
Alamy

14

"THAT JAMES TAYLOR THING"

Carly Simon had been around the block. She was in many ways a female, half-Jewish alter ego of the male, WASP heritage of James Taylor. Born to immense wealth, her father was Richard Simon—whose three brothers and sister were all named after British monarchs—the cofounder of the mega–publishing company Simon & Schuster in 1924. His wife, Andrea Heinemann, was, in fairy-tale fashion, a switchboard operator at the company. Growing up in a sprawling manse in the Fieldston section of Riverdale, the tony northern part of the Bronx, Simon also had a competitive relationship with her siblings, all of whom would become quite successful, beginning her musical career singing folk tunes with Lucy and Joanna Simon (the former to become a Broadway composer, the latter an opera singer), and with Lucy as the Simon Sisters, who attracted attention playing around the same Boston/Cambridge folk houses that Taylor frequented in the mid-'60s. They recorded three albums during the decade, appeared on TV dance shows, and had a minor hit setting the kiddie poem "Winkin' Blinkin' and Nod" to folk in the manner of "Puff the Magic Dragon."

The trio disbanded when Lucy got married and Carly, who began singing to mask a stutter, had blossomed into a statuesque beauty who could sing, write songs, and act, all of which she did in the 1971 Milos Forman film starring Buck Henry, *Taking Off*. She was signed by Jac Holzman to Elektra Records the previous year and made an immediate noise with the breakout hit in '71 from her debut album, "That's the

Way I've Always Heard It Should Be," written with *Esquire*'s film critic Jacob Brackman. Unlike Mitchell's delicate sonnets, Simon's style was to take no prisoners, splaying her fears and resentments of her parents' alleged coldness and rotted marriage, though when she famously sang of her father sitting with no lights on, cigarette glowing in the dark, it had to have been projection, since Richard Simon died in 1960. The first track of that first album, the song served notice that folk rock could go beyond personal travail, all the way to something like musical patricide and matricide, with the related observation that her married friends from college were also suffering through "silent noons, tearful nights, angry dawns," their children hating *them* but no more than they hated themselves, closing the wounds with alcohol. Yet, in the end, she was resigned to marrying, too, and winding up in the same wretched dead end. With this melodramatic bewailing, Simon had found the magic formula—the deconstruction of idealism—which music writer Chuck Klosterman would dub the "Carly Simon principle," that is, a singer—even a filthy rich one—projecting ordinariness to etch an "espoused reality" through which people could "construct meaning."

James Taylor, of course, had done that, too, in excelsis, though he was far too private—too *nice*—to grind an ax with his own *parents*. (He had never known what it was like to have college friends.) Though he rarely bothered to put other artists' albums on a turntable, nor his *own*, and from what he'd heard of it disliked her music, when he caught Simon's Troubadour performance in April 1971 he was mesmerized that a woman as shy as he was, and so stunning and smart, could be so insecure and yet so ballsy—even more than "Mussolini Mitchell"—as to lay it all out there, proto-feminist style, angrier but also *sexier* than anyone had heard from a woman in song before.

Like the two other women he had called his girlfriend, sometimes at the same time, Simon was older than he was, by three years—either a coincidence or possibly some kind of oedipal thing. He recalled having seen her when she performed with her sister around the Vineyard and thinking "she was quite attractive," but even with his appeal to older girls, thought she was way out of his league. Now, the age difference no barrier, he was about to fall in love—again, only months after having told *Newsweek* that he had "serious feelings" for Joni Mitchell.

It took a while for him to meet Simon. She detested L.A. as he did, recording in New York at Hendrix's Electric Lady studio with Jimi's producer Eddie Kramer and ex-Yardbird and then Cat Stevens producer Paul Samwell-Smith. He went to the Troubadour in 1971 to see her open for Cat Stevens, then connected with her by happenstance months later, in November, when he was in New York for another prestige engagement, at majestic Carnegie Hall on the ninth, with Jo Mama opening for him (but not Carole King, who was about to give birth again). Simon, in the audience, had arranged with his lawyer, Nat Weiss, to go backstage and meet Taylor after the show. According to Simon, "It seemed as though we'd known each other for a long time." Seeing them talking and playfully flirting, Danny Kortchmar says he and Lee Sklar smiled and said to each other, "*Mrs. Taylor.*"

At one point, Carly coyly told him, "If you ever want a home-cooked meal . . . "

Not at all coyly, he replied, "How about . . . tonight?"

They would teasingly refer to their first time together on a joint *Rolling Stone* interview a year later, with Carly saying, "James came up and embraced me upon first meeting and then we went in the bathroom and fucked." Doing his own riff, he added, laughing, "Actually, we never made love until we were married." Neither was the case. When Simon wrote her autobiography, she related that it happened that same night, but not in a bathroom. At 3 AM they left together after a postconcert party at the Time Life Building. She then took him over to Jake Brackman's apartment where the three of them smoked weed. James, in a haze, mistakenly put on Brackman's shoes, prompting the latter to quote the seething line in Bob Dylan's "Positively Fourth Street" about "If you could stand inside my shoes, you'd know what a drag it is to see you." Brackman thought he was being clever, but as Simon remembered, "the words hurt James's feelings," admitting that the "hurt little boy coming out was very appealing to me."

Next stop was her place on Lexington Avenue in Manhattan's midtown Murray Hill section, where she fixed him eggs and toast. He then said, "Can we go lie down on your bed?" and she joined him on it, wearing "a black silk camisole and white cotton underpants." After she kissed him, she recalled, "I lay on top of him like a gun in a holster, ready to make a move." For her it was the culmination of a fantasy—"This was the same preadolescent, knobby-kneed boy who had been subconsciously making his way around my dreams for years," Yet his response to it was hardly the stuff of romance novels. "We should just go to sleep," he said, and soon was out cold. Putting the best spin on that odd moment, she wrote, "Awake still, I was left alone with my desire, but I felt a merging of a part of our union that went much closer."

The next morning was a different story. Taylor, she said, "woke up amorous" and "I let his lips surround mine [and] I returned his love." Merging as they did, she likened it to two "perfectly complementary and harmonized notes," and "the sound of an oboe cutting through the breathy rise of an alto flute." She thought they would make beautiful music like that forever after. With this Rubicon crossed, they grew immediately close, each publicly flaunting the other like a prized possession. They enjoyed being seen together, holding hands and cooing to each other like giddy teenagers. He even seemed to make an effort to cut ties with the women he was stringing along, but this was not a laughing matter to Carly, given how cruel he could be toward other women.

Hearing him speak on the phone to Maggie and even Joni after he had found his new soulmate, Carly would recall how his "callousness had stunned me," such as when he icily told Maggie "not to call him ever again, and when he hung up the phone he started swearing. . . . What had she done, what had gone so terribly wrong, that she deserved to be guillotined like that?" When Joni had called, he let the same blade fall on her neck, dispatching the woman who had immeasurably helped him gain ascent by sneering, "You shouldn't call here anymore," after which, as Simon wrote in her memoirs, he "looked steely and furious." These were signs of cold, indifferent self-absorption and calculation. And Carly took no comfort in what he apparently believed were grand displays of loyalty for her benefit, fearing they were symptoms of a cavity in his soul that might one day unleash steel and fury at her as well.

This was not the James Taylor who sang of the nobility of being a friend and just wanting to make it through another day. But then, Taylor never claimed he had sorted out his pathological flaws. And Simon knew that was the Taylor she had signed on to. Even so, she was, as she would come to admit, "transfixed by my own innocent conceit in believing James belonged to me now, and that words so icy, and so final, could never, ever fly in my direction."

Opposites that they were, Taylor and Simon were united by receiving the exact same critical praise, or skewering—Christgau reviewed her album, saying, "Since affluence is an American condition, I suppose it makes sense not only for the privileged to inflict their sensibilities on us, but for many of us to dig [their] calculated preciosity and false air of discovery. . . . If Carly's college friends are already old enough to have alienated their children, her self-discovery program is a little postmature anyway."

Not incidentally, on her way up the totem pole she'd also been romanced and left by Cat Stevens, Kris Kristofferson, and the biggest babe hounds in Hollywood, Warren Beatty and Jack Nicholson—Taylor *wanted* to be in such fast company. At the beginning, Simon was more cautious than he about getting serious. Not least of all, there was the Taylor family and their *eccentricities*, the sort that she soon would see were handed down by generations of those "Taylor men." Simon wrote in her autobiography that she had heard from friends that it was a rather inbred brood, as she called them, "a strange family" that "mainly socialized with one another," the father "a brilliant doctor but an alcoholic." James, who they all called "Jamie," seemed to be an eternal man-child, not fully matured, still socially awkward and naive in many ways. "Jamie" led her to recall an old Mark Twain adage, that "everyone is a moon, and has a dark side which he never shows to anybody." But he was also, as his brother Alex had told her, a man who could "charm the ugly off an ape," and she grew into the idea of an extended relationship once he had moved into her apartment and she into his home on the Vineyard. It was during one spell up there that he won her over; when Kate Taylor was being threatened by a guy she was dating, said to be a huge man with a black belt in karate, James burst from his pacifist shell and ordered the guy out of Kate's house.

Later that night, chopping wood in the moonlight, he began to croon, "Carly! Carly! I love you!" At that, she would say, creating new English, "I fell cementedly in love" with and "addicted" to him. It was easy for them to say, *very* easy; as Dan Kortchmar says with a laugh, as carefully as he can, "When you're so talented and so attractive, it makes the rest of us look like we're in another league, and they know it. It's a turn-on. The problem is, all that talent and all those looks can't make something last that really shouldn't ever be taken on in the first place."

Not to mention that other conquests, doable conquests, are always there. Indeed, Taylor may have unwittingly facilitated Simon soon adding another famous notch to her lipstick case. She was scheduled to record her third album in London in the fall of '72, the coyly titled *No Secrets*, produced by Richard Perry, who had pleaded with her to let him produce her. Taylor went with her and sang backup vocal on one track, "Waited So Long," a song that couldn't possibly have been about him, being that it dealt with her losing her virginity; and Simon also covered "Night Owl" on the album. But, apparently, her mind was on the time she had spent with a bigger rocker than Taylor. As the story goes, Taylor, who had known Mick Jagger through Peter Asher, met up with him in London and bragged about being involved with Simon. After he introduced Jagger to her, Mick apparently became instantly infatuated. When Taylor split to go record in L.A., Jagger and Simon, neither bothered by guilt, had some sort of affair, a fling with major consequences.

By coincidence, the Simon sessions were at the same Trident Studios in London where Taylor had made his heralded but humdrum Apple album, and where she came in one day with a song that titillated millions of people, "You're So Vain," her lament about falling for a bounder like . . . *who*? As clever as the song was, this dumb riddle sustained it, and still does—was it Mick? Warren? James?—with Simon's smug perpetuation, as if it were a state secret who wore that apricot scarf, flew his plane to Nova Scotia for an eclipse, and would think the song was about him. (For what it's worth, and all it matters, her most recent hint was that it's some guy she only identified as "Dave.")

Again, Christgau winced, writing, "If a horse could sing in a monotone, the horse would sound like Carly Simon, only a horse wouldn't rhyme 'yacht,' 'apricot,' and 'gavotte.' Is that some kind of joke?" At least Taylor could be relieved that she made clear right away it wasn't him—although, amusingly, Taylor had actually once flown in a plane to *Nova Scotia*, and, she acknowledged, "James suspected that it might be about him because he is very vain"; but, as she said, "it wasn't a Lear so he's off the hook." (To be clear, she may well have been singing about *no one* in that song, too, having also said it "was taken from my imagination. I don't know anybody who went to Saratoga and I don't know anybody who went to photograph the total eclipse of the sun.")

When "You're So Vain" started pouring from radios, Carly was back in New York with Taylor, informally engaged, as they both told people, but her heart was still back in England with the emaciated Stone whose famous lips matched hers and who had sung background vocal on the song that *could* have been about him. Taylor, who shut out gossip and rumors, knew none of what had happened. But by now Bianca Jagger, who'd been married to Jagger for a year, had put two and two together—she'd also found love notes, and when he returned to their home in the south of France, she greeted him with a gun and threatened to blow him away before she cooled off. The next thing she did was place a trans-Atlantic call to Carly Simon's apartment, to be answered by James Taylor.

"You know my husband and your fiancée are having an affair," she told him.

Simon would later recall the moment, saying he replied, "That's not true." Adding, "He defended my integrity beautifully."

A caveat here: As befits gossip, there are other versions of this story, one being that Taylor, made aware of the canoodling, called Jagger and warned him to cease and desist. If so, rather than grabbing a firearm or even confronting her, in typical fashion he brooded for a while but, given his own unabated philandering, didn't press the matter when she insisted, as she still does today, that she'd simply "spent time together" with Mick but that she "really didn't want to be with anyone but [James]." Nothing more was said about it. But both of them agreed the only way to guard against such temptation and complication—the kind of worry Jagger would never have had, and with cause since Bianca would put up with his *affaires de coeur* until 1979—was for them to bite the bullet and marry. In fact, it was *she* who first suggested it, when they were in London.

As Taylor would tell it, his response was, "There's really no reason to get married. We love each other and we've been living together." A few hours later, after thinking on it, he was ready to say, "Maybe we should." They left it at that, but when Mrs. Jagger made that phone call, it probably wasn't only the general temptation but also his worry that Mick would still be on the make for Carly that led him to the decision. Looking back, the sudden conversion was amusing for her. "There's nothing that gets men so crazy as other men pursuing their women," she said. "Boy, did we decide fast!"

As the story of postmodern romance with its ambiguous models of sexual control grew, Taylor faced a crucial juncture. After "You've Got a Friend," Warner had seen fit to not release another single until, in October 1971, it had tried "Long Ago and Far Away." When it stiffed, going no higher than number 31, it would be over a year before another Taylor record appeared on the market. In the interim, Taylor toured some, made time with Simon some, and retreated to the Vineyard, trying to get over a mental block he had contracted in writing songs. He would not be ready again to record until the late summer of '72, and came in with so little new material that it necessitated he record the album in an experimental way.

He would record the songs in his home studio in the still under-construction Vineyard house, with huge speakers and amps suspended by cables and even duct tape from beams on a high cathedral ceiling that always looked about to collapse. With only Kortchmar, Sklar, Kunkel, and Doerge, he cut basic tracks and his leads, with Carly Simon, Carole King, and singer Abigale Haness (Danny's new wife) doing harmonies, then took the tapes to L.A. for him and Asher to flesh out. It was a long, meticulous process. At times the studio swelled with musicians, twenty-three in all, including his usual core, plus Simon; Alex, Kate, and Hugh Taylor; Linda Ronstadt on vocals; John Hartford; guitarist John McLaughlin (who wrote the song "Someone" for the album); Dash Crofts on mandolin; and horn men George Bohanon, Arthur Baron, and Randy Brecker. There were also sound effects such as a saw played jug-band style by Mark Paletier.

Warner knew how to deal with the lag time; it would frame the album as having been "a year in the making," which was a stretch but true. It had a harder time with what would be the core of the work, a nine-track ten-minute "sing cycle," ranging from 0:29—the chantey he made out of the "Mescalito" line he thought up during his recovery from the motorcycle crash—to 0:55 ("Instrumental I"), 1:00 ("Little David"), 1:13 ("Jig"), 1:35 ("Chili Dog," "New Tune"), 1:41 ("Instrumental II"), 1:42 ("Fool for You"), 2:07 ("Dance"), and 2:10 ("Woh, Don't You Know," written with Kortchmar and Sklar).

This was a carryover from *Mud Slide Slim*'s two attenuated tracks, which were not throwaways but part of his fancy that pop need be confined not to the two-and-a-half-minute AM single nor to five-minute-plus FM entry, and that within the album format almost anything could work as binder or transition between tracks. The longest, at 3:10, was the title cut, "One Man Parade," like *Mud Slide* a jokey title that would see his pet bull mastiff David on the album cover, in a photo taken by Peter Simon, the dog at the feet of Taylor, in a tie, standing oar in hand on a raft rolling on a lazy river. (He had toyed with the idea of using "Farewell to Show Biz" as the title but nixed it when Carly Simon disliked it.)

The theme of the work, such as it was, spilled from side 1, track 1, "One Man Parade," a wistful desire to waste time on the simplest of pleasures, walking a dog, pouring rain, checking out an occasional garbage can. The upbeat track, aided by a trippy conga beat by Kunkel, was his most carefree yet, but it wouldn't have been Taylor without a tell, here about the secrets he was hiding and that "I'm right good at holding on, holding on, holding on."

"Nobody But You"—the title referring to Simon, though he would say the content "isn't about anything" and "the song is nonsense"—preceded the "sing cycle," with "Chili Dog" an actually laugh-out-loud blues parody in the "Steamroller" mode—"I ain't trying to fool youse / Don't bring on no Orange Julius"—which set the tone for a progression of tunes sprinkled with congas, Doerge's electric piano, giggles and little touches like Asher on woodblock guiro, and perfectly placed electric licks by Kortchmar. It had the Taylor sentimentality and redemption—"Someone" was a gorgeous ballad, with Taylor's playing Flamenco-like, asking where that someone was and testifying that life was worthless without love, "the force from which all beings live," his heart a "magnet for your love." In "Fanfare" he celebrated that he was "unafraid to be free"—a veiled reference to his love for Simon—as a spectacular chorale surrounded him. "Hymn" was almost a baptism, Taylor finding his place in religion by being dipped in "sweet sweet music," basted by "Sergeant Pepper"–like horns.

At times it was downright funky and certainly less country, *white*, and depressing than usual. "Woh," with Alex and Hugh Taylor backing him, was a fetching gospel-style rocker, "One Morning in May" a dreamy, folky echo of "Sweet Baby James" with a quiescent harmony vocal by Ronstadt. "Jig," the final cut, was a salsa-seasoned hat dance that featured *three* trombones. Even "Mescalito," which he finally found a context for, was presented as a life-affirming mantra about the drug that opened his eyes and that he renounced. If it was intended to show that James Taylor could be as light and lively as the next guy, the structure confused the issue. Some of the tidbits would stop dead just as they were spreading out, or seamlessly become the next one. Bewildered, the folks at Warner wondered why some of the similar song fragments couldn't be combined into regular-length tracks, and they certainly could not be happy that only one track seemed to have hit potential, "Don't Let Me Be Lonely Tonight," that sad and terrific chain link of lonely-man rock, updating "Heartbreak Hotel" and "Only the Lonely."

This was classic Taylor, a plaint about isolation and rejection burrowing deep into the soul but with a forgive-and-forget generosity—"Do me wrong, do me right / Tell me lies but hold me tight." Adding to the au courant nature of the work, Asher would record in the quadraphonic format, which had been around since the '50s on four-track reel-to-reel tapes and progressed to eight-track encoding in 1970. Rockers had gotten into quad in '67 when Pink Floyd performed a concert in early surround sound in London's Queen Elizabeth Hall. There was even an FM radio station in San Marcos, Texas, KRMH, calling itself "Good Karma Radio," that broadcast in "Quad Stereo" in the early 1970s. For trivia freaks, Taylor beat the Who's earthmoving *Quadrophenia* album by a year (though the latter was never actually released in quad; Pete Townsend used heavy multitracking but said it was quadraphonic only "in a creative sort of way"). Not that many music buyers had anything like quad sound in their living rooms—the world was still lo-fi, and it would be years until the album was properly heard by most—and whether Taylor went in this technical direction because he didn't have many complete songs, he didn't intend to go there lightly. Although some of the tracks had never been played nor rehearsed before they were laid down in the studio, he put great care into the work. Though even today, according to AllMusic's retro-review, "a lot of it was sketchy and seemingly unfinished."

Jon Landau renewed his original stamp of approval, albeit with his quibble that Taylor came with a "patrician arrogance" that

> accounts in part for his popularity while it at the same time explains the critical resistance to his work. Those who see themselves championing mass tastes can't accept the individualized point of view—the supremely autobiographical quality of his work—even while the audience they presume to speak for has made his modest output of albums among the best sellers ever released by his record company. . . . Here it is that each of us must find his own happiness because there is no external force or power that can provide us with it. He has stopped questioning and started dealing with his reality. In the process, he has created an album that

> exudes self-acceptance, exultation, celebration, and personal triumph not unlike (in spirit) Van Morrison's *Tupelo Honey* or Dylan's inferior *New Morning.*

The social-climbing critic believed the album did in fact hang together, that Taylor had "turned in his best singing performance . . . with fire, force, and enthusiasm," that "Lonely Tonight" "shows James reaching for some of that jazz and pop he seems to enjoy so much," and he even heard "Fanfare" as a potential Top 40 hit, with "its picture of industry gone mad and its conclusion that [dog-eat-dog] 'doesn't apply to you and me . . . we are living in the deep blue sea.'" Not so sure was the decades-later review in the *Rolling Stone Record Guide*, which could only muster two stars out of five for the album.

One Man Dog and "Don't Let Me Be Lonely Tonight" were released November 1, 1972, around the same time as Simon's *No Secrets* album and "You're So Vain" single. Two days later, Robert Christgau (who raked the album in exactly four sarcastic words: "James Taylor with panache. C+") went to another enormous milestone performance by Taylor, a midnight concert at Radio City Music Hall, a spectacular victory for Taylor and Peter Asher, who had lobbied the Rockefeller family hard to allow the stage they owned to be used for the first time to host a rock-and-roll act—then wrote: "Let us be candid about this. James Taylor's immense popularity has had only negative effects among fanatical rock and rollers like myself." He claimed he had taken "the poster from his third album and ripped it into four or five pieces. Then I hung the face on my wall and scrawled upon it slogans from imaginary Maoist comic books, e.g.: 'Eat felt-tipped death, capitalist pig!'"

Yet Christgau had to admit that "if James Taylor weren't so famous, he would be inoffensive, even likable. Upon sane reflection I recognize that he is a master of folk guitar, and that I even like some of his songs. . . . His midnight performance won me over to several old compositions that I'd heard without listening, especially 'Knocking 'Round the Zoo.'" The closing number, "Steamroller," was "a brilliant parody of the macho white-blues fantasy, at once so attractive and so repellent." What's more, the suckers he blamed for lapping up Taylor were now given a nod for their *politeness*:

> His audience responded with a muted enthusiasm that never bordered on the rambunctious. Everything was polite. Taylor even introduced his sound man by name, and when his amplifier made an incontinent noise, he promised that it wouldn't happen again. There are rock stars who pretend that every electronic squawk is the word of God made manifest among us, and rock stars who can't remember their sound man's name when they want to bum a cigarette off him. Understandably, Taylor and his audience react to such pretension and egomania. They are intelligent and liberal and good. They work for McGovern.

In passing, Christgau noted, "Several of his admirers remarked that he looked elated." And why not? After all, it was only hours since he'd gotten hitched to the sexiest singer in the world.

That world-shaking decision had been made only two days before, following months of dithering. The wedding was thrown together so fast that after a license was hastily obtained and a judge arrived at Simon's Murray Hill apartment for the ceremony, she was still calling her sisters to tell them. Only the respective mothers, Trudy Taylor and Andrea Simon, were there—one might have wondered if James was snubbing his father (and perhaps if Simon was still crucifying hers in his deathly repose; on *No Secrets* she had sung of him as "a frightening and devilish kind of figure"). Jacob Brackman acted as best man for both bride and groom. Not even Peter and Betsy Asher could make it in quickly enough, though Betsy was given the job of calling Joni Mitchell and telling her about the nuptials; her response was, "Oh, okay." It's not clear if she also gave the news to Maggie Corey, who would at long last be free of his on-again/off-again attention and would go on to become an actress (she died tragically young, in 1997, at age fifty-four).

These two children of fortune paid for each other's rings—$17.95 a piece. The press was kept in the dark. The world at large didn't know it until Taylor announced it during the Radio City show, to gasps from some in the hall. The nuptials made all the papers, and even the *New Yorker* magazine. They would take a brief cruise to Hawaii, then they had to go out on the road, separately. After all, they still had product to move. Always, it seemed.

The bad news was that Taylor now seemed to be swimming upstream, according to those who had their fingers on the musical pulse. Robert Plant in '72 had mused, "It's a shame that the whole solo singer-songwriter concept had to degenerate into that James Taylor thing of taking things so seriously. Actually there are a lot of good ideas going around now." And yet, he added, "Actually this'll probably sound strange, but ultimately I can envisage Pagey [Jimmy Page] and myself ending up doing a whole Incredible String Band–type thing together. Very gentle stuff." This often happened when Taylor was the subject: grudging tribute. But even ambivalence in rock breeds rash conclusions. An article in *Good Times* in November 1973 claimed that, the preceding year, "when all the Rolling Stones had to offer was *Exile on Main Street*, and when certain people decided that James Taylor was a worthless junkie, it became the norm for rock n roll fans to latch on to Bowie." And, to be sure, the thin white duke in his shlock Ziggy Stardust alter persona gained traction for the same reasons the glam-rock grease of T-Rex had, by poking "safe" rock in the eye. This rumbling led some of the hoarier folk poets to some curious pronouncements, Leonard Cohen, for one, perhaps the most turbid troubadour of all, who said: "For a certain kind of nature that is prone to melancholy, my music has a salutary effect. For others, it has the opposite effect. . . . I can't stand it. Rock has become so wordy and inane. So trashy."

John Lennon, too, had a new complaint. The chimerical "Imagine" aside, he now was in his back-to-the-roots, drunk-every-minute-of-the-day phase, every reason to trash the troubadours for not acting like punks in public. "I want to take all the new singers, Carole and that other one, Nipples. I wanna take them all and hold them tight, all them people that James Taylor had . . . I wanna suck their nipples." God only knows what the hell the man was talking about—was Simon "Nipples" and if so, why?—but then he was working on an album in L.A. with rock's malevolent munchkin Phil Spector, who shot a hole in the ceiling of the A&M studio, so he had cause for spillover derangement. The soul outpost of pop music seemed to have its own directive for oversensitive pop bards, with the warning of Sly and the Family Stone's "Dance to the Music"—"All the squares go home!"

Jackson Browne defended the brethren. "After Dylan," he said, "there really wasn't much going on except for Joni and, I suppose, Neil. And these people used their own lives to discuss things that touched on all of our lives. Today there isn't this overwhelming universality. It's no longer this highly flashy and blindingly spectacular dissertation by one person on the quality of life existence for us all. There are no more James Deans, no more Bob Dylans. I prefer that to there being one central figure who outshines everybody with a way of thinking about life. I'd rather see everybody acting out their own feelings of how they should live."

In this skew, it was no crime that Taylor had not become "the next Dylan"; his role was that he had opened doors to other pilgrims of self-revelation. Ironic, then, was that the most hard-core opposition to Taylor was actually melting somewhat, and grudgingly. Lester Bangs, in a February 1973 *Creem* review of *One Man Dog*, no longer looking for Taylor with a broken Ripple bottle, wrote:

> When in the course of rock drought you cast about desperately for something to listen to, why not let your defenses down and try James Taylor? I know he wears his neuroses on his sleeve, solicits his audience's sympathy, and holes up in a Martha's Vineyard bungalow far more than is healthy for a growing boy. . . . On the other hand, everybody needs a little vicarious pain. . . . So what makes James any different? That he was a spoiled rich kid, makes it with Carly Simon (woo woo) and sings wimp? Well, that's not enough.

And:

> James Taylor's a real *punk*, when ya get right down to it. He never had any shame in the first place; he just sits around and gets fucked up all the time, just like most of us, and I betcha when he's not being a Sensitive Genius he's a getdown dude who don't give a shit about nothin'.

In Bangs-speak, that was a *good* thing. And, this time, he was right.

15

"A FUNCTIONAL ADDICT"

"Don't Let Me Be Lonely Tonight" hit the December 2 singles chart at number 60 en route to a peak rank of number 14 (number 4 on the easy listening list) in mid-January 1973, the same time that *One Man Dog* topped out at number 4. As it happened, *Billboard* could report in the January 27 issue that "James Taylor and his bride Carly Simon have just received gold records for their recent recordings," *One Man Dog* and "You're So Vain." And while William Ruhlmann's AllMusic retro-review has it that the album and single went gold "largely on the momentum of Taylor's career . . . it disappointed fans," *Dog* was anything but a disappointment. Though it would not reach platinum levels—meaning that in the superficial, always fretting mindset of the Canyon it was a dud—he got his gold record and hit single out of it and the bits and pieces were sort of a mini-album on the FM stations, where the scalpel-like incisions of personal pain were like diary entries.

Largely because of "Fire and Rain," easy listening music no longer was synonymous with torch ballads or stringed, big-band numbers like "Moon River" or "Theme from a Summer Place." Now, balladeers could divulge themes of darkness, inhumanity, even death, could bring both AM and FM listeners to tears but still leave them with a peaceful afterglow. Such was the case with "Don't Let Me Be Lonely Tonight," which played on both sides of the dial. The problem, as ever, was that at moments like this his first impulse seemed to be to ruin it all: the need to score some doojie.

Though it had taken Peter Asher a while to confront the truth about Taylor, by the mid-'70s his thoughts had moved from how to enable his meal ticket's smack problem to, as he says, "How do we keep him alive and not have him be another boring dead junkie?" Yet if by stopping indulging him, any of his inner circle believed they were setting him straight, all it did was make him play the role of a cleaned-up junkie, a role he had learned to play remarkably well. For the next decade, he did that, fooling a lot of people, even Carly Simon for stretches of time before she figured out that she was being played. One might call those years "Taylor's latency drug period," when he lived as "normally" as a junkie can—and many have, for even longer. He had, as well, carried on a public sham, speaking in very stark and unnerving terms about heroin—about how he was *over* it.

That implication was evident when he had told *Rolling Stone* in '71, "I have friends, some of whom are dead now, who've been at it for years, who've really paid dues, and I almost feel as if I'm cashing in on some sort of glory. I'm not that proud of it. But it certainly is something I did, and it was central to me for about two years, too." He also said, with great moral probity: "And Jesus, I don't mean to say that taking junk is all right. I don't want a kid out in Nebraska to read this and go out and say well, I'm gonna go pick up on some soul and take some smack just like James did. I tend to be loathe to talk about smack and being on junk, 'cause a lot of people boast about it."

Whether or not he regretted coming on so preachy, or laughed about it afterward knowing he was getting away with his deceit, he was in worse shape than ever. Out on the hustings, the easygoing, affable if sullen Taylor persona became that of an ashen, emaciated, dead-eyed zombie. Years later, Taylor would refer to himself during all of the '70s as "a functional addict," and that was true for long periods of time. But there would always come a fall. "If you're an addict, it controls your life and your life becomes uncontrollable. It's boring and painful, filling your system with something that makes you stare at your shoes for six hours." The staring happened again, then again. There were times when he did what Ray Charles once said he had done when trying to kick heroin—"I vomited and vomited and vomited until there was nothing left to vomit. And then I vomited some more [until] I was heaving up poison"—but simply couldn't go through the agony and went looking for a needle and a pusher.

More than the physical ordeal, however, he seemed even less committed to remove the crutch that the drug provided for him, relief from the "painful place" his songs sprung from. "That's my problem," he once said. "That was the manifestation of my problem. Junk, in itself, isn't the problem with me. It's a symptom of unexpressed and inexpressible anger, in a nutshell. It's a way of retreating from the world. It's a way of finding comfort and consistency in a chemical and I guess I have an addictive personality." He also surmised that he would regularly return to heroin because of the pressures of recording, and the anger he would also feel knowing that "I *have* to perform." In fact, after going cold turkey for the last tour he did with Carole King, when he began another solo tour, in the fall of '72, in Williamsburg, Virginia, he would recall:

> I was sick . . . and it went lousy. And I ran into a chick who I had scored from in London earlier that summer and she took me to Richmond and we copped from this guy there named Hangdown [who] sold me enough to keep me until we got to Chicago. It kept me for about two weeks . . . I was high all the time. . . . When I got to Chicago, I got in touch with a doctor who was a friend of mine and he got me methadone somewhat illegally.

This might have been the Chicago drug-scrounging interlude Asher refers to. But who really knew with Taylor, there were so many; *everyone*, it seemed, had a story of Taylor being oblivious to the world around him, a sure tip-off to his filling his veins with flea powder. Scot Eric Barrett, who on and off acted as his road manager, as he had with Hendrix, recalled:

> I spent an evening with him in a bar in New York while the place was burning down around us. They had to pull us out before it collapsed. We hadn't finished our drinks and James didn't want to leave. He just didn't care if the roof fell in. And James is a very persuasive cat so I would've been in the rubble, too. Listen, the only reason he wore clothes at all was to stop him being arrested or getting cold. He just didn't care about what a star was supposed to be doing or looking like. Never saw anyone in his position that completely unconcerned with anything materialistic or what his image should be.

Barrett saw this as a mark of honor, admittedly naive that much of the antiheroic pose was really just a heroin haze.

Whatever the confluence of circumstances and causes, and changing names in the cast of characters of his life from Bobby and Smack to Hangdown, every minute was hell on Simon, who tried hard to believe the stories she was hearing from others were just rumors because that's what he wanted, expected, her to do. But how long could *that* go on? He wasn't *that* good an actor. Indeed, Taylor recalled the autumn shoe-staring shows as an "awful tour . . . because I was wasted. I was just totally abusing myself all the time. I was in bad trouble. I was taking a lot of drugs."

He would come out, sing, play guitar, say little, and leave. For loyal audiences, these sort of perfunctory performances were rarely held against him, his endearing "shyness" providing cover—he would say in 1973 that "my act is the most unburlesque imaginable. I sit in a chair and don't move for two hours," with not a thought of any real sexual vibe. Then, too, he wouldn't for years appreciate or even feel the affection of his own fans. Seeing how distanced he was from them, Livingston would get all over him for it. "Livingston saw me feeling uncomfortable once onstage about the applause I was getting, and he said, 'What the fuck are you doing? These people love you. Why don't you enjoy it?'" All he really ever did was analyze the nature of the performer-fan dynamic, coldly, without simply letting himself hear those cheers.

Even so, he did hear the jeers and catcalls on that tour, and it would bring him down even further. He would claim he went on methadone after the tour, and would stay on it for two years—hardly a walk in the park, either. And if it was rough on him, it would be torture for Simon, dealing with his devils and hers at the same time. In this light, marriage was just as tortuous as she had sang it was, leaving *her* to sit alone with no lights on, cigarette glowing in the dark of a penthouse. Neither, however, seemed to want to admit they were wrong about the other. For Taylor, avowals of real love and reclamation were a lot easier than making an honest effort to kick smack.

Despite this enormous complication that some always knew would be the fatal Achilles heel of the marriage, this most peculiar love story, a conjunction of bitching and moaning times two, seemed at the start to sail in champagne bubble bath water. It was a postmodern fairy tale of a cover boy and a cover girl, both from the right side of the tracks, both with the most instantly recognizable voices of the new order. They were even more different than he and Mitchell had been—with the *woman* now the less breakable one—but were both neurotically abnormal people, and by coupling they ensured they would need to endure nothing but attention, one-upping the paparazzi's priority even for Liz and Dick. Rumors of their sure-to-be-soon divorce and warmed-over drug stories drove him into a media shell, scrimping on giving interviews. In truth, both Taylor and Simon would bridle as lost souls swimming in a fishbowl year after year. But she would be better at being stalked by paparazzi setting off explosions of flashbulbs as they entered or exited studios, clubs, restaurants, concerts, whatever, arm in arm. The result was normally a shot of Simon's dancing eyes and blinding wraparound smile contrasting Taylor with his clenched jaw around a dangling cigarette, eyes glaring. In the new trope of rock and romance, with both on equal levels—the new Sonny and Cher, or more veraciously given all their neuroses, the Burtons—she was the sophisticated city woman of means, he the hillbilly of means, something like the not very convincing image projected on the *Mud Slide Slim* cover.

As Hollywoodish as it seemed, and as natural considering that both their voices would be heard on so many of each other's records, the union actually further defined the soft-rock genre as capable of manufacturing fables to be punctured with darkly ominous gossip as an opiate for the masses who would eagerly read of the couple's picture-perfect existence and their mountain of neuroses, psychoses, and addictions. For the couple, it wasn't nearly as entertaining. Rather, the concept of marriage became a sobering sentiment, indeed. Yet they pushed on, with Taylor even foretelling that, as Simon recalled he told her, "We'll have children and give them names like Ben and Sally."

For the better part of two years, the winds of rock blew pretty much all in one direction, sweeping together various idioms. Bill Withers's "Lean on Me" was a prominent example of this idiom bleed, matching up the soft, romantic soul that was now oozing out of the Gamble-Huff studio in Philadelphia with the soft, personal reflection of folk rock, the song a thinly veiled cop of "You've Got a Friend." But now the Taylor model was getting barbed, mostly because of the female folk-rock singers who were seemingly turning the top tier of soft rock into an insipid game of musical Clue. It seemed almost a relief when Linda Ronstadt had a number one hit with "You're No Good," produced by Peter Asher. It was a cover of a song first recorded in 1963, meaning no male on either side of the Atlantic could think the song was about him, no doubt disappointing many who wanted to be as dickish as Warren Beatty. Or James Taylor.

But Simon was swept into a new wind, too, an ill wind she hadn't bargained for. It was hard dose of reality that after only a few years, her castle in the air was being tested, and taunted, daily. For Simon, the realization that she had bought into the life of a less-than-perfect prince upset all the dreamy pretensions. Early clues arose when he would seem to belittle her intellect for no real reason beyond cruelty. Once, when she remarked that the bathwater in their beach house was dirty and left a scum on her skin, she recalled, "James stared at me, his face pinched and condemning, blurting out, as if in response to the most egregious comment ever uttered by anyone ever, 'Haven't you ever heard of *emulsification*?' . . . James, schooled in physics and chemistry, knew a term that I didn't, and had pounced on me, humiliated me by deliberately making me feel dumb . . . leaving me confused, embarrassed, and feeling rather bullied." To the point that she made a list of words and phrases he might catch her off guard with. But at least during those moments he was interacting. Worse was the distance he kept, at times isolation, even when they were under the same roof. When she would step out of the apartment, she would wonder if he even knew she was gone.

On a more serious level, there soon were increasing signs of his dependency on drugs. She had known nothing of his heroin addiction and saw nothing amiss when they carried out the usual rock and roll indulgences, smoking pot and popping prescription pills. During a joint trip to Japan, they sweated out a tense few minutes going through customs after she forgot to dispose of the pill she had in her coat, thought she was able to explain it away. She became aware of his far more ominous drug of choice in a typically bizarre turn, when she stumbled across him during one of his periodic failed attempts at going cold turkey. Apparently he had become so committed to kicking heroin that he not only didn't try to hid this addiction from her but spared her none of the gruesomeness of it, inviting her to witness, almost ceremoniously, what he intended as his last fix. It happened when they were staying in L.A. in a posh suite at the artsy rock and roll in-spot, the Chateau Marmont Hotel on Sunset Boulevard, where John Belushi famously would a decade later die after a spree of heroin-and-cocaine speedball injections. Walking into the bedroom, she watched as Taylor matter of factly opened a suitcase and withdrew a piece of rubber. As she would write in her memoir, she thought, "*OH SHIT*, what was he doing?"

His explanation was, "This is what I do. Watch, I can't have you and the habit at the same time. I just can't. I've got to get rid of this. Maybe if you see me do it, it will take away the cat-and-mouse game. You have to watch me. I have to let it all go."

He then proceeded to go through the meticulous and hideous ritual of the junkie. He took a syringe and a bag of white powder he had kept in a bag in his suitcase, went into the kitchen and melted it on a spoon over a burner, and filled the syringe with the viscous liquid. As this slow waltz of the damned went on, Carly could only stare. "My mouth began to dry up and my heart went into panicked rhythms." Perhaps fascinated as well on some level, she watched silently as he fastened the rubber around his arm, his veins becoming "purple and frightening," then walked to the bed, sat down, and shot up. "It took five seconds," she said, "and then he fell back on the bed. When he pulled the needle out of his arm, he exhaled and made some sounds like that of an animal being freed."

She went on: "A few minutes later, during which time I was as still as a corpse—in shock and trying not to show it, just sitting there leaning on one elbow—James got up from the bed and flushed everything down the toilet. All the medicine was gone. He threw the rubber arm strangler into the hallway chute to the incinerator [and] we clung to each other like apes, and closeness got hold of us in a painful but towering way." She told him she would cancel her plans and stay with him, but "he assured me that the crisis was over and that he was all right. He was beyond it. Everything was so much better."

"It's over," he told her. "I don't need it anymore."

She wanted to believe it, for his sake. But she wasn't fooling herself that such scenes were indeed over; or that this hadn't been merely another show for her benefit. She wrote in her diary that day: "I was angry and totally depressed. Was he shattering an illusion of what I wanted him to be? . . . [A]n addict will always lie to protect his disease. Life is barren without the drug. Was I asking for too much?" Sensing there would be more pain to come, she added, "Mainly, I didn't want him to die. I was so scared that he would, just like my father. I was even getting to that familiar habit of knocking on wood."

In the Olympic river of celebrity marriages, they would be swimming upstream, against the tide of inevitable failure, comforted and deluded by being able to pretend it was a wonderful idea, overflowing with love and music. When they did give interviews, it made for piquant quotes and images few could forget, if only for how excruciatingly sexy Simon was; in a book-length, cover story Q & A in the January 4, 1973, *Rolling Stone,* the magazine was able to acquire photos taken by her brother Peter on their honeymoon cruise ship, leis around their necks, the cover shot in profile, the pair staring across the sea, over The Honeymooners. A better shot on the inside had them leaning against a guard rail, the ocean and sky behind them, she in the skimpiest of bikini bottoms, mesh top tight around her torso. If anyone noticed the tall, skinny guy in the white linen suit beside her, Taylor, looking breezy in an open-necked shirt and white shoes, cocked his head to her, cigarette jutting, himself seeming rather amazed at what was now his.

Writer Stuart Werbin helpfully noted that "Carly is an excellent, provocative cook, James is fair on the dishes." But a subtext of the interview was the competition between the two, and whether the marriage could embrace that, with Taylor swearing, "We love to shine, but on the other hand, we don't like it so much that we want to sacrifice everything to it, including our personal lives. . . . It's been a man's world . . . controlled by the man's outlook. That's changed a lot too." She admitted that "it worried me terribly" that he had shown little interest in her work, though he said, "I heard as few songs of yours as I'd heard of Dylan's . . . or of anyone's. I just don't listen to music. . . . I never listened to mine, either." Then, apologetically, "I don't know honey," adding, "I'm very much interested in not seeing Carly behind the kitchen stove." Yet he still betrayed a tad of irritation that, of the two, she was the lightning rod and that he was "very seldom recognized."

"People don't recognize you out of context," Simon reminded him. "People don't expect to see James Taylor out in Sayville."

"Yeah, but people recognize *you.*"

Bouncing out of wimp mode, at one point he noted, "She's a piece of ass. . . . If she looks at another man, I'll kill her," which sounded like as much of a joke as he probably thought it would coming out of his mouth. Taking the edge off it, she returned the compliment. "And I think James is a nice piece of ass," she said.

They were the new culture's foremost man and wife, full of self-conscious froth. But never far behind Taylor was the dark side. He again had to discourse on his heroin habit, no matter his hypocrisy when taking the media to task for bringing it up. Living with him already through all the phases from addiction to methadone to cold turkey and back, she said, had had "a reverse effect on me. I snorted cocaine a couple of times but it was never as bad to me as it seemed when I saw James getting into it. Now I have a horror about cocaine. I was never tempted to try heroin or acid. . . . I haven't smoked grass for the last four months." Then: "I've felt often in our relationship that I've been addicted to James and I have a dependency on him that's almost like a drug I couldn't do without. Maybe that's what addiction is all about."

For his part, he said all the right bromides about addiction being "an amazing downhill slide" with high "emotional guilt" and that "after a while it perpetuates itself as nothing perpetuates itself," that it was like "trying to get away from a feeling that you cannot control and that you cannot in any way express. . . . Either it's anger or fear or a combination of the two." But the tell this time was that, asked about cocaine, he replied: "Sometimes it can be very refreshing. If you do it once a week, for instance, or once a month, when someone comes around, you're having a party, you're doing this thing, that thing, and say here, have a little blow of this. But the trouble is that the damned things always escalate, so it's better left behind."

He didn't say he had kicked junk; but neither did he say he *hadn't.* And in this game of self-delusion, when conceits seemed to make more sense than reality, he insisted what brought them together was something like *religion*, within his parameters, which seemed to come off a Hallmark card: "My love for Carly is a very religious thing, to me, because sometimes I just exchange with her completely and I don't know where I end off and she begins." In this prism, religion was the antidote to feeling controlled by societal conditioning. Religion, he said, "is just the opposite of that. It's the idea of throwing yourself away," thus explaining why he had also thought to call the album *Throw Yourself Away.*

Simon asked him, "I am wondering what connotation Jesus had for you."

"Rhymes with *cheeses*," merrily said the man who had begged Jesus to look down on him and guide him to salvation.

He would try to prove how much he wanted her to be as successful as he, by playing and singing on her albums, as she did on his, her efforts adding a more pungent flavor than Joni Mitchell had.

Simon acknowledged that "there are predictable problems" in living with Taylor, "the old-fashioned chauvinistic idea that the man has to be on top, has to be better than the woman if they're both working in the same field. If James and I have albums out at the same time and mine does better than his, there's this tremendous insecurity on his part and anger at me. And I kind of feel the same way." There were other repercussions as well, stemming from her own family clefts. While the Taylors, she wrote in her memoirs, "were a family who knew how to support one another," her sisters seemed to pull away from her. There had, she said, "always been a natural amount of sibling jealousy among us, which wasn't helped by the fact that I was now married to a famous prince, and getting the princess treatment. The more that happened, the worse, and guiltier, I felt." But so intent was she on making the marriage work that one song that went on her 1975 album, *Playing Possum*, she called "Slave," which she said, "I'm sure is gonna cause a lot of women to be really down on me," inasmuch as that, at times now, "I feel just like a slave to my *own* chauvinistic emotions."

She was also lovestruck enough, or so she believed, to attest without shame years later that "James was my muse, my Orpheus, my sleeping darling, my 'good night, sweet prince,' my something-in-the-way-he-moves."

In truth, given how consumed each one was with their careers and their own neuroses, objectively the marriage was a perfectly horrible idea. And if one looked closely enough at Taylor, the seeds of the disaster this union would be were already visible. As self-possessed as Carly was, she had no idea how to go about dealing with it, playing mother hen and nurse to a heroin junkie not being what she believed she was signing up for. The good thing—and very bad thing—was how functional he could be on the junk. It never had taken a toll on his writing or studio work, that is, *when* he was ready to go in. In this race he was nearly running parallel to Eric Clapton, whose métier, American blues, led him to conscript one of those American James Taylor–type singer-songwriters as a muse, Tulsa-raised J. J. Cale, who was languishing in L.A. when Clapton covered his bluesy "After Midnight," slinky electric guitar riffs and all, in 1970, and mellow warning about the drug he equated with the lure of a woman, "Cocaine." He would record in America, at producer Tom Dowd's Miami studio and Muscle Shoals, recording "Layla" with Duane Allman backing him on side guitar. But Clapton, too, was walking the edge, his heroin jones alternating with music as the thread of his life, not to fully kick it until 1987. At this point, there was no reason discernible to either man why they should need to go that extra mile. Looking back, Clapton related the same feeling Taylor surely was harboring, that his creativity was tied to the lowest form of existence. "I thought that if I stopped drinking and I stopped using drugs I would not be able to play anymore," he said. "In other words, those were things that were necessary for inspiration."

Still, Taylor was finding inspiration harder to come by. His follow-up to *One Man Dog* was delayed for over a year as he went about playing househusband, moving with his bride to a new, bigger apartment on Central Park West, and trying to knock her up and actualize all those premonitions of fatherhood. Simon's own timetable slowed as well: she did no recording for a year. Then, after she learned she was pregnant in the spring of 1973, she prepared for a new album, which would be called *Hotcakes*, shuttling with him that autumn between studios in L.A. and New York. Taylor contributed guitar and backing vocals, most notably on her cover of "Mockingbird," the novelty song that Charlie Foxx and his younger sister Inez recast from the traditional lullaby "Hush, Little Baby," its first verse about how "Momma gonna buy you a mockingbird" and if it didn't sing, "Momma's gonna buy you a diamond ring." As it happened, Taylor had seen the Foxx siblings, who were from Greensboro, North Carolina, perform the song after it was a number 7 pop and number 2 R & B hit in 1963 and suggested that Simon cover it, writing some new nonsense lyrics for it. The two recorded it in a percussion-filled, hip-hop style, with New Orleans boogie-rock master Mac Rebennack—"Dr. John"—on organ and Robbie Roberston on electric guitar, Taylor with a faux New Orleans–style blues dialect that made "have you heard" come out "have you *hoid*."(Amusingly, Sheila Weller in her panting book about Simon, Carole King, and Joni Mitchell, *Girls Like Us*, mistakes this as Taylor's stab at a *Yiddish* accent!)

The song marked a distinct change for Simon, a welcome break from her grim autobiographical songs, which continued onto this album but now with a whiff of optimism and even traditionalism in the virtual love letters she composed to James—"Forever My Love" (cowritten with him), "Mind on My Man," "Think I'm Gonna Have a Baby," and "Haven't Got Time for the Pain" (with Jacob Brackman), the latter a sentiment she never would have expressed in years past. Wedded bliss, if that's what it was, worked well to soften her sound and image. And the album cover of her, pregnant and beaming in their country kitchen, was out of a fairy tale. The album flew out of stores, selling a million copies, reaching number 3 on the chart, and sending "Pain" and "Mockingbird" high up the pop and adult contemporary lists. (Not that Simon, the classic Nervous Nellie, could live with that; she deemed it a failure because it hadn't racked up to the chart and sales success of *No Secrets.*)

Taylor, on the other hand, was wracked by indecision and inertia. Their first child, Sarah "Sally" Maria Taylor, was born on January 7, 1974, just as Simon's album dropped, and the last thing he wanted to do was go back in the pressure cooker, not when he was giving another shot at going cold turkey. But with Warner demanding he return to the studio, as they always seemed to be, he gave in, scheduling sessions at the Hit Factory studio on West Fifty-Fourth Street in Manhattan, and once again cutting demos in his home studio at the Vineyard. As Taylor recalled, he was tired of his previous work, though not for the reasons most would have had for that. Those albums, he said, "were very whimsical, very unself-important and not taken very seriously on my part." Now, feeling as if "the walls were closing in on me," he didn't want to proceed "in as free and light-hearted a way as I had been before." Aside from what it said about him that he could construe things like addiction, mental illness, and suicide as "light-hearted," he now wanted to broaden his messages.

Seeking inspiration where he could, he took the birth of his daughter as a kind of rebirth and reclamation. This was something he had been bandying about with Peter Asher, who had needed to be talked into the experimental nature of *One Man Dog* and wanted to return to the minimalist approach of "Fire and Rain" and "You've Got a Friend." Hits were getting tougher to come by, Taylor was flagging, he needed some of that old voodoo. But Taylor seemed to shift the blame onto his old confrere. Indeed, in the Taylor-Simon *Rolling Stone* interview, he seemed gratuitously hard on Asher, saying that "Peter's not an accomplished musician. He is a musician from a certain point of view. . . . There's a difference between Carly's working with the producer and my working with one." Allowing that Asher was "very helpful" and a "fantastic organizer," he nonetheless added, "I don't know if there would be much difference between what I do were

I producing myself, and what I have done on my last two, maybe three albums. . . . Aside from the music that is made, Peter is responsible for the environment in which I record. The word producer can mean many different things. It can mean someone the company hires to time the tracks. It's too vague a term. . . . The other role of a producer is someone who sits behind that glass and says 'OK' or 'Do it again.'"

Asher insists the artistic differences between them were all too normal for an artist and producer, and that he had no problem with Taylor finding someone else back east to produce the album. Indeed, he said, "We never really discussed it," his communication with Taylor often being nonverbal, in which "a nod is as good as a couple of paragraphs. A lot of stuff is understood." Seeking a more pointed, jazzier sound, and less of an autocrat, Taylor hired David Spinozza, the superb New York session guitarist and arranger who in '71 had, with fellow guitar player Hugh McCracken, helped Paul McCartney see through the recording of his second solo album, *Ram*, which, while reviled by critics who held McCartney to blame for the Beatles' crack-up, spilled off his first number one solo hit in the United States, "Uncle Albert/Admiral Halsey." Spinozza had also worked with John Lennon on *Mind Games* and Yoko Ono's *A Story*. Rather than summoning Danny Kortchmar, Russ Kunkel, Lee Sklar, and the other regulars, he called in some top East Coast sidemen such as McCracken, percussionist Ralph MacDonald, keyboardists Don Grolnick and Kenny Ascher, drummer Rick Marotta, and horn men Barry Rogers, George Young, and Alan Rubin. Another notable get—Paul McCartney—repaid Spinozza by singing backup and playing bass on a couple of the tracks. Simon also sung backing vocals.

Right from the first words sung on track 1, "Walking Man," the Taylor "sound was essentially re-trademarked as a two-for-one," with he and Simon harmonizing about "moving in silent desperation" toward "the holy land, a hypothetical destination," with Taylor to lament walking—or, as he sang, stumbling drunk—past what really matters in this life, like frost on the pumpkin. The concept of the song, which would give the album its name as well, he explained, "was a combination of my father and the fall of the year and winter coming. October is my favorite month, but I used to have a terribly strong reaction to fall and the end of summer, and I still have it." The languid ballad, which featured a Vox Humana, a new age studio gimcrack that gave vocals an organ-like timbre, was also a clue that the album would feature far louder instrumentals and hip-hoppier touches that played off resounding horns and hazy, swirling strings. It was a poppy, funky, almost Doobie Brothers style he seemed to be after; on his paean to his blues roots, "Rock 'n' Roll Is Music Now," and "Me and My Guitar," horns blew in time with wah-wah guitar licks, electric pianos, and itchy drum fills.

Within the progression of song tracks, it was clear Taylor made sure not to encroach on too sentimental ground, that being allowed only on a few numbers, the mandatory "lullaby" song "Daddy's Baby," his valentine to Sarah, its whisper-like vocal buffed by Simon and a gorgeous lush chorale, and "Hello Old Friend," its sad sense of loss and weeping horns to be cribbed seven years on and contoured to the "1812 Overture" in Dan Fogelberg's "Same Old Lang Syne." And as a *real* change of pace, Taylor slipped in his first "message song," not with the old folk fervor but a pop hook, one repeated over and over in the title phrase "Let It All Fall Down." This was his diss of Richard Nixon—"for whom the bell is tolling," he sang—as he floundered in the Watergate swamp of his own making, Taylor sidestepping his own caution to sing not just slagging Nixon but the lazy American populace that had twice elected him:

I just now got the news
He seems to tell us lies
And still we will believe him
Then together he will lead us
Into darkness, my friends

However, if he had much to say with these songs, which paid tribute mostly to family and the warmth and benediction of nature, it seemed that they were just this side of contrived, at times a mile wide and an inch deep. A wonderful idea such as covering Chuck Berry's cadge of "The Wabash Cannonball," "The Promised Land," lost any bite as a railroad boxcar song when the vocal, curiously, ended early, giving way to a swelling doubled electric guitar and soulful organ straight from out of the TV show *Good Times*. Arguably his best vocal, a soaring, emotional wail on the scenic folk ballad "Migration," which nicely integrated the new rock prop, the Moog synthesizer, was coated by a weirdly too thick echo and smothering choir. The closing track, "Fading Away," put a clever bow on the work, taking his disillusioned "walking man" back from his walkabout migration to his center of gravity, the innocence of love. The tune was also a reminder of the original Taylor formula, recycling the singsong delivery and countryish feel of "Sweet Baby James," but his refrain, "You can hardly see me 'cause I'm fading away," could have been taken as a parable for *Taylor* himself after the intervening years—as could his sentiment on the Spinozza-written "Ain't No Song" that went "I'm a man of few words / Trying to find a rhyme / And finally it occurred to me / That I'm wasting my time."

Walking Man's cover, a noirish black-and-white photograph by his old friend Richard Avedon, was a portrait that struck the ironies Taylor had carried from the start, with darkness stalking him, even here in a seemingly tepid pose, clean-shaven, freshly scrubbed face, and wearing a preppy wool sweater, his long hair for a change neatly coiffed. If one looked hard enough, one could see an open-faced pocket watch was in his hand. Taylor would say this was symbolic of time moving him onward, to a different stage of darkness. And there was no doubt it did. Again, it being seemingly impossible for a Taylor album to lack any merit, and a lot of it, Stephen Holden's *Rolling Stone* review was a rave, calling *Walking Man* "Taylor's most unabashed rock efforts to date," one that hinted at even more religious overtones in its "apprehension of one's personal destiny being ultimately a matter of will." The softly biting "Let It All Fall Down" was, he wrote, "one of the most cogent and sobering musical expressions of thwarted political idealism to come out of the Nixon era." In sum, this was, he wrote, "the first album in which James Taylor has sounded more warm than sullen, more confident than confused," its achievement "the communication of personal happiness. It is a pleasure to share it with him." Time, however, would not be as kind; in William Ruhlmann's retro-review on AllMusic, it was "a more considered effort than its predecessor that managed to be just as trivial but even less interesting. . . . Somehow, a songwriter who had seemed in 1970 to have as precise an idea of the national mood as Bob Dylan had had in 1965 now seemed to be a man without a country." Robert Christgau didn't even bother to review it.

At the least, what the album showed was that for an absolutely disassociated artist like Taylor there were dangers bowing to the prevailing wind instead of trying to march through it. Even world events let him down. Indeed, within weeks of June 1, 1974, the date that "Daddy's Baby"/"All Fall Down" was released as the album's first single, the man who insisted "I'm not a crook" would resign from office, just two years after a historical landslide victory, removing the sting of "All Fall Down," such as it was, from the song. Neither side as much as charted, and the next song put out, "Walking Man," made it to number 26 on the adult contemporary chart but not into the Hot 100. What's more, Taylor was bested by a better anti-Nixon song, Stevie Wonder's "You Haven't Done Nothin'," its veiled thematic statement very similar to "Let It All Fall Down" but with the added zing of funk, anger, and the Jackson 5 singing the famous "*doo da wop*" chorus; released two days before the resignation, it rose hard and went to the top of the pop *and* R & B charts. Timing, which had always been Taylor's kindest ally, was seemingly taunting him now. *Walking Man* would go as high as number 13 but not chart at all in England, where none of his albums ever would again. It would not go gold—and has not to this very day.

Good intentions aside, Taylor took the chilly reception hard. During the recording of the album, not only he but also the musicians had a vague uneasiness; the craftsmanship was exemplary, the songs good, the spirit high. But, as Don Grolnick said, "something did seem missing but nobody wanted to come out and say it." As crazy as it seemed, he added, the best material on the work "probably would have done better if they were released by another artist." That wasn't a knock on Taylor; it was a recognition that he was a truly gifted songwriter but that when he sang, a certain sound, tonality, and *mood* were expected. Since no one can do the same song forever and Taylor was growing further distant from the "Fire and Rain" framework, he was in a real bind now, needing to adapt to the changes in music and having much on his mind he could write about, but with no slack for not quite getting it right. Some days during the monthlong tour in support of the album that commenced in mid-July, he seemed as if he just wanted to drop into a hole and disappear—which is one way many concertgoers would have described his performances. According to some, he was basically run off the stage by his Asher stablemate Linda Ronstadt, who was there to open for him; the surly Taylor, saying nothing, singing poorly, and at times cutting short his set after half an hour, would exit to another chorus of boos.

Nearing the midpoint of a rapidly moving decade he had defined in so many ways, new modes were bubbling up all around music; old listening habits were wearing thin. Now, one had to wonder if James Taylor was just another morning glory about to close up in the evening sun. Could it be that, at all of twenty-six, he was exactly that proverbial walking man, walking right out of the picture? If the thought occurred to Taylor, the coming few months would determine just how far he could continue walking.

16

"HE GOES AWAY FOREVER EVERY DAY"

Music had indeed come a long way since Bob Dylan's folk-rock period; Dylan himself had strayed from the persona of the beatnik bard to go introspective, too. About the only contemporaries of his still doing socially conscious music were Tom Paxton (who slighted folk rock as "folk rot"), Phil Ochs, and Dave Van Ronk. Other kinds of singers had been bred during the war, such as Kris Kristofferson's "Viet Nam Blues" and Creedence Clearwater Revival's "Fortunate Son" and "Who'll Stop the Rain." John Lennon, dilettante or not, was getting down with "Power to the People." The highly selective and downplayed activism of James Taylor, meanwhile, was not much altered by his Nixon song. Bonnie Raitt, signed to Warner Brothers in 1970 and with two blues-rock albums to her credit so far, reflected that "the public expects you to play a role and often literally kill yourself for them. So it's either destroy yourself or withdraw. I was raised with a political outlook to know better, but people like Dylan and James Taylor just withdrew. I'm not planning to let it happen to me, and I guess that sets me apart." It surely did from Taylor, who would adopt a classic cop-out when he said of political activism, "I'm not a student of social trends. My credentials are only as a musician who entertains people."

Still, with Nixon blessedly gone back to San Clemente, most of the entrenched bad guys from the 1960s were history, and with the presidential inheritance of the last surviving Kennedy brother left in the splinters of a bridge in Chappaquiddick, not far from James Taylor's home turf, folk rock seemed to be getting less edgy still as the retrenchment of the '70s now embraced even softer, less cerebral music. Thus did the appetite for John Denver/Kenny Loggins somnolence grow, and with it more stirrings of backlash to the cerebral Taylor mode. A '50s refugee like Ricky Nelson, all grown up and a country rocker now, sold a huge number of records with the strikingly ingenuous refrain that you can't please everyone so you've got to please yourself—one that Taylor noted himself was the essential truth of life—which one music writer, Todd Everett, said was far easier to stomach than "the infinitely sappier existential angst of the likes of James Taylor." Perhaps if Monte Hellman had let Taylor do some speaking, he and not Kristofferson, in the 1972 movie *Cisco Pike*, could have played a dissipating L.A. rocker—perfect casting!—who is told in the flick "that California shit ain't happening no more."

In truth, the California shit was just shifting to a different plane, with a whole lot more money to be made through existential angst. Hell, even *Elvis* saw the advantages of covering Taylor; in 1973 he had performed a version of "Steamroller Blues," its hunk o' funk riffs right in his wheelhouse, on his *Elvis: Aloha from Hawaii* TV special that year. Not that some of those who had risen *weren't* adrift, running on empty, running blind—but while Jackson Browne may have felt that way in song, he was not really in that bind, and in fact was just starting to take off in the capitalist enterprise that was seeking new faces. His eponymous 1972 debut album for Asylum was, as Barney Hoskyns said, "blandly James Taylor–esque" but its lyric writing "impressive—introspective but chiseled." When Linda Ronstadt signed to Peter Asher's management company in 1973, Asher skillfully positioned her as next in line through the revolving door of sexy folk-rock females right behind Mitchell and Simon.

Yet one more scion of wealth, raised on a ten-acre ranch in Arizona, Ronstadt's father the head of his own machinery company, what set her apart was that she sought no catharses from real or fancied alienation; neither did she write songs, only sing, her hypnotic, plaintive voice and three-octave vocal range heavily influenced by Mexican *ranchera* music, Hank Williams, Billie Holiday, and Maria Calas. She recorded her second solo album, *Silk Purse*, entirely in Nashville, something that might have behooved Taylor had Asher—who after she signed with Asylum began producing Ronstadt's country-flavored songs—given him the same leeway in the studio that he gave her. It was almost as if the munchkin Brit fell under her spell, as did every other man on earth, though few knew of her temperamental outbursts and controlling nature, and Asher could even take a bow for keeping it all platonic. "It must be a lot harder to have objective conversations about someone's career when it's someone you sleep with," he said with a twinkling eye.

Indeed, with Ronstadt winning notice as a harder Joni Mitchell and softer Carly Simon, able to melt men with her sizzling, part-Latino swarthy looks, she stood on the verge of skyrocketing stardom. Her first number one hit, "You're No Good," in '75, would win her a spot on the cover of *Rolling Stone*, and a spate of enormous success with some original songs written for her but mostly covers of Motown. One could forgive Taylor for believing that Asher was more territorially invested in her than him, on the what-have-you-done-for-me-lately premise. Still, while Taylor had veered from Asher to find some autonomy of his own in the studio, he was beholden to the man as his manager and guru. Indeed, while Taylor was taking more control of what songs he wanted to record, he listened hard when Asher counseled him to redo some of those Motown standards as well; a decade past their shelf life, they were gold to the aging baby boomers, he told him.

Asher, having won great repute as the man behind James Taylor, was now in the cradle of power in L.A. His office was now fairly opulent digs at 644 North Doheny Drive, hard by Santa Monica Boulevard, cradled by the mountains of the canyon, and even with his small client list—essentially Taylor and Ronstadt, with Kate Taylor having quit the business—the business they generated was beyond his capacity to handle himself. He hired the giant Gibson & Stromberg entertainment public relations firm, some of whose clients were the Rolling Stones, Pink Floyd, and Neil Diamond, to oversee the endless demand for Taylor interviews, almost none of which were now granted. Turning entrepreneurial, in 1973 he became one of the founding investors in the Roxy Theater in West Hollywood, partners with David Geffen, Elliot Roberts, Elmer Valentine, and Lou Adler. When Asher advised Taylor to get out of his rut by living in L.A. for a while and recording his next work there, James thought it a good idea, as did Simon, who had become a tad stir-crazy in those apartments and his always disheveled house. In the early summer of 1975, the Taylor clan packed up and went west, Asher having found them a house to rent on Hazen Drive in Beverly Hills, a rented Mercedes-Benz at their disposal.

Though Taylor had not put in much time in L.A. the last few years, the rock scene out there was still in ascendance. Everywhere one looked around the town, *something* was crackling. The biggest noise now was being made by the Eagles, Geffen's concoction of strangers thrown together in 1971 almost literally from the crowd hanging at the Troubadour bar when Linda Ronstadt needed a temporary road band. Only in a soulless but magical kingdom could a band be formed from musicians who had not known each other before. In fact, before Glenn Frey and Don Henley had ever written a song in tandem—"Desperado" would be the first—the list of those who could contribute material to the band emanated from the Laurel Canyon rock commune directory. Jackson Browne, who lived in the same cottage as Frey, cowrote their first hit, "Take It Easy," and several more songs for them, as did John David Souther, erstwhile Byrd Gene Clark, country songwriter Jack Tempchin, folk writer David Blue, and Tommy Nixon. Their eponymous debut album, recorded in London and produced by former Beatles engineer Glyn Johns, set the tone for the deluge to follow. Robert Christgau's review of their second album, the pseudo-cowboy rock *Desperado*, wrote that "the country orientation bespeaks not roots but a lack of them, so that in the end the product is suave and synthetic—brilliant, but false."

That could have gone for much of the L.A. rock scene, the qualities Taylor hoped to avoid but now needed to exploit. High professionalism, though, even with an insincere product, was a formula for world domination, and Henley and Frey perfected it. But no more so than Geffen, who could merge Asylum with Elektra. Busy as Geffen and Roberts were counting dollars—and with Geffen, whom Barney Hoskyns dubbed "the Croesus of LA rock," luxuriating in his success—they handed the Eagles off to Irving Azoff, yet another pit bull, whose growl had been held in abeyance, confined mainly to managing Dan Fogelberg. Though no one could be certain how high the Eagles would fly back in '72, at a time when CSN was losing a bit of altitude and seeming a tad dated—and tiresome for the public spats the Eagles would learn to keep private, for a few years anyway—L.A. had its signature band for the new order. It was just the sort of coldly contrived coup of behind-the-scene string-pullers that had been presaged as ultimate victory in a growing sense of impersonal corporate vacuity. Little wonder that with each successive album kneading the soft clay of the L.A. genre into different shapes—from cowboy rock to smugly contrived country, hard rock, folk (even covering Tom Waits), and Castaneda hot air, all seemingly wrapped in very pretty-sounding sexist preening and posturing—they would fly right past James Taylor, who now needed to prove he still belonged.

That indeed was an objective he seemed more interested in than being at home in his glitzy Beverly Hills retreat, where he rarely set foot. Simon, who had to live with longer absences from him as time went by, often felt like a single mother. Sounding like a lyric waiting for a new song, she said she would lament to her new set of friends, "He goes away forever every day." It was no way for a princess to live.

The last James Taylor single, "One Man Parade," released two years ago, back in March 1973, had wheezed its way only to number 67. Warner would not release more than the two singles from *Walking Man,* hoping for much stronger (read: *commercial*) material when he handed in his next album. Still, high or low tide, it was impossible to shunt him out of the way, nor ignore that, as one rock scribe put it, "The best singer-songwriters are all sons and daughters of James Taylor, giving up on the larger issues and concentrating on the inner social order." As for the record industry, it needed no excuses to keep expanding soft rock as far as it could before the dam might break. The results, as proven by the Eagles, were often sapless, but not for the account books of corporate power. For the artists seeking to find a way in, it was never a bad idea to follow Taylor down his road. His imprint could be seen not just on his own work but in the small print of others', as if engraved in the scripture of the new reality. John Denver, moving toward a lead role in the caste, seemed to be using Taylor as a lever. Back in '70, Denver covered "Carolina in My Mind," his first successful single; also that year was "Take Me Home, Country Roads," the last two words channeling Taylor's publishing company, Country Road Music. Two years later, Denver recorded a live album called *Carolina in My Mind.* Denver found a niche with anthems to pristine countryside, snow-capped mountains, and the big blue sky, but he hadn't gotten there first.

But just what *was* the nature of soft rock now that Taylor had to follow, not lead? Aside from the group dynamic and harmonies of the

Eagles and their cohort—England Dan and John Ford Coley, Seals and Crofts, etc.—the troubadour torch now seemed to be changing hands from Taylor to Jackson Browne. The more hunky, less broody singer-songwriter was playing the game to perfection in the Canyon. Not only had he shown a knack for saying the same kind of things Taylor did with a swingier beat and blues-jazz kick, he was there to scoop up Joni Mitchell after Taylor split, though he would not allow himself to be seen or portrayed as Joni's pet or object of long-term ownership. Browne was not running on empty as he would soon be singing, but on a quick-rising geyser, his third album, *Late for the Sky*, going to number 14 in '74 and earning him a Grammy nomination. Its cover art, a knock-off of Rene Magritte, was as riveting as the usual Canyon checklist of alienation, and life as, in the title of one of its tracks, a "Fountain of Sorrow." With a sharper poetic pen, the Browne model of personal travail seemed fresher and more joyous than the suddenly gauche "Fire and Rain."

Browne also found his own studio cats, including fiddler/steel guitarist extraordinaire David Lindley and string arranger David Campbell, with Don Henley and J. D. Souther singing backup—and producer Al Schmitt. Linda Ronstadt would self-contain as well; even as Asher produced her, only Russ Kunkel from the Taylor crowd was a regular; her band was led by Andrew Gold on keyboards, guitar, and backup vocals and Kenny Edwards on bass. Ronstadt's fifth solo album, the 1974 Grammy-winning *Heart Like a Wheel*, her last for Columbia, was the first of three consecutive number one albums, something only equaled by Carole King, en route to becoming the top-selling female artist of the decade with eight platinum albums overall. Unlike King and Simon, Ronstadt was unpredictable, guided by her own instincts and influences, in effect turning Asher into a pupil, since the Brit had little sentience of country music. But she could pinball from covering Hank Williams's "I Can't Help It (If I'm Still in Love with You)," which won her her first Grammy for Best Country Performance and went to number 2 on the country chart, to covering Martha and the Vandellas, Buddy Holly, and Warren Zevon. Like Taylor and drugs, Ronstadt could be too cute with her protestations of hating to be a sexual object—she had no objection posing for the cover of her 1976 Grammy-winning LP *Hasten Down the Wind* in a sheer white dress, noticeably braless. Still, she had no time for collecting and showing off boy toys and her self-reliance, as opposed to Mitchell's and Simon's need to be claimed by a man, did much for gender equality in the industry, though the stereotypes and games of control hardly disappeared, and if anything may be worse today.

As of the mid-'70s, the cultural softening of the folk-rock tell-all mania had taken the idiom even more down the center of the road, its personal confessionals more obscured by sprightly arrangements and harmonies that didn't bring anyone down. This trend swept the Eagles into their moneymaking maelstrom of lyin' eyes and women who were the daughters of the devil and angels in white. A new entrant, a migrant from Long Island, Billy Joel, was getting gigs as Bill Martin, a troubadour with melodrama in his voice and verve in his piano runs, most notably on the most harrowing heroin song ever, "Captain Jack." The Canyon was still buzzing, the great driving force the almighty dollar. Danny Kortchmar had risen to the role of studio god. He would record three instrumental albums for Warner with Kunkel, Sklar, and keyboardist Craig Doerge as the Section.

"It did feel like the center of the universe," says Kortchmar. "All hell had broken loose, and we were on fire. We were cutting records all the time, every day."

For Sklar, the effects of being on that first Taylor session was like an "explosion, the phone started ringing and hasn't stopped to this day."

As for the visionary who had given them this lucrative life, he was typically depressed. On the surface, he had little to brood about. He had more money in the bank than Ike Taylor ever had. His albums were assured of at least going Top 20. His songs were still the gold standard of soft rock, and many were actually compatible with disco, their lonely but lilting anthems fitting the "I Will Survive" motif of the syncopated era. Both the Isley Brothers and Sylvester covered "Don't Let Me Be Lonely Tonight" in that era, of which a reviewer wrote, "When James Taylor sings his tune he sounds like he's pleading with his mother to tuck him in and leave the night-light burning, but Sylvester and the Hot Band ignite it into a torrid rocker that milks it for all its erotic potential." But now there were serious doubts about him. *Melody Maker* boldly asserted about Taylor in 1974 that "having peaked early, he seems to have leveled out and slid backwards." His embedded unhappiness was worsened by heroin and booze. He *had* backslid, personally, so much so that despite his warm visions of fatherhood, his absences from home and general grimness was a self-fulfilling propecy he himself had predicted back in 1971 when, the names of his as yet unborn children already picked out, he said, "I fear that when my child grows up, when little Ben or Sarah get to be 40, they'll live in a filthy world. They'll live; they'll survive. But the land will be dirty and the ocean will be putrid. The food they eat will be yeast."

Of course, he didn't know the half of it—that he would live to hear about the polar ice caps melting from greenhouse gases trapped in the atmosphere. What he did know in 1975 was that the world had slapped him down somewhat by reacting coolly to *Walking Man*, creating a crisis and a crossroads when he was ready to go into the studio again, something that gave him cold shivers. Again, he shut out Asher, turning to Russ Titelman, a onetime teenage protégé of Phil Spector who had worked in the Brill Building corral as a songwriter then back in L.A. as a guitarist on George Harrison and Lowell George sessions. Titelman then formed an alliance with his boss, the head of A & R Lenny Waronker, a real industry go-getter—his father, Si Waronker, was a concert violinist for the 20th Century Fox orchestra in the '30s who in 1955 founded one of L.A.'s hardiest independent record labels of the rock era, Liberty Records, of Eddie Cochran, Bobby Vee, and Jan and Dean fame. Apprenticing at Liberty, Lenny Waronker was subsequently hired by Mo Ostin, his main project being another scion—Randy Newman, whose father had played in the same Fox orchestra with Si Waronker. Now, after shaping Newman's wry, bitingly laconic slices of life, he and Titelman would have at Taylor, in something of a rescue mission, one that brought him back to the bosom of the Canyon. Their solution to his blues: more, better blues and R & B—that is, not just blended willy-nilly into the mix as on *Walking Man* but as the new James Taylor mien.

Kortchmar, Kunkel, and Sklar would be back, and Simon was there for backing vocals, as were David Crosby, Graham Nash, and Valerie Carter. Others included David Sanborn with his jazzy sax and Randy Newman on what was called a "hornorgan." The dates went down at Warner's own shop in North Hollywood, with additional sessions at the Burbank Studio. Tracks would be produced in a whirl, on a whim, with whatever sidemen were around; in all, there would be three drummers—Kunkel, Jim Keltner, and Andy Newmark—and Willie Weeks on bass. Another synthesizer, called the Solina String Ensemble, was used, along with real strings, mandolin, flute, clarinet, oboe, and harp. Nothing was left to chance.

The sessions ran through March and April 1975, with no wasted time. It took a visit to the Central Park Zoo, following what he said was "a fight with Carly," that gave him his theme—that of the highly metaphoric gorilla. The song with that title, and subsequent title of the album, borrowed from Simon and Garfunkel's "The Zoo," with Taylor skipping from literal ("He's got a nose like a doughnut") to figurative ("He rides my El Dorado"), making apelike noises along the way. While Taylor wrote all the tracks except for his bubbly cover of the Holland-Dozier-Holland's "How Sweet It Is (To Be Loved by You"), Marvin Gaye's biggest crossover hit until "I Heard It Through the Grapevine," and there was obligatory grousing—in "Angry Blues" he sang, "I can't help it if I don't feel so good"—one reviewer thought the songs "didn't seem to be about Taylor, or if they were, as in the extended metaphor of the title track, the connection was so oblique that it was hard to say what the point was." Actually, what came through most were his loyalty oaths to Simon, such as "You Make It Easy" ("Heaven knows I love my woman / Just bound to fuss and fight . . . You supply the satisfy and I'll supply the need") and "I Was a Fool to Care," in which he confessed:

Had I listened to the grapevine
I might have had my doubts
But I did my level best
Just to block them out
Cuz love is so unwise
And love has no eyes

It was all easy listening and lighter than air, acoustic guitar smothered in schmaltz ("Sarah Maria" and "Love Songs" were two more sonnets for his daughter, the latter attesting "I reckon I must be just an old softy / 'Cause I still believe in love"), synth-pop, and slow jams. Listeners would be left humming the vanilla-flavored soul of "How Sweet It Is," he and Simon in perfect tandem with each other and Sanborn's delirious sax, and the happy-feet melody of "Mexico," a meaningless song written on a short trip south of the border but lit up by a conga-seasoned, faintly Latin beat and chorus hook ("Oh Mexico, it sounds so sweet with the sun sinking low") again fattened by Simon—who was, it was clear, his best weapon now, a distinct property of his best songs. One could not have imagined Taylor would ever record a song as unabashedly optimistic as "Music," with its wish to "let the music fill the air" and put a "symphony inside you," or the string-coated acoustic bauble "Wandering," which he vowed never to stop doing.

Kick-ass, it wasn't. It wasn't rock, Lord knows, nor folk nor country. Yet, in retrospect, the album set the template for the postmodern James Taylor, the one the world would easily live with the rest of his career, but never really deem a rock *star.* And it was a more important work than it's been given credit for, because if one looks beyond the continued slide of Taylor down the rock ladder, his work here set a sonic tableau for romantic electro-pop that would come to brand the next decade and all soft pop since then. It was, as well, time-capsule fodder, the vocals on "Lighthouse," with its all-world chorus of Simon, Crosby, and Nash, the best proof that the harmonies of the '70s were what made the decade and the era what it was. It came out on May 1, its cover a photo not of a gorilla, alas, but of Taylor clad in one of those blasted white Gatsby suits—itself another subject of parody—and sandal-footed, dispensing advice comically to an invisible person (or maybe a gorilla).

His work done, he prepared for a tour to support it, not knowing if he'd get many big bookings. Then first reviews came in and he could breathe easier. In *Rolling Stone*'s notice on July 17, Bud Scoppa ventured: "Taylor is well on his way to staking out new ground. What he's hit upon is the unlikely mating of his familiar low-keyed, acoustic guitar-dominated style with L.A. harmony rock and the sweet, sexy school of rhythm and blues." Scoppa wrote that "You Make It Easy" was "the most overtly urgent vocal he's ever recorded" and concluded, "Taylor is too cool and contemplative to become the singer/songwriter sector's answer to Gaye but the influence has given Taylor new life by placing a healthy dose of happy eroticism (what's that about the sugar cane, James?) into the space vacated by his dark melancholy." Robert Hilburn's verdict was "*Gorilla* is a soothing beast . . . [his] best album in four years."

Released as the first single, "How Sweet It Is" hit the chart in June and ran to number 5 on the Hot 100, number 1 on the adult contemporary (the first since "You've Got a Friend"), number 1 in Canada. The angle that developed as sales began to take off, pushing the album to number 6 and, again, gold status, was that *Gorilla* was Taylor's "comeback" vehicle, one that reclaimed him from the has-been heap. Lester Bangs, in self-imposed exile, apparently couldn't bring himself to deliberate on Taylor any more, but Robert Christgau had an ambivalent grumble; *Gorilla*, he wrote, was "better than *Walking Man* [but] so is *The Best of the Cowsills*. Basically a solid piece of singer-songwriter product—I might actively enjoy 'Lighthouse' or 'Angry Blues' if someone else sang them, and I enjoy 'Gorilla' and 'Mexico' now. So why do his devotees regard it as a heartening comeback? Because its desecration of Marvin Gaye has propelled it into the top ten? Or because they never cared about his agonies or ideas either?" Indeed, if it wasn't hard to accept that Taylor was back on track, it almost strained credulity that the folk-rock demon had climbed to his feet again in a very odd guise: James Taylor, soul man.

Taylor, with some relief that his brand was renewed, had embarked on the new round of touring an album; a May gig at Carnegie Hall, with Carole King and David Crosby, was a highlight (a duet of him and King singing "You've Got a Friend" would appear on the latter's 1994 *A Natural Woman: The Ode Collection* album), and in the fall would expand to three months more of appearances. He finally had a new guitar, too, a custom acoustic beauty built by Mark Whitebook to replace his old Gibson, which would be placed in a case as if hermetically sealed, never to be discarded, and toted along on tours today with some dozen other guitars, more like some sort of voodoo amulet. He had no such talisman when it came to his marriage, though.

The Taylor-Simon union was always one step from going under. It was probably because everyone expected it any day that they toughed it out, or tried to, using the normal remedies of holding together a bad marriage. However, whether it was because of his endless heroin treadmill or because Simon had given his recording depth and purpose, in writing and studio actualization, he was now in a zone, songs springing to fruition. And with this resurrection, he would have yet more profound impact on the inner and outer layers of the music industry in its reformation from hot to cool, before the manic days of this splintered and self-centered decade would reach its finish line.

17

MOCKINGBIRDS

Tom Wolfe, as only a popinjay could, gave the '70s its identity when he wrote the August 23, 1976, *New York* magazine essay, "The 'Me' Decade and the Third Great Awakening." He didn't mention specifically the arts, but the poet-rockers, and a certain one in particular, could have been what he meant by those who "begin with . . . 'Let's talk about Me' [and] begin with the most delicious look inward; with considerable narcissism. . . . It's exhilarating!—to watch the faithful split off from one another to seek ever more perfect and refined crucibles in which to fan the Divine spark . . . and to *talk about Me.*"

When James Taylor recorded "Fire and Rain," he could never have imagined that West Coast soft rock would within a decade bloom into a monster that became too big to fail. It seemed the immediate sector of the music culture most taken with its connecting of personal sin with a forbearing Jesus were the restless country rebels of Nashville. Kris Kristofferson, for whom religious awakening was a salve for *his* drug and booze addictions, had written "Why Me" in 1972, echoing Taylor ("Lord help me, Jesus, I've wasted it so / Help me Jesus I know what I am") on what would be Kristofferson's only number one country hit as a singer, and two years later he rang in with "One Day at a Time," a song that has been recorded by some two hundred artists, with the similar refrain ("One day at a time, sweet Jesus / That's all I'm asking from you").

Of course, "Fire and Rain" would be covered nonstop itself. The British songbird Petula Clark, well into her forties and long past the swinging '60s and her "Downtown" prime, was one example. Seeing her perform it during a show at New York's Empire Room in 1975, John Rockwell wrote in the *Times* that it "was about the most extraordinary disjunction of singer and song this listener has heard in years." Increasingly, Taylor felt the same about himself. The song had come to represent to him a corporate albatross, an obligation of mercenary cynicism, something that was palpably worsening, the election of a humble Democratic peanut farmer in 1976 only a temporary wedge in twenty years of Republican rule. America was nearing the Ronald Reagan/"Greed is good" decade, and no one had to lecture men like David Geffen and Irving Azoff on *that* subject. Even if the Eagles floundered through the decade nearly drowning in drugs, internal dissension, and dissipation—they released a mere two albums over the last four years of the '70s, half of Taylor's output—the market ignored out of hand the critical stoning they took. When *Hotel California* came out in '76, the *Circus* review assailed it as "weary . . . loaded with sermons about Hollywood's rat race, and its gloom not particularly attractive. . . . I'm willing to believe these guys are trying. I'm just glad I'm not buying. Don't you become one of their statistics, either."

The album, of course, would be bought in ridiculous numbers, and if that wasn't enough the first Eagles greatest-hits package would go on to sell more than any other album ever made, save for Michael Jackson's *Thriller*. The Azoff blueprint of massive beer- and car-company-sponsored worldwide touring was being followed by high-visibility megabands like Journey, Foreigner, Rush, Boston, Chicago, Aerosmith, Kansas, Supertramp, Cheap Trick, and on and on. On the capitalist chain this was "corporate rock," causing so much revulsion that the movement to get back to the feral instincts of music began to gush with the unkempt three-chord rock of the Ramones, Television, the Voidoids, and the Sex Pistols. Lou Reed's David Bowie–produced *Transformer* mainstreamed transsexuality, drugs, and backroom blow jobs by "sugar plum fairies" and took "Walk on the Wild Side" into the Top 20. Out in L.A., meanwhile, former pornographer Frank Zappa's Mothers of Invention had back in the late '60s seeded L.A.'s underground scene. One of Zappa's circle, Kim Fowley, who abhorred James Taylor—but dated Kate Taylor for a time—would profoundly change the face of rock by founding the first all-female punk band the Runaways in '75, saying the impetus for such radical notions as punk and glam was "Taylor, saggy tits and granola."

Fowley, who sadly died as this book was being written, railed about "castrated hippies with no skin tone making music with no rock 'n' roll stink to it" and recalled in the present tense, as if it were still happening, "James Taylor sits on a stool and begets all kinds of men and women sitting on stools wearing overalls and flower-print dresses singing about Laurel Canyon dogshit." He would say, "I can talk about James Taylor all day and all night," and then do so, with streams of invective. In 1973, Fowley produced a glam-punk-*whatever* album under his name called *International Heroes,* his bizarre lantern face on the cover in Bowie-style makeup and lipstick. Reviews were mixed; but Fowley was particularly gratified by one that called the work "a more perfectly crafted exposition of love/sex than any of those whimpering folkies like James Taylor have ever presented." That alone made the effort seem worthwhile.

In the end, even if Taylor was indirectly responsible for sparking a new punk idiom that was Fowley's salvation, rock's Don Quixote never stopped grimacing about him. His requiem for the music that dominated the '70s was this: "It was horrifying and it wasn't rock and roll."

Taylor himself wasn't a granola eater, and saggies certainly weren't his thing—witness his missus—and not with all those sweet young perky things so available when away from home. And if the backlash wave in music believed they would write new rock-and-roll law, the reality was that all such offshoot idioms soon became a money stream in the corporate ocean. Furthermore, they probably knew that Taylor would outlive them all. In '75, with his comeback album putting him back in the game, he was in a groove, or in musician-speak, in the pocket, a phrase that seemed to fit his mood when he would go back in the studio in the late fall. Rather than brood in isolation, however, he now found himself *eager* to be on the road. As Kortchmar recalled of the routine, "We played mostly sitting down, but after that album was out we'd do a *show*—James would dance around and we'd open up the arrangements, let us all stretch out and make the best known songs breathe more. Before that, when James would go onstage, it was like his skin was on fire, with his eyes on his toes and an 'Aw, shucks' terror about the sets. Now we had fun."

With this élan, Taylor encamped in Warner's Burbank studio, again with Titelman and Waronker to oversee the production, with enough musicians to begin an army; over three months of sessions, thirty-three people would contribute in big or small ways to *In the Pocket*, including Simon of course, on four tracks; Art Garfunkel, Stevie Wonder, David Crosby, Graham Nash, and Bonnie Raitt on one each; as well as über–studio guitarists David Lindley (one) and Waddy Wachtel (two). Kortchmar would only play on two tracks himself, one on mandolin; Kunkel and Sklar, two; Doerge, one. Stevie, who had loved Taylor's Marvin Gaye cover, played harmonica on and cowrote "Don't Be Sad 'Cause Your Sun Is Down," an echo of "Brighten Your Night with My Day." Indeed, much of the album was guided by Stevie, who brought along Malcolm Cecil, his producer and inventor of the largest version of a Moog synthesizer the world has ever seen, which as he liked to clarify was a multitimbral polyphonic analog synthesizer. Looking like the deck of the Starship *Enterprise*, the unit, called "The Original New Timbral Orchestra" (or TONTO), was a key element of all those Grammy-winning '70s albums like *Innervisions.* Now, TONTO was put in service for the Lone Ranger of soft rock, on "Don't Be Sad 'Cause Your Sun Is Down," a classic Stevie plea for higher ground—"The night doesn't need your sorrow / Don't be sad 'cause the light is gone / Just keep your mind on tomorrow and carry on."

With so many influences, eclecticism was obvious in the material, with more of an edge to the sprightly soul of *Gorilla.* The range was such that the twelve tracks found common ground both in his and Garfunkel's duet on "A Junkie's Lament"—the first use of such a blunt term in a Taylor song title—and his and Carly Simon's harmonies on the unblushingly upbeat "Shower the People," in which he owned up to "playing the fool" for so long and sung about himself: "You can play the game / You can act out the part / Though you know it wasn't written for you." As Russ Titelman recalled, Taylor would come into a session brimming with ideas, some ingenuous, some nutty.

> He had all sorts of little inventions and ideas. His brain never sleeps or goes on hold; it's always fully occupied with *things*, not just related to writing songs but how to make them sound the way they do inside his head. When you work with James, you have to go deep inside his head

> with him, hear what he envisions for each song, each note, each bridge, and sort out the fanciful from the functional. It's a long trip sometimes—longer now, because he had so many more ideas and the technology is so much more advanced—but the journey is always worth it.

For "Shower the People," his brainstorm was to devise a sort of "voice organ," singing one certain note that would be transferred onto two twenty-four-track tape machines and sound like forty-eight notes; then, Titelman says, a technician at Warner Brothers, Al McPherson, constructed a keyboard to play the same notes. The result was the "shower" of ethereal rhythm heard throughout the song. Each song took a listener on a similar archaeological dig through chords that rang or were snubbed; even passages of silence and trailing echoes were planned down to the fractions of seconds. In the less ethereal area of commercialism, "A Junkie's Lament" obviously was designed to get attention. However, those looking to hear an updated confessional of his "Fire and Rain" demons would be let down; the narcotizing effect of Taylor and Garfunkel's tender harmonizing all but obscured fleeting references like "A junkie's sick / A monkey's strong / That's what's wrong" and "They wind him down with the methadone / He's all on his own." As well, the chorale's swelling fade-out, intended as a sad/happy funeral march/dirge, numbed the message altogether. There *would* be a reprise of his trademark phrase, in "Money Machine," but only as a put-down of his own place in the rock-and-roll rat race, channeling the Gamble-Huff-style syncopated soul of the O'Jays' "For the Love of Money," its lyrics spilling out:

When I began the game
See me singing 'bout fire and rain
Let me just say it again
I've seen fives and I've seen tens

Much of the album was like a checklist. "Slow Burning Love" was the slow jam, a hazy blend of synthesizers and high harmonies bathing another story of lost love dying "like the sun on the edge of the western sky." "Everybody Has the Blues" turned the funk, assuring, "Everybody gets to sit and cry / Everybody gets to wonder why." The long-way-from-home song was the effusive ballad "Daddy's All Gone," addressed to Carly and Sally, to whom he was "just the same old well-known stranger." The soul cover was "Woman's Gotta Have It," Bobby Womack's sweaty 1972 R & B number one hit, the white Southern boy trying hard to do some heartbreak testifyin'—"A good friend of mine / Told me to tell y'all what I say today." "Captain Jim's Drunken Dream" put him in his sailor's cap, singing "All I need is the sea and the sky . . . nearer my God to thee." The acoustic entry was the rolling "Nothing Like a Hundred Miles" (backed by Crosby and Nash), which was what he hoped to put "between me and trouble in my mind." The gospel stab was "Family Man," which suggested the theme song of *The Jeffersons.* The schmaltz was the closing track, "Golden Moments," a shimmering ballad yearning for that slice of heaven, its mantra-like hook:

No one's gonna bring me down
No one's gonna stop me now
No one's gonna reach me here
No one's gonna know I'm gone

It is striking how these tracks portended the feel of what would be '80s pop, an era of technical proficiency but little daring. This perhaps was not surprising, Taylor consciously following the path of Stevie Wonder, whose own progression from the most profound socially conscious songs of the '70s to saccharine pop in the '80s was fed by overuse of the synthesizer. Stevie's harmonica solo on "Don't Be Sad" was a dead ringer for the one he would play on the future middle of the road '80s megahit "That's What Friends Are For." The bigger problem for Taylor was that, aside from the blatantly commercial "Shower the People," he was perhaps a little blasé about what would be hit material in the '70s, *for him.* The album—with Norman Seeff's cover photograph of an angular Taylor seen from the rear against a white background, holding open one side of his sport jacket, the back cover a reverse shot of him facing front wearing a T-shirt with the cover of *Gorilla* on it, and a very crowded group shot of all the musicians on the inner sleeve—was released in June. Two months later, as it and "Shower" were scaling the charts, *Rolling Stone*'s Kit Rachlis (later editor of *The American Prospect*) clobbered *Pocket.*

Taylor must have wondered where Jon Landau was when he needed him, as Rachlis tore into the work as "a cool, impersonal, slick piece of work . . . a curious retreat behind the barriers of pop convention . . . a series of autobiographical ballads that rely on production tricks, inspirational songs in the form of Dear Abby bromides, and R & B send-ups that embarrass their sources [that] drip with wordiness and cliches." The hyped "Junkie's Lament" was, he wrote, its "principal failure . . . rife with platitudes, sung with all the commitment of a bounced check." Indeed, "he has failed to write a single memorable melody, and on a record that is more than 40 minutes long, the result is inevitable—boredom." The savage review, worthy of Lester Bangs, ended: "To say that a performer hasn't taken any risks has become the prime cliché of rock & roll criticism, but there is no other way to describe James Taylor's current failure. If *In the Pocket* were his first rather than his seventh album, it would hardly cause a ripple or receive a review of this length."

Taylor would overreact to this review, which laid him low for months as he questioned himself. In truth, the album was not nearly that wretched, nor a failure. Decades later, the AllMusic retro-review believed that Taylor "took on a surprisingly rough set of issues in his typically gentle style" and that the album was "a respectable effort for an artist who was evolving into more of a craftsman than a virtuoso." Because Taylor had gone firmly middle road, it wasn't entirely a slap that the LP only made it to number 16 on the album chart (his lowest ranking of the decade), and "Shower the People" to number 22 on the Hot 100, since the single rose to number 1 on the adult contemporary list (in the United States and Canada) and the album returned him to gold record status. However, when Warner released "Everybody Has the Blues" and it didn't make any chart, it went back to *Gorilla* for another single, giving "You Make It Easy" a shot. When that failed, it returned to *Pocket* for "Woman's Gotta Have It," which made it to number 20 on the AC chart.

Mo Ostin and his boys didn't know just what a bankable Taylor record was anymore. All they knew was that they had to have him around. Never did they think he would stray. But if his music was unpredictable, it was no more so than the man himself was.

On January 22, 1977, Taylor's second child was born, a son named Ben, just as he had said it would be, into the lousy rotten world he fretted about. The boy looked astonishingly like his father, and it was now that Taylor began to offer a half-hearted rationale for reforming his self-indulgent habits, for the sake of family. He reflected somberly to *Rolling Stone*:

> It gets to the point sooner or later where you start to think about your kids: "What does your daddy do for a living?" "He plays the guitar and he talks about his drug problems." It's embarrassing to read the drivel that comes out of your mouth sometimes. So I guess maybe the question is, why am I doing this [giving an interview] in the first place? And honestly, I suppose I'm doing it because I'd like to promote my record.

In reality, Taylor would spend scant time with his children, for whom Simon curtailed her own album tour duties, something easy enough for her to do with her stage fright, which did not keep her 1975 album *Playing Possum* (featuring Norman Seeff's cover shot of Simon, on her knees, a black negligee barely covering her behind, in black stockings and black high-heeled boots—the twentieth best album cover of all time, according to *Rolling Stone*) from going Top 10. Taylor gave much of himself to the album, on which Carole King also contributed backing vocals on the hit "Attitude Dancing." Taylor's vocals on the ensuing single "Waterfall" took it to number 21 on the adult contemporary chart, a market that for Simon, too, would become a nice sinecure. They were still a riveting couple. When he would go out on tour, he would make room for her on his stage, usually when he would call out "*Mock—*," at which point there would come a disembodied female voice singing "*yea-uh,*" then "*Ing—*," and "*yea-uh,*" then "*Bird*" and "*yea-uh,*" whereupon Simon would come wiggling onstage to finish "Mockingbird" with him, during which they would hold hands and do an awkward dance across the stage, to the rabid squealing of the crowd. To limit the competitive side of the union, they had a compact: there would be no gold records on the walls of their homes, no pictures of them in performance, no playing of their songs except when working out an arrangement for an upcoming session. Uneasily, they tried to keep their work out of their conversations and merely be husband and wife.

In '75, she had insisted, "I have trouble writing songs about James, or Sarah, or my married life. . . . I really don't know why. It seems so terribly terribly personal to me. It seems so terribly private. There's a part of my life which I do not want to invade for the commercial market. I've written many songs and poems about James which I wouldn't necessarily want to publish."

As for exposing the kids to his living drug hell, Taylor himself had come to the convenient deduction that any strides he had made in his songwriting, or even being able to write at all, was tied to the fact that he had gone back on heroin. However, that wasn't the half of it. Anyone can be trapped in the physical eddy of drug dependency and the loss of conductive reasoning. It was what he *never* spoke of that were the bigger threats to the family: his *voluntary* behavior, which spoke not to addiction but to disrespect and humiliation for his wife and children.

Despite his renouncement of adultery in "You Make It Easy," he had no intention of following through on it. The fact was, he was far more self-indulgent when he took other women to bed, or didn't come home at night, leaving Simon to wonder if he'd cracked up on the road for the last time—but more likely he was zonked out unconscious in some chick's bed. There were also his childlike temper tantrums and verbal abuse of her that alternated with bouts of stone-cold silence, when he'd go off in the snow in the dead of night. At first somewhat clueless about his habit—she thought it could be cured, "like a virus"—and then in denial about it, Simon was given a hard tutorial in the vagaries of living with a junkie. A possibly apocryphal story is that after she found a telephone number on a piece of paper one night, she dialed the number and a guy on the other end revealed that he was Taylor's drug dealer. Freaking out, she swore she'd "destroy" him for what he'd done to her man, whereupon the pusher told her, "Lady, if I go down, your husband goes down with me." Fable or not, many other moments and telltale signs made it evident he was back on smack. When she would confront him about it, he would tell her to fuck off, stop lecturing him, and insulted her looks and intelligence.

This then was the troubadour king, circa the mid-'70s, the sensitive and gentle artist whose shy and awkward veneer made women in his audiences swoon and weep. It was that persona that he was able to reanimate when he and Simon appeared together, did their little Virginia Reel onstage during "Mockingbird," and tried to make the world see how much in love they were. Talk about *mocking.* Away from the spotlight, both were finding new ways to piss off the other.

Don Grolnick told of "screaming matches" during sessions, noting that the Taylors were "two of the most obstinate people you'd ever want to meet." Simon for her part rubbed it in his face that she was having no trouble making hit records while he struggled, which naturally caused him to get more defensive. Everything they did seemed to accelerate a cycle of inevitable clashing. Worse, they knew well that they were living a fable that was a lie.

Despite this, any joint appearance by them was a happening. They did a TV sit-down on October 14, 1977, on the *Dick Cavett Show,* now a weekly discussion show on PBS, sans studio audience. Both seemed ill at ease, Taylor especially, fidgeting nervously in his seat. When they sang "Devoted to You," she gazed lovingly while he avoided looking at her even once, doing his shoe-gazing thing and remarking at the end, "A sobering sentiment." At least it was the way he sang it (he was more comfortable while performing "Secret o' Life," musing about its "pretentious title"). This somber appearance affected the usually glib Cavett, who didn't seem to know what to ask them. At one point, referencing that Simon had said she was the "unattractive" sister growing up, Cavett noted, "That's like saying Niagara Falls isn't wet."

"She's bloody moist, I'll tell you that," Taylor broke in, and she blushed at whatever that meant.

About the only time he sounded awake was when talking arcanely about music, such as that "Secret o' Life" had utilized a certain chord change—"from the A-major 7 to the B-minor 7"—that he said he had come to use so much that it was "a hereditary chord change," one he had been playing "over and over again" through the years.

Simon, who had teared up while he sang the song, remarked, "I was very touched and moved by your performance."

"Well thank you very much," he said, again fidgeting.

Cavett, ending on an obsequious note, remarked, "It's people like you who give marriage and success a good name."

That enough people actually believed this confirmed they were the perfect selfish exemplars of the culture they had exploited so well in their songs, while in truth they deserved the reputation they were acquiring for trying to out-crazy each other. When Simon's success began to slow, she began having seemingly paranoid delusions that David Geffen, after the Elektra-Asylum merger, was holding her back. Her theory, if it can be followed, went like this: Geffen, who before he came out of the closet years later boasted of how many female stars he bedded, including Simon, was doing Joni Mitchell, post–Jackson Browne, and Joni's resentment toward *Taylor* and her jealousy toward Simon led Geffen to pay back *Simon* with neglect and snide remarks. As she said, "There were several incidents in which I got my feelings hurt." Once, Geffen allegedly called her a "spoiled rich kid." Other jibes, she said, were "vitriolic."

According to a reported story, Taylor, who was one of the few L.A. rockers not under Geffen's thumb, advised Simon to hang tough, that Geffen would do more good than harm. But Geffen had actually quit Asylum in 1975 to become vice chairman of the Warner Brothers movie studio, not to return to the music business until 1980. Moreover, Simon had a lava flow of vinyl released all through the '70s, eight in all, two platinum, three gold. In '77 she sang the theme song for the James Bond movie *The Spy Who Loved Me,* "Nobody Does It Better," which went to number 2 on the pop and 1 on the easy listening lists, her biggest hit, earning two Grammy nominations.

But the silliness about Geffen was an indication that such conspiracies were ripe for assimilation in the minds of Mr. and Mrs. Taylor, who when they actually were together must have had some whacked-out conversations. No one doubted that these were two of the strangest people that could be found, even in Hollywood.

None of which mattered to their overlords. In 1976, a long-delayed Taylor greatest-hits package was released by Warner. Unable to acquire licenses for the Apple recordings, and having hankered for years to rerecord some of them in the intimate context they should have been at first, Taylor, with Peter Asher logically producing the songs he had not fully presented the first time around, recut "Something in the Way She Moves" and "Carolina in My Mind" at L.A.'s Sound Factory early in the fall. The album also included a live version of "Steamroller," the audience reaction fully bringing out its blues parody. The big hits were there, filled out by "Country Road" and "Walking Man." Released in early November, it repeated that same odd tendency for Taylor albums to jog rather than race up the chart; it climbed to number 23, stalled, fell off, then in August returned to it, its second go-around taking it to number 15. Refusing to leave for long, it would loiter on and off the chart for years, selling over eleven million units to date and going platinum an amazing *eleven* times. Even Robert Christgau's real-time review grudgingly admitted that "his voice you can get used to—it's soulful in its way, and he can phrase."

Few would have called him James Dean–ish any longer, nor ascribed him godly powers. Indeed, for some, he was still the Antichrist. *Melody Maker*'s take on *Greatest Hits* was:

> James Taylor has been responsible for inspiring some of the most pretentious crap that's ever masqueraded as music . . . signal[ing] a deluge of inarticulate, self-pitying singer songwriters obsessed with their own personal hang-ups. . . . "Fire and Rain" was—and is—a great song . . . and "Sweet Baby James," a work of significance. . . . Sadly, Taylor hasn't gotten within a mile of it since; in fact at times he's seemed of little more value than the wimps who followed on his heels. . . . Taylor produced nothing of note between 1971 and 1975. It's only comparatively recently—since Taylor dropped his traumatic self-examination in favor of less intense, more commercial, funkier music—that he's recovered some of the earlier impact.

Much of this was British hokum. The idea that the recent funky material could have revived the impact of "Fire and Rain" was preposterous, a good example of much of the critical hooey about Taylor—call it Ire and Disdain—and which never had a tangible effect on his staying power. Indeed, John Rockwell made a point to note that in the larger prism of the times, "Rock and disco are supposed to be at the center of the pop-music scene these days. But . . . the supposedly dying genre of introspective singer/songwriter isn't finished yet." The genre, though, and Taylor were in a different phase. By mid-decade he had stopped touring with Carole King. For her 1976 *Thoroughbred* album, he did harmony vocals on "There's a Space Between Us," but the tandem seemed old, and it would not be rekindled until both were capitalizing on the profitability of nostalgia for golden-year baby boomers. For King it would be a rough ride. Lou Adler went into movie producing. She divorced Charlie Larkey and married songwriter Rick Evers, with whom she cowrote songs for her first album for Capitol, *Simple Things*. But the LP, an ill-advised attempt to go disco, was a crime, named "The Worst Album of 1977" by *Rolling Stone.* Worse, Evers then died of a cocaine overdose, sending her into a tailspin.

Carly Simon's husband, meanwhile, was still pushing *his* luck with the same old heroin-methadone dance of death. Yet there were still some mighty powerful people around L.A. who wanted nothing more than to pay James Taylor a boatload of money to have him in their charge. One of those people was of course Mo Ostin. He had turned Warner Brothers/Reprise into a thresher, the arm-length list of top acts he had signed in recent years including Fleetwood Mac, Van Morrison, Neil Young, Randy Newman, Frank Zappa, the Grateful Dead, Eric Clapton, Bob Marley, the Eagles, ZZ Top, and Rod Stewart; later signings would bring John Lennon and George Harrison. Yet by '78, Warner was losing market share, most of its roster aging as punk and disco were cutting into rock's always most desirable demo—young buyers. Still, Ostin was adamant about re-signing Taylor when his contract ran out after the greatest-hits package was done, considering him a reliable earner even if he seemed more valuable in name now than in deed.

Ostin had no reason to think this wasn't a done deal. Taylor had become close to him and always said Ostin had made his career. Mo had never shorted him of funds nor attention, even when an album tripped up, and he believed in Simon, too, as her sire at Warner/Elektra/Asylum, not flinching when *she* bombed, a glaring example being "Waterfall," the second single from *Playing Possum*, which prominently featured Taylor on harmony vocals but went no higher than number 78 on the pop chart. Still, Ostin was no sugar daddy, and when for the reasons men like him generally do—because they *can*—he refused to not immediately renew the option on Taylor's contract, he outsmarted himself. He apparently had no clue that Peter Asher had another offer in his pocket, from within the Canyon fraternity of leprechaun-like scavengers. Over at CBS Records, the bombastic, bearded president and CEO, Walter Yetnikoff, decided he'd like to add Taylor to his own burgeoning rock roster.

A lawyer by trade, and CBS's general counsel, Yetnikoff had sprung into the industry rat race in the early '70s after Clive Davis was fired as CBS Records boss when it was discovered he had dipped into CBS coffers to pay for his exorbitant lifestyle, including a lavish bar mitzvah for his son. Yetnikoff, who already had homegrown rising stars like Billy Joel and Bruce Springsteen, and for more middle road tastes Barbra Streisand, had a battle plan to lure top acts from their labels, and perceived Taylor as a major linchpin. Yetnikoff was not without his enemies—this is the record industry, after all. But for Asher, the lovably crazy "Uncle Walter" was a most helpful ally. When Taylor's lawyer Nat Weiss confided in him that James felt neglected by Warner, believing all the play there was on Fleetwood Mac, Yetnikoff knew what to say: "Tell James I'll give his career my personal attention."

Weiss arranged a meeting with Taylor and, as Yetnikoff recalled, "We hit it off," rhapsodizing, "You had to like James Taylor. . . . He had that feeling-healing aura that calmed the most tumultuous soul, even mine. As a man, he had manners, charm, and elegance. In those days he also liked to get high." As did Yetnikoff, who would battle cocaine and booze addiction for decades until cleaning up in the 1990s with the help of a Catholic priest friend. He didn't explain what his reference to Taylor's addiction meant, but clearly it wasn't a disqualifier—has it ever been in this industry? In any case, Yetnikoff sweet-talked Taylor into an oral agreement, the details of which were worked out with Weiss and Peter Asher. By then Asher had turned against Mo Ostin. That happened when he told Ostin, "You need to renegotiate with us," and Mo replied, tartly, "No, we don't."

Neither had it helped Ostin that the absurdly tangled contract he'd given Taylor had not worked out well for the artist. The royalty-by-stock terms had seriously undercut Taylor's earnings. The advances and postalbum payments were good and, as with any act, touring proceeds went straight into his pocket, along with half of the publishing and writing royalties. However, he may have lost twice what he made when, as could have been predicted, the Warner stock fell from forty-four dollars a share to just seven—meaning that, now, making forty-four dollars meant making about a seventh of that in return. It was, he once told Tim White, "depressing to be at a company and making them a whole bunch of money and not making anything off these records." He had thousands of shares in Warner Brothers stock, yet after his accountants had gone over the books, he was told that he had no money at all from records sales. Literally zero, he said. By exiting Warner he would be able to sell off his Warner stock, every penny of it.

With this as backdrop, it didn't take much from Yetnikoff to steal him, even though Ostin lost his bravado and finally began negotiating with Asher, forcing Yetnikoff to escalate his offers to *three times* Warner's, $2.5 million a year for five years—Rolling Stones kind of bread. Yet, typically, Taylor began to feel guilty about jilting Ostin and Warner Records VP Joe Smith and got cold feet at the eleventh hour, when Mo became obsessed with keeping him. On the night the signing was to occur, at Weiss's New York apartment in mid-December 1976, Taylor and Asher were no-shows for hours, keeping everyone waiting and making Yetnikoff extremely impatient and surly. Not coincidentally, Ostin was flying in from the coast that night to make a last-ditch plea to Taylor. Finally, after midnight, Taylor and Asher showed up, both looking exhausted. Taylor, whom Yetnikoff describes as looking "ashen," said he *still* was undecided. Asher pleaded with Yetnikoff to keep his cool, that Taylor was going through hell. Yetnikoff asked why.

"The Warner people have been working him over," he said. "They've been lobbying him to stay."

"Tell those assholes the deal is done," Yetnikoff replied.

Now Taylor spoke up. "It isn't done, Walter," he said. "I have feelings about this."

Yetnikoff no doubt was less enamored now with the "feeling-healing" artist he had praised while pursuing him, but was learning fast how much such mercurial feelings meant to Taylor. While it was really Asher's job to be the one worked on and lobbied, not his client, Taylor felt a personal bond with Ostin. And, now, he seemed on the verge of tears having to choose sides.

"You have to respect James's feelings," Asher said. "It's a very big decision for him."

"What about *my* feelings," Yetnikoff came back. "We've been working this deal night and day. You're getting everything you want."

"I want my integrity intact," Taylor said.

"And that's what I'm buying—your integrity as a great artist."

"The Warner people helped make my career."

"And we're taking your career to another level. Look, James, this is no time for kvetching."

When Asher again interceded, saying he had told Taylor to take as much time as he needed to make a decision, the volatile Yetnikoff exploded, grabbing him by the collar and screaming, "Shut up, you redheaded English traitor!"

Still, Yetnikoff agreed to allow Taylor a walk around the block. Taylor, who Yetnikoff says was on the verge of tears, made for the door, turned around, and bowed, Japanese-style, to the CBS honcho. As Yetnikoff recalled the bizarre moment, "The gesture was neither gratuitous nor sarcastic. It was the gesture of a gentleman." An hour went by, then another. Up in Nat's place, a beyond exasperated Yetnikoff remembers telling Asher and Weiss, only half in jest, that Taylor would either sign the contract or "die by my hand." At around 3 AM, Taylor reappeared, still ashen and even more disheveled than a man should ever look. He walked to a table where the contract sat and signed it the only way he thought he could.

"I'm writing 'James,'" he said, but not 'Taylor.'"

It was fine with Yetnikoff. "Put an X if that makes you happy, but take the check."

He did both.

But still his guilt wasn't relieved. Walking on Mo Ostin played havoc with his conscience, giving him a few sleepless nights. However, cashing out his Warner stock cost him far more than he believed he'd lost—Asher, who sagaciously held onto his stock, enjoyed a windfall when the price again rose. Taylor, on the other hand, would say he "basically took a bath," estimating that, with the straight royalty, he had to settle for a puny forty cents per record. If one takes the *Greatest Hits* album as an example, sales of around eleven million copies to date (excluding another three million or so for worldwide sales) would translate to a return for Taylor of $4.5 million, maybe half that after taxes, much of which could be avoided on stock transactions.

Still, he had a new beginning. And the question was: Now what?

18

SPARKS IN THE DARKNESS

James Taylor by 1977 had already bent to several winds. He had done the panting folk, the MOR soft rock, the poppy-preppy soul. Others cast in his mold of personal confession were doing more ear- and gut-grabbing music amid the general din of soft rock and the empty clatter of corporate arena rock. Jackson Browne had overtaken Taylor as the main man of the Canyon, with a new way of folk rock with jazzier, louder hooks and no brooding allowed. Browne even made coke addiction sound bright and cheerful in "Running on Empty," the best autobiographical song ever written, which could have described Taylor's life as well, only where Taylor had walked down the road of life, Browne ran down it, blind, into the sun, always running behind.

Now, it seemed, *everybody* was admitting to far more than Taylor ever had in song; there were lines on the mirror (Eagles), too much coke and too much smoke (Lynyrd Skynyrd), and digging one's own grave with a silver spoon (Fleetwood Mac). Similarly, the alienation thing could not go much further, or do much better on the charts, than when Andrew Gold stepped out of Linda Ronstadt's shadow with "Lonely Boy," mimicking Browne's autobiographical journey; and Browne, in "Doctor My Eyes," also had a Taylor-esque slant, with a big beat:

Doctor, my eyes have seen the years
And the slow parade of fears without crying
Now I want to understand

Having cleared much of the underbrush for this sort of music, Taylor could not revisit it and hope not to sound like *he* was the thief.

As Browne sang, it was later than it seemed for him. Having looked into the future of music with his last two albums, he had probably neglected to look at the present, just down the road a little. But Walter Yetnikoff was a hands-on type of record boss and the two of them had long conversations about what CBS expected of him, which was a return to the essential Taylor, the one with the edge, with some more rock, not funk. It's unclear whether Yetnikoff brought up the touchy subject of drugs, a subject usually addressed within this drug-infected industry with a wink and a nod, but while Taylor still had no intention of cleaning up permanently, he certainly seemed more committed to work than during his periodic pullbacks from '72 to '76.

He was up to the task. Over March and April 1977 he and, at Yetnikoff's urging, Peter Asher went into Hollywood's Sound Factory studio, this time with not much more than his old core of Kortchmar, Kunkel, and Sklar, with Sanborn on sax, Clarence McDonald on keyboards, and David Campbell arranging strings. Carly Simon, Linda Ronstadt, and Leah Kunkel did backup vocals. With this streamlined operation, the work was done with far more dispatch than his last two albums, and he came out with a beaut of a CBS debut, titled succinctly and confidently *JT*. No pastiche this time, the material once again flowed in a cohesive stream. Seemingly effortlessly, he bridged idioms but without overstating the case. Track 1, "Your Smiling Face," was the old softie in him, the usual valentine to either or both Carly and Sarah, the smiles and pretty little pouting of whom could always convince that "no one can tell me that I'm doing wrong today."

According to Asher, however, *he* had to tell him that. When Taylor broke into a strained falsetto on the first take, Asher says, "I wasn't completely happy with it and I wanted to cut the track again, so we did it again and everything was great except that he didn't sing such great stuff at the end. I ended up taking only the vocal off that early take and dubbing it back in and trying to get it in sync. The early take turned out to be a little slower tempo, so I had to take little surgical incisions, little pieces of tape out between phrases so the tempo changed. It took a lot." Such is the hidden craft of producing that turns good music great, and people like Asher into millionaires—not that artists like to admit it wasn't all them—and may help explain why Taylor's records seemed to lack that little extra fillip without the little Brit behind the glass.

The lullaby song of *JT* was "There We Are," a gorgeous ballad with the strongest Taylor vocal he may have ever sung, its moods lurching and retreating, the piano and steel guitar blending bittersweet sentiments like:

Here we are
Sparks in the darkness,
Speaking of our love
Burning down forever and forever.

The rocker was "Honey Don't Leave L.A.," written by Kortchmar as a kiss-off to a French woman he had a fling with in L.A. who left him to go back to France. With Kootch letting loose with some delicious guitar licks and Sanborn's sweaty sax behind unabashed Jackson Browne–style vocals and yodeling, Taylor reveled in parodying something he never thought he would—being loyal to the place he detested most. There were, to be sure, moments of Taylor unrest; in the very sad Carole King–like "Another Grey Morning" might be the most telling thing he ever uttered—"She said 'make me angry / But just make me cry / But no more grey morning / I think I'd rather die,'" which one could easily imagine Carly Simon saying to him. "I Was Only Telling a Lie" was as down and dirty as he could get, his Don Henley–ish guttural vocal a convincing admission that too often his words of love were just that, a lie. The gushy ballad "If I Keep My Heart out of Sight" put his heart in competition with his cynicism that saying "I love you" only ruins a good thing ("You couldn't say no tonight / If I keep my heart out of sight").

What would really break out hardest was the least self-conscious track, his cover of Jimmy Jones's 1960 hit "Handy Man," a classic post-doo-wop hip-shaker ignited by Jones's falsetto, whistling, and scatting, that went to number 2 on the pop chart. Urged by Kortchmar to use it as his now regular soul tribute, Taylor slowed and stripped it down into an acoustically sensuous, hip-grinding ballad, his and Leah Kunkel's sharp vocals revealing the original, boastfully sexual intent of the song Jones and Otis Blackwell wrote that, in 1960, had to be fudged for the market. But the real message he wanted to spread was in another beautiful ballad, "Secret o' Life," an unapologetic toast to simple truths—the secret being "Enjoying the passage of time / Any fool can do it / There ain't nothing to it." However, typically, he didn't exactly say he *was* enjoying it; indeed, he judged that since we're all on the way down, and here only for a while, we "might as well enjoy the ride." This was about as optimistic as he could get, and another in that vein was "Looking for Love on Broadway," his requisite "lonely" song in which he declares he's "had my fill of self-pity." If only.

His "journey" song, "Terra Nova," cowritten with Simon, who sang a lovely solo on the break, told of burning off the haze to find what really matters: to "come home and stop yearning" for what wasn't there. A cathartic aside was Taylor's reach into the mists of the past:

I miss my lovely mother
And I love my lonely father.
I know I owe my brothers one thing and another
I hear my sister singing.

Even a throwaway track, "Traffic Jam," a sub-two-minute gospel-blues wail, the vocal semirapped and semigiggled, the last line having him "driving down the road to ruin," set toes to tapping. All in all, it was a fresh breeze, so honest in its affection for music of all shades that "Bartender's Blues"—which might have been meant as a send-up of Merle Haggard country barroom soul drowning, with lines about honky-tonk angels, lighting up smokes and laughing at jokes—would even make the country chart, a first for him, and he would later do a duet of it with George Jones. Released in June, the cover a black-and-white head shot of an earnest Taylor, not quite smiling, not quite frowning, *JT* had smooth sailing. The *Rolling Stone* review by Peter Herbst fawned that the work "illustrates Taylor's evolution rather neatly. . . . Taylor is actually a pretty convincing rock singer here." "Handy Man," Herbst wrote, "is a masterpiece of adaptation and singing" and the album "the least stiff and by far the most various album Taylor has done. That's not meant to criticize Taylor's earlier efforts—I'm a fan of even his most dolorous work. But it's nice to hear him sounding so healthy."

It would certainly wear well. William Ruhlmann's retro-review grades it the "best album since 'Mud Slide Slim & the Blue Horizon' because it acknowledged the darkness of his earlier work while explaining the deliberate lightness of his current viewpoint, and because it was his most consistent collection in years." And the brackish Robert Christgau's take was damn near a rave:

> James sounds both awake—worth a headline in itself—and in touch; maybe CBS gave him a clock radio for opening an account there. "Handy Man" is a transcendent sex ballad, while "I Was Only Telling a Lie" and "Secret o' Life" evoke comparison with betters on the order of the Stones and Randy Newman, so that the wimpy stuff—which still predominates—sounds merely laid-back in contrast. Best since *Sweet Baby James*, shit—some of this is so wry and lively and committed his real fans may find it obtrusive.

CBS, though it had bought a folk-rock giant, could not resist putting the clever "Handy Man" out as the album's first single, and was handsomely rewarded. It hit the chart in June and ran hard to number 5 on the pop chart the week of September 3, the same week it hit number 1 on the adult contemporary chart—where it would stay one week before being knocked out by . . . Carly Simon's "Nobody Does It Better," on its way to a seven-week run at the top. Indeed, Taylor was giving a lot of himself to his wife's work, in direction and sound, his vocals as integral to her as hers was to him, a key to her next two albums, *Another Passenger* and *Boys in the Trees,* on the latter of which they recorded a winsome duet covering the Everly Brothers' sugary "Devoted to You," repeating the alchemy of "Mockingbird," the song going to number 36 pop and number 2 on the adult contemporary list, a neat follow-up to Simon's first hit single from the album, the Top 10 pop "You Belong to Me."

Riding high with his own oldie cover, "Handy Man" itself remained on the Hot 100 for twenty weeks, longer than any other Taylor song. In the tunnel of time, the song, which today sits less than five thousand copies from million-selling status, would be indicative of how Taylor had tapped into his cover songs with a rare way of making them uniquely his. Another AllMusic retro-reviewer, Jason Elias, calls the tune "so laid back it's almost somnolent" but says that Taylor's unhurried version "has the benefit of allowing him to shade the words in new ways." It would also win Taylor his second Grammy, for Best Pop Male Vocal. Wasting no time to cash in further, CBS released "Your Smiling Face" in early fall, and by the winter it peaked at number 20, the best back-to-back chart performance he'd had. The LP, meanwhile, soared to number 4 and crept its way to becoming his biggest selling album, at 3.5 million to date, and being certified three-time platinum. It also earned him his second Grammy nomination for Best Album, though he (and the Eagles for *Hotel California* and Steely Dan for *Aja*) would lose to Fleetwood Mac's *Rumours.* (*JT* also lost to *Aja* as Best Engineered Album, though Peter Asher won for Producer of the Year.) Needless to say, Walter Yetnikoff was a contented man, every minute he had waited in Nat Weiss's apartment worth the return. As he would gloat: "I'd pulled it off. I'd acquired one of the premier talents in pop music. Columbia Records was richer for the acquisition. . . . Fuck Warner."

With albums flying out of stores and its songs constantly being spun on AM (the two hit singles) and FM stations ("Terra Nova" and "Secret o' Life" particular favorites), an extensive tour was scheduled. James Taylor was hip again. Even before *JT,* he had found a place in the quickly evolving culture when an opening episode of the second season of *Saturday Night Live*, hosted by Lily Tomlin, featured him as the musical guest. Between skits such as one depicting a debate between Gerald Ford (Chevy Chase) and Jimmy Carter (Dan Aykroyd) and Weekend Update "news" about Legionnaire's disease and crustaceans hijacking airplanes, he sang "Shower the People," "Sweet Baby James," and Junior Walker's "Road Runner." A fringe benefit—or perhaps not—of being around the cast of brilliant rogues for a week was that he established a kinship with the most brilliant and roguish of them all.

Actually, he already knew John Belushi, who also had a home up in the Vineyard but was introduced to Taylor out in L.A. Like seemingly everybody else the rotund, rubber-faced comedian was invited to one of Peter Asher's home soirees. Danny Kortchmar, who knew Belushi, a knowledgeable R & B buff, took him over to meet Taylor. After the two again bisected during rehearsals for the show, they began to meet up periodically: at clubs, at Belushi's apartment where he built a soundproof room for blasting his record collection at max volume, the Taylors' apartment, and around the Vineyard. Clambakes and beach parties included the Taylors, Belushi and his wife, Judy, and guests like Dan Aykroyd, who'd arrive on his giant Harley. Belushi of course would soon make the best statement ever about "sensitive" folksingers like Taylor without saying a word—when he smashed Stephen Bishop's acoustic guitar to smithereens in *Animal House.* But these two polar opposites had, besides a love of American roots music, one thing in common: intensely addictive inner mechanisms, something that worried Simon, who wanted James to keep a safe distance from the aggressively reckless comic.

Taylor that year had written three songs for Stephen Schwartz's much-honored but short-lived Broadway musical *Working*, "Millwork," "Brother Trucker," "Traffic Jam," and the music for "Un Mejor Dia Vendra" (cowritten with Matt Landers, one of the cast members, and Graciella Danielle). All dealt with the play's theme of finding a modicum of pride living with hopeless working-class drudgery, but it was the first song that became Schwartz's favorite number, a transfixing self-portrait through the tired eyes of a female laborer chained by life to her "machine"—"For the rest of the morning, for the rest of the afternoon, and the rest of my life." Taylor's own stark and plaintive performance of the song, which he retitled "Millworker," was an affecting throwback to the Woody Guthrie era of folk tales of the underclass and the scarred rise of labor unions. But, having agreed to the job at Yetnikoff's behest—the cast album would be released by Columbia—Taylor was tarred by the show being one of the all-time Broadway bombs, even though many critics singled his songs out for praise. Never one to take any pleasure from a failed project, he would not again moonlight on such ventures, saying, "I think I'll stick to what I do best . . . writing my own music and performing live." However, he had no compunction performing "Millworker," which has become an anthem of class inequality and union solidarity, covered by Bette Midler, Emmylou Harris, and Bruce Springsteen.

He did some touring over the summer, including a July gig at the Hollywood Palladium, and an extensive tour was scheduled for the New Year. But, again, Taylor couldn't keep himself in one piece long enough to keep things rolling. In February 1978, shortly before the Grammy presentations, he and the family were off on a vacation to Tortola in the British Virgin Islands when, cutting the meat out of a coconut, the knife slipped and slashed his left palm between thumb and index finger, severing a nerve. Even though it only required minor surgery, the lack of feeling in the hand made playing guitar impossible for almost a year, and kept him off the road for nearly two, since he refused to go out just as a singer. During this downtime, hunkering down at home or straying to secret hiding places, he worried that he might never be able to play guitar as well as he had.

Taylor's stunning defection, meanwhile, had enormous repercussions in the industry, touching off a war between his new and old labels, which took to raiding each other's rosters. Paul Simon, who had broken Stevie Wonder's seeming lock on the Grammys by taking the Best Album Grammy in 1976 (Stevie had won the previous two years) with *Still Crazy After All These Years,* was another of Ostin's acquisitions, and Simon so believed Yetnikoff was trying to ruin his career to exact retribution that he sued him late in '78. CBS would win the war (not that Ostin had to ask for any charity); not only would Taylor be a winner long into the future but Yetnikoff convinced Paul McCartney in '79 to give CBS the North American distribution rights to his albums, as well as hit the mother lode, taking Michael Jackson away from Motown, and his solo albums and collaborations with McCartney redrew the lines of industry profit.

Yetnikoff, like most everyone else, found Taylor to be a strange bird. Taylor had insisted when he signed with CBS that money wasn't the biggest reason for coming over. Yetnikoff, an effusive guy with his acts—the story he liked to tell was that he gave Billy Joel complete publishing rights to his music as a birthday present—wanted to give Taylor a bonus when *JT* and "Your Smiling Face" were big hits. One day he bought him an expensive lunch, then had his limo stop at a swanky car dealership. Taking Taylor inside, he grandly told him, "Pick any one you want." Taylor said no thanks, that the wheels he'd just bought—an old former taxicab, a big yellow one, just like Joni Mitchell sang about—were good enough for him. He would tool the streets in Manhattan, sometimes stoned, and people would even try to hail him! One of his friends said it was something out of a Cheech and Chong movie, not the first time his life seemed to be. Far more edifying for him than a fancy gift was that Yetnikoff signed Kate Taylor, who hadn't recorded since '72 and like the other siblings was fading. James was so intent on justifying the signing that he spent months producing and backing Kate on her eponymous 1978 CBS album, a flavorful stew of folk, rock, and soul for which he wrote the song, "Happy Birthday, Sweet Darling." He was delighted to no end that she had a Top 50 pop hit with her cover of the old Betty Everett 1964 evergreen "It's in His Kiss (The Shoop Shoop Song)."

To those who knew him, his strangeness was a mark of his singularity and head-in-the-clouds artistic obsessions. But the elephant in the room, as it was with a good many rockers, was what was never spoken about in the circles he ran in—his addiction. This was surely how Taylor wanted it; that way, it was always up to *him* to talk about it, with the appropriate disclaimers that he was off the stuff, for good now. It was good enough for Yetnikoff, who for years was slowly killing himself with booze and drugs and wouldn't clean up for another two decades. All that really mattered to his new overlords was presenting them with another album like *JT.* As with following *Sweet Baby James,* it was a tall task. After another long gap—his last single, "Honey Don't Leave L.A.," had come and gone a year ago, reaching number 61 on the pop chart—he returned to L.A. in February 1979 to convene at the Sound Factory studio with Peter Asher and his newest posse, including engineer Val Garay, Kortchmar, Kunkel, Sklar, Schuckett, Grolnick, David Sanborn, David Spinozza, Waddy Wachtel, and pedal steel master Dan Dugmore. String arrangements would be charted by the incomparable Atlantic Records producer Arif Mardin, with backing vocals by Simon, Alex Taylor, Graham Nash, David Lasley, and Arnold McCuller.

The album would be titled *Flag,* one of those abstruse Taylor references one would need to look to the cover of the album to decipher—though it's possible even *he* had no clue that the stark geometric pink and yellow flag pattern was, according to the international maritime code, telegraphy for "man overboard," since he would explain away the cover as a simple, undefined "personal statement" that he "ran up the flagpole." To be sure, given the eventual content, there were other flag designs that would have worked just as well as semaphores, including "Negative," "Keep clear of me, I am maneuvering with difficulty," "I'm dragging my anchor," and "I wish to communicate with you."

He wasn't exactly drowning, that was obvious by his huge comeback and scads of CBS's money. But there seemed to be a distress signal coming from many of the album's cuts, and the songs he closed out the '70s with were not nearly as happy, soulful, or carefree as those on *JT.* Indeed, he decided to rerecord "Rainy Day Man," one of his first compositions about heroin. And the two songs he included from

Working also set the tone for an earthier, more earnest work, his voice not soaring but more labored, grabbing for some of that old intimate emotion. Track 1, "Company Man," a duet with Simon of varied tempos, could have been about Yetnikoff or Ostin, or all record bosses who had enriched and complicated his life, warning prospective artists, "If there's something you do well / Something you're proud of / Better to save some for yourself / If that's allowed." As he would say of the song, it "couldn't have made the record company very happy," though just what sort of exploitation he was suffering with that $2.5 million deal wasn't quite explained. Wading into murkier waters, "Johnnie Comes Back" was perhaps his darkest and certainly sickest parable about drugs, centrally about, as he said, "some guy who gets a little girl off the street strung out so she'll keep coming back . . . a seedy little love story." The lines were fearless—the girl "Always comes back for more / Hanging her head and banging my door [saying] Johnnie be good / 'Please give me some medicine man.'" His aside that "My God, she must despise me" was a thin mask, on some level an admission that he despised *himself*.

He had reached a crossroads with songs like these. Before, they were always about *him*. Now, reality was inverted, transmuted to fictional characters. Asked in 1979 if he was tired of writing about himself, he answered, "Yeah, I think perhaps I am. I think I probably just about covered it . . . or else I filled whatever need I had to write about that kind of stuff." But that was pure conceit; whatever he wrote was in some way about himself. In the punchy "I Will Not Lie for You" he put himself in the shoes of a friend who will no longer cover up his misdeeds and betrayals of friendship and love. "Brother Trucker," his paean to the big-rig drivers cruising the highways hopped up on pills and making their own rules, had a rich harmony vocal by Alex Taylor and, aside from the gauche CB lingo, gathered momentum as rock and country jam, its hook repeating, "Roll, roll, roll brother trucker."

There was the obligatory bluesy throwaway, "Is That the Way You Look," a romp through the remains of doo-wop, and the sugarplum filler "Chanson Française," sung entirely in French. Yet even the "lullaby" song was a minefield. This was "B.S.U.R.," his tribute to the playful literary devices of *Shrek!* creator William Steig's children's books/puzzle games *CDB!* and *CDC*, in which letters and sounds were guessing games as to the meaning of a phrase. This was a format also long used by soul/funk singers like Sly Stone in songs like "Thank You

(Falettinme Be Mice Elf Agin)," though the mainstream media would usually anglicize it in print. However, "B.S.U.R." needed no guesswork: it was an obvious pin prick of Carly Simon. As bizarre a pair as they were, public pissing matches like these had the *approval* of the other party; he would insist, "I don't take it seriously," that putting "business on the street" and "messing with someone" was "a risk you take in a relationship." Thus, when Simon recorded one of *her* indictments of *him,* "Fairweather Father" ("Wants his wife to be the truck driver / Wants his wife to be the gardener / And still look like a Hollywood Starlet") Taylor sang backup, as did she on "B.S.U.R.," shorthand for "Be as you are, as you see as I am I am" (thus the parenthetical addition to the title, "S.U.C.S.I.M.I.M."). But if his point was that deprecation (e.g., "trying to take control / watching every little thing I do") and admitting that they were "Strangers at this masquerade / Pretending to know each other" could only strengthen the marriage, then the song rightly should have been called, simply, "B.S."

Again, it was the relief—or at least *putatively* so—from the dark side that would serve him best, even if this too seemed to perpetuate his suffering. His first-ever Beatles cover, "Day Tripper," led his gritty vocal to break into a harsh, jarring falsetto—a grudging concession to disco, arguably the most depressing moment of the album. More notable was his ornate version of Carole King and Gerry Goffin's "Up on the Roof," which she had pulled out of mothballs on her early *Writer* LP, with Taylor on guitar. He had sung the song acoustically as far back as his 1971 Fillmore East gig and with King at her Carnegie Hall show in 1971, and now put his stamp on the immortal 1962 Leiber and Stoller–produced Drifters hit, in which beleaguered men could claim a small piece of land—high up on a big-city roof—to flee jobs that kept them in servitude (which out of black singers' mouths gave it a mildly racial element; that those who most needed such escape were black men). Taylor's take was racially neutral, its mounting swirl from acoustic calm to stirring orchestral pomp bloating the simple premise into a Broadway-style schmaltz-fest of paradise lost, existing only in the memory.

That was in line with the album's cri de coeur of very little to live for in the present. The closing track, "Sleep Come Free Me," was jarring. Taylor had written it after a terrifying incident when, blitzed out on angel dust, he recalled, he "blacked out a whole rampage of awful behavior," most of which he couldn't remember, though he could recall biting a large hole in a friend's guitar. Written in the guise of a killer on death row in Alabama who had committed murder during a blackout rage, it was a pained and painful wail for relief or, perhaps, death, its last grooves fading out with eerie chants of "*Pleeeeease* set me free," and the unsettling sound of a door being slammed shut, lock bolted.

If Yetnikoff had wanted from Taylor a rebranding of his old grim self, he soon realized that with these songs James had buried himself in unexplained depression and anger. Fortunately, Taylor had given himself some wiggle room with "Up on the Roof," and with no serviceable single fodder among the brooding tracks, "Roof" and *Flag* went out in May without great fanfare and with the sense that chart rankings were now insufficient to judge the value of the man. Stephen Holden, in reviewing *Flag* in *Rolling Stone,* put his finger on the new nature of Taylor songs, their darkness not titillating but an honest discomfiture of his aging generation. Wrote Holden:

> The James Taylor who gazes out from the gatefold of *Flag* is an emaciated, jaundiced Yankee eccentric glaring at us with cold, eagle-eyed skepticism. The picture is almost the negative of the movie-star-glamorous photo on the cover of *JT*. . . . But the aesthetic shift from last year's debonair to this year's dour isn't just a gimmick. Whereas the material and tone of *JT* suggested a similar mellowing of Taylor's personality, *Flag*'s thorny songs and hard, tense arrangements bear witness to the stark and piercing artwork. . . . [It] peels away the glamor to expose the flinty marrow of a hostile stranger . . . a grim self-portrait of a chronically depressed man with a monkey on his back, as Taylor relentlessly accumulates correlatives to his own despair. [His] beautiful version of . . . "Up on the Roof" is also the saddest ever recorded.

But if this seemed like the predicate for a pan of a review, Holden segued, arguing that the work was "exquisitely crafted," and that Taylor's voice "never sounded better," adding that the songs were "as evocative an exploration of one strain of the American character—the Puritan sensibility under extreme stress—as pop music has yet offered." He concluded: "*Flag* is the aural equivalent of an Andrew Wyeth painting: austere, meticulous, its palette the color of cracked, dried mud. . . . With Bob Dylan in decline, James Taylor has risen to become the foremost vocal exponent of Appalachian folk and Southern blues classicism."

No question, Taylor was now in rarefied air, able to summon up all the cool literary and pop culture references a happening critic could think of—or continuing scorn. Robert Christgau's verdict was much briefer and less academic. His review read: "What's wrong with most of these songs is that Taylor is singing them. He can sing, sure—the 'Day Tripper' cover and 'Is That the Way You Look' show off his amused, mildly funky self-involvement at its sharpest and sexiest. But too often the material reveals him at his sharpest and most small-minded; John Lennon might get away with 'I Will Not Lie for You,' but JT's whine undermines whatever honesty the sentiment may have." The AllMusic retro-review relegates it now to scrap, as "pointless," "inconsequential," "a hodgepodge," and "a snooze." The consensus in real time was somewhere in between. But it wouldn't be the critical reaction that proved if rock's Andrew Wyeth could still move records. It was the ever-evolving music audience.

By late June, the single and the album were running up charts that were now dominated by disco songs—Donna Summer had two in the Top 5, "Bad Girls" and "Hot Stuff"—leaving "Up on the Roof" to climb highest on the adult contemporary list, peaking at number 7 for four weeks in late June and early July, when the top spot was held by Anne Murray's "Shadows in the Moonlight," then Maxine Nightingale's "Lead Me On." By July 28, "Roof" was ebbing, having risen to number 28 on the pop chart, and *Flag* to number 10. The album would sell its million and go platinum. But the numbers were an augury of where James Taylor stood at the end of the decade: still bankable—even if Carole King had to rescue him again—but now, disco had its own Top 80 chart and "hot soul singles" was the chart to watch. Taylor's niche was the demographic that had gone from marches to Muzak in ten years. And if not overly solicitous of his tormented visions, his fans were still unable to keep from laying down a few bucks to slap it on a turntable or in a cassette player.

Taylor was still a hot property. On May 12, he was back as the musical guest on a *Saturday Night Live* episode hosted by Michael Palin, the one with the classic "Raging Queen" sketch, with John Belushi captain of the all-gay ship on its journey to "Mykonos, Kronos, and San Francisco!" and Dan Aykroyd, as Jimmy Carter, presenting the "Boulevard of Proud Chicano Cars." The show was—just like Taylor—moving toward the end of its golden era, with Belushi and Aykroyd soon to join the already departed Chevy Chase as full-time movie stars. Taylor sang "Johnnie Comes Back," "Up on the Roof," and "Millworker" preparatory to going out, backed by the Section—Sanborn, Grolnick, Wachtel, Lasley, and McCuller—on a six-week, seventeen-city summer tour, with stops in L.A.'s Greek Theater, Berkeley's Greek Theater, and Madison Square Garden. He would also reappear in the pages of *Rolling Stone*, in a September cover story interview with Peter Herbst, his steely blue eyes glaring on the cover and a two-page spread on the inside of him shirtless, staring blankly as a pair of shapely female legs and arms *not* Carly Simon's wrapped around him, a blurb beneath the image reading, "I wanted to perform, I wanted to write songs, and I wanted to get lots of chicks," his original reason for going to England, a mission surely accomplished.

But, being James Taylor, he was not without the usual fears and insecurity. He admitted it had made him a little crazy to read Kit Rachlis's now yellowed *Stone* rip job of *In the Pocket*, which he said had "really changed my opinion of the album. . . . It sunk me, and I've decided two things about critics since then. I've decided that it's not worth my while to read them until somebody tells me it's okay to read them. And the other thing is that it's okay for people to not like what you do. It's okay to put out an album that nobody likes at all." If that was a reach, so was his latest suggestion that his drugged-out, depressed days were done. "I'm not saying I'm depressed, because I've learned to deal with that largely. My tendency is to crawl into a hole and poison myself, intoxicate myself." But, "my family—not only the children, but Carly—has moved me away from the way I used to deal with it, which was my completely overtouted drug problem."

Taylor was highly skilled now in the art of deception about this subject; while not *saying* he was off drugs, the inference was couched in careful language that a politician could envy. For example, he said he had "gotten off methadone in '74" and that "I've been careful to make it work for me" ever since, whatever that meant. Other bromides included, "If I wanted to get really drunk and all fucked up, I'd have to worry about whether or not I would hear the baby crying if it fell out of the crib." And, "I'm not saying that I'm free of all my problems, because there's always that temptation, and some people say that it may even be hereditary [but] I think that a jump rope can be as helpful to a depression as two years on methadone maintenance or five years in psychotherapy." Performing, too, was a prophylaxis; among his preparations for a tour was "no smoke, no coke," one reason why his voice was always so pristine. What about *after* a tour? He forgot to say.

He was, as well, quite adept at the art of the self-put-down, claiming it was harder than ever for him to write, even focus, now, that he could never write another "Fire and Rain," given his "complacency," and moreover, had grown rather bored with himself: "I've written a hundred songs . . . and I think that's a lot of songs. A lot of them are repetitive and a number of them are lightweight. . . . I was gonna open this tour with 'Blossom,' but 'Blossom' sort of bothers me. It seems so floral, so cute. Actually there are so many songs that came after it in that mode that are really a drag."

If so, it was this unsettled, gnawing unease that would keep him writing and performing for the next four decades. Indeed, that he suffered for his work was, he admitted, partly why the competitive nature of his marriage had caused "tensions" between himself and Simon, tensions that might not be worth the grief.

"Maybe I shouldn't be out here trying to rock and roll for the people anymore," he mused. "You know, I've got a wife, I've got a couple of kids, I'm getting older. I'm not a country artist. Maybe I can't do this forever. I used to think of the age of thirty-five as being the cutoff point. But I don't know if that makes sense or not."

For all their private turmoil and mutually assured destruction, the Taylors were still the couple most likely to make people agog. It was always an electric moment when they were seen together, such as when Vineyard residents were up in arms in 1980 that a McDonald's was going to open there. Suddenly forgetting his working-class sensibilities on *Flag*, Taylor and Simon were aghast that the delicate beauty of the seaside town would be spoiled. Then, too, Hugh Taylor, now married and a father of two (his son named Isaac), had forsaken music to get into real estate in the Vineyard, where Kate and Livingston were also raising families. Isaac Taylor, too, was not far away, living in Boston and at the Vineyard with his new wife, Suzanne Sheats, a much younger woman and a lawyer; despite his heavy drinking he was a dutiful husband, siring two more sons and a daughter. He was, as well, director of the Boston University Medical Center, in addition to his continuing role at the UNC medical school back in Chapel Hill. Chapel Hill was where Trudy Taylor remained, but even she would soon complete the family's renunciation of Carolina and move permanently to the Vineyard as well. Thus, property values were much on James's mind. Notwithstanding the jobs the fast-food joint would provide for less-than-rich denizens, he and Carly actually consulted Tom Hayden, the former "Chicago Eight" activist who, with his wife Jane Fonda, was in their L.A. circle. On Hayden's peculiar sense of what "people power" meant in this case, they went door to door gathering signatures from their wealthy neighbors, vowing to boycott the restaurant should it open. When the corporate giant surrendered, a huge party was thrown at their home, where the swells celebrated victory over the encroaching Big Mac empire.

At such events, and of course in public, Simon was always the one who grabbed the attention, which despite Taylor's insistence that he was no party animal, began to bug him, especially since her recording output was greater than his, even if she too was seeing uneven chart rankings—her 1979 LP *Spy* barely crept into the Top 50 and *Come Upstairs* a year later, her first of three albums for Warner, was only marginally better, at number 36, though it did spawn "Jesse," mercifully, a non-Taylor-related song that ran to number 11 on the pop chart. She was also giving her own interviews, and seemingly digging into his ego and sexist impulses, such as saying that he was the type whose idea of womanhood was having his wife stay home and "bake pies." She wanted to come off as merely rakish, but Taylor felt the bite of such words. He knew he was no bargain; he could be a real prick, given to what he called "black moods . . . a type of despair that I experience as being very deep." He credited Simon for coping with it, acceding when he would tell her to "answer the phone for me" and "ask her for some reassurance. And she's good at that; she's very supportive. She's also subject to phobias and anxiety attacks. . . . But we can be relatively supportive of each other." He seemed to pity her—but then he *had* to, openly, knowing his market base was women.

"Carly's having a rough time right now," he said. "She feels hurt and disillusioned, and I don't blame her," he said. "It's harder for her to do it without many other outlets, and also feeling . . . much more restricted by family life and raising children than I appear to be."

But when he would read a Simon interview in, say, *People*, he'd throw the magazine down with an expletive. Their friends could feel the bitterness growing. Taylor did not seem to object to the continuing A-list status he had. He also was serious—in his own limited way—about having two young kids to raise, but seemed to have a phobia of giving too much of himself and his time even to his family. Heroin, on the other hand, he always had time for, even after one of his endless promises to Simon to go to rehab, for real. Simon apparently was going out of her mind trying to raise the kids with him coming in and out, sometimes late, late at night with people she did or didn't know, all of whom were as jacked up as he was. One time, according to Jacob Brackman, Carly walked into the living room to find James and Betsy Asher snorting coke—his own manager's *wife*, at a time when Peter Asher was insisting on shutting down Taylor's drug use. (Whether or not related to any of this, Asher would divorce her in 1983.) Simon, who was at her wit's end, recalled that "in not knowing *how* to help, I became even more helpless and foolish and more of a deterrent to his stopping," given how he turned on her whenever she would issue ultimatums.

Simon went through their houses and apartments daily on bloodhound hunts for drugs, flushing whatever she found down the toilet. She tried to preserve her sanity by spending most of her time living with the kids in her sprawling twelve-room Central Park West apartment, keeping their distance from his rustic digs up at the Vineyard or the rented house out in Beverly Hills. When he was home, things could get hairy. Despite Taylor's oft-stated aversion to being a party animal, there were more than a few at his house, which friends describe as "wild." One attendee told of seeing "a couple openly fucking on their kitchen floor" and said that "there was always a lot of drugs." If so, that would have made Simon a hypocrite, even if she didn't join in on the drug rituals, just for allowing these shindigs to happen in her presence. Regardless of fault, it was all sick and twisted, and the only question now was how much they could hurt each other before she lost her sanity, or he his life.

In rock, it seems, all things come full circle, as Taylor would find out, long down his October road. In the last year of the decade, Lindsey Buckingham, who had cut his guitar teeth on the banjo of John Stewart in the '60s and then had ascended into the rock elite with Fleetwood Mac—extending tattletale rock to a group dynamic of intraband amour and dissolution—repaid Stewart by playing that funky bluegrass folk guitar on Stewart's only hit as a belated rock star, "Gold," in '79. But even now, a decade older, James Taylor was still on the A-list, and always up for a spot on a big protest venue to help make the case he was big time. With Vietnam now a rotting memory and Bangladesh apparently fed, rock centralized around one big cause: antinukes. Taylor, having been there at the forefront of that chic movement, at Amchitka in 1970, immediately signed on to the roster of acts that would stream through five Musicians United for Safe Energy (MUSE) concerts at Madison Square Garden in New York City in September.

These concerts would form a triple-LP album released in December—the final Taylor product of the 1970s—and the 1980 Warner Brothers documentary *No Nukes,* distinguishing the careers of Bruce Springsteen, Jackson Browne, Graham Nash, John Hall, Bonnie Raitt, Tom Petty and the Heartbreakers, the Doobie Brothers, Poco—and Mr. and Mrs. James Taylor, whose duet/dance while performing "Mockingbird," Simon in a form-clinging striped pantsuit, was a standout moment. For Taylor, who also sang "The Times They Are A-Changing," "Honey, Don't Leave L.A.," and "Captain Jim's Drunken Dream," and harmonized with John Hall on the latter's "Power" and with the whole entourage on the Doobies' "Takin' It to the Streets"—another, "Stand and Fight," would be in the film—it served as a delayed rebuttal to Raitt's complaint about him withdrawing from political consciousness, though in truth, this was the only cause that he was willing to embrace, saying, "I'm into the nuclear thing because it's so clearly insane."

Looking at the film, one could almost sense liberation in the man's voice and body language. Here was a Taylor supremely self-confident and satisfied with where he was in the rock sphere. On "Takin' It to the Streets," he seemed almost joyous to let go of his inhibitions and vamp wildly on the chorus; missing a cue to take his turn on a verse, when John Hall begins, he sheepishly hastens to the microphone and bangs out, "Wherever *peeee*-pull live together," in a breathier, more muscular vocal than he ever sang. Taylor would single out Michael McDonald as a singer he wished he could sing like, as close to soul as a white man could sing. But Taylor hadn't done badly in that idiom, either. And Michael McDonald could not have sung country or folk anywhere near as convincingly as Taylor did soul.

In an objective light, in fact, James Taylor had done enough by the end of the 1970s. Of everything. More than enough, making what was to still come perhaps parenthetical but always intriguing and sometimes important, although at best really an epilogue to the dizzying twists and turns of the decade that—whatever else can be said about it—certainly had an overarching identity thanks to him. He had a long way to go still, but would stay essentially the same artist, the same guy, with improvements both major and minor, but now having earned a deep and significant niche of his own. In the long lens of history, James Taylor's past would now be prelude to trends that would again shape the music and cultural landscape. If he wasn't going to be the main man, he'd still be wise, old, brilliant JT. And it would be reassuring to know that, if nothing else, he was simply *there*.

19

NEVER MIND FEELING SORRY FOR YOURSELF

James Taylor began the 1980s by winning another Grammy, or at least sharing in it—not for disillusioned angst but unspoiled adolescent fantasy. The first recording he made in the new decade was a pet project by Carly Simon's sister Lucy, who had sold Warner on the concept of getting various popular artists to write and record children's songs, aided by Jim Henson voicing his lovable Muppets, and had recruited some big-name acts, some of the biggest in her own family. Kate Taylor, who that year also recorded an album in Muscle Shoals, wrote and sang with all the other Taylors the title song for the work, *In Harmony: A Sesame Street Record*. Livingston did "Pajamas"; James, "Jellyman Kelly"; Simon, "Be with Me"; others featured included Linda Ronstadt, the Doobie Brothers, Bette Midler, Al Jarreau, Dr. John, George Benson, and Libby Titus. The album did not sell well but reeled in the Grammy for Best Children's Recording, and a sequel would come a year later.

It was a breath of relief for James Taylor, who was facing an uncertain future with conflicting signals. Almost eerily, the man who gave the '70s its sweet and low flavor began the '80s by having a brush with the crackpot who further stilled the '60s, not with song but a bullet to the chest. On December 7, 1980, Taylor, who had given up the Hollywood house and taken an apartment on Manhattan's Upper West Side just for himself, was in the West Seventy-Second Street subway station when a meek-looking guy with glasses recognized him. As Taylor recalled, he "pinned me to the wall, glistening with maniacal sweat, and tried to talk in some freak speech about what he was gonna do, and stuff about how John was interested and how he was gonna get in touch with John Lennon." He thought little of it, having been buttonholed by many oddballs, until the next night when the world learned Lennon had been shot and killed just down the block in the courtyard of the creepy Dakota apartment building on Central Park West by a drifter named Mark David Chapman—the same guy who intercepted him in the subway. Taylor was shaken. "It was surreal to have contact with the guy 24 hours before he shot John," he said, knowing that Chapman, who spoke with Lennon the day before, too, was packing the same weapon he'd use the next day.

That was how fickle life was; Lennon, on an upward path, was taken away. Meanwhile, Taylor's life continued to crumble. That summer, his son Ben, sickly since birth, became sick, his weight shriveling and his body weak and feverish. Simon took him to several doctors who insisted he was fine, a diagnosis shared by her husband, whose response to her doting on the boy was to say, "Leave him alone!" But he grew sicker and weaker, and after James made a rare call to his father to discuss it, Ike called the best pediatric doctors he knew and arranged for one at Columbia Presbyterian Hospital in New York to see Ben. That's when the problem was found: a dysplastic, or abnormally formed, kidney, which was putting strain on his other kidney.

He needed delicate, risky surgery to remove it, but during the unbearably tense and frightening hours he was in surgery, his father wasn't there because he was driving his latest plaything, a Japanese dancer named Evelyne, to the airport. Simon, trying to keep it together for the sake of her son and her sanity, was furious. Eventually James arrived, but as if too scared to face his son's life and death ordeal, he sat on some stairs outside the hospital, alone, zoning out, a pitiful, forlorn figure. When Carly's manager, Arlyne Rothberg, saw him and began screaming at him to go upstairs, "he didn't react to anything I said."

Eventually he snapped out of it and was at Ben's bedside when he awoke, the surgery a success. As he recovered, both parents made an effort to put their bickering aside while tending to him. But the artificial comity was short lived. After that horrible chapter, Simon was beyond the reach of any of the horde of psychiatrists she had turned to for help—as had Taylor years before deciding that they were of little value. It quickly became all too clear that even the peril of their child wasn't enough to resolve all the resentments they harbored against each other, and the fatigue of always having to deal with it. After nearly a decade of marriage, Simon still didn't fully know him, and aside from his work, he could seem like a helpless child himself. Taylor, she said in 1981, was "an odd mixture of dependence and independence" and could be "aloof and closed off," a trait she thought was borne of his childhood, when his "great need to be connected to a home and his parents became critical and traumatic." He was, she said, "a dreamer. He's not well organized and usually lets people plan his day for him." In this light, his own children were little more than dependents.

Even now he didn't stay with the recovering Ben for long before going back out on the road, and thought nothing of trading in the dancer for an actress, Kathryn Walker, with whom he now began spending most of his time. Carly was out of options—if the near death of their son wasn't enough to reform his frat-boy sensibilities, then *what*? She would be up-front about his straying in interviews. While she believed it was good for James to be out playing music, she told *People*, guaranteeing millions of eyes would read it, "It's still difficult for his children, especially Ben." Her friends, too, were dropping hints. Songwriter Libby Titus said: "Their ship has sprung some leaks, and now they're deciding whether to patch things up or abandon ship. . . . Anger and frustration are beginning to come out."

It was more like a flood, and getting worse once he took up with Walker. Another bright and intellectual woman older than he, by five years, she was very much in the mold of Maggie Corey; Phi Beta Kappa at Harvard, she had earned a master's in Celtic studies and studied at the London Academy of Music on a Fulbright fellowship. Starting in TV soap operas, she also won an Emmy in 1975 playing Abigail Adams on the much-acclaimed PBS series *The Adams Chronicles*; she appeared in two other Emmy-awarded PBS series that starred Bette Davis and Katharine Hepburn, respectively. She had also been in several movies, including *Slap Shot* with Paul Newman, *Blade*, and *Rich Kids*. The latter was an apt entrée to James Taylor, whom she met through John Belushi following the unexplained death of her lover Doug Kenney, the *National Lampoon* editor who cowrote and had a bit part in the megahit *Animal House*, before cowriting and producing the almost as popular *Caddyshack*. Kenney, however, was a deeply troubled soul, success deepening *his* longtime depression and use of booze and cocaine. Walker, herself a recovering alcoholic, had accompanied him on a vacation to Hawaii in August 1980 but had to leave early. The next day, he mysteriously fell, or perhaps jumped, from a cliff to his death, his body not found for three days. His death was ruled an accident. In his room a note was found attesting to his deep love for Walker.

Taking refuge in the Vineyard, Walker, who was about to film the comedy *Neighbors* as Belushi's wife, was clearly suited to a train wreck like Taylor, who while he was consoling her fell in love. Not coincidentally, he was fond of the fast circle in which she ran, an assortment of *Lampoon/SNL* alumni—the sort of people Carly Simon generally loathed for their self-destructive habits and parochial sexism. Belushi, she thought, was the worst of them, a man-child who spouted horrible slurs about women (in 2011 Belushi's former *SNL* costar Jane Curtin told Oprah Winfrey that he was a "misogynist" who had during the show's run "sabotaged pieces written by women"). And Walker's ambition was palpable. Simon would later say of her, "She was fierce, a fierce woman, who wanted James at all costs. She knew exactly what she wanted."

Before the crisis with Ben, Simon had recorded her *Come Upstairs* album, from which came the million-selling "Jesse," about a man she dreaded, but needed, coming back to her. In it she admits "I've sunk so low"—which seemed to say it all about her marriage, though she denied it was. Now, in late autumn, with Ben's recovery going well, she hit the road, sapped from the stress and down to 114 pounds. She was onstage in Pittsburgh when she suffered an attack of acute cramping brought on by premature menstruation and collapsed in front of a gasping audience. Taken offstage, she began to hemorrhage and was rushed to a doctor, whereupon she canceled the rest of the tour. Incurring lawsuits by promoters, she held firm, and would not tour again for another decade.

Taylor came off the road to be with her, during which time they recorded the *Sesame Street* album. But she believed their son's ordeal had actually pushed him further away, such was his natural tendency to run from personal travail, normally into the pit of heroin. She also believed that Walker was egging him on to leave her, conspiring with Trudy Taylor, who, as many mothers no doubt would, apparently blamed his son's famous wife for his deepening descent into drugs. (Sheila Weller quotes an unnamed associate of James who believed that "Trudy eventually ruined *all* her kids' marriages. She couldn't help it. She loved her kids too much. She was married to a madman herself, who left her. Trudy was going to do everything she could to 'save' those kids of hers." If so, it must have given more bite to Taylor's oedipal assumptions about his relationship with his mother.)

Fed up, their arguing making the children cry, Simon told him to leave. In turn, Simon just as brazenly stepped out on *him*, first with recording engineer Scott Litt, then inveterate womanizer John Travolta. People around the Vineyard would see Simon literally dancing on tabletops with the much younger *Saturday Night Fever* and *Grease* star. (Trying to uncover *any* bedsheet, or cemetery plot, Ian Halperin's biography of Taylor claimed that Simon was also "reported to be having a tryst" with Pablo Picasso at the time, which could have only happened had she been a necrophiliac; the legendary artist died in 1973.) Simon began some bizarre name-dropping to the media, as well. For example, when she ran into Woody Allen, who lived next door in the Vineyard with Mia Farrow, she told the press, "I'd give Woody just the tiniest little toot of cocaine to give him that extra confidence to be a great conversationalist."

Such "help" of course was exactly the *opposite* of the vigilantly anti-drug pose she struck with her husband, and made her plaints about not doing drugs herself seem laugh-out-loud comical. Both Taylors were living large, making the Vineyard scene, hobnobbing with their own cliques. And within his crowd, Taylor's drinking had become as grave a problem as smack, something Simon hung on Belushi, who was seeing his career take a dive and, apparently needing to escape reality, constantly called Taylor to go carousing with him. As a result, Taylor acknowledged around that time, "I don't have much moderation in my drinking. If I get intoxicated, I lose control. And I've sometimes made mistakes when I was too high that I deeply regret. I can get real sad thinking about things I've said to people and ways I've made people I love feel because I was so out of it."

Simon, meanwhile, not denying her adultery, was acting like a schoolgirl around Travolta, openly speaking of his "magical way of knowing when I am in need." She actually thought she might divorce Taylor and marry Travolta, before the latter walked away. And though Taylor had no right to object, he nonetheless felt humiliated by Simon's public exhibitions. Now, he had reason to say that *she* was a bad influence on the kids, and there was no reason why he should stop playing around. One night he sauntered into the Manhattan nightclub Trax and announced, "Jezebel kicked me out, so I'm up for grabs," as if that hadn't always been the case. For *the* showbiz couple of the era, the glamor had long worn off. What were left were merely two broken people waiting for a merciful end.

All during this unseemly soap opera, Taylor's work seemed almost an afterthought. Following the decent but too brief run of *Flag* and "Up on the Roof," CBS chose not to release any other singles, and Taylor went on his way toward irregular albums and appearances. He made another on *Saturday Night Live*'s one hundredth show on March 15, six shows before the end of the original cast's run, singing three duets with Paul Simon, "Cathy's Clown," "Sunny Skies," and "Take Me to the Mardi Gras." His first post-'70s album was still awaited, and when he got around to it in the early fall of 1980, it was more of a cudgel against Carly Simon, his title, *Dad Loves His Work*, a cheeky—or just plain nasty—riposte to what had been Simon's ultimatum to cut back on touring and spend more time at home. Recorded back in L.A. with Peter Asher, *Dad* was still proudly, rigorously, his type of music, with no great concession to pop music beyond what he had already embraced. It dished up quite serviceable pop, with the usual dashes of Taylor salt, pepper, and sweet cream, with mercifully few references to personal travail—mainly on track 1, "Hard Times," an easygoing groove pleading for an end to the "Angry man, hungry woman / . . . Driving each other crazy" nature of his marriage, but while his attestation that "I may be wrong for you baby . . . but I love you just the same" and refrains of "We've got to hold on, got to hold on" made for a good hook, the song was a sham, he having decided there was nothing to hold on to.

Taylor's voice was notably vibrant, even fevered on "Stand and Fight," which he had performed at No Nukes, before falling back on serene generic shimmer, recycling the faintly Caribbean beat of "Mexico" on "Sugar Trade," cowritten with Jimmy Buffett, another of Taylor's latter-day pals. The lack of Carly Simon's backing vocals was minimized by Jennifer Warnes's crisp and loud harmonies. And the prize in the Cracker Jack box was "Her Town Too," written with J. D. Souther and Waddy Wachtel, performed as a live duet with Souther and a beat Taylor called "a relentless bolero quality," backed with high harmonies like something off *Hotel California*, on which Souther had cowritten "New Kid in Town." The lyrics here too seemed to be about him and Simon—"It used to be your town / It used to be my town, too / You never know 'til it all falls down / Somebody loves you"—though Taylor claimed it was about the nasty split of Peter and Betsy Asher. Other tracks were expertly crafted and quite haunting, such as the last two, "London Town" and "That Lonesome Road," tempering loneliness with a rejection of self-pity:

Carry on
Never mind feeling sorry for yourself
It doesn't save you from your troubled mind

When the LP was released in March 1981, reviews were tepid; Don Shewey in *Rolling Stone* called it "simple and memorable" but slammed Taylor's seeming reluctance to mix it up as "infuriating . . . seal[ing] off an interestingly turbulent world of emotion, keeping half-hidden the impulses that made the songs worth writing in the first place." Shewey dissed "Her Town Too" as "a catchy mindless ditty" and concluded, "Those who admire James Taylor for the depth and craftsmanship of material like 'Millworker' have come to expect more than mild-mannered pop crooning from him." But the Taylor brand was strong enough to move it as high as number 10 on the chart on its way to platinum status, propelled mainly by the nerve-calming "Her Town Too." Hitting the same note as "Up on the Roof," this, the first single, rose to number 11, pop; 5, adult contemporary—the best result since "Handy Man," and the last time he would find his way inside the Top 20 on the Hot 100. A second single had not come off of *Flag*, but *Dad* put three on the charts, the others "Hard Times" (72, pop; 23, AC) and its flip side, "Summer's Here" (25 AC).

While the album was easy listening comfort food, its creator was his usual mess, and the first to admit it. Interviewed by Tim White in *Rolling Stone*, the cover photo of him by Aaron Rapoport showed a rapidly balding, crazy-eyed man with a sardonic grin over the cover line "James Taylor Grins and Bears It"; the inside photo cast him bare-chested under a ratty tweed sport jacket looking like a skid row bum. Taylor didn't mince words. "This past year has been the worst in my life," he said. "I see myself, basically, as a depressed person who tends to hole up and shut systems down. And a lot of things have been happening at once." White, as had Tim Crouse a decade earlier, visited Dr. Isaac Taylor, who sensed in his son's new album the same ambivalence about needing his parents to love him but also needing to love his work. Taylor added, "They miss me, but I'm having a good time." But that word, *love*, was no easier for Ike's son.

"I'd like them," he said, "to think fondly of me."

Indeed, his stable place in the rock-and-roll landscape, despite his decayed state, was impressive, since he had no intention of following men about the same age, like Bruce Springsteen and Billy Joel, into the new universe charted by a new television network on cable TV. When MTV dawned on August 1, 1981, its first entry was not anything that came out of the previous decade but the prophetic song by the unknown techno–new wave group the Buggles, "Video Killed the Radio Star." The signature of the music channel was images of an Apollo 11 astronaut beside an American flag planted on the moon's surface. For Taylor there was quite a bit of irony in this, given that he had been onstage at Newport when a human took the first step on that surface. Yet the powerful visual images that were now necessary to the meaning of any given recording—rendering lyrics, and pondering what they meant, almost immaterial—augured brutal new generational realities for people like Taylor.

They were at a grim disadvantage; none of them had ever made a thematic video or had a song that suddenly didn't seem a thousand years old. The closest Taylor had come was a ninety-minute "In Concert" Showtime cable TV special in 1979, produced by Peter Asher, filmed before a crowd of twenty thousand at the Blossom Music Festival in Cuyahoga Falls, Ohio. Among those who could possibly "play the git-ar on the MTV," Taylor would be downgraded most, since he saw no need or ability to pretend that the teenage offspring of the boomers, the MTV target market, would ever believe he was a new age rocker. While Taylor had actually acted in a movie, he chose not to do what the nonactors—Browne, Henley, Elton John, the Stones, John Mellencamp—were able to, turning videos of their songs into three-minute micromovies, in which they might not sing or even lip-synch a note, just look like they were thinking something heavy (Taylor's *specialty*!)—or, to Bruce and Billy's misfortune, dancing.

Taylor could have handled the brooding poses, but doing what Don Henley did in his excruciating Fellini-light videos would have made him cringe. In the diversified, greatly overpopulated cable galaxy, a handful of Taylor videos would be seen, fleetingly—only one made in the early years of the era, "Her Town Too," five more through the decade, but not until the late '90s would he take it seriously—ironically, when his songs were too sclerotic for MTV and even its nostalgic sister channel, VH1. The best was the video for "Enough to Be on Your Way," filmed in the New Mexico desert, with him walking hand in hand with, and convincingly kissing, actress Barbara Hershey. Still, his idea of videos generally were the string of a half-dozen "video albums" made of live concerts to date, all now released on DVD and all spellbinding in their identical formats of music interwoven with rustic anecdotal revelations. (Arguably the best are 1993's *Squibnocket* and the 1998 platinum-selling *Live at the Beacon Theatre.*) But even with a less than dazzling video footprint, and though Taylor had once said "Things don't last forever, nothing was meant to," he would find himself very much a lasting property as he was becoming progressively lost in a thicket of younger, hip-hoppier, rappier, higher-tech, and more superficial idioms and production. His loyalty to the style that had bred him, it was now obvious, wasn't as much about the '70s as it was about *him.*

His beliefs had come through the '70s intact. Now, if only he could rid himself of the other lingering albatrosses around his neck, beginning with his marriage.

Simon enjoyed the fantasy-like aspects of finding her brilliant and hunky "Orpheus." His artistry fascinated her, seeming like he was in a mystical spell. "When James was writing a song," she said, "guitar in hand, head bowed down, in a trance almost, he often uttered the most delicate, profound things. I've never seen anyone reveal himself so mysteriously, yet approachably, at the same time . . . touchable and remote, the flashes of his dream world open[ed] his listeners' eyes to the lonely spinning galaxy he believed was his true home." However, at times this ritual could seem just another way of spinning her out of it. To be sure, he seemed less taken with sharing his own solitary fables. As she wrote, "Many years later he would accuse me of loving him for 'being James Taylor,' which ironically he meant disparagingly. But it was right on, and a very accurate description of the way I felt."

At the same time, the *other* drug he was addicted to—sex—inversely dimmed in importance. Simon hinted as much in writing that they had become a famous couple "more in print and in the imagination of our fans, maybe, than in our bedroom and living room," and that "the same fire that ignited our relationship could turn to icy silence." Taylor ceased to exist on a soulmate level, physically disappearing to continue his impulsive and conditioned habits in isolation and psychologically punishing her with his ever-distant moods and sullen, silent, glaring episodes—a very prophetic repeat of the scenes she had once sung about in her parents' disintegrating marriage. As she wrote in her memoirs, "Angry dawns, indeed."

Simon's fantasia about the marriage reached its limit by the summer of 1980. She recalled the time she came into their bedroom one night and murmured to him, "I love you so much, my darling man." She took for granted that it would fall on deaf ears. As she would write, "Of course [he] didn't hear me. He was dreaming, no doubt, about his own fascinating rhythms and moods." Which by now she had come to accept did not include her, or their children. Later that year, she would reference this very vignette in her song "From the Heart," a moment that, the song goes, "interrupted the war / That's the way / these cold wars are / I love you, we said / Or one of us did." However, as with Joni Mitchell's retrospective songs about Taylor, such assumptions about love just not being enough, even if it was implicit in the soul, came after the love was gone.

In September 1981, they felt compelled by their status to announce that they'd separated, with a joint statement released to the press reading that "our needs are different; it seems impossible to stay together." Still, they made room for one last ride. Winding up alone in the kitchen of her apartment after he had visited the kids, James, recalled Simon, sat at a table, "a lit Camel in his hand, either drunk or stoned, or both." Without a word, they moved closer, and closer, until the great romance poet of song had a brief command.

"Strip, bitch."

This it either a joke or a bluff, Carly called it. Soon they were in bed one final time. For her, interchanging the gender roles, "I felt I was Orpheus leading Eurydice out of the underworld, not daring to look back until we had at least reached the upper air. But unlike the myth . . . I never looked back, and James still disappeared."

Time had run out on the marriage, and as the final dissolution was being worked out and people took it as perhaps some sort of symbolic ending to another decade—the union having been the ultimate conceit of the "Me Decade"—the fact was, they had fully expected, and planned for, such a denouement. With fatalistic intuition, they had signed an agreement when they married stipulating that in the event of divorce, "all possessions would be distributed to both parties," meaning their respective personal estates were entirely separate. Simon would say years later of the agreement, "I still have this sweet, sad document," which seemed a lot sadder than sweet.

As he moved away from his addiction to Simon, Taylor knew he could not live easily unless he grew up and got the hell off heroin. His last excuse for resistance had been the heroin-cocaine overdose death the previous year of

John Belushi after a frantic night of speedballing at the Chateau Marmont. For Taylor, only a few months older and living just as recklessly, "Initially, John's death was a shock and just a very sad thing to have happened. But it made me look at my own life and the way I was behaving. It brought home the danger of self-abuse."

Of course, he had said things like that before. But if he did look at himself, what he saw had to scare him. His life was still a carousel of pain, and living it had made him old beyond his years. A human coat rack, he came into the '80s with his skin stretched thin on his face, eyes dead, verve drained from his abused veins. Even a suntan he wore on tour late in '79 seemed like it had been sprayed on a skeleton. And now he *did* get serious about kicking heroin, which went hand in hand with ending his existentialist bullshit about dying young as a self-fulfilling prophesy, something pounded home by Belushi's death and that of his old costar Dennis Wilson, who on December 28, 1983, dove drunk into Marina del Ray and drowned at age thirty-nine, barely a month after Taylor had run into him on an L.A. street, with Taylor recalling later that the grizzled Beach Boy looked "absolutely wild, in some altered state."

When Belushi's time came, Taylor had been scheduled to do a few European dates but canceled them when Judy Belushi asked him to help her arrange the funeral. During the ceremony, he stood beside the open casket with what Judy called "a long, very intense, sad look at John." When the casket was taken to Abel's Hill Cemetery in Chilmark, where Belushi was buried under a tombstone that was inscribed, "I may be gone but Rock and Roll lives on," Taylor brought the small inner circle around the grave site to tears with a hushed, poignant rendering of "That Lonesome Road."

Two days later, he was in Ft. Lauderdale for a concert, sadly announcing onstage that he had just come from burying his friend John Belushi. When he returned to New York, it was with a new purpose: saving his own wretched life. He went off methadone—again—and began working out regularly at a West Side studio, where they did aerobics to disco music and where the sight of the elongated superstar in baggy sweats must have been a surreal sight. He brought his jump rope on tours, saying, "It makes me feel good to try and pump it up every day. It helps my singing and it helps to have that extra energy and stamina when you're out on the road." Kathryn Walker was of no small importance in getting him straight. Simon was right; she was fierce, in all ways, and stayed on him, even when he seemed to indeed be making her as crazy as he'd made Simon.

During detox, when he would need around-the-clock support, waking up from nightmares in a cold sweat, launching into screaming fits, or puking all over his apartment, she was severely tested. A friend told of her exclaiming, "This is too much! This is impossible!" She hung on, later describing the ordeal as "a very wrenching and very ugly thing neither of us wanted to go through but had to." He got past the worst of it, which he knew never would have happened had she not been there. This time he stayed off methadone, and heroin, and surprised himself that he could do it. He had secretly checked into a Manhattan drug rehab hospital for what was to be a four-month stay. Instead, after nineteen days, he woke up and had no withdrawal anxiety, aches, pains, or physical torture. He had never gotten this far before, and after he checked out, Walker was not going to let him backslide. Looking back in 2010, he said: "I cleaned up in 1983 . . . and the shocking thing was to see that a lot of, something like fifteen percent of people who are seriously addicted get any kind of meaningful recovery at all; eighty-five percent of people die from this disease. I've been a lucky guy, it's a day at a time."

Carly Simon, who had endured years of futility trying to accomplish what had just happened, had not wanted to divorce Taylor, and she now begged him to reconcile, at one point telling him, "Please! We're affecting our children's lives here!" She might as well have played for him her 1980 song "James," which went: "Sing to me / Sit on the edge of my bed as when we first spent nights together / Your body wrapped around your guitar." But if that had worked back then, it didn't now. He was just as much fighting to rid himself of *Simon* as an addiction, no doubt with motivational pep talks from Walker. Still feeling she had betrayed him, he hastened to file divorce papers.

The marriage officially dissolved, after eleven hellish years, in the summer of 1983. On the day the final dissolution was granted, Simon came into the courtroom and quietly took a seat a row behind Taylor and Walker. Her head full of emotions, she found her gaze strangely—was there any other way for her?—fixated on Taylor's *ankle*, later saying that "the way his ankle bone turned, and where his pant leg stopped, and his sandal" was exactly the same as their son Ben's leg looked. "That image—it still stays with me."

Even though their lawyers were sicced on each other, in the end no money was divided, each having their own fortune. By mutual consent, Simon received full custody of the kids she had been nearly mother and father to, with liberal visitation rights reserved for Taylor. Although it had to bridle him, the house that he had built with his own hands in the Vineyard was also given to her. He soon bought another home, on the edge of Menemsha Pond in Chilmark, where he moved with Walker. Sally and Ben Taylor would have to find their own way, as their father had, in spite of paternal neglect and resentment, and they would find it the same way he had—in song. Simon, typically, felt the need to put her dirty laundry on a public clothesline. Her next album, *Torch*, echoed Joni Mitchell during *her* breakup with Taylor, the selection of songs pointed, including Hoagy Carmichael's "I Get Along Without You Very Well," "Hurt," "What Shall We Do with the Child," even, à la Mitchell, "Blue of Blue."

The first new man Simon took up with wasn't far from the tree—none other than Russ Kunkel, who wasted little time pouncing on the new divorcée even at the risk of offending the man who had taken him on a long and profitable ride. When Simon was asked how they had gotten together, she gave a typically outré answer. "Well, we'd just taken a lot of drugs—no, just kidding," she joked in the worst of taste considering the victim pose she'd struck for so long. For Kunkel, it was the best of all words, including business. He would play on and coproduce her 1985 *Spoiled Girl* LP, and be the subject of its opening song, "My New Boyfriend." However, living with Simon in James Taylor's old house could not have been easy, separated from the children he had from his defunct marriage. Just before the album was released in June, the couple became engaged.

However, it never happened. Kunkel, whose red hair now receded, making his long locks frame his head like Bozo the Clown's, also coproduced her next LP, *Coming Around Again*, in 1987, but shortly thereafter, still not ready to walk down the aisle and feeling suffocated by Simon's overwhelming aura, he ended it and returned to the Canyon, another painful crack-up for her. The man she would next marry was, probably wisely, a *non*music type, businessman James Hart, later in 1987, a union that would last for almost two decades. Finally getting back to making music that had nothing to do with James Taylor (though Hugh sang backup vocals), and she had started fresh with Clive Davis at Arista Records, and *Coming Around Again* sold two million copies. She won Oscar, Grammy, and Golden Globe awards for "Let the River Run" on the *Working Girl* movie soundtrack.

As for her ex, he had to take the first steps of his life as well, the life he thought he'd never live to see.

Taylor spent the first year after the divorce waiting for the writing spirit to grab him, but he could think of nothing to write about, alarmingly. "I've never really had this kind of silence before," he said of his writer's block. "This is as bad as it's gotten. . . . I'm at the point of desperation." He said he would sit himself down for four hours every day to "come up with something." If not, he said, Yetnikoff would just have to wait until he did. He added high-tech digital recording equipment to his home studio. He ran six miles a day in the woods. He tried to jump-start by going to Montserrat, the British territory island in the Caribbean that the Rolling Stones and Elton John had made the "in" place to record, but after a few dry sessions at George Martin's AIR Studios, came back home.

Then Asher received an invitation from promoters in Brazil for Taylor to appear at the "Rock in Rio" outdoor festival from January 11 to 20, 1985, which was held as a celebration of the first election in Brazil in twenty-one years. Taylor took the gig, and was stunned by his tumultuous reception. Originally, he was a second-tier act behind Queen, Rod Stewart, AC/DC, Yes, and the American soul singer–guitarist George Benson, each of whom were to headline for two nights. However, when Taylor's opening set on January 12 ran so long due to repeated encores, Benson graciously gave Taylor top billing on his next show two days after, when he again rocked Rio. The vibe clearly rejuvenated him; he spoke of "the spark of insight and vitality I got from the Latin music I was exposed to in Brazil," not to mention the rush of "democracy flowering in the air." By the spring, after a four-year drought, and contractually obligated to get an album in the can, he had at least broken through enough to book time at Right Track studio in New York, his producer and engineer mainly Frank Filipetti, with some tracks completed in L.A. with Asher, adding background vocals by Don Henley, Graham Nash, Deniece Williams, and Joni Mitchell, with whom, once he was free of Simon, he was collegial again. Russ Kunkel was back on drums, though Kortchmar was not around, replaced by the pungent steel guitar of Dan Dugmore.

The work was titled *That's Why I'm Here*, the why apparently being not to wallow anymore. Where once he would have sung about Belushi's death as figuratively dying himself, he sang of it in the title track almost jauntily—"John's gone found dead / He dies high he's brown bread"

(Cockney rhyming slang for dead) and it "hits us like a ton of lead," yet the comforting electric piano–flavored rhythm was meant to back his new rule that to "'learn not to burn' means to turn on a dime." As he had in "For the Love o' Money" he referenced the song that had made and nearly broken him, singing that "fortune and fame" meant "strangers . . . pay good money" to hear him sing "'Fire and Rain'"—"again and again and again." But there was no cynicism in his voice, and the point seemed to be that he *would* sing it, again and again and again. And amen to that.

The ballads were, as ever, gorgeous, the sentimental "Song for You Far Away" dreamlike as he crooned, "Sittin' here thinkin' of you." "Only a Dream in Rio," a paean to the recent trip when his "heart came back alive," was just as shimmering, seeking no more than a "samba floating in the summer breeze" with a heavenly chorale singing, in Portuguese, *Quando a nossa mea acordar*. There was bouncy white funk ("Turn Away"), catchy pop ("Going Around One More Time"), a torch song ("My Romance"), the bluesy "Limousine Driver," the country, fiddly "Mona." One oldie cover was Buddy Holly's lullaby-like "Everyday," filling in the original spare classic with layers of foamy cream and neat little rhythmic changes. Another, the old Gene Pitney movie tune "The Man Who Shot Liberty Valance," was given a blues feel, juiced by Mike Brecker's sensual sax solo, a perfect underscoring of the tune's cynical parable of deceit and reality merging within a culture of hero worship.

He had again stayed true to his formula, with its limited bending to the times and plenty that touched the nostalgic—"Only One" sounded for all the world like one of his lilting duets with Carly Simon, though the harmony was provided by the woman he dumped for her, along with Don Henley. And with it, he had surrendered to the realities of "adult contemporary." Whitney Houston could easily have covered many of the songs here. It may have been too calm, too sticky, too toothless. But it was the Taylor you'd get now, which seemed to some a better deal than you might find with his '70s cohort. Joni Mitchell, as it happened, released her barbed, issue-oriented *Dog Eat Dog* (with a jolting Edvard Munch *Scream*-style image of her on the cover) around the same time, produced in part by the British techno-pop star Thomas Dolby and featuring Taylor singing backing vocals with Don Henley on three cuts: the title track, "Tax Free," and "Shiny Toys." *Newsweek*'s Bill Barol reviewed them together, writing, "Her new sound rings false to the ear. Personal stability needn't dull one's musical edge; Taylor proves that. He may not be 'Sweet Baby

James' anymore—but, he says with calm assurance, sounding like a man who is slowing down at last, 'I'm reasonably happy with the ticket I've written myself.'" The consensus was that Taylor had grown up, finally seeing things for what they were rather than what they weren't, even if some critics now were pecking at him for not being heavy *enough.* Taylor agreed.

"I spent a lot of time with a feeling of negative faith," he said, "an assumption that the world had a nasty surprise just around each corner. But I'm comfortable now. I don't have any investment any longer in things turning out badly."

That's Why I'm Here did not turn out badly, making it to number 34—and, in time, the usual platinum status—and "Everyday" made it to number 61 on the pop chart, number 3 on the adult contemporary. Two subsequent singles, "Only One" and "That's Why I'm Here," went Top 10 on the AC. For the post-1970s James Taylor, this was all that was needed to stay a thing. Comfortable as he was with that, he was ready to settle down again, at least as much as possible for a man with his roving eye. On December 14, 1985, he and Kathryn Walker wed at the Cathedral of Saint John the Divine—an event that, as Simon theorized it, was Taylor's answer to her engagement to Russ Kunkel. Other than Taylor's splendid tux with a wraparound ascot, the day was memorable as the time that Walter Yetnikoff chose for a profound change in his own life, the Jewish-born CBS honcho converting to the Church of England at an adjunct ceremony. It seemed that spiritual rebirth was the keynote of such warhorses in the mid-'80s, and for Taylor it would actually seem to work.

Taylor and his contemporaries had allowed their corporate patrons to become unconscionably powerful, and beyond wealthy. Unleashed by the Eagles, Irving Azoff's power rose like a vector, his ego hanging over the Valley like thick smog. He was able to make deals that brought him and his clients outrageous monetary gain, earning Azoff the moniker of "The Poison Dwarf"—from his own associates. (Another was coined by Don Henley, who would say Azoff "may be Satan, but he's our Satan.") Azoff had begun his own management firm, Front Line Management, and his rise inevitably ran him up against his onetime boss, David Geffen, who had himself become obscenely rich, when he sold his management company and became vice chairman of Warner Brothers' movie division. After a cancer scare, he returned to music in 1980, forming Geffen Records, anchored by Donna Summer, John Lennon, Elton John, Cher, and Aerosmith.

Taylor's own Svengali was flourishing as well. Peter Asher had had his ups and downs with his discovery but his grip on Taylor was indisputable, even if Taylor sometimes bridled about it with subtle digs. In a *Rolling Stone* profile of Asher in 1977, both Taylor and Linda Ronstadt laid on hands about the carrottop sprite, though with enough hedging that writer Ben Fong-Torres mused that Taylor had "a tough time explaining just what it is Asher does." Asher, who remarried a woman named Wendy Worth, would ride Taylor and Ronstadt into the 1990s, though his role as the top-dog producer had been eclipsed by men like Russ Titelman, who went on to work with Chaka Khan and Paul Simon, and win three Grammys, two with Eric Clapton, one with Steve Winwood.

Danny Kortchmar also prospered, reaching a heady level beyond even James Taylor. Not incidentally, the two old buddies still had not patched up the old resentments about Taylor's heroin escapades that helped sink their Flying Machine. Nor, despite all their success, had Kootch ever particularly felt he was playing the music that turned him on when he soldiered with Taylor.

"I *hate* folk music, I always have," he says. "I don't want it to sound like I'm making disparaging remarks about all those people, but one of the functions I've always performed is to make sounds that are a little more outrageous than the other players. Give songs an *edge*. But still, you know, neither James or Carole are rock and roll at all. So it's always been challenging for me to play with them. I've had to hold back quite a bit."

Now Kortchmar would escort Don Henley into massive solo success. No one was more pivotal than Henley for unpacking a sound for the new decade, and in coproducing Henley's grown-up version of the Eagles' themes, Kortchmar bathed the ex-Eagle's sandpapery but soulful voice in what could be called arch versions of Taylor's sparser odes to alienation, rejection, forgiveness, nobility (even if he had to say so himself), and hopeless explorations for "the heart of the matter." Henley, a, shall we say, *self-important* fellow, would take as much heat from new- and old-generation rock critics still pining away for stripped-down, primal rock and roll as the early stirrings of punk, new wave, grunge, and the like grew louder—witness Mojo Nixon's hysterical "Don Henley Must Die."

The '70s had cleared the underbrush for punk, grunge, alienated funk, rap, and untold offshoots of each. But Taylor had hung in, one tough nut to discard. He no longer was the ligature that held together an entire movement; the movement had entrenched itself, not needing to score huge hits to soothe now middle-age baby boomers' nerves. Taylor, contractually obligated to record a new album only once every four years, could freely come out of hibernation for those good, safe causes. On June 12, 1982, one of the largest rallies ever held in the United States, another antinuke concert, filled Central Park's Great Lawn with around a million people to see Taylor, Bruce Springsteen, Jackson Browne, Linda Ronstadt, and Joan Baez perform—the stars now being Springsteen and Browne, who sang several duets during the concert, which was simulcast on radio stations across the country and later released as the documentary *In Our Hands.*

Taylor was long cemented into a fold of politically aware rock elders, helping to keep his profile elevated. His private life was still a matter of interest in the tabloids, if with lesser hysteria, which was all right by him. For a few years he and Walker lived an idyll, she replacing Simon on his arm at events, his eyes not diverted but longingly meeting hers. They had pet names for each other that made people gag: he calling her "Kitty," she calling him "Bim" for whatever reason—thus explaining the last verse of "That's Why I'm Here" about "Kitty and Bim / He loved her / And she loved him," an encomium to Walker having gotten him through rehab by waking him up in the middle of the night to "Tell me / Everything's all right." He seemed to finally be able and willing to enjoy his domesticity—but only until history repeated. Walker may have helped him kick heroin but as she feared, he could no more keep his attention and passion confined to her than he had with Simon. When he began spending more time on the road, the worst of it each summer when he strung together a seamless three months performing in beatific settings in mainly rural amphitheaters and country fairs, her feelings of abandonment grew apace. Her sad, oft-repeated refrain to her friends echoed Simon's nearly word for word—"James is going away again." In a replay of the Taylor-Simon contretemps, his resentment over what he thought were ultimatums to stay home more produced the same results. Arguments became shouting matches, usually with Taylor simply turning on his heel and walking out, not to reappear for days.

As this new personal crisis boded ill, Taylor ended a three-year dry spell (a second Taylor greatest-hits package *Classic Songs* was released in European markets, his Warner songs on side 1, CBS songs on side 2) to cut his twelfth album. He hunkered down again in the studio with Lee Sklar;

Dan Dugmore; sax man Mike Brecker; drummer Carlos Vega; guitarist Jeff Mironov; keyboardist Bill Payne; and backup singers Arnold McCuller, David Lasley, and Lani Groves (one of Stevie Wonder's regulars); with Don Grolnick elevated to producer. Grolnick, a jazzman by nature, added a swingier beat, funkier guitar riffs, and electric-acoustic riffs to the usual electric piano/synth-pop mood, separating Taylor ever so slightly from the overproduced mainstream at a time when the pounding backbeats of Michael and Janet Jackson were fading and music was again splintering: pop-tart and kiddie-band fluff on one end, screeching hair metal bands on the other, the melodic heavy metal of Guns N' Roses and Metallica about to break. But Taylor always seemed to be able to find a middle ground between his own template and the era he was in, keeping his vocals and his lyrics crisp and adhering to perfectly crafted structures.

He titled the album with the latest Taylor aphorism—*Never Die Young*, twitting the mantra of the Catholic Church that he had been baptized to accept—only the good die young—which he never could, not when he had been so bad so young. Billy Joel had struck this theme with mocking irony. But Taylor's title track, which seemed to be a sort of "Don't Fear the Reaper" calmness about dying young, was actually a roundabout irony about finding a proverbial heaven on earth, worth all of the pain it takes to "sail on to another land beneath another sky," urging almost selfishly, "Let other hearts be broken / Let other dreams run dry." Taylor and Grolnick made use of some funky arrangements, such as in "T-Bone," cowritten with Bill Payne, that had an electrified *accordion*, and a resonant saxophone solo in "Baby Boom Baby," a bright ballad he had cowritten long ago with Zach Weisner, the last line of which—"What do I do if my dream come true"—was now fully ironic given that he had not dared dream when it was written.

On "Runaway Boy" he sang heartily of "putting down roots" and wanting "To soak up sun / And stay right here until my days are done." Even his old friend, the darkness, was replaced by a new metaphor—"Sun on the Moon," a near-hip-hop/gospel run with an impatient 6/8 beat, Taylor ragging on the "saddest people," those "Living in a hole, body and soul / Strung out on the company dole." Not so for him—"My ducks are all in a row," he boasted, with "nowhere to go." One of the more ambitious songs one can find in the Taylor catalog, written with Timothy Mayer, was "Home by Another Way," in which the tale of the biblical magi—the three wise men—who bore gifts for the baby

Jesus then avoided the evil King Herod by "returning home by another way" was knitted into a catchy, melodic parable of individual determination of which way to go and whom not to obey—"Mustn't let King Herod haunt you so / Or fantasize his features when you're looking at a friend," sang the wise man of rock, "Steer clear of royal welcomes / Avoid a big to-do / A king who would slaughter the innocents." And even that line was coated in rose-colored optimism and a conviction that "tomorrow is another day" and "we can make it another way." Taylor may have been in a biblical state of mind after his close friend and biblical scholar Reynolds Price, during treatment for a cancerous tumor that left him a paraplegic in 1984, swore he had a mystic vision in a dream in which he met Jesus at the Sea of Galilee.

The album ran an economical ten songs—including Taylor's only overt paean to sex, "First of May," which he sheepishly admitted bordered on "being rude" with lyrics like "A rite of spring / A horizontal thing / The sweetest sort of dance / Hidden in among the plants." William Ruhlmann wrote years later in his AllMusic retro-review that this was James Taylor riding on "a sea of yuppie contentment." In real time the reviews were lukewarm. *Never Die Young*, noticed the *Los Angeles Times*' Connie Johnson, "is strewn with fewer broken hearts than it was during his 'Fire and Rain' days. Most of these sweetly tender tunes are written from the perspective of a man satisfied with the hand life has dealt him." While the album cover was a striking photograph of a hungry wolf baying at the moon, the vibe was more that of an old bloodhound sleeping in the afternoon sun. This time there were no covers of old ditties as radio fodder, and yet when it was released in January 1988, the single of "Never Die Young" died at number 80 on the pop chart—Taylor's final trip to that chart to date—and *Rolling Stone* passed on giving the LP a review. But, with very little play, "Never Die Young" rose impressively to number 3 on the adult contemporary list. Its flip, "Baby Boom Baby," made it to number 16. The album went as high as number 25, en route to platinum status.

The way *he* kept rising every four years, on *his* list, finding his way home by whatever means he chose, James Taylor was now much like a different biblical character—Lazarus.

20

HOURGLASS

A year into yet another new decade he would need to find his way through, America had been fighting another war far from home, blood being spilled for oil in the Persian Gulf, and James Taylor had another album to serve up to now graying baby boomers who were no less needy for the comfort he could bring from headlines that had never seemed to get any better since the '60s. Having handled the passage of time, he was able to give them exactly that sort of comfort. However, despite successful albums, he frequently doubted himself as he aged.

"I had a dark reaction to my music—that I'd perhaps stayed too long in one place, being a horse in a familiar harness," he said, the problem being to convert from a junkie-eye view of life—when he was, he admitted, "caught in a tiny little trap" of obsession—to a "relatively conscious and sober-minded" grasp of all the facets around him that had equal weight. That would take work, energy, effort. And he didn't have it.

Something indeed seemed to have drained from him after kicking heroin. His appearances were exercises in lassitude. Taking the easy route by playing mainly his oldies, it got rough out there; after a 1987 gig at the Pacific Amphitheater the *L.A. Times*' Gina Arnold wrote, "Taylor's songs, once celebrated for their sensitivity, now sound almost wimpy, not to mention dated. Tune after tune about loneliness and love, interspersed with Taylor imagery of leaves falling and rainbows ending, wore as thin as Taylor's hairline long before the end of the first set . . . [he] seems to be a classic case of a talented person who had a lot more to say earlier in his career. Now that he's successful there doesn't seem to be a lot on his mind."

He always seemed to need something to rejuvenate him, and it happened again, from without. In the spring and summer of 1991, after having watched in horror the jingoistic patriotic fervor of the first televised war, and then all that ritualistic camaraderie fade to the hard realities of economic recession, he composed songs for a new album. Taylor didn't go into it halfway. For one thing, he had not simply allowed his precious voice to age without protection, or improvement. Having become hoarse on occasion when he had to scream to be heard over strings and horns, he studied with vocal coaches to temper it, and to not shout onstage. Now a better technical singer than ever, he made the new album a major project, recording tracks at four different studios, the Power Station and Skyline Studios in New York, A&M, and Studio F in L.A., then mixed at a fifth, Sterling Sound in New York. Nearly thirty musicians in all played, including cellist Yo-Yo Ma and three drummers: Carlos Vega, Steve Jordan, and Steve Gadd. Don Grolnick and Clifford Carter played the synth; Jerry Douglas, a resonator guitar. Mike Brecker and Jimmy Johnson were back, but now too was Danny Kortchmar, who Taylor had beckoned to not only be in the band but also act as coproducer with Grolnick. He also, for the first time, wrote a song with Kootch, who produced the funky blues rocker "(I've Got to) Stop Thinkin' 'Bout That."

New Moon Shine, the name of the work, was a pun for the moonshine (recalling "Carolina in My Mind") back in the hills of his childhood in North Carolina and, as Taylor explained it, "the certain light coming from a new moon, the contradiction of darkness and radiating something out of it." The theme, he said, was "the necessity of redemption," something he knew well. The opener, "Copperline," was perhaps Taylor's finest, most transfixing song of his post-'70s work. Written with Reynolds Price, it is a stunningly visual trip home to his childhood in the smoky hills of North Carolina, with its memories of "Creosote and turpentine / Sour mash and new moon shine," his towering vocal pulsing with sadness and anger that towns like Copperline, half a mile down from Morgan Creek, were now paved with condos and highways—"I tried to go back, as if I could / All spec houses and plywood / Tore up and tore up good," he sings, backed by fiddles and steel and acoustic guitar licks that weep with him.

"Down in the Hole" channeled Woody Guthrie in a chorale about life in the mines but on a broader level about severe depression that made one crawl in a hole and hide. "The Frozen Man," the other track produced by Kootch, and on which he played acoustic guitar, originated with a story Taylor had read in *National Geographic* about the viability of cryogenics; the song he wrote played off *The Elephant Man*, of a guy being revived after decades in a frozen state and manipulated as a freak, robbing his dignity and soul. The message was to fight for that dignity, and there was a classic Taylor line—"Thought it would be nice just to visit my grave / See what kind of tombstone I have." He had often felt that way about himself. Just like the Walking Man, Taylor was also the Frozen Man.

Notably, Taylor did not shrink from political unburdening. "Slap Leather," a term for country line dancing, borrowed the machine-gun rhythm and word salad of "Maggie's Farm" to skewer the man he called only "Ron" for the inevitable crash of the '90s—by keeping people out in the cold while spending billions on "weapons you can never use" and feeding a "Hoover the future in the land of greed / Sell the Ponderosa to the Japanese." It went on like that for a delirious two minutes, with cameos for "Storming Norman" (Gulf War commander General Schwarzkopf), phone sex, Big Macs, and a knowing "slap" at the news media for turning the world into a TV show—a still quite applicable complaint. A more direct hit was "Native Son," a dirgelike embrace of homeward-bound soldiers, laced with sardonic lines like "Damn the darkness, speed the dawn / They lost, we won / Try to find your way back home / Native son."

These tracks, and his belated tribute to Martin Luther King, the tabernacle-like "Shed a Little Light," rejecting the "clenching of a fist" for "ties of hope and love, sister and brotherhood," made the album breathe harder, smartly cushioned by his lightly Latin-seasoned cover of Sam Cooke's "Everybody Loves to Cha Cha Cha" (emulating Cooke's closing "who-oh-oh" riff). Appropriating another familiar sound, "One More Go Around" was a copy of the bass-heavy beat of the Talking Heads' cover of Al Green's "Take Me to the River." The very familiar chords of "Fire and Rain" could be heard in his gorgeous version of an old Scottish folk ballad, "The Water Is Wide."

New Moon Shine was far more poignant and gifted than the uplifting *Never Die Young*, its cover posing Taylor, clad in black, leaning against a wall, arms folded, heavenly lights crawling down the wall. But did Taylor fans want poignant and pointed? Or merely light? As the *New Rolling Stone Album Guide* put it, his post-'70s albums "offer little beyond pleasantry," seriously underselling *Never Die Young* but fairly proving that even Taylor fans now appreciated him more on tone than substance. "Copperline" would become a concert fixture, because it could send one into the near-trancelike state of "Fire and Rain." As well, "Slap Leather" would get a call, too, not as an anti-Reagan piece but as a hillbilly-style hoot, with Taylor rolling out another of his thingamajigs, a nonelectronic, self-playing drum kit made of wood with about a hundred moving parts. More important, though, new songs were making the cut of his stage act now, coexisting with the evergreens that audiences might have preferred he stuck to. And he had another album that would go platinum and put three singles on the AC chart, "Copperline" (number 13), "Stop Thinkin' 'Bout That" (28), and "Cha-Cha" (19). (Of historical note, *New Moon Shine* was Taylor's first work not to be released on vinyl, except in Brazil where he was now an idol.)

With this success, Taylor was certainly back in the game. When Sting and his wife, Trudie Styler, initiated a yearly (now biannual) springtime concert at Carnegie Hall in 1991 for the Rainforest Foundation, Taylor was busy. But having missed the signal '80s convocations like Live Aid and Farm Aid, he agreed to participate in the '92 Rainforest affair and hasn't missed one since, helping turn this event into rock's biggest ongoing benefit event, raising around $30 million to date. The concerts also have seen some mind-blowing duets. At the 1995 edition, Taylor performed "Obsession" with Sting, "The River" with Springsteen, and with Elton John they all teamed on "It's a Wonderful Day." It was, Sting said, "an incredible feeling" to sing with Taylor.

Such triumphant and politically correct venues became the nucleus of his public life. One even brought about a short-lived rapprochement with Carly Simon, at the 1995 Livestock benefit concert for the Martha's Vineyard Agricultural Society. Each had reservations but, prodded by their children, they came onstage and embraced each other before singing, a sight few who knew them believed possible. For Walter Yetnikoff, scenes like these were quite helpful. He was still profiting handily from *this* old dog. In August 1993 came the release of Taylor's first live album, a double-CD set, thirty-song jubilee of old, new, and not-before-released material including George Jones's 1962 number one country hit of Dickey Lee's "She Still Thinks I Care" and another collaboration with Reynolds Price, "New Hymn." Not only did the album reach number 20, a cropped version called *Best Live* followed later in the year. All were signs that he was still a leader of at least *his* pack. Even in the '90s, then, he was a kind of reference point, good and bad. The *New Rolling Stone Album Guide*, for example, in reviewing the Blake Babies' singer-songwriter, wrote, "Juliana Hatfield . . . [is] the James Taylor of '90s alt rock: a decent enough writer and performer, but one who consistently lacks the fuel to turn sparks into fire." And REM's lead guitarist, Peter Buck, said in 1994, "I feel we're perceived as being a folk-rock band, mellow dudes who sit on a stool, like a '90s James Taylor, and nothing could be further from the truth."

For James Taylor, life was too rich, still too challenging to care about any slights—after all, he had heard them all. But his charmed longevity was not shared by his brother Alex. On March 12, 1993, James's forty-fifth birthday, Alex was in a studio in Sanford, Florida, recording an album for King Snake Records, a redneck punk and blues label owned by Bob "Rattlesnake" Greenlee, who played bass for Root Boy Slim and the Sex Change Band in the '80s. It was a long way down the ladder for Alex, who had cut his last album, *Voodoo in Me*, for King Snake in '89, five years after performing with Dan Aykroyd on a live album with what was called the Blues Brothers Band. The once robust, surfer-boy-looking Alex was now jowly and weathered, drinking prodigious amounts of booze. During the session, he fell asleep, drunk, on the floor, stopped breathing, and no one could awaken him. Pronounced dead of a heart attack at forty-six, he left a wife, two sons—one of course Sweet Baby James—and four granddaughters. Said his brother James: "When Alex died we all went down to Florida to say goodbye. The day after we flew home a giant mother hurricane followed us north through the Carolinas, trashing everything in its path and finally raining record rains on Martha's Vineyard."

A song would come out of that awful day, "Enough to Be on Your Way," which James wrote in Paris a year later, a heart-rending eulogy to Alex, though not overtly, for some reason changing the gender to female, in the manner of Suzanne Schnerr. Taylor dipped into that same well to summon the same emotions when he had walked his mind to an easy time and turned his back toward the sun. Now, he wrote, the sun "Rolls across the western sky / And back into the sea / And spends the day's last rays / Upon this fucked-up family." Then: "So long old pal."

His marriage to Kathryn Walker had become tenuous. Seeing it unraveling, and Taylor making the same effort he had to keep himself closer to home and hearth with Carly Simon—none—Walker realized that there was perhaps a rough limit any woman could ever hope to make it through with him; for Simon it was eleven; for Walker, nine. She was still amazed by him, the magnetism he had for so many. When she met him he was the only voice she could bear listening to after Doug Kenney's death. During the marriage, she said, "he got so many letters from people in mental institutions. . . . The light shines through. It's beyond just being talented." Yet he almost never responded to those letters; it was as if his voice existed in an ether above him, a separate identity from the man who himself probably had not received the care he needed in institutions like that. In many ways, he was dysfunctional, unable to coexist with *himself*, much less a mate or even his own children. Simon once said that he lived in perpetual fear of "imminent doom." By 1995, he surely knew his marriage was doomed, and was ready to move on without Walker.

With far less rancor than last time around, by mutual agreement they signed divorce papers, Walker also agreeing not to speak about the marriage to the press. She made no property or creative claims, though he had publicly credited her with naming the *Never Die Young* album and making other creative decisions, as well as urging him to tour with a full symphonic orchestra, a move that leavened his music as "serious." Indeed, feeling stale again, in 1994 he had played a concert at L.A.'s Irvine Meadows that did not go well. During his set, hundreds of fans began to leave, not even stopping when he sang "Fire and Rain." When next he went out on the road, accompanied by the symphonic pops orchestra, and came to L.A., it was a different story. The *L.A. Times*' Mike Boehm wrote: "When Taylor sang 'Fire and Rain' conductor Edward Cumming and the orchestra helped him turn it into a grand, swelling anthem, writing large the song's ultra-familiar, but still-arresting portrait of a man struggling in a moment of shock and grief to hang onto his fragile mental balance."

Taylor and Walker divorced, without lawyers issuing public statements, few stories about it in the media, and Taylor agreeing to what was called a five-figure settlement payoff. They would remain friendly, though decreasingly, as Walker too moved on. In 1997, she became the Rothschild Artist in Residence at Radcliffe College and soon after produced the six-part documentary series *The Millennium Journal* on the PBS-owned Metro Arts cable channel, as well as numerous theater pieces for the Ninety-Second Street Y's theater, on Manhattan's Upper East Side.

Taylor would not be eager to repeat another plunge into matrimony. He kept touring and during these excursions he made an effort to establish connections with his neglected children. He would take Ben on vacation with him to places like Madagascar and Glasgow—where he later also paid for Trudy Taylor to see him perform in the land of Ike's ancestry. Ben and Sally, both of whom went to the Tabor Academy prep school in Marion, Massachusetts, went white-water rafting with him, and he took them on a trip to climb Er Mei Mountain in China, where he wrote the song "Up Er Mei," which would go on his next album. With both of them having set off on singing careers, both grabbing attention as he had, being tall, extraordinarily good looking, and hugely talented, he sometimes gave Sally the experience of singing onstage as part of his backup group. And while these bonding rituals still came between long absences, this was the new Taylor "dynasty." Ben, who wore the same laconic, droopy-eyelid look as his father, cut his first song in 1995, "I Will," which was on the soundtrack of the movie *Bye Bye, Love.* Within a few years, both would have bands: Sally with two Tabor schoolmates calling themselves the Slip, and Ben playing what he defined as "neo-psychedelic folk funk."

As for the original singing siblings, few now called them the first family of rock. A signal moment for them had come on August 5, 1981, when all five of Ike Taylor's children sang together, including Hugh Taylor, who had not gone after a musical career but rather owned the Outermost Inn in Aquinnah, at the western end of the Vineyard. James, Kate, Livingston, Alex, and Hugh appeared at the South Street Seaport Museum in Lower Manhattan that day, at a "Save Our Ships" concert. Livingston would sustain well, recording eleven studio albums (the most recent, *Blue Sky*, in 2014), several compilations, and three live albums, with five singles on the pop chart and "Going Round One

More Time" covered by James on *That's Why I'm Here.* His real job, however, would be teaching as an artist in residence at Harvard College and then at the Berklee College of Music, where James received an honorary doctorate in 1995 and would be a guest lecturer at his brother's stage performance classes, as would Jimmy Buffet, Steven Tyler, and John Mayer. When Livingston would be required to sell his home on the north shore of the island overlooking Gay Head Lighthouse as part of a painful divorce in 2003, he sold it to a neighbor who leased it back to him. With Trudy now living full time in the cottage the family would spend the summers in, painting seascapes, the brood was closer now than they had ever been. After losing Alex, James began to spend more time with Livingston.

"I got the early attention," James Taylor said, "but there is no real reason that it couldn't have been Liv. We could easily have swapped. Our sense of the world is informed by each other."

But such was the receding interest in the once-heralded "other" Taylors that when James went on the *Regis and Kathie Lee* morning show in 1997, the clueless Kathie Lee Gifford insisted that she loved his siblings' work, then asked, "How's Alex doing?"

Taylor blinked. "I wish I could say he was doing well," he said. "Alex died about four years ago."

Dr. Isaac Montrose Taylor II, lost in his own miasma of alcoholism and grief, seemed to simply give up on life. After his wife and son died, and unable to properly take care of three young children, he slipped further into the bottle and illness, growing more infirm by the day. He eventually contracted pneumonia and was taken to Mass General, slipped into a coma, and on Sunday, November 3, 1996, with the cold winds beginning to gather in Martha's Vineyard, he took *his* last breath, in the same building where his second son James Vernon Taylor was born forty-eight years earlier. He left behind his four surviving older children and his three younger ones. James, who had seen him deteriorate and knew the end was near, made the announcement of his father's death to the media a few days later, when the *New York Times* obituary was headlined "Isaac M. Taylor, 75, Prominent Physician." The funeral was held on Sunday morning, November 30, at the Church of the New Covenant in Boston's Back Bay overlooking Bunker Hill, its

Tiffany stained-glass windows and puddingstone exterior and steeple to be declared a national landmark in 2012. Having shunned religion all his life, he was celebrated in a Presbyterian service by hundreds of his friends and colleagues. When his second son delivered the eulogy, he quoted Scripture.

"I saw a new heaven and a new earth," James Taylor said, "and I saw the holy city, New Jerusalem, coming down from God out of heaven." They were the kind of words almost never spoken or heard in the Taylor household, but they seemed appropriate for the son who flirted with the concept of God in his songs, if not his own life, never fully accepting it. Later, he would say he chose the passage because Ike had a sailboat named "New Jerusalem," which seemed to him Ike's late-coming embrace of something bigger in his life than material gain as he faced his mortality. Indeed, as the patriarch had grown older and more infirm, his son had tried to bridge the gap between them and blunt the old resentments, trying to express the love for Ike buried deep beneath the alienation. After a visit with him, he had written "Only for Me" for *Dad Loves His Work*, telling of seeing Ike, his mind "In his whiskey / And his body in a folding chair / Far beyond repair," but that being together was "a wonderful sight . . . from one who was lost and found." As he watched Ike near death, he wrote "Up from Your Life," in which he sang, "For an un-believer like you / There's not much they can do," and assured him that death was his deliverance, so he should "look on up" even "In the middle of your sadness / The everyday madness."

Ike wasn't the only loss that Taylor had to bear. That year, too, on June 1, Don Grolnick, with whom he had become close, had died from non-Hodgkins Lymphoma at forty-eight. Worse, having to bury such important people in his life would become a regular, and always traumatic, ritual, almost as if he had to pay a price for his survivability.

Taylor's continued relevance surprised no one more than himself. He could not deny that he was "older and . . . not as emotionally intense." Besides writing, he added, "I've found other solutions—emotional solutions in my life. . . . I think songs need to come out of—really out of a state of boredom almost as much as anything else. You need to have empty time in order to receive them. I'm much more distracted now and there's less time for them to come through." Back in the '80s he started to feel he was writing not from "the inside out" but because "the songs are somewhat being pulled out of you as something that's expected of you." He also said, "I really didn't anticipate that anyone would hear it, you know? I mean, the motivation for writing it was quite pure. And that's not the case so much anymore."

Still, here he was, *gaining* in his status as an elder. Peter Asher's unseen hand was still at work through the '80s and '90s hawking Taylor ditties for use on TV shows and movies. Asher however would soon be gone from his affairs, as well as Walter Yetnikoff. CBS Records had been sold in 1988 to the Japanese-owned Sony Corporation—after which Yetnikoff was given a golden-parachute retirement buyout—touching off frenetic mergers and acquisitions of American businesses by Japanese entertainment corporations, and in 1995 Asher was made senior vice president at Sony Music Entertainment. In the shuffle, Taylor's publishing royalties owned by CBS through April-Blackwood went to Sony/ATV Music Publishing (the result of another merger, with ATV, owned famously by Michael Jackson, giving Jackson control of the Beatles' song catalog). Country Road Music also was absorbed by Sony/ATV. Asher would rise higher. In 2002, he became copresident, then president, of Sanctuary Artist Management, managing among others Pamela Anderson. The old rocker could even turn the clock back as a lark, reuniting with Gordon Waller for a series of concerts before the latter's death in 2009, and was awarded the Commander of the Order of the British Empire in 2015.

Taylor now went with L.A.'s Borman Entertainment agency run by agents Gary and Ann Borman, and moved ahead to his next album, six years on. He had holed up in a rented house on the Vineyard writing and making demos of songs and when he had enough he booked time in December 1996 at Right Track Studios in Manhattan, before again taking the tapes to L.A., to Westlake Studios for dubbing and mixing. He called back Frank Filipetti to produce and reassembled much of the mob that had made *New Moon Shine*, along with Stevie Wonder to play harmonica and Branford Marsalis on sax. He also added the remarkable octave range of Kate Markowitz to the chorale of David Lasley, Valerie Carter, and Arnold McCuller. While *Moon Shine* had intimate moments, the new work—titled, in a perfect trope of a man whose life seemed like sand through one, *Hourglass*—was meant as serious introspection in the aftermath of his brother's and father's deaths.

The songs were "spirituals for agnostics," as he put it, a neat phrase for the dichotomy he still hadn't fully resolved.

His pseudosecular elegy to Alex was "Enough to Be on Your Way," the song he had written after the former's funeral, with "Alice" the proxy for Alex, which he explained came to him after "we all went down to Florida to say goodbye. . . . In Paris, a year later I changed his character to a hippie chick named Alice and the location to Santa Fe but my soulful older brother is still all over this song like a cheap suit," a song that he said was "almost fuck-free." Indeed, the arrangement was near beatific, its violins and the broken heart behind Taylor's vocal surely the saddest song he had ever sung, clearly suggestive of "Fire and Rain"—"It woke me up on a Sunday / An hour before the sun," he sang. "They brought her back on a Friday night / Same day I was born / We sent her up the smoke stack / Yes, and back into the storm."

The tracks on the record were a barometer of wistfulness—"Another Day," "Little More Time with You," "Up from Your Life." There was also a cover of Livingston Taylor's "Boatman," from the latter's 1996 album, *Bicycle*, an oblique metaphor for their father (a more direct tribute from Livingston Taylor was a song he wrote called "My Father's Eyes," which he had sung at Ike's funeral and would later be on his 1999 *Snapshot: Live at the Iron Horse* album). Ike's ethereal presence also seemed to be like sands through *Hourglass*, the agnosticism of which clearly had the edge on the religious; in "Gaia," inspired by environmental futurist John Lovelock's 1965 "Gaia hypothesis" that all organisms form a self-regulating system of survival on earth, he identifies as "a poor, wretched unbeliever," who gave faith a last shot, in vain; in another song, "Up from Your Life":

So much for your moment of prayer
God's not at home
There is no there, there
Lost in the stars
That's what you are
Left here on your own

Another, "Jump Up Behind Me," flavored by a Calypso beat and bongo accents, was a dreamlike recitation of when Ike had come and rescued him from that New York hell, taking him back home where he "Felt the darkness fall away / Even as the world was turning."

Even an innocent rendition of the 1930 evergreen "Walking My Baby Back Home" was hued in despondence; and his yee-ha cowboy turn, "Hangnail," whip cracking in the background, seemed to suggest a waiting tombstone. "Another Day" could make one wonder whether he meant Suzanne Schnerr when he sang, "Oh, wake up Susie / Put your shoes on / And walk with me into this light . . . / Just to know that life goes on." When Taylor sang in "Jump Up Behind Me" that "I know now / Only one thing matters in these days / One thing, true love," he could be believed. There were a few hard edges. "Line 'Em Up," the first track, retro-devoured Richard Nixon, recalling his resignation, with a "tiny tear in his shifty little eye" (he also parodied himself again—"I've seen corn in Kansas / And I've seen picket fences / And perfect cowboy dances"), and "Yellow and Rose" told of Britain's populating the Botany Bay penal colony in Australia, where "Everything changes for the strangers on the shore / They are blue and green no more / They are yellow and rose," his odd allegory for a world where "Seeds of the universe ever endeavor to grow / Tiny pieces of everything into the water they go."

The surprise was that the album was not a downer but an honest plaint of a man aching all over but learning to be strong. "I've had my fun . . . and my chance to be free," was another trenchant line—his way of saying a taste of honey is *better* than none at all, and that the chain of time never stops, nor does nature. In "Boatman," with pedal steel guitar weeping, he yearns to "forever run free" and asks, "Can you deliver me?" None of these messages came with any fancy dressing; all his usual influences—postmodern pop, blues, country—were there, but kept unobtrusive so that his lyrics were free to cut to the chase. *Rolling Stone*'s Elysa Gardner thought she had heard the voice of the current generation in the album: "As young singer/songwriters from Joshua Kadison to Eddie Vedder continue to prove, earnest, introspective men can stoke the hormonal urges of music fans just as handily as their more aggressively seductive peers. Earnest guys also tend to age better. While stars like [Robert] Plant often become parodies of their more youthful selves, Taylor, who never had much of an edge to begin with, can settle comfortably—even radiantly—into middle age. . . . *Hourglass* is a case in point."

Other reviews were more effusive. Stephen Holden in the *New York Times* found a Taylor who had a "Zen-like embrace of life's simple pleasures." *Time* said he "blend[ed] ironic detachment with persona reflection" and reported that in the studio during the making of "Enough to Be on Your Way" "there was a long silence in the room every time he finished playing it." The AllMusic retro-review commends the "pleasant, melodic, simple songs about love, family, and social activism. That's not necessarily a bad thing, since Taylor has a gift for such material, and [here] he sounds as good as ever."

Accordingly, the album caught a strong breeze and went to number 9 amid scattered reviews, some suggesting it was his "best ever," a quite fanciful notion that would be repeated for every new Taylor album. On this trail of huzzahs, he agreed to sing and tell the genesis of his songs on the VH1 *Storytellers* program, and his performance of "Little More Time with You" from the album was used as an oft-played video on the channel, helping send the single of the song to number 3 on the AC chart. When the Grammy nominations came down, *Hourglass* was nominated for Best Pop Album and Filipetti for Best Engineered Album.

Taylor was in Norway on a skiing trip when he learned his album had won both Grammys; indeed, the awards that year had a distinct skew toward the premise that old was new again. Also nominated for Best Pop Album were Fleetwood Mac's *The Dance*, and Bob Dylan was the big winner that night taking home three, including Album of the Year, for *Time out of Mind*, besting by one his son Jakob, who won two as front man of the Wallflowers. (Not all of rock got with the program; announcing the Album of the Year winner, Usher called him *Bill* Dylan.)

However, these rites of industry self-congratulation never fazed Taylor much—more fulfilling to him that year was when the new age guitarist Alex De Grassi recorded *Interpretation of James Taylor*, a dreamlike collection of acoustic covers (to this day a top-selling album in Bolivia)—and his newest "comeback" did little to stint the cold, hard realities of life. Death seemed to mock the album's success. Besides Alex and Ike, Tim Mayer, his collaborator on "Home by Another Way," had died at forty-four from cancer only months after *Never Die Young* was released. Now, Taylor's drummer Carlos Vega, who he had just returned from a European jag with and was to accompany him that day on the *Oprah Winfrey Show* and then at the Rainforest concert at Carnegie Hall, shot himself in the head at home in L.A. and died at age forty-one, leaving a wife and two daughters. As with Alex, Taylor had not seen it coming, and it shook him terribly, coming as it did just before the *Hourglass* tour was to commence. He had been to too many funerals, seeing other men unable to endure what he had.

Says Danny Kortchmar:

> We like to pretend we know it all as young artists, but looking back, James and I knew nothing. We faked it. We never knew, or cared, what the future would bring. When he wrote "Secret o' Life," that was a big moment, him saying the secret of life was "enjoying the passage of time." Once he got clean, he could do that. For a lot of us who'd seen him go through hell, it was something. You tend to feel guilty when people you love die and you live, and there was some of that, you can hear it in those songs on *Hourglass.* But each time it happened he came away a stronger person, more into what life meant to him. That was really when he grew up. We all waited 'til we were old to grow up.

The pit bulls of the Canyon were in clover by the new millennium. David Geffen's vanity label made the first big noise of the '90s when Nirvana broke out of the Seattle grunge scene. Geffen sold his label to MCA in 1990 but continued to run it until '95, whereupon it became barter in the game of corporate mergers and acquisitions, today residing within the Universal Music Group. Geffen meanwhile cofounded the DreamWorks SKG movie studio with Steven Spielberg and Jeffrey Katzenberg—the music division of which was run by another familiar corporate potentate, Mo Ostin, after thirty-two glorious years at Warner Brothers. Geffen sold out in 2008 and now mainly buys and sells yachts from his mansion in Malibu. Irving Azoff kept pace, returning to Front Line Management in the '90s, still managing the Eagles as well as Christina Aguilera, Neil Diamond, Fleetwood Mac, Van Halen, and dozens more. He produced movies, was CEO of Ticketmaster and Live Nation, and by 2012 was, according to *Billboard,* the most powerful man in the music industry. Under his watch, the Eagles, Linda Ronstadt, and Jackson Browne divided no less than $7 million for *one* show, on the millennial New Year's Eve, at the Staples Center. This was certainly in line with the philosophy defined by a fifty-something Glenn Frey, repeated to audiences—"You're paying, we're playing."

Taylor played out the century on a far less starry stage, a typical gig for him being the sellout concerts he gave on July Fourth at the famed Tanglewood outdoor amphitheater in the Berkshires. As the *New York Times* reported it: "As they looked around, more than a few of those squeezed into the middle-aged mosh pit at the foot of the stage or sprawled on Tanglewood's plush lawns must have wondered where were the legions of the young—vagabonds or simply weekenders—who gave the Berkshires much of their coltish spirit in those days. Of course, Mr. Taylor is now 51 and most of his longtime fans are lawyers, managers and entrepreneurs, people who, if they do wander about, do so in Lexuses and Ford Explorers."

And *that* was a decade and half ago.

For James Taylor, time could be measured almost in dog years. Way back in 1985, *Newsweek* had noted: "The next time you're tempted to forget that the years are rushing by, focus your reading glasses on this: James Taylor is 37, and Joni Mitchell is 42. Doesn't seem possible, does it?" In 2000, Sweet Baby James—the one he had immortalized when he was born, was a thirty-two-year-old man with a wife and family. But for his uncle, there was still work to do. That year, Gary Borman hired Barbara Rose, who had managed David Crosby and Graham Nash, to manage one client, James Taylor, who broke into the new millennium seeing another album begin a slow ascent to gold status, the sixteen-track *Greatest Hits Volume 2* package. Hardly forgotten, months before, in March, he could bask in the sort of rites he had hated but come to an accommodation with when he was inducted in the same Rock and Roll Hall of Fame class with Eric Clapton; Bonnie Raitt; Earth, Wind and Fire; and the band he had succeeded at the Night Owl, the Lovin' Spoonful.

As cynical as he was about the Hall of Fame concept—"I don't know exactly what that means or where the Hall is . . . maybe in Cooperstown," he jibed during its endless construction in Cleveland—or injecting rock even deeper into corporate self-congratulation, at the whim of overlords like Ahmet Ertegun and Lou Adler and the now upper-crust Jann Wenner, he could not rightly object when Paul Simon had asked him in 1990 to deliver the induction speech for Simon and Garfunkel—the same night Carole King and Gerry Goffin went in, inducted by Jon Landau—or when Crosby, Stills, and Nash asked him in 1997 to do the same for them; each time he did so nearly off the cuff, saying of the former that he had "a very close affinity for them and their music" and of CSN that they "helped me identify myself as a singer and songwriter," though he misidentified "Ohio" as "Kent State." Joni Mitchell was also inducted into the Hall that night, and Taylor performed, rivetingly, "Woodstock." And when she was voted into the Canadian Songwriters Hall of Fame a decade later, he flew to Toronto to be onstage with her

Now, when his turn came for induction he asked Paul McCartney to do the honors for him, saying, "I wrote him a letter." McCartney's speech went over the familiar lines of Taylor's career, including of course the Apple train wreck he insisted, grinning, that he had nothing to do with, and ended with him saying, "I love him. He's a really beautiful guy." Taylor, rising to the stage in his loose-fitting tux and still not completely reconciled to why such an award was even necessary, told the packed ballroom, "I'm very grateful," then, with a glint in his eye, "I only hope this never falls into the hands of someone desperate enough to use it."

That he came into the new century prepared to make things right that he had screwed up in the past was evident by the woman he escorted into the Waldorf-Astoria Hotel that night, who was beautiful and blonde but unlike his famous past consorts. In 1993 he had met Caroline "Kim" Smedvig, the public relations and marketing director of the Boston Symphony Orchestra, after he sang with the accompaniment of conductor John Williams and his assemblage. Pert and six years younger than him, the divorced Smedvig was not the usual Taylor "type," but perhaps her distance from the rock and showbiz "in" crowd was a refreshing change now that he was beyond the need to be "in" himself. She thought so, too. One time, she said, "I drove down to pick him up and there he was standing at a pay phone at this little convenience store, cutting quite a dashing figure. Needless to say, that was it."

For years they shadow danced, not allowing themselves to jump too quickly into a relationship, but her warm smile and quick wit had him hooked. He took her to Ike's memorial service, she moved in with him in his newest home, in Brookline, then on Christmas Eve 1999, he actually got down on bended knee and proposed with an antique diamond ring from Tiffany's. During his Hall of Fame speech, he referred to her as "the love of my life" and "Snookums." After several postponements the wedding was on February 18, 2001, at a church in Boston, attended by fifty friends and family members. John Williams gave Smedvig away and Sir Andre Previn and Yo-Yo Ma performed at the ceremony. Soon after, Taylor performed at her behest at the centennial anniversary of Symphony Hall with the Boys Choir of Harlem. Later in the year, at fifty-three, Taylor became a father again, the result of in vitro fertilization with a surrogate that resulted in twin sons, Henry (named after his maternal grandfather) and Rufus, who unlike Sally and Ben *were* the center of his life. Now, when he mentioned family, he meant it. Better still, he lived it.

Taylor had no way of knowing it but his music was about to find a new context, too, the result of America's worst day. Like the rest of the world, he was stunned and sickened by the horrifying images of planes crashing into the soon crumbling World Trade Center towers on his TV the early morning of September 11, 2001, when over three thousand died. When the country needed a friend and a sense of serenity among the terror, he was there, performing at the Concert for New York City on October 20 at Madison Square Garden, the proceeds going to the families of the first responders and victims of the attack. Introduced by Bill Clinton, he sat on a stool in khakis and a white shirt and began a slow, mournful rendition of "Fire and Rain," as people in the crowd held up pictures of dead fathers, brothers, and sons, and wept. It was then that this hardy song found a literal context, every word seemingly describing this tragedy—fire and rain, sweet dreams and flying machines in pieces on the ground, and an almost unbearably touching "I always thought I'd see you somehow one more time again." Then he rose and sang with a grand orchestral accompaniment "Up on the Roof," which also could be metaphoric of those tall buildings, saying it was "a song that's very much about New York."

Less than a month earlier, at the Hollywood Bowl, he had chosen not to sing these and most of his old songs, prompting Robert Hilburn to castigate him, "You can sympathize with Taylor for refusing to build his show around the songs that first brought him stardom three decades ago, but in a time of national anxiety, you also wanted to feel the cleansing beauty of his best work rather than the far less distinguished material that has characterized his albums since then." Taylor took that to heart. He had long become tired of his signature song, and believed so had the music public, even fans. As far back as '81, he had joked that when he sang "Fire and Rain" in concert, "I think someone in the audience is thinking, 'Aw, you poor guy. You got so upset you had to take *two* Valiums, eh?'" But the need to hear it post-9/11 imbued it with a new life, and now he had a new relationship with it. Singing it in the figurative burning embers of America's worst day, he was "reanimated in a way . . . maybe because it's a type of emotional connection people were feeling, suddenly everything you touched, everything you did, resonated way down deep to the taproots."

Nearing his midfifties, he was still learning lessons about his own music, not that he was convinced he had gotten it right. He told Charlie Rose on *60 Minutes II* in 2000 that this "rock-solid image of sanity, you know, it doesn't feel that way to me, especially when I wake up at, you know, 5 o'clock in the morning, you know, you know, anxious." Many of his songs he now said had "fallen short of the mark," but it now meant more than he ever could have imagined that "we got close enough."

That was made clear when, long ex post facto, Warner Brothers went back to its long-standing drawer full of Taylor hits and in April 2003 issued *The Best of James Taylor*, a twenty-song compilation of hits and detritus left in the Warner vaults, including previously unreleased takes of "Carolina in My Mind," "Steamroller," and "Country Road," and a new song, "Bittersweet," that he was allowed to cut for the album. Nostalgic Taylor fans lapped it up, pushing it to number 11 and, by 2005, platinum status. To AllMusic, these evergreens, hoary as they were, "do not seem to age; they feel as immediate and relevant in the 21st century as they did in the 1970s." This was some trick, and the way Taylor pulled it off was by keeping himself injected into each changing of the guard, and *sounding* a lot like that guy from the '70s.

James Taylor and Carly Simon wound up on opposite ends of Massachusetts: Taylor on two hundred acres of cloistered land in Pittsfield deep in the Berkshires near Tanglewood, not far from where Oliver Wendell Holmes Sr. and Henry Wasdworth Longfellow wrote poetry, Herman Melville wrote *Moby Dick,* and Elizabeth Sprague Coolidge began the Berkshire Music Festival at South Mountain in 1918. Simon, who divorced James Hart in 2007, still lived in the house Taylor built in the Vineyard, before leaving it semiabandoned when she bought a new one. Their two children are both singer-songwriters like their parents, recording albums with little help, by design, from their parents. In the late '90s, when Simon was diagnosed with stage one breast cancer and had a mastectomy, he lent his support.

But the chill between them would never really thaw, and apparently he still could not stop saying nasty things that got back to her. By 2008, fully recovered from cancer, she told an Associated Press reporter that she had been able to finally wipe the slate clean of Taylor. "I'm so erased, so erased," she said, but added, "I don't think James has forgotten in any way. If he had forgotten, he wouldn't be behaving in the way he is." And *she* couldn't keep from slagging him for having been an "absentee husband and father who cares just about himself." In the end, she said, "I don't think I would have changed anything except that I wish that James would have been happier with himself."

Taylor's next studio album was the 2002 *October Road*, released as both a single CD and in a limited double-CD set with three tracks of old material, an alternate-version "Don't Let Me Be Lonely Tonight," a previously unrecorded song about his first son, "Benjamin," and an alternate version of Mark Knopfler's "Sailing to Philadelphia," on which he had done harmony with Knopfler on the latter's 2000 album of the same name, with Knopfler doing the same here. Once again it was a lavish production, produced by Russ Titelman and drawing on no less than fifty-five musicians and singers, including a full string section, new drummer Steve Gadd, Ry Cooder, Yo-Yo Ma—and both Sally Taylor and Kim Smedvig on backing vocals. The title track, with Titelman doubling his vocal on a country-rock feel, was as good a statement as any of where his head was:

Oh, promised land and me still standing
It's a test of time
It's a real good sign

The sound was folkier, hesitant to let loose, and save for the cocktail-lounge blues of "Mean Old Man"—the bridge was a wondrous solo by jazz pianist Larry Goldings and guitarist John Pizzarelli—most tracks were done at the same midtempo pace with a few percussive flecks, and the themes were certainly familiar—how could they *not* be by now?—family (there was a love letter to Kim, "Caroline I See You"), the earth and sea, roads to "carry me on my way," optimism, and some passing *shpilkes* such as his allegory of gun running and tribal feuds on "Belfast to Boston." It was nothing if not a pleasant, swaying middle road sedative, the chant of "Lie down, lie down, lie down" in "September Grass" an apt command for anyone playing the album.

On "My Traveling Star," another of his secular hymns, he crooned beside a very sad violin and rising chorus: "Watch my back and light my way / My traveling star, my traveling star / Watch over all of those born St. Christopher's day." On "Baby Buffalo," he sang almost in a whisper, "Hold on to now till you have to let go / Easy through your fingers, ever so." "On the 4th of July" was another wonderful trip back in time, when concepts mattered such as "Freedom and freedom's land / And the kingdom of God and the rights of man / With the tiny tin voice of the radio band / Singing 'love must stand.'" "Have Yourself a Merry Little Christmas," an oddity on an album to be released in the summer, was his metaphor that, in the wake of 9/11, bonds should be timeless, not an obligation at holidays. Heavy-handed and preachy, yes—and one critic would call it "morose"—but who could argue the point?

It seemed few were in the mood to now. Dissections of Taylor albums were getting briefer—the *Rolling Stone* review ran two short paragraphs, saying *October Road* was "much more subtle than those peak-era LPs; what's more [it] is a hit album without any obvious hit songs," and that "at a time when veteran stars are routinely propped up with upstart guests and gimmicky grooves, Taylor and Titelman's tasteful restraint is refreshing." The AllMusic retro-review said it showed "strong hints of a man who feels he's been rescued." By rote, it would go platinum, bettering *Hourglass* by going to number 4 on the chart. Five years after his last single, "On the 4th of July" (number 16), "Whenever You're Ready" (21), and "September Grass" (25) all charted on the AC. And when his Christmas song went out as a single over the holidays, it made number 4 on the AC, prompting the recording of a full-scale Christmas album in 2004 that went platinum and put two singles, "Deck the Halls" and "Winter Wonderland," in the Top 10 of that chart; another, "Santa Claus Is Coming to Town," got to number 12.

It seemed that whatever Taylor touched had a market.

Yet he would not record original material again for years—"If it's not gonna be a major effort and represent a valid thing for somebody in my position, then why bother?" he explained. "There's no reason to just get something out to fill a slot in the marketplace"—but was reliably all in whenever a good cause or a good Democrat needed him, such as John Kerry. Yet, as was always the case with Taylor, activism had a ceiling. In 2002, he had done a show for Country Music Television with the Dixie Chicks, who had revered him growing up. (One of the trio, Emily Erwin Robison, told him, "I used to kiss the cover of *Mud Slide Slim*.") However, when their lead singer, Natalie Maines, said in 2003 after the "war of choice" in Iraq had begun, "We don't want this war, this violence, and we're ashamed that the President of the United States is from Texas," they were despicably banned from many country stations around the South and their concerts canceled. Taylor said nothing by way of outrage, joining too many of his peers in intimidated silence—a very notable exception being the old bush dog Merle Haggard, who said, "I don't even know the Dixie Chicks, but I find it an insult for all the men and women who fought and died in past wars when almost the majority of America jumped down their throats for voicing an opinion. It was like a verbal witch-hunt and lynching."

Other, newer causes were now on the radar screen. The Dixie Chicks, for example, supported gay rights and gender equality. Taylor, meanwhile, stayed in the pocket of safer causes. He later appeared with the Chicks on a 2004 Vote for Change tour and a 2005 benefit for victims of Hurricane Katrina. He campaigned heavily for Barack Obama in his two campaigns, performing at an inaugural ball in 2009 and again in 2012, moments before Obama took the oath of office. Right there on the Capitol steps with his guitar, in front of hundreds of thousands of people, just feet behind him a smiling Sonia Sotomayor softly swaying and a stone-faced Clarence Thomas. Sometimes it seemed no charity affair went on without him. He did stem cell benefits for Michael J. Fox, and even gave Nancy Reagan props at a 2004 Beverly Hills dinner when the former first lady was honored for her commitment to stem cell research. He dutifully performed at the Rainforest concert every year. Horrified by gun violence in his region, he performed at benefit concerts after the Newtown, Connecticut, school massacre and more recently at Boston Strong concerts after the marathon bombing. For this child of the '50s, activism was a duty, but it still came with a sense of caution.

The Taylor dynasty had long been played out. Kate and Livingston were only semiactive. Kate recorded her first album in twenty-four years in 2003, though it had a tragic epilogue when her husband and manager, Charlie Witham, who wrote most of the songs, died just before it was released, making the final track, "Auld Lang Syne," arranged by James, a threnody. And Sally Taylor had stepped away from music to do philanthropic work and move to Colorado. Ben, now a solo act playing soft folk rock, recorded three albums in four years, the last, *Another Run Around the Sun,* in 2005, with his parents and sister singing backup vocals and the actor Kevin Bacon producing the work and playing bass; like his dad, as well, he was doing some acting. That year, father and son sang before the men's final match at the US Open tennis tournament in New York; six years later they would sing onstage together on an eight-show swing through the Midwest.

The rites of simply *being* James Taylor seemingly were played out on an endless tape loop. Some of the appearances were tacky, others blissful. In 2006 he was named Person of the Year by the MusiCares Foundation, the National Academy of Recording Arts and Sciences' own charity wing, assisting musicians financially with needs like housing and drug rehabilitation. At its annual event some of the biggest artists performed Taylor's music—Bruce Springsteen on "Millworker"; Jackson Browne, David Crosby, and Sheryl Crow on "Mexico"; Bonnie Raitt on "Rainy Day Man"; the Dixie Chicks on "Shower the People"; Keith Urban on "Country Road"; India Arie on "Secret o' Life"; Allison Krauss on "Carolina in My Mind." Watching from a side table, Taylor, in an open-necked tux, held one of his twin sons on his lap, clapping and whistling his appreciation, then closed out the show (which is available on DVD from Rhino Records) by singing a duet with Carole King. Taking the microphone, he thanked everyone, down to his road manager Mark Robinson and stage manager Ralph Perkins, reading the names off a Saks Fifth Avenue underwear package cardboard, including his family, saying, "Love you, Liv." Then, trying to put the event in perspective, he said, "Strange to be at an event like this and still be alive."

He had stayed alive long enough to be a grandfather, when in October 2007 Sally gave birth to a son, Bodhi Taylor Bragonier. He also had seen marketing strategies change in the industry, and took advantage of it. His final CBS/Sony album had been the 2006 *James Taylor: A Christmas Album*, but with his wide swath he had been allowed to cut his original Christmas album on the label of Hallmark Cards and sold exclusively through the gift shop company's four thousand Gold Crown stores, limiting its sales though it still found its way onto the album chart at number 22. (His 2006 Christmas album, *James Taylor at Christmas*, released on the Columbia label, peaked at number 16 on the *Billboard* album chart and number 3 on its holiday chart, with another edition out in 2012, yet ironically while it went gold the Hallmark work has over time gone platinum.) Now, rather than re-up with CBS, he went in a totally new direction—with a label under the aegis of the Starbucks coffee corporation in conjunction with Concord Records, an old jazz label. Called Hear Music, it had been given heft by its first signing—Paul McCartney—its concept being a forum for soft music played and offered for sale exclusively at the coffee shop "media bars," a concept that seemed made for Taylor, who no longer needed to deal with high-pressure vipers in the industry—though his entrance helped Hear grow, reeling in Joni Mitchell and Carly Simon, proving that in music, nothing good stays small forever.

With Barbara Rose having left for other pastures, he was now being handled by a small but burgeoning agency in Vancouver, Macklam Feldman Management, who began by representing the Chieftains and grew to include Elvis Costello, Diana Krall, and Ry Cooder. Thus fortified, he embarked on his first album for Hear, the 2007 nineteen-song, near-unplugged live CD/DVD set *One Man Band*, which was recorded at the Colonial Theater near his home in Pittsfield and released in an advanced-for-the-time digital surround sound format, as well as being the first Taylor album to be made available for downloading on iTunes. It charted at number 17, went gold, and garnered him a TEC award, which is presented each year for technical innovation. A PBS *Great Performances* film of the concert, which Taylor produced in association with Don Mischer and Sydney Pollack, was nominated for an Emmy Award. A year later Taylor released *Covers,* his interpretation of songs from the '50s, '60s, and '70s. Recorded over ten days in January in a converted barn in Weston, Massachusetts, the selections were eclectic, to say the least, finding room under the same roof for songs made famous and semifamous by Elvis ("Hound Dog"), Junior Walker (["I'm a] Road Runner"), Eddie Cochran ("Summertime Blues"), Buddy Holly ("Not Fade Away"), the Drifters ("On Broadway"), Leonard Cohen ("Suzanne"), John Anderson ("Seminole Wind"), the Dixie Chicks ("Some Days You Gotta Dance"), and George Jones's first chart hit ("Why Baby Why"). It was a convincing and clever homage to all his influences, and while no one would have confused him with David Ruffin, his surprisingly gritty and soulful cover of the Temptations' "It's Growing" eased its way to number 11 on the AC, and the album to number 4, earning Grammy nominations for Best Pop Vocal Album and, for his even more laid-back version than Glenn Campbell's of Jimmy Webb's "Wichita Lineman," Best Male Pop Vocal Performance.

Doing promotion, he went on numerous TV shows. On the *Colbert Report* he answered a question regarding his philosophy by simply performing "(I'm a) Road Runner" in its entirety. This successful lark of a project led to bonus tracks being issued for a sequel edition in 2009 called *Other Covers.* But he clearly gave his critics ammunition, and a boost to the sort of crude commercialism he liked to rag on when he appeared on, of all things, the home shopping channel QVC to hawk the bonus CD/DVD of the album, with his band, on two segments. Let the record show that he sold over fourteen thousand copies this way, a small but profitable sellout. And he was doing no apologizing for it.

The reunion with Carole King in 2007 was a stroke of genius by Peter Asher, who had resigned from Sony in '06 to produce independent projects—such as Taylor and King's six-show run at the Troubadour in November 2007 on the venerable club's fiftieth anniversary. The joke Taylor told, and would still tell, is "We played here in the early

'70s, repeatedly . . . evidently." They were backed for the engagement by Kortchmar, Kunkel, and Sklar, who had played on the original recordings. With a double CD/DVD of the show announced for a 2010 release on Hear/Concord, a joint "Troubadour Tour" was booked for the spring of that year, during which the *Live at the Troubadour* package was released in May. In demand out of the gate, it would rise to number 4 on the album chart and sell a million copies—meaning that Taylor had notched a Top 10 album in every decade since the 1970s. It was, Taylor said, "like one of those dreams where you go back to school. Usually I'm naked though." The reunion tour ran through North America, Australia, New Zealand, and Japan, making a fortune. For Asher, who would next turn to producing Elton John's fortieth anniversary reissue of *Goodbye Yellow Brick Road,* the Taylor-King reunion was a final—probably—payback on an IOU long in coming.

"I owe James a great debt of thanks," he says, "because I bet my career on his."

The most ticklish irony for Taylor was that the prose of the rock critics who had labored in vain to undercut him—or cut him to pieces with a broken bottle—seemed far more dated and small than he was now. Lester Bangs, the head would-be executioner, lived only long enough to see Taylor endure into the '80s, his last days misspent as a widely ignored punk band front man before he bit the dust, dying in 1982 at thirty-three, accidentally overdosing on Darvon, Valium, and cold medicine—the sort of improvised cocktail that once might have gotten Taylor through a night without heroin. Taylor, on the other hand, had grown to such stature that he would be honored with Quincy Jones and jazz saxophonist Sonny Rollins with the National Medal of Arts at a ceremony in the East Room of the White House in March 2011, the medallion draped around his neck from the man he helped put in office.

Although he was not too proud to do goofy things like ride a float in the Macy's Thanksgiving Day parade, mostly his presence aided a charitable cause or nostalgic appearances by him and other stalwarts from his era. He was there in the greet line when the Dalai Lama came to Boston. He did a New Year's Eve show on Stowe Mountain in Vermont to benefit the Spruce Peak Arts Center Foundation (top ticket: $1,000). He sang with Randy Newman on the Oscars show, performed at Eric Clapton's Crossroads Guitar Festival in Dallas, sang "Sweet Baby

James" on Jay Leno's last *Tonight Show* (in his first stint), and appeared on *David Letterman* six times. He sang with Crosby, Stills and Nash "Love the One You're With" at the Hall of Fame's twenty-fifth anniversary concert, and at tributes to Carole King when she was awarded the Gershwin Prize at the White House in 2013, feted by MusiCares in '14, and was a Kennedy Center honorée in 2015.

He did all this not for the bread but because he *could.* To be sure, a good many of his contemporaries *couldn't.* Joni Mitchell, who had been releasing an album every few years into the new century, apparently retired from music in 2002 but returned to record her *Shine* album in 2007 on the Hear label, peaking at number 36 on the album chart and winning a Grammy for Best Pop Instrumental for "One Week Last Summer." The album was a hypnotic echo of her most affecting and dreamlike songs, and Taylor pitched in on acoustic guitar on the title track. But shortly thereafter, she developed Morgellons disease, a rare condition that she said makes her skin look like "mushrooms after a rainstorm"; on March 31, 2015, the seventy-one-year-old legend was found unconscious in her home and hospitalized; she recovered but remained in ill health, unable to speak. Linda Ronstadt, who also was a no-show at *her* Hall of Fame induction, said in 2013 that she had Parkinson's disease and could "no longer sing a note." Both she and Mitchell live in the kind of hermetic isolation one might once have assumed awaited Taylor. Instead, he was booking concerts as far ahead as he could see, including a July 4, 2015, gig at Tanglewood—his twenty-fourth there—and an appearance a month later with Bonnie Raitt at Fenway Park. The "lifelong Red Sox fan," as he called himself, watched from his box seat as they won their first championship in eighty-six years, prompting him to write "Angels of Fenway," which he said was going on his next album of original material.

"I got out of the habit of writing songs for about 10 years," he said by way of explanation. "I hadn't been able to convince my manager, my wife and my kids that this had to be a priority. But I said to them, 'If I don't get this record written, I don't know what's going to happen.' And then they let me go." And: "I have no idea what releasing an album even means anymore. Friends of mine say, 'James, you have to adjust your expectations. People don't buy these things.' Not to be presumptuous, but Vincent Van Gogh sold just two paintings while he was alive. If that's what your medium is, you simply must do it."

The promised album, *Before This World*, finally rolled out in June 15, 2015, two months after word of it had been released to *Rolling Stone*, which wrote of the project as "James Taylor's Mellow Rebirth." Taylor had been working alone writing songs in a rented apartment in Newport, Rhode Island. He then honed them in the barn behind the house, recording demos with Steve Gadd on drums and Jimmy Johnson on bass. He began performing some of the songs in concerts that fall, his rendition of "Wild Mountain Thyme" having been tabbed as one of the album's songs, and "Today Today Today" planned as a single. When he was satisfied, he went into Sterling Sound Studios in New York with producer Dave O'Donnell and engineer Ted Jensen, his backing musicians members of his touring band. The ten songs were mainly laid-back tunes with bite like "Watchin' Over Me," in which he reached back to tell about his recovery from addiction, chanting, mantra-like "I hope someone's watching, watching over me." "Stretch of the Highway" was his latest metaphor of finding God's work on earth, thanking "the man that planned the land" and "towed the load," in this take lionizing some off heroes—"Eisenhower, Mr. Dwight D., General Motors, Big Ol' GMC," though in this take the pastoral could extend to the carnal pleasure of "first-class poontang." On "Today Today Today" there was some typical Taylor ambivalence, optimism tempered by fatalism, its first lines: "Today, today, today I'm finally on my way / The time has come to say goodbye, goodbye, goodbye," but came down on the former, averring: "Somehow I haven't died and I feel the same inside / As when I caught this ride when first I sold my pride." "Angels of Fenway," as promised, was included, its meaning now clear as his late grandmother's hopeless devotion to the Red Sox. "You and I Again" was his paean to past love, as if a confession to all his exes that he never realized "how fierce you are" or "how serious you are," nor that they had been "standing on Holy Ground."

Clearly, he had come to an accommodation with his God, who loomed over many songs in the majesty of the land and the sky. While "Watchin' Over Me" was the most literal expression of this, in "Montana" he sequestered himself "high on my mountain and deep in the snow," asking rhetorically, "Who can imagine the scale of the forces that pushed this old mountain range up in the sky? / Tectonic creation, erosion, mutation; somethin' to pleasure God's eye." Yet here too he admitted he hadn't quite seen the light—"I'm not smart enough for this life I've been livin', a little bit slow for the pace of the dream / It's not I'm ungrateful for all I've been given but nevertheless, just the same." Indeed, if he could muster up some of that old dancing under the sun and palms escapism of "Mexico" on "Snow Time," riffing "Ay caramba, one-note samba, la la la la bamba, lighting me up inside," he saved one track for his most salient distress signal, a sorrowful, stinging antiwar statement as jarring as it was brilliant.

This was "Far Afghanistan," a history lesson of doomed incursions into that godforsaken country dating back to "old Alexander" and repeated by the Russians and the Brits. "And after 9/11 here comes your Uncle Sam / Another painful lesson in the far Afghanistan." As seen through the eyes of a soldier from Indiana, the song opens with the observation that an American is taught to hold his liquor, a woman, and a rifle, "but nothing will prepare you" for "the hills of Kandahar" where similar young men of the Hindu Kush, the Band-e Amir, the Hazara are taken to the mountains and taught to kill and die on orders from their God. All soldiers talk to God, but the American realizes "that crazy bastard talks to God and his God talks back to him." This might well be the first, and only protest song of the wars in the Middle East, and it was a little late in coming—thirteen or so years late. But that it came from Taylor in his old age meant that adult contemporary wasn't a pass to stop being morally outraged.

Still, the album was meant as a good vibe to be had by all. He eschewed the blues and tricky chords for the exercise of wide-eyed optimism. The title track, which in its complete form was "Before This World/Jolly Springtime," crafted like an old English/Celtic folk tune, wailed: "Let the resin risin' up in the tree, make the green leaf bud / The bird and the bee and the fish in the sea, feeling it in my blood." If there was an overarching epigram for Taylor's declaration of (almost) joy, it was the line from "Today Today Today" that went:

Somehow I haven't died
And I feel the same inside
As when I caught this ride
When first I sold my pride

There was something in these evolved grooves that particularly found a place within a music culture lost in superficiality and redundancy, a condition that had been building for years, helping to keep

Taylor relevant. But, now, his soul-searching lyrics stood in stark contrast to the preen-a-lot, say-little maw of pop-tart, hip-hop superficiality. In a sense, Taylor's songs had come full circle, providing something similarly simple but connective tissue as the country was again charting its way after years of chaos and confusion. Afghanistan wasn't merely fodder for a song, it was the same unlearned lesson that marked the Vietnam years, one that trapped even a Democratic president elected because of *opposition* to war in the Middle East. There were immigration battles, refugee battles, politicians stoking fear and xenophobia. For James Taylor and his legions, it all seemed familiar.

And so the album propelled him to a place where even he had never been. Greased by good reviews, word got around fast. Stephen Thomas Erlewine's AllMusic write-up called it "something unexpected: a record as relaxed as the average James Taylor album but one that's also riskier and richer, the right album for him to make at this date." *Rolling Stone* was cooler, quibbling over "a few slightly cornball moments . . . and an occasional over-reliance on gauzy harmonies that threaten to depersonalize the songs, *Before This World* is sweet grown-up James." Then came the deluge. The album sold ninety-six thousand copies it first week in release and was number 1 on the *Billboard* album chart the week of, appropriately enough, July 4 (though actually *October Road* had sold 154,000 its first week, en route to number 4). In what seemed like a jaw-gaping anomaly, or culture clash, it sat above Taylor Swift's *1989*, Adam Lambert's *The Original High*, Ed Sheeran, and Hilary Duff's *Breathe In, Breathe Out.* Only Tony Bennett had waited longer than Taylor for a top-ranked album, fifty-four years, nine more than Taylor, and its marketing campaign spawned several special editions, one sold exclusively at Target stores with bonus tracks—Woody Guthrie's "Pretty Boy Floyd," Hank Williams's "I Can't Help It (If I'm Still in Love with You)," and the folk standard "Diamond Joe." There were as well a bonus CD with five demo and live tracks, and a bonus DVD. The album, which was also (as had been *October Road*) released on vinyl, proving that the more things change the more they don't, charted in fourteen countries, going to number 4 in England.

The album kept him traveling. Even before it came out, he was a blur, performing two concerts on the *Queen Mary 2* during an idyllic, eight-day voyage from New York to Southampton. With the classic Taylor dreamy-eyed insouciance, he said, "There's something romantic about departing on a boat and seeing the water, and actually experiencing every nautical mile. It sort of makes a connection back to another time and place." Of course, the same could have been said about the album. Or even merely by saying his name.

When Carly Simon's long overdue autobiography came out late in 2015, it showed that Taylor will likely always be pierced with residual slings and arrows for his past. If he could come to a friendly homeostasis with Joni Mitchell, he apparently will never enjoy the same accommodation with Simon, who filled pages with victim-like self-pity about, as Janet Maslin wrote in her *New York Times* review of the book, "a mostly bleak marriage to James Taylor, with whom she is apparently not in communication. On the evidence of Ms. Simon's fulsome descriptions of their intimacy and the terse, angry, distant spouse she describes, he is not apt to be one of her enthusiastic readers." She believed Taylor would not and cannot be happy. But maybe somewhere along the line he did become, if not happy or completely self-confident, then at least *comfortable*, finding an answer to the question he had once sung—yes, it *was* amazing that a man like him could feel this way. In April 2014 at the Rainforest Fund's twenty-fifth anniversary benefit concert at Carnegie Hall, Taylor, who during a 2006 Rainforest concert came onstage clad in a British army uniform and shorts, had entered wearing a lamp shade on his head and with Sting and actor Kevin Spacey performed a kitschy rendition of the show tune "What a Swell Party" while clowning around, Three Stooges–style, Taylor applying a plastic cup over Spacey's mouth while Sting bit Taylor's hand. Sting was so taken with him that even as he was starring in a play on Broadway, he appeared at a Taylor tribute show at the 54 Below theater on West Fifty-Fourth Street, singing "Shower the People."

As he turned sixty-seven in 2015, James Taylor was even now a quirky, distant sort of rock daemon. His mother, Trudy Woodard Taylor, her long and fruitful life lived out quietly in the Vineyard, died that autumn at ninety-three, James making the announcement on October 15. In her final days, her son seemed more at peace than she had ever seen him; his wife and twin sons were more a part of his life than he had thought could be possible in his selfish years. Yet even as he became less self-contained, he is even more controlling, restricting outsiders having access to him or even his image on film. Elissa Kline, who was hired as the official photographer of the Troubadour reunion tour, had to accede to some strict demands. "Although I technically own the photos," she says, "I am under strict limitations as to their use. I have signed agreements to clear any photo use with both Carole and James's managers. Even if one inch of his face is in the background and blurred, it's off limits [laugh]. Or else."

One would never know of this hard side by visiting Taylor's website, on which he says, even if he really doesn't believe it: "I've written maybe 150 songs. But really what I've done is written 25 songs ten times. That's what I do. I write different versions of the same thing. There are themes I will write about." He also waxes with childlike ardor about doing something he always has wanted to do—give guitar lessons, which he does in an online course, a *free* online course. There is a video on the site in which he displays the innards of his tour's wardrobe trunk, which includes a bag with honey and vinegar for his throat, a mini–music box that plays "Happy Birthday," shoes, boots, emery boards, and other fingernail supplies like fiberglass and glue for a "good, healthy, finger-pickin' nail." Of the old trunk, he says coyly, "It's got a few more tours left, I think."

If not exactly a saint, he is a sort of ambassador, or so it seemed when Secretary of State John Kerry, whom Taylor has known around the Vineyard for decades and for whom he campaigned in 2004, visited France after the 2015 *Charlie Hebdo* killings—belatedly, having taken heat for not attending a memorial service immediately after the tragedy—and brought with him one James Taylor, to sing to the French "You've Got a Friend." Oh, he took some heat for *that* from the horned toads on the right, though not as much as he had in 2013 when Taylor, still haunted by Sandy Hook, spoke out on gun control, telling a right-wing website that "we need to make some sacrifices to our freedoms, if that's the way to put it. We need to make some sacrifices to what we might want to have, in order to safeguard our children." *That* no doubt made Bonnie Raitt approve, as would "Far Afghanistan." And for some who had lived through decades waiting for James Taylor to be less safe, maybe it wasn't too late, after all. Yet it really wasn't anything political that had brought Taylor to his elder statesman role.

Rather, it was the fact that in a time of need, his voice and sense of sincerity and integrity were so reassuring. Having lived through yet another convulsion—the terrorist attacks in Paris in November 13, 2015—he appeared days later on the Stephen Colbert *Late Show* and sang a quiescently moving version of "The Marseillaise" in flawless French, one of his backing vocalists Kim Smedvig Taylor. But he also on that show engaged in a scripted segment, the premise of which was that he had seen a lifetime of things after he had seen fire and rain. He then began to sing, alternating with the host, verse after verse in the song's meter of sights such as as calzones, slim-fit jeans, and "almost every episode of *Friends*."

"How many verses are there left?" asked Colbert in mock frustration.

"Seventy-five," Taylor deadpanned.

True indeed was that he had seen a *lot*. And while there were few honors left that he hadn't been given, the last one to fall, the most significant, was in December 2015. After appearing at other storied artists' ceremonies upon receiving the Presidential Medal of Freedom, he finally had the medal hung around his neck by Barack Obama, his fellow recipients that day including Steven Spielberg, Itzhak Perlman, Stephen Sondheim, Barbra Streisand, the late human rights activist Minoru Yasui, Senator Barbara Mikulski, former congressman Lee Hamilton, Indian rights activist Billy Frank Jr., and Willie Mays.

Not that his audiences ever doubted he deserved such high honors but they will buy their Taylor albums and their Taylor tickets for a more basic reason: to hear him demonstrate his simple creed, "I want to be in tune. I want to sing pretty, I want to sing sweet. You find a way forward," he said, "if your audience keeps showing up."

And so they do. In places like Sunrise, Florida, where tonight they have had parking lot picnics and cried to "You've Got a Friend."

"Great show, wasn't it?" a woman from one of the picnic groups said after the show as she found her way to her car. "Never sounded better." She reached into her handbag and pulled out a piece of wrapped cheese.

"Here," she says to the stranger whose name she never asked to know. And he took it with a hearty thank-you, asking only one thing.

"And the wine?"

"Oh, no. That was gone, long ago. We couldn't have snuck it past the guards anyway. It ain't 1970 anymore."

She sounded sad when she said it. Then she slid behind the tinted windows of the passenger side of her BMW and it disappeared into the night, leaving 1970 inside the arena until the next time James Taylor came through, or at least until "Fire and Rain" came on the radio for the eight-millionth time.

REFERENCES

AUTHOR INTERVIEWS

Tony Bramwell
Kim Fowley
Robert Hilburn
Elissa Kline
Danny Kortchmar
Russ Titelman

BOOKS

Beam, Alex. *Gracefully Insane: The Rise and Fall of America's Premier Mental Hospital.* New York: PublicAffairs, 2001.

Brackett, Nathan, and Christian Hoard. *The New Rolling Stone Guide.* 4th ed. New York: Fireside, 2004.

Bramwell, Tony. *Magical Mystery Tours: My Life with the Beatles.* New York: St. Martin's, 2006.

Davis, Stephen. *More Room in a Broken Heart: The True Adventures of Carly Simon.* New York: Gotham; reprint edition, 2012.

DeCurtis, Anthony, James Henke, and Holly George-Warren. *The Rolling Stone Album Guide.* 3rd ed. New York: Random House, 1992.

Emerick, Geoff, and Howard Massey. *Here, There and Everywhere: My Life Recording the Music of the Beatles.* New York: Gotham, 2006.

Evans, Tom, and Mary Anne Evans. *Guitars: From the Renaissance to Rock.* New York: Paddington, 1977.

Fong-Torres, Ben. *Not Fade Away: A Backstage Pass to 20 Years of Rock and Roll.* Backbeat Books, 1999.

Halperin, Ian. *Fire and Rain: The James Taylor Story.* New York: Citadel, 2000.

Hoskyns, Barney. *Hotel California: Singer-Songwriters and Cocaine Cowboys in the AL Canyons, 1967–1976*. New York: Harper Perennial, 2007.

———. *Waiting for the Sun: Strange Days, Weird Scenes and the Sound of Los Angeles*. New York: St. Martin's, 1996.

King, Carole. *A Natural Woman: A Memoir*. New York: Grand Central, 2012.

Kubernik, Harvey, and Henry Diltz. *Canyon of Dreams: The Magic and the Music of Laurel Canyon*. New York: Sterling, 2009.

Kubie, Lawrence S. *The Riggs Story: The Development of the Austen Riggs Center for the Study and Treatment of the Neuroses*. New York: Paul B. Hoeber, 1960.

Mitchell, Joni. *Joni Mitchell: In Her Own Words*. Toronto: ECW, 2014.

Price, Reynolds. *A Whole New Life*. New York: Scribner, 1995.

Simon, Carly. *Boys in the Trees: A Memoir*. New York: Flatiron Books, 2015.

Spitz, Bob. *The Beatles: The Biography*. New York: Little, Brown and Company, 2005.

Summers, Anthony, and Robbyn Swan. *Sinatra: The Life*. New York: Random House Digital, 2006.

Thompson, Dave. *Hearts of Darkness: James Taylor, Jackson Browne, Cat Stevens, and the Unlikely Rise of the Singer/Songwriter*. New York: Backbeat Books, 2012.

Von Schmidt, Eric. *Let Me Follow You Down: The Illustrated Story of the Cambridge Folk Years*. New York: Anchor Press, 1979.

Weller, Sheila. *Girls Like Us: Carole King, Joni Mitchell, Carly Simon—and the Journey of a Generation*. New York: Atria, 2008.

White, Timothy. *James Taylor: Long Ago and Far Away*. London: Omnibus, 2001.

Yetnikoff, Walter. *Howling at the Moon: The Odyssey of a Monstrous Music Mogul in an Age of Excess*. New York: Broadway, 2004.

ARTICLES

"1955: The Year R&B Took Over Pop Field." *Billboard*, August 13, 1955.

Ackerman, McCarton. "Eric Clapton Gives a Shout Out to Sobriety." *Fix*, March 11, 2013. www.thefix.com/content/video-clapton-talks-kicking-his-addictions.

Allis, Sam. "Still Singing the Blues: Despite a New Album and a New Woman, James Taylor Can't Avoid the Loneliness of Being Human." *Time*, May 19, 1997.

Altham, Keith. "Cat Stevens: The Honest Way for It to Happen." *Record Mirror*, June 5, 1971.

———. "James Taylor." *Petticoat*, October 23, 1971.

Asher, Peter. "James Taylor." Apple Records website. www.apple records.com/#!/albums/Album_JamesTaylor.

Bangs, Lester. "James Taylor Marked for Death." *Who Put the Bomp*, June 1971; reprinted in the posthumous Bangs anthology *Psychotic Reactions and Carburetor Dung*, edited by Greil Marcus. New York: Knopf, 1987.

"Beatles Lawyer and Close Brian Epstein Friend Nat Weiss Has Died." *San Francisco Examiner*, August 4, 2013.

Billboard, May 8, 1971; May 22, 1971; May 29, 1971; June 24, 1971; July 31, 1971; January 27, 1973.

"Billboard Power 100: Irving Azoff." *Billboard*, January 26, 2012. www .billboard.com/biz/articles/news/1099262/billboard-power-100 -irving-azoff.

Brady, Thomas J. "James Taylor Is Engaged to Orchestra Exec." *Philadelphia Inquirer*, January 15, 2000.

Braudy, Susan. "James Taylor, a New Troubadour." *New York Times*, February 21, 1971.

Buk, Askold. "Rolling Thunder: Lindsey Buckingham 90's Magazine Guitar Tips." *Guitar World*, May 26, 2012.

Burton, Charlie. "Sister Kate, Alex Taylor with Friends and Neighbors." *Rolling Stone*, May 13, 1971.

Canby, Vincent. "Cross-Country Ride and a Chase in Spain." *New York Times*, July 8, 1971.

Canning, Corrine. "James Taylor to Perform on Cunard's *Queen Mary 2*." *USA Today*, August 7, 2014.

"Carlos Vega: 1957–April 7, 1998." *Drummer World*. www.drummer world.com/drummers/Carlos_Vega.html.

Caulfield, Keith. "After 45-Year Wait, James Taylor Earns His First No. 1 Album on Billboard 200 Chart." *Rolling Stone*, June 24, 2015.

Cocks, Jay. "Wheels: Hi Test." *Time*, July 12, 1971.

Cromelin, Richard. "Sylvester and the Hot Band: *Bazaar* (Blue Thumb)." *Phonograph Record*, December 1973.

Crouse, Timothy. "James Taylor: The First Family of the New Rock." *Rolling Stone*, February 18, 1971.

Crowe, Cameron. "Joni Mitchell." *Rolling Stone*, July 26, 1979.

Demorest, Stephen. "*Hotel California*." *Circus*, March 17, 1977.

"The Eagles, Linda Ronstadt, Jackson Browne: Performance: New Year's Eve." *Rolling Stone*, February 17, 2000.

Ebert, Roger. "Two-Lane Blacktop." *Chicago Sun-Times*, January 1, 1971.

Everett, Todd. "Rick Nelson: You're Not a Kid Anymore!" *Phonograph Record*, December 1972.

Farber, Jim. "Rainforest Fund Benefit Concert Celebrates 25th Anniversary with Sting, Paul Simon." *New York Daily News*, April 18, 2014.

Fisher, Bob. "*Martin Mull*." *Cream*, June 1975.

Fong-Torrez, Ben. "Peter Asher Presents Platinum Diggers of '77 Starring James Taylor and Linda Ronstadt." *Rolling Stone*, December 29, 1977.

Gans, Charles J. "Carly Simon on Painful Past and James Taylor Ignoring Her." *Huffington Post*, May 20, 2008.

Garvey, Marianne, Brian Niemietz, and Oli Coleman. "Sting Will Squeeze in a Tribute Show for James Taylor While Starring the Same Night in 'The Last Ship.'" *New York Daily News*, December 30, 2014.

Gillett, Charlie. "Joy of Cooking and Carole King: *Tapestry*." *Ink*, June 12, 1971.

Gioia, Ted. "The Red-Rumor Blues." *Los Angeles Times*, April 23, 2006.

Greene, Andy. "James Taylor's Mellow Rebirth." *Rolling Stone*, April 9, 2015.

Gross, Mike. "Taylor-Made Discs, Songs Grab Action." *Billboard*, February 6, 1971.

Herbst, Peter. "James Taylor: The *Rolling Stone* Interview." *Rolling Stone*, September 6, 1979.

———. "Peter Asher Talks About Producing." *Rolling Stone*, December 29, 1977.

Hibbert, Tom. "Crosby, Stills, Nash and Young: *American Dream*." *Q*, December 1988.

Hinckley, David. "PBS Documentary 'Troubadours' Features 1970s L.A. Soft Rock Scene, Greats Carole King, James Taylor." *New York Daily News*, March 1, 2011.

Hoberman, J. "Contact Sports." *Village Voice*, September 26, 2000.

Hochman, Steve. "They've Still Got Friends: Memories Were in the Air at James Taylor and Carole King's Troubadour Show." *Los Angeles Times*, November 30, 2007.

Hodenfield, Jan. "The 10th Annual Folk Festival Lacked Excitement and Direction, Though James Taylor Nearly Broke Through." *Rolling Stone*, August 23, 1969.

Hopkins, Jerry. "James Taylor on Apple: 'The Same Old Craperoo.'" *Rolling Stone*, August 23, 1969.

"Interview with Peter Asher." Rock and Roll Hall of Fame website. http://rockhall.com/blog/post/10245_interview-with-peter-asher-of-peter-and-gordon/#sthash.yV2Io0DK.dpuf.

"Give a Hoot." *It's All in the Streets You Crossed a Long Time Ago* (blog), August 4, 2005. http://streetsyoucrossed.blogspot.com/2005/08/give-hoot.html.

Irvin, Jim. "R.E.M." *MOJO*, November 1994.

"Isaac Taylor, 75, Prominent Physician." *New York Times*, November 8, 1996.

Jahn, Mike. "Leonard Cohen: Rock Poetry Had a Lot of Promise, Back Five and Six Years Ago." *New York Times*, June 9, 1973.

———. "Taylor's Folksongs Stir Recollections with Rich Fullness." *New York Times*, July 19, 1970.

"James Taylor: The Family Way." *Melody Maker*, May 11, 1974.

"James Taylor Crash: Breaks Both Hands." *Rolling Stone*, November 15, 1969.

"James Taylor on Gun Control." *Daily Caller*, January 22, 2013.

"James Taylor Strolls Down 'October Road.'" *Billboard*, July 12, 2002.

"John Belushi a Misogynist? Jane Curtin Tells Oprah Star Sabotaged Women's Work." *Huffington Post*, April, 13, 2011. www.huffingtonpost.com/2011/04/13/john-belushi-sexist-jane-curtain_n_848646.html?.

Kalish, Jon. "Taylor's Bill Is One of Clean Health." Reuters, December 14, 1985.

Kaye, Lenny. "To Live Outside the Law You Must Be Honest." *Cream*, November 1971.

Kent, Nick. "A Whole Lotta Rock 'n Roll." *New Musical Express*, December 23, 1972.

"King of the Nighttime World: Kim Fowley." *Rock's Backpages*, 2000. www.rocksbackpages.com/Library/Article/king-of-the-nighttime-world.

Kohn, David. "James Taylor: Through Fire and Rain: Songwriter Writes About His Life, Personal Struggles." CBS News, December 11, 2000. www.cbsnews.com/news/james-taylor-through-fire-and-rain/.

Kovall, Burt. "James Taylor: Sunshine and . . ." *Saturday Review*, September 12, 1970.

Kutulas, Judy. "That's the Way I've Always Heard It Should Be: Baby Boomers, 1970s Singer-Songwriters, and Romantic Relationships." *Journal of American History*, December 2010.

Lavender, Paige. "John Kerry Decides the Best Way to Apologize to France Is to Have James Taylor Perform." *Huffington Post*, January 16, 2015. www.huffingtonpost.com/2015/01/16/john-kerry-james-taylor-france_n_6486050.html.

"Lead Belly—Bad Nigger Makes Good Minstrel." *Life*, December 30, 2011.

Mansfield, Brian. "Linda Ronstadt Has Parkinson's Disease." *USA Today*, August 23, 2013.

Maslin, Janet. "Review: In Carly Simon's Memoir, Few Secrets Left Untold." *New York Times*, November 25, 2015.

"Message from James." James Taylor official website. www.jamestaylor.com/guitar/a-message-from-james/.

Murray, Charles Shaar. "Joni Mitchell: A Tender Dignity." *New Musical Express*, January 6, 1973.

Nolan, Tom. "Carly Simon: Attitude Dancing." *Phonograph Record*, May 1975.

Oberbeck, S. K. "That Lonely Feeling." *Newsweek*, February 8, 1971.

Oliver, Myrna. "Doug Weston, Troubadour Founder, Dies." *Los Angeles Times*, February 15, 1999.

"One Man's Family of Rock." *Time*, March 1, 1971.

Partridge, Rob. "Randy Newman." *Melody Maker*, June 15, 1974.

Paul, Donna. "A Quiet Place to Make Music and Putter." *New York Times*, April 23, 2009.

"Ray Charles Gets 5-Year Probation, $10,000 Fine." *Jet*, December 8, 1966.

Riegel, Richard. "Lester Bangs: Liberation Critic." *Throat Culture*, 1990. Archived at www.rocksbackpages.com/Library/Article/lester-bangs-liberation-critic.

Robertson, Sandy. "Kim Fowley: *International Heroes.*" *Sounds*, 30 July 1977.

———. "Lou Reed: *Growing Up in Public.*" *Sounds*, May 3, 1980.

Rockwell, John. "The Pop Life." *New York Times*, July 8, 1977.

"*Rolling Stone* 500 Greatest Albums: The Velvet Underground and Nico." *Rolling Stone*, November 1, 2003.

Schaak, Art. "*James Taylor and the Original Flying Machine.*" *Rolling Stone*, May 12, 1971.

Shelton, Robert. "Singer-Songwriters Are Making a Comeback." *New York Times*, July 5, 1968.

Siegel, Jules. "Midnight in Babylon." *Rolling Stone*, February 18, 1971.

Silverton, Peter. "Devo: *Q: Are We Not Men? A: We Are Devo.*" *Sounds*, August 26, 1978.

Stanglin, Doug, and Michael Winter. "Chapel Hill 'Rocked' by Killings of 3 Muslim Students." *USA Today*, February 12, 2015.

Staunton, Terry. "Jim Croce: *The Way We Used to Be.*" *Record Collector*, November 2004.

Tiven, Jon. "The Rise and Fall of David Bowie: All That Glitters Is Not Gold." *Good Times*, November 7, 1973.

Toop, David. "Surfin' Death Valley USA." *Collusion*, February 1982.

Traum, Happy. "The Swan Song of Folk Music." *Rolling Stone*, May 17, 1969.

Turner, Steve. "CSNY: Graham Nash and David Crosby." *New Musical Express*, November 1, 1975.

———. "Jackson Browne." Unpublished article for *New Music Express*, 1976.

Valentine, Penny. "James Taylor Comes to Town." *Sounds*, October 31, 1970.

———. "The James Gang." *Sounds*, October 17, 1970.

Walsh, Ben. "Vanity Case: Will Carly Simon Reveal the Identity of the Mystery Man in Her Seventies Hit 'You're So Vain'?" *Independent*, March 11, 2010.

Waters, Harry F. *Newsweek*, November 4, 1985.

Weisbard, Eric. "Limp Bizkit: *Significant Other.*" *Village Voice*, July 14, 1999.

Werbin, Stuart. "James Taylor & Carly Simon." *Rolling Stone*, January 4, 1973.

White, Timothy. "James Taylor." *Rolling Stone*, June 11, 1981.

Wolfe, Tom. "The 'Me' Decade and the Third Great Awakening." *New York*, August 23, 1976.

Young, Charles M. "Hell Is for Heroes: The Eagles: Slow Burn in the Rock and Roll Inferno." *Rolling Stone*, November 29, 1979.

Zimmer, Dave. "Danny Kortchmar: The Standup Rocker." *Record*, March 1983.

REVIEWS

Aizelwood, John. "*October Road.*" *Guardian*, August 9, 2002.

Arnold, Gina. "James Taylor's Singing Has Something to Say, but It Was Said Long Ago." *Los Angeles Times*, November 16, 1987.

Barol, Bill. "Grown-up James, Adult Joni." *Newsweek*, November 4, 1985.

Boehm, Mike. "Taylor Warm, Appealing with Orchestra." *Los Angeles Times*, November 6, 1995.

Browne, David. "*Before This World.*" *Rolling Stone*, June 16, 2015.

Christgau, Robert. "Carly Simon." Robert Christgau official website. www.robertchristgau.com/xg/cg/cg19.php.

———. "James Taylor." Robert Christgau official website. www.robertchristgau.com/xg/bk-aow/taylor.php.

Elias, Jason. "Handy Man." AllMusic. www.allmusic.com/song/handy-man-mt0001447243.

Erlewine, Stephen Thomas. "*Before This World.*" AllMusic, www.allmusic.com/album/before-this-world-mw0002842975.

———. "*Hourglass.*" AllMusic. www.allmusic.com/album/hourglass-mw0000023236.

Gardner, Elysa. "*Hourglass.*" *Rolling Stone*, May 29, 1997.

Gerson, Ben. "*Mudslide Slim and the Blue Horizon.*" *Rolling Stone*, June 24, 1971.

Gilbert, Jerry. "*Mud Slide Slim and the Blue Horizon.*" *Sounds*, May 1, 1971.

Herbst, Peter. "*JT.*" *Rolling Stone*, August 11, 1977.

Hilburn, Robert. "Taylor in West Coast Debut at Troubadour." *Los Angeles Times*, July 10, 1969.

———. "Taylor's 'Gorilla' a Soothing Beast." *Los Angeles Times*, June 24, 1975.

———. "You've Got a Friend Still, but with a Twist." *Los Angeles Times*, October 8, 2001.

Holden, Stephen. "*Walking Man.*" *Rolling Stone*, August 15, 1974.

Hoskyns, Barney. "*One Man Band.*" eMusic.com, November 2007. Archived at www.rocksbackpages.com/Library/Article/james-taylor-one-man-band.

"*James Taylor's Greatest Hits.*" *Melody Maker*, January 29, 1977.

Johnson, Connie. "*Never Die Young.*" *Los Angeles Times*, March 13, 1988.

Jurek, Thom. "*The Best of James Taylor.*" AllMusic. www.allmusic.com/album/the-best-of-james-taylor-2003-mw0000593194.

Landau, Jon. "*James Taylor.*" *Rolling Stone*, April 19, 1969.

———. "*One Man Dog.*" *Rolling Stone*, January 18, 1973.

Planer, Lindsay. "*James Taylor.*" AllMusic. www.allmusic.com/album/james-taylor-mw0000264104.

Rachlis, Kit. "*In the Pocket.*" *Rolling Stone*, August 12, 1976.

Ruhlmann, William. "*Flag.*" AllMusic. www.allmusic.com/album/flag-mw0000192161.

———. "*In the Pocket.*" AllMusic. www.allmusic.com/album/in-the-pocket-mw0000199229.

———. "*JT.*" AllMusic. www.allmusic.com/album/jt-mw0000097545.

———. "*Never Die Young.*" AllMusic. www.allmusic.com/album/never-die-young-mw0000198428.

———. "*October Road.*" AllMusic. www.allmusic.com/album/october-road-mw0000225967.

———. "*One Man Dog.*" AllMusic. www.allmusic.com/album/one-man-dog-mw0000311475.

———. "*Walking Man.*" AllMusic. www.allmusic.com/album/walking-man-mw0000194605.

Scoppa, Bud. "*Gorilla.*" *Rolling Stone*, July 17, 1975.

Shewey, Don. "*Dad Loves His Work.*" *Rolling Stone*, May 28, 1981.

Walters, Barry. "*October Road.*" *Rolling Stone*, September 10, 2002.

RADIO

Adams, Noah. "Musician James Taylor Discusses His Song 'Fire and Rain.'" *All Things Considered*, NPR, June 26, 2000.

TELEVISION

The Dick Cavett Show. PBS, October 10, 1977.

"JT Shmoozes About Paul McCartney." YouTube video excerpt of *Charlie Rose.* www.youtube.com/watch?x-yt-ts=1422327029&x-yt-cl=84838260&v=hVd6cGKfLa4.

VIDEO

Carole King and James Taylor Troubadour Reunion. PBS, 2007.

Troubadours: Carole King/James Taylor and the Rise of the Singer-Songwriter. PBS American Master series, March 3, 2011.

INDEX

Songs and albums that are not followed by an artist attribution were performed by James Taylor.

LINDENHURST MEMORIAL LIBRARY
3 1801 00569 5063